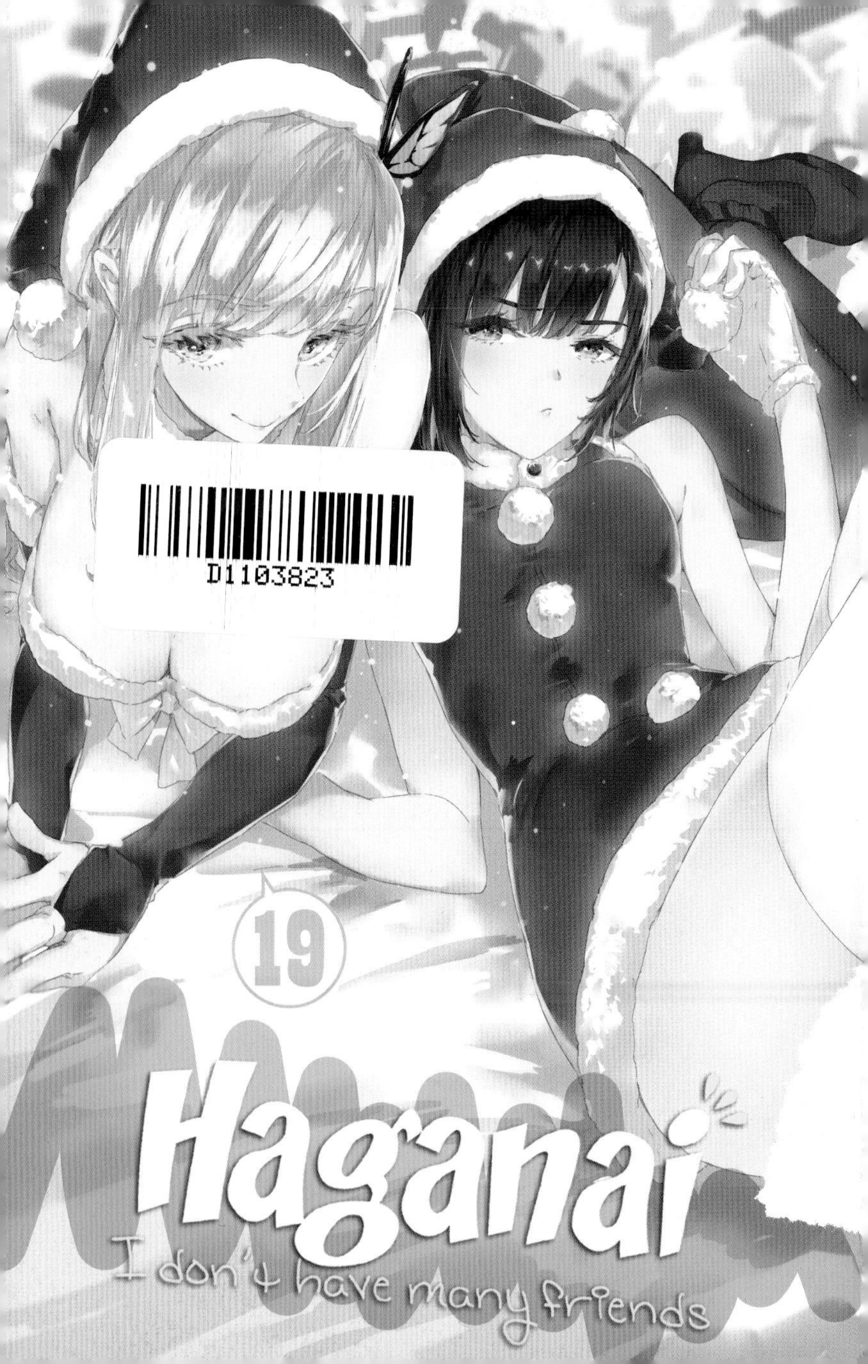
19
Haganai
I don't have many friends

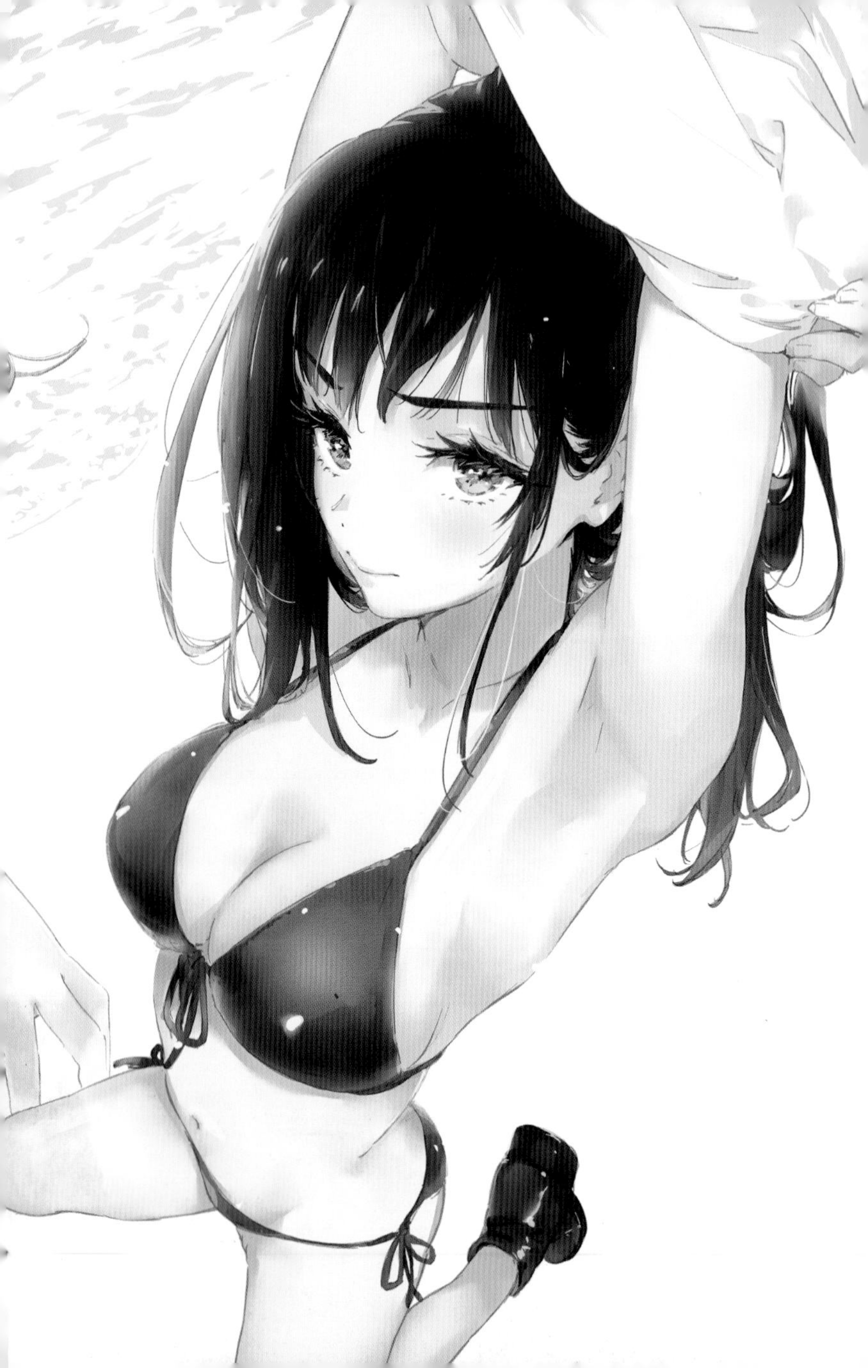

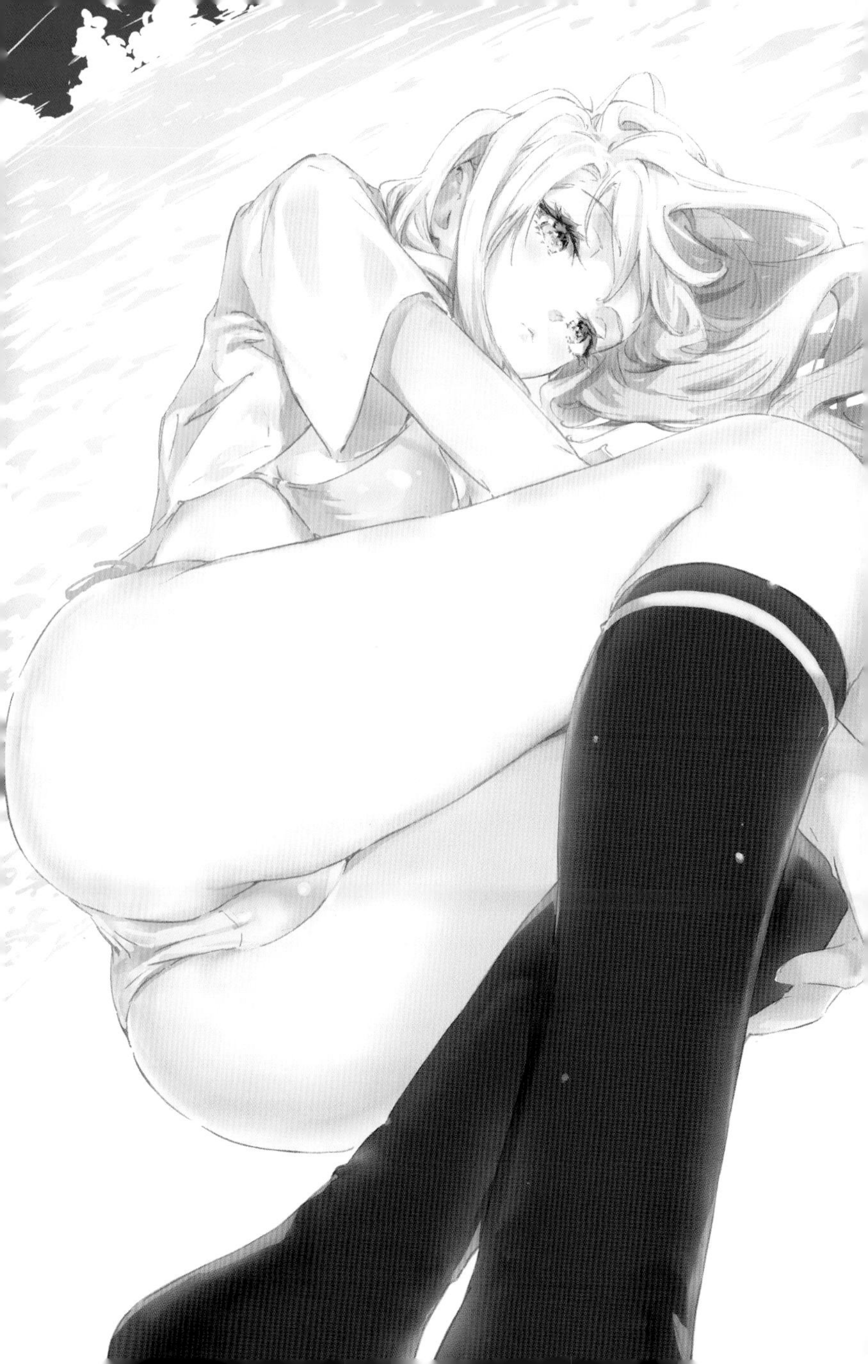

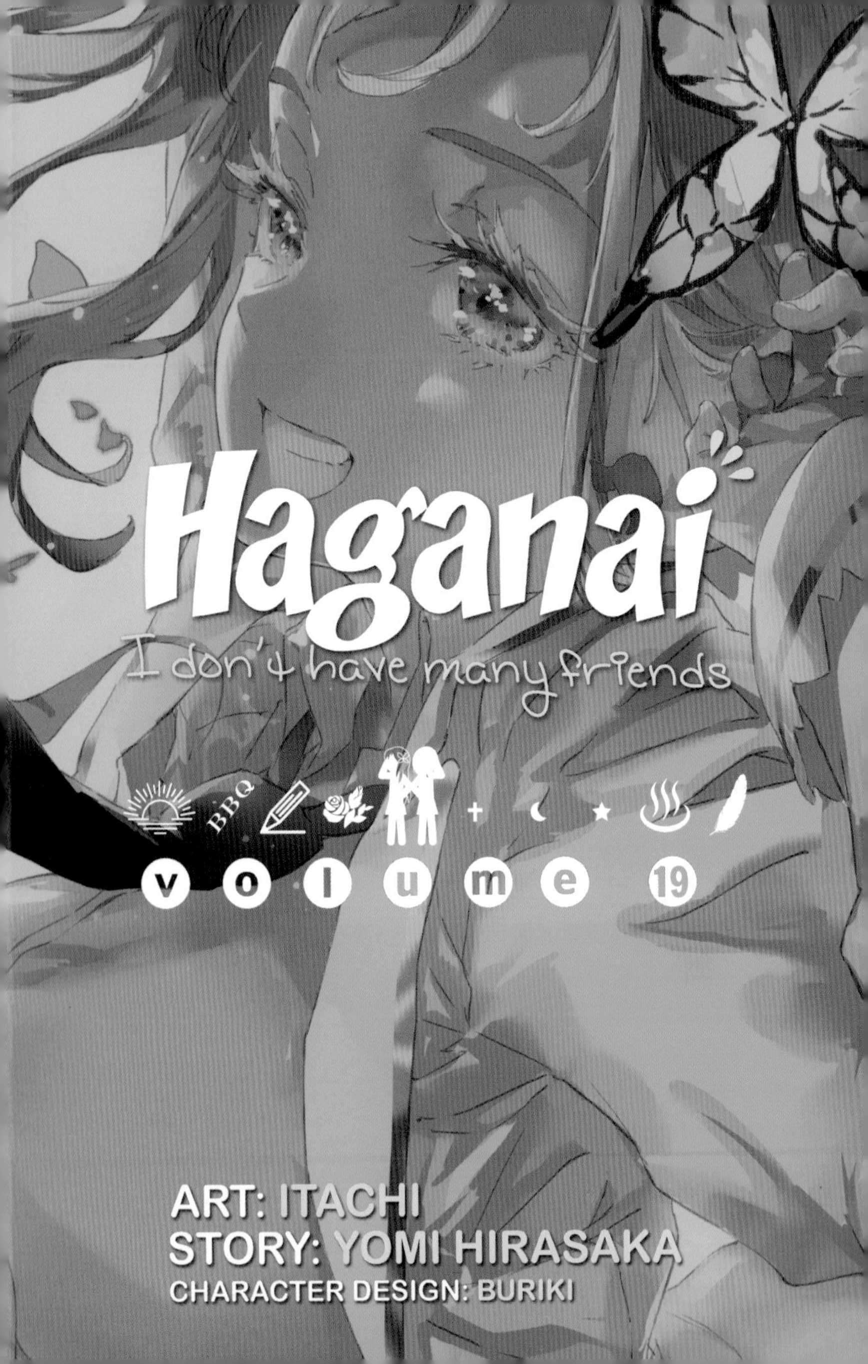
Haganai
I don't have many friends
BBQ
volume 19
ART: ITACHI
STORY: YOMI HIRASAKA
CHARACTER DESIGN: BURIKI

Haganai

MEET THE CAST

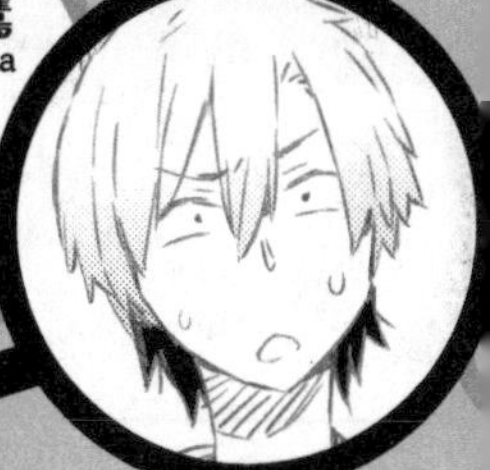

羽瀬川 小鷹
Hasegawa Kodaka

A second-year student at Saint Chronica Academy. He looks like a thug. Doesn't have many friends.

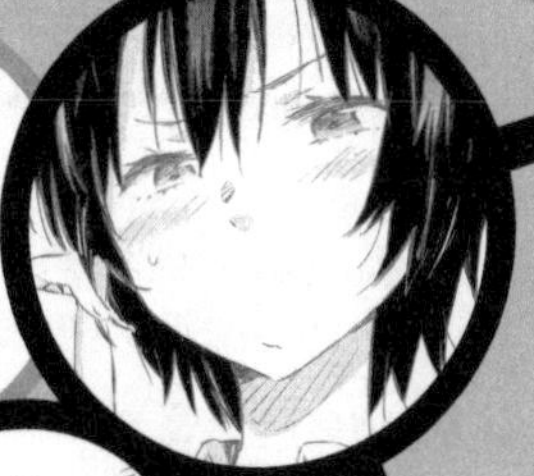

三日月 夜空
Mikazuki Yozora

Kodaka's classmate. Other than her looks, she doesn't have much going for her. Doesn't have many friends.

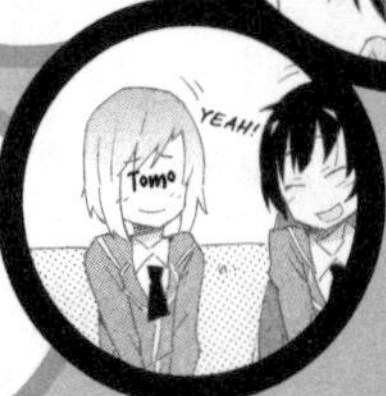
YEAH!
Tomo

トモちゃん
Tomo-chan

Yozora's "air friend."

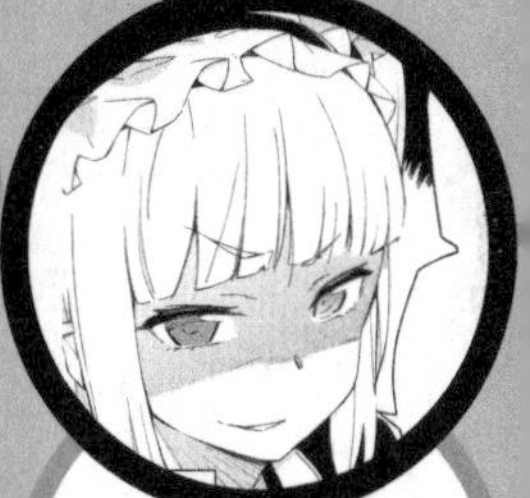

羽瀬川 小鳩
Hasegawa Kobato

Kodaka's kid sister. She's a student at Saint Chronica Academy's middle school, and she has some... unfortunate ideas. The unusual way she dresses and speaks stems from her persona as a "Great Ancestor" vampire.

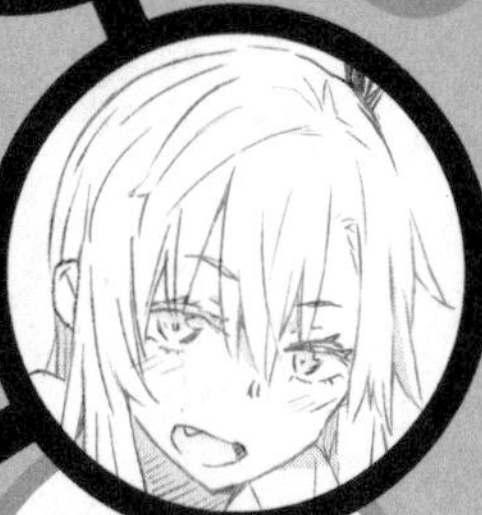

柏崎 星奈
Kashiwazaki Sena

The daughter of Saint Chronica Academy's director. Perfect in every way...except for her personality. Doesn't have many friends.

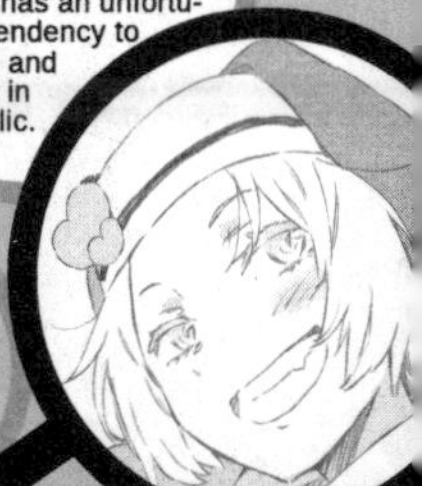

高山 ケイト
Takayama Kate

A beautiful nun who behaves like a middle-aged man. She's Maria's big sister, and has an unfortunate tendency to belch and fart in public.

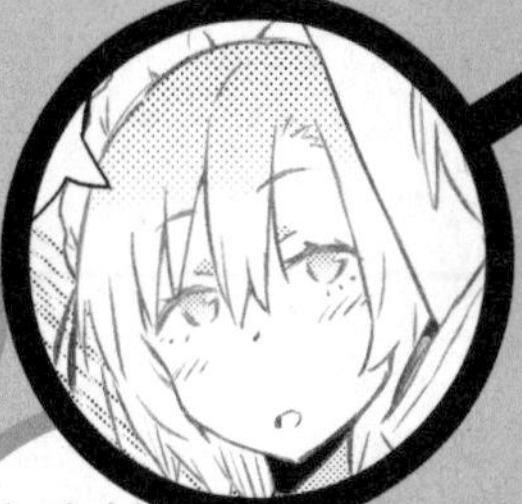

楠 幸村
Kusunoki Yukimura

A first-year student at Saint Chronica Academy. A kouhai to the rest of the club. Don't be fooled by the maid costume--Yukimura dreams of being a "fine Japanese boy."

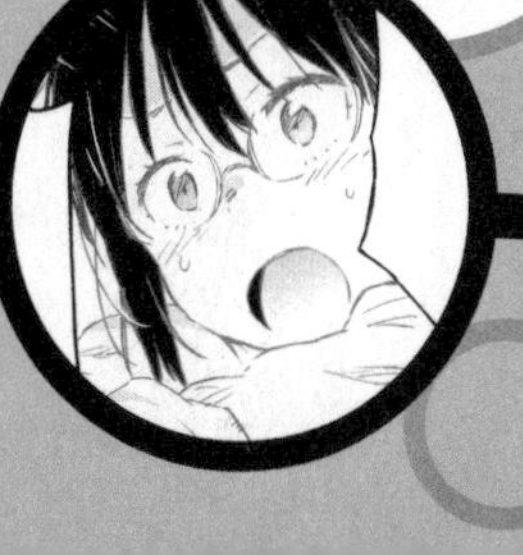

志熊 理科
Shiguma Rika

A first-year student at Saint Chronica. She's a genius inventor, and also a perverted yaoi fan who wastes her intelligence.

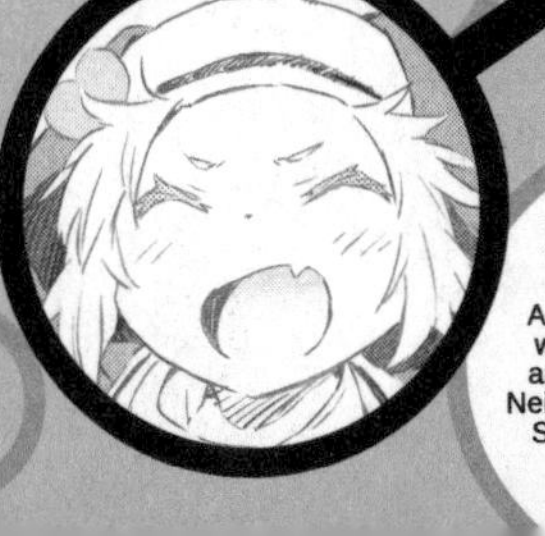

高山 マリア
Takayama Maria

A ten-year-old girl who wears a nun's habit... and happens to be the Neighbors Club's advisor! She loves both potato chips and Kodaka.

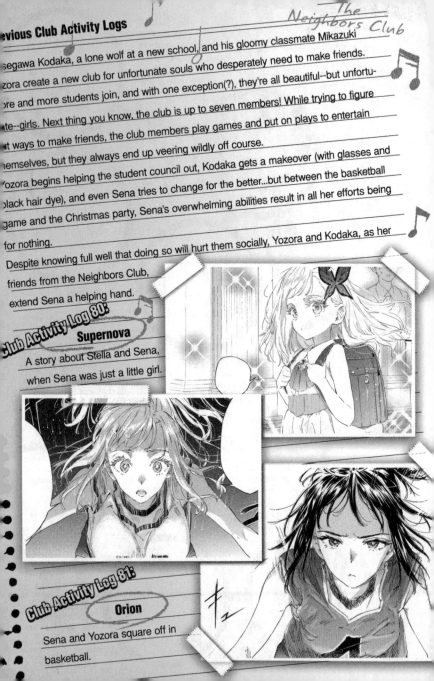

The Neighbors Club

evious Club Activity Logs

segawa Kodaka, a lone wolf at a new school, and his gloomy classmate Mikazuki

zora create a new club for unfortunate souls who desperately need to make friends.

ore and more students join, and with one exception(?), they're all beautiful--but unfortu-

ate--girls. Next thing you know, the club is up to seven members! While trying to figure

t ways to make friends, the club members play games and put on plays to entertain

hemselves, but they always end up veering wildly off course.

Yozora begins helping the student council out, Kodaka gets a makeover (with glasses and

black hair dye), and even Sena tries to change for the better...but between the basketball

game and the Christmas party, Sena's overwhelming abilities result in all her efforts being

for nothing.

Despite knowing full well that doing so will hurt them socially, Yozora and Kodaka, as her

friends from the Neighbors Club,

extend Sena a helping hand.

Club Activity Log 80:
Supernova

A story about Stella and Sena,

when Sena was just a little girl.

Club Activity Log 81:
Orion

Sena and Yozora square off in

basketball.

Club Activity Log 82:

God's Blessing on This Wonderful Holiday!

The Christmas party begins.

Club Activity Log 83:

The Dark Knight Rises

We give up on reinventing ourselves.

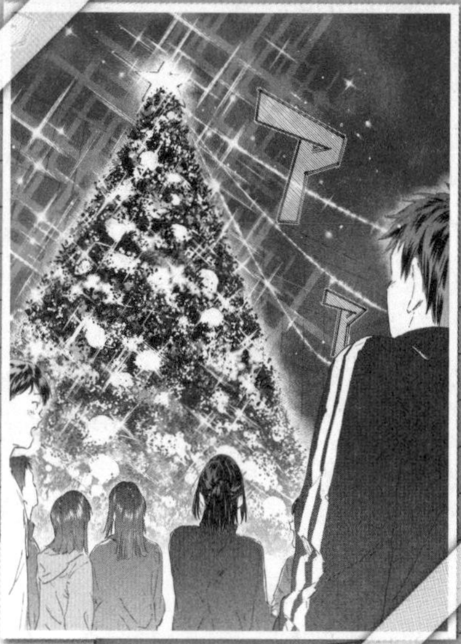

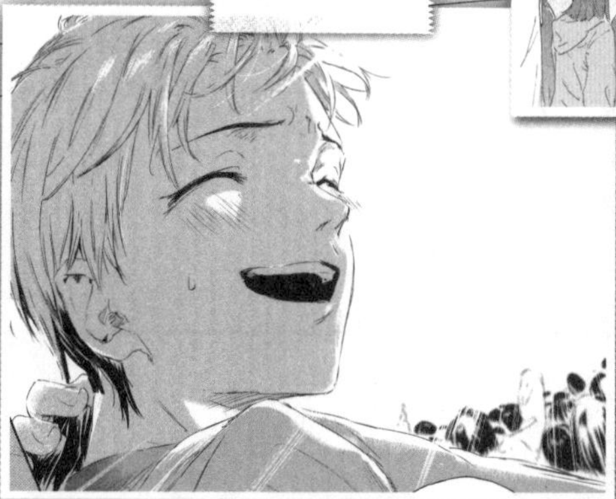

Club Activity Log 78:

Be My Friend

Sena and Yozora become friends.

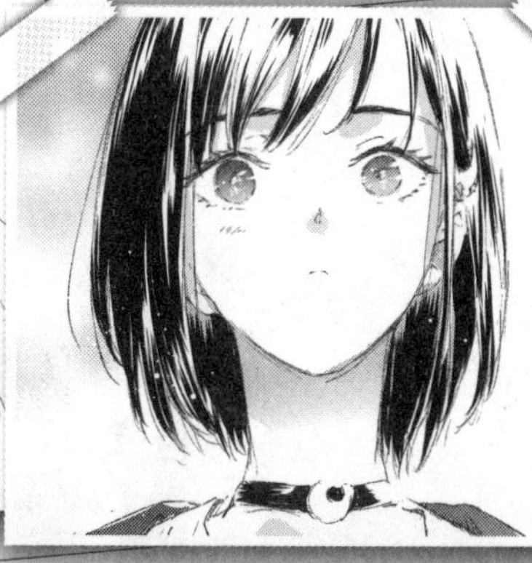

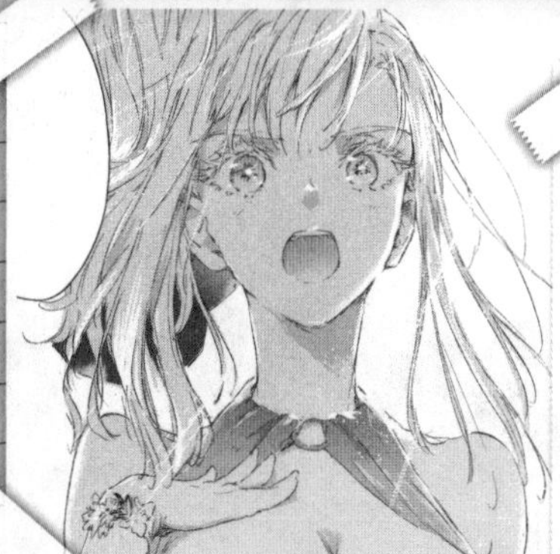

Haganai

I don't have many friends

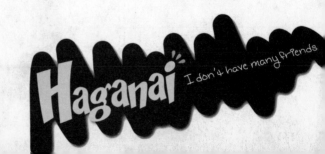

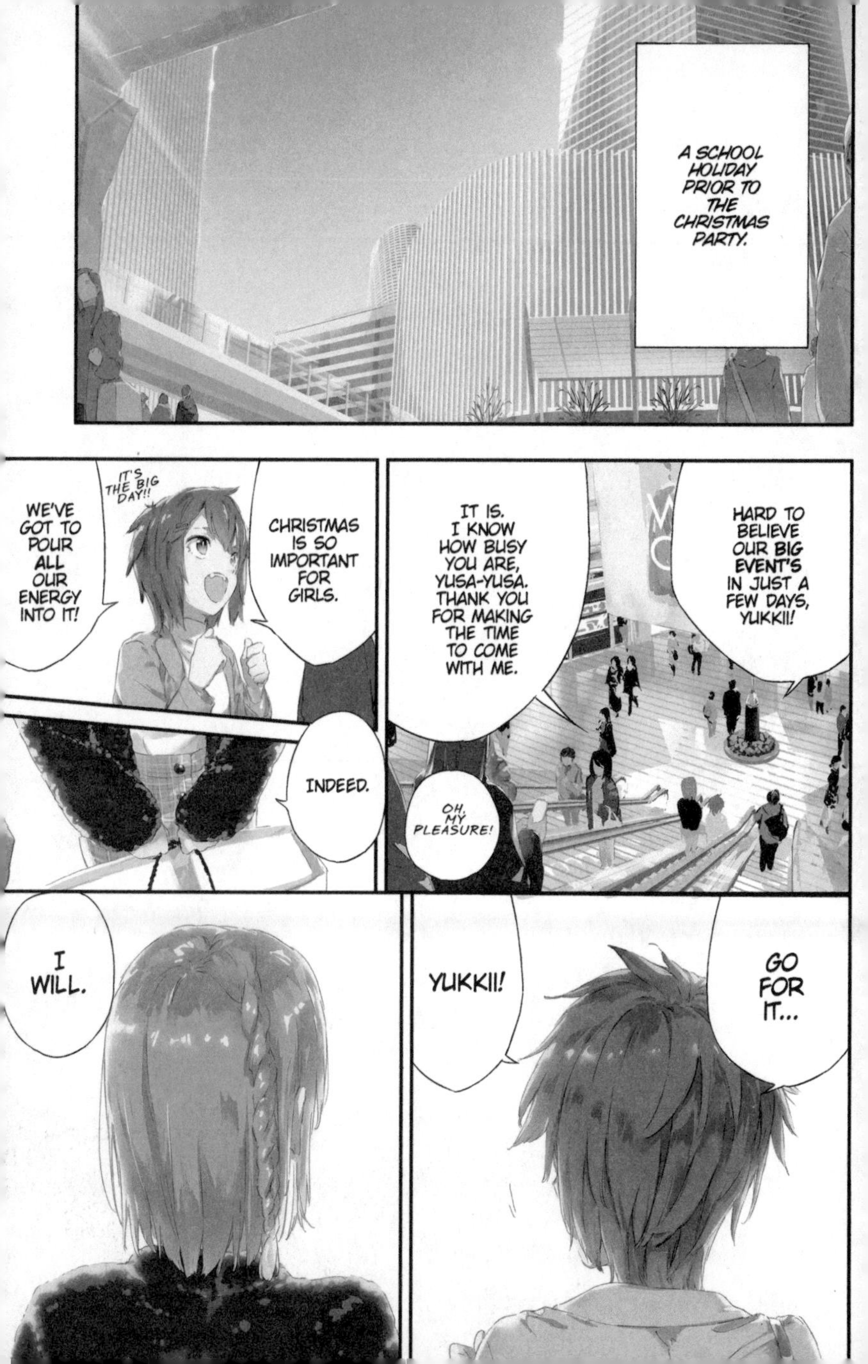
A SCHOOL HOLIDAY PRIOR TO THE CHRISTMAS PARTY.
HARD TO BELIEVE OUR BIG EVENT'S IN JUST A FEW DAYS, YUKKII!
IT IS. I KNOW HOW BUSY YOU ARE, YUSA-YUSA. THANK YOU FOR MAKING THE TIME TO COME WITH ME.
OH, MY PLEASURE!
CHRISTMAS IS SO IMPORTANT FOR GIRLS.
IT'S THE BIG DAY!!
WE'VE GOT TO POUR ALL OUR ENERGY INTO IT!
INDEED.
GO FOR IT...
YUKKII!
I WILL.

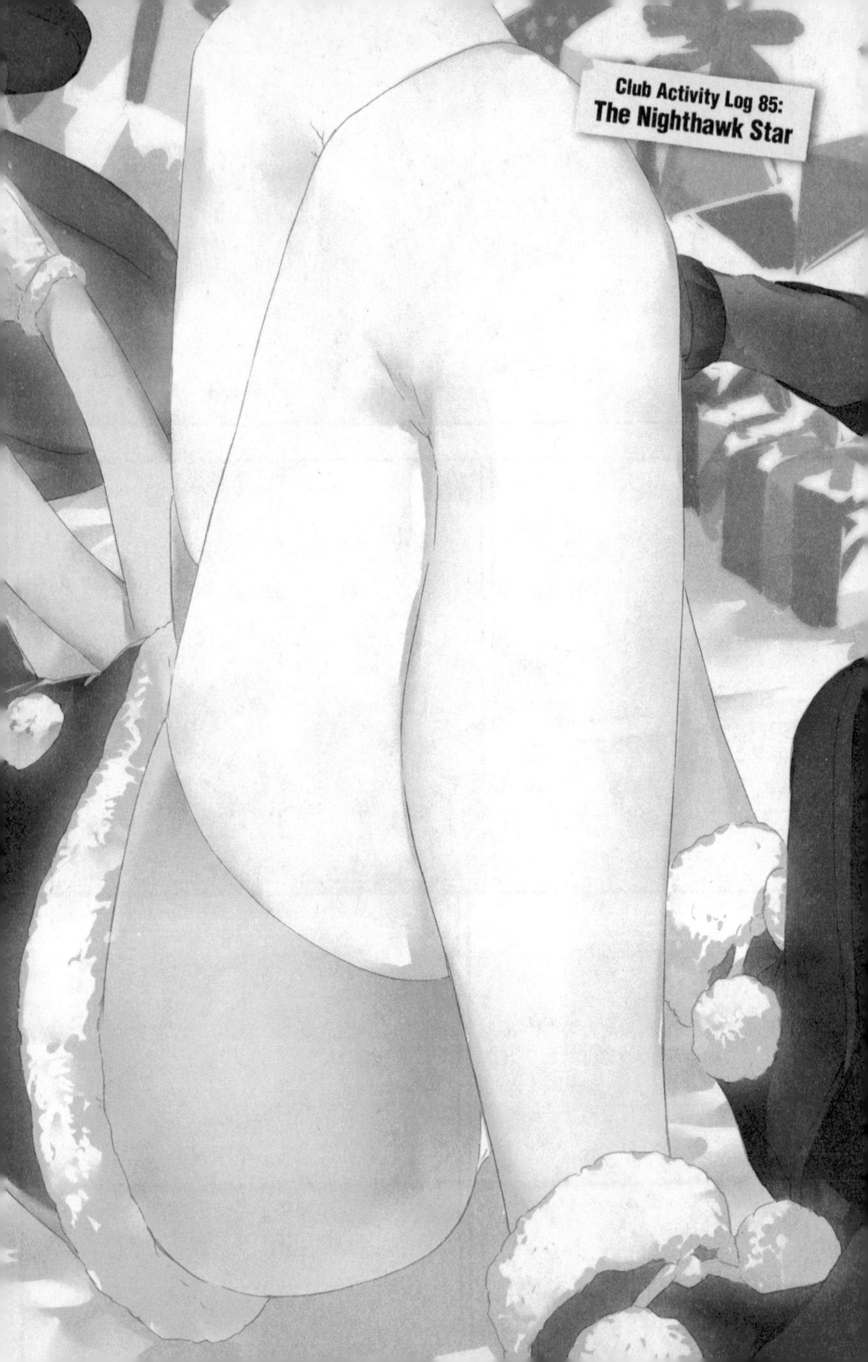
Club Activity Log 85:
The Nighthawk Star

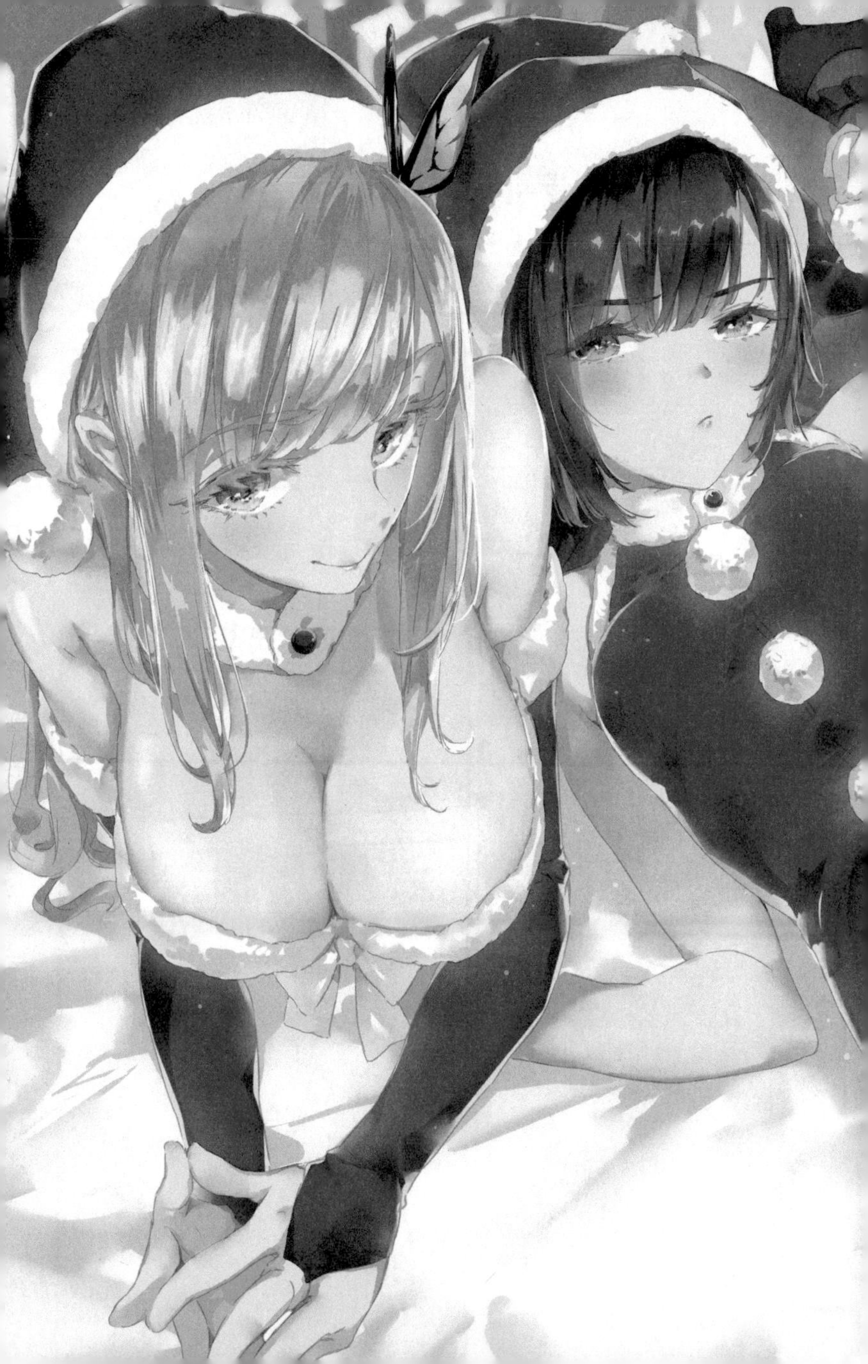

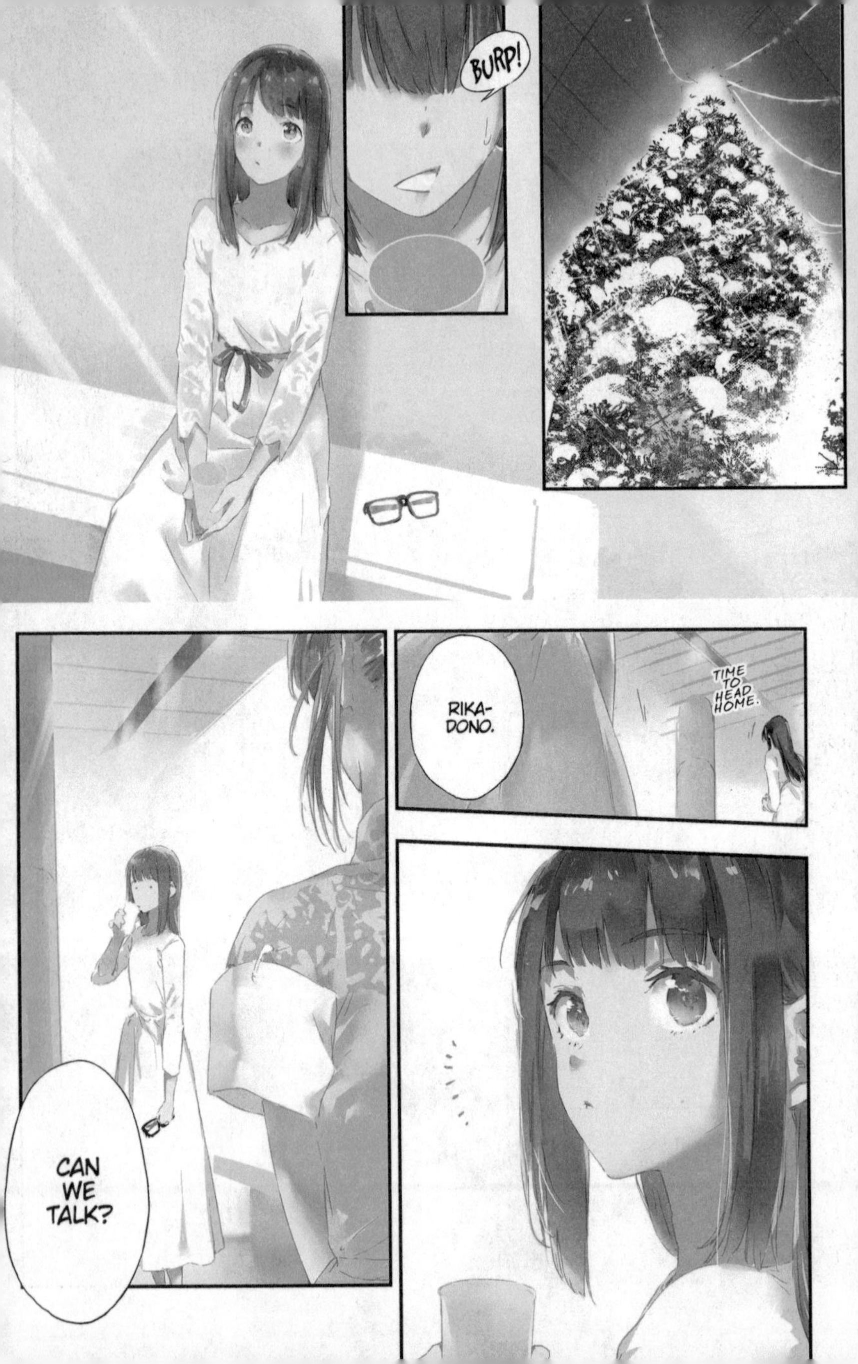
BURP!
TIME TO HEAD HOME.
RIKA-DONO.
CAN WE TALK?

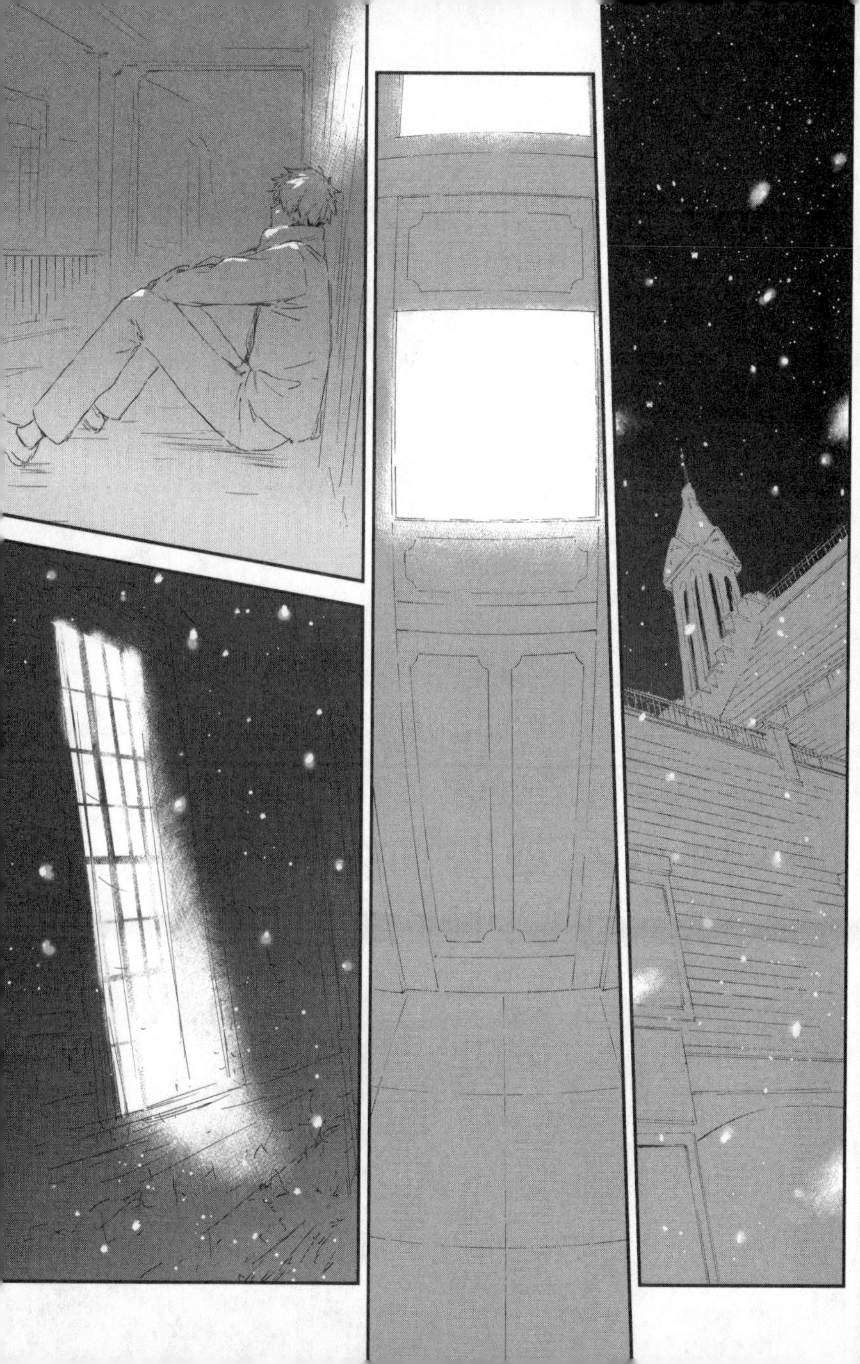

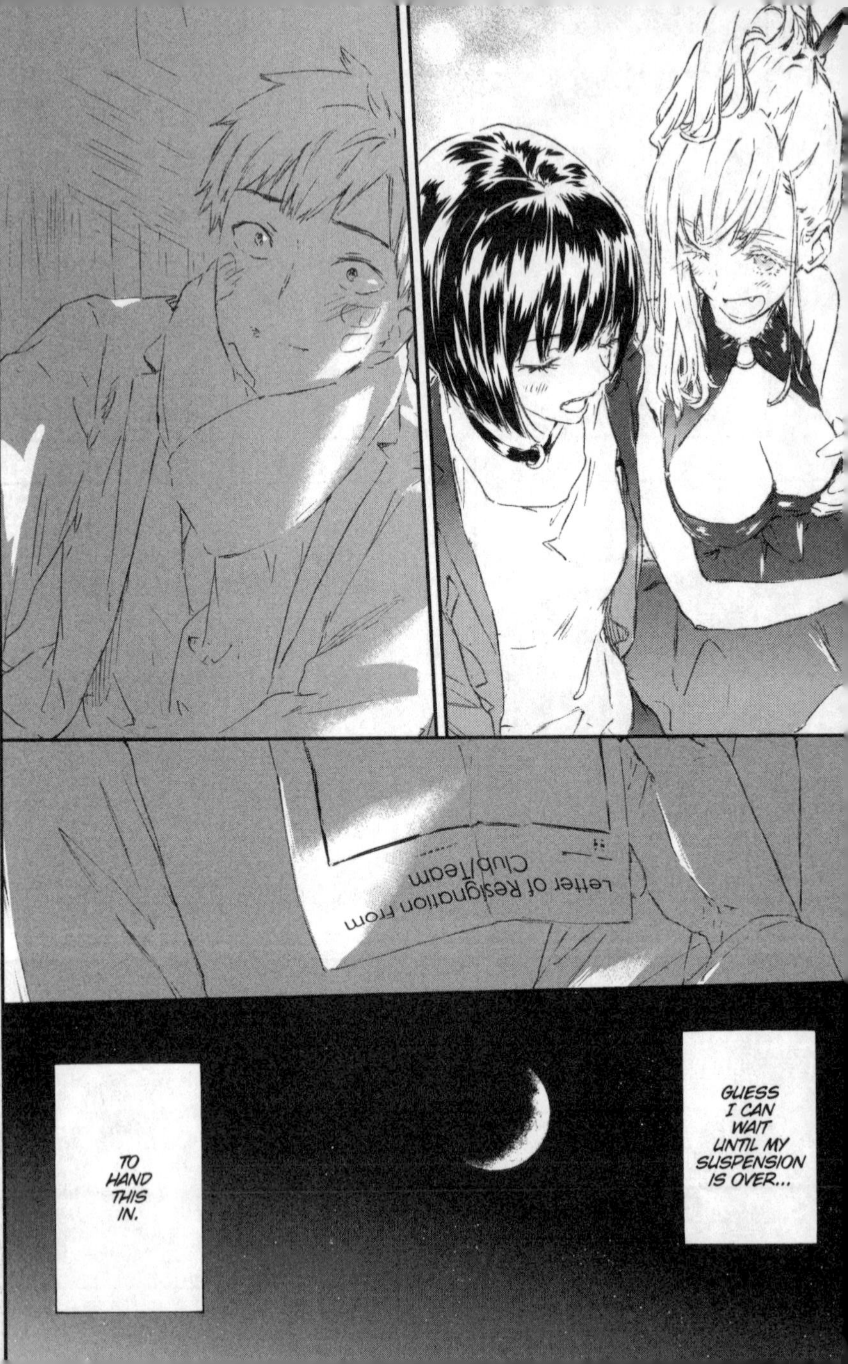
Letter of Resignation from
Club/Team
GUESS I CAN WAIT UNTIL MY SUSPENSION IS OVER...
TO HAND THIS IN.

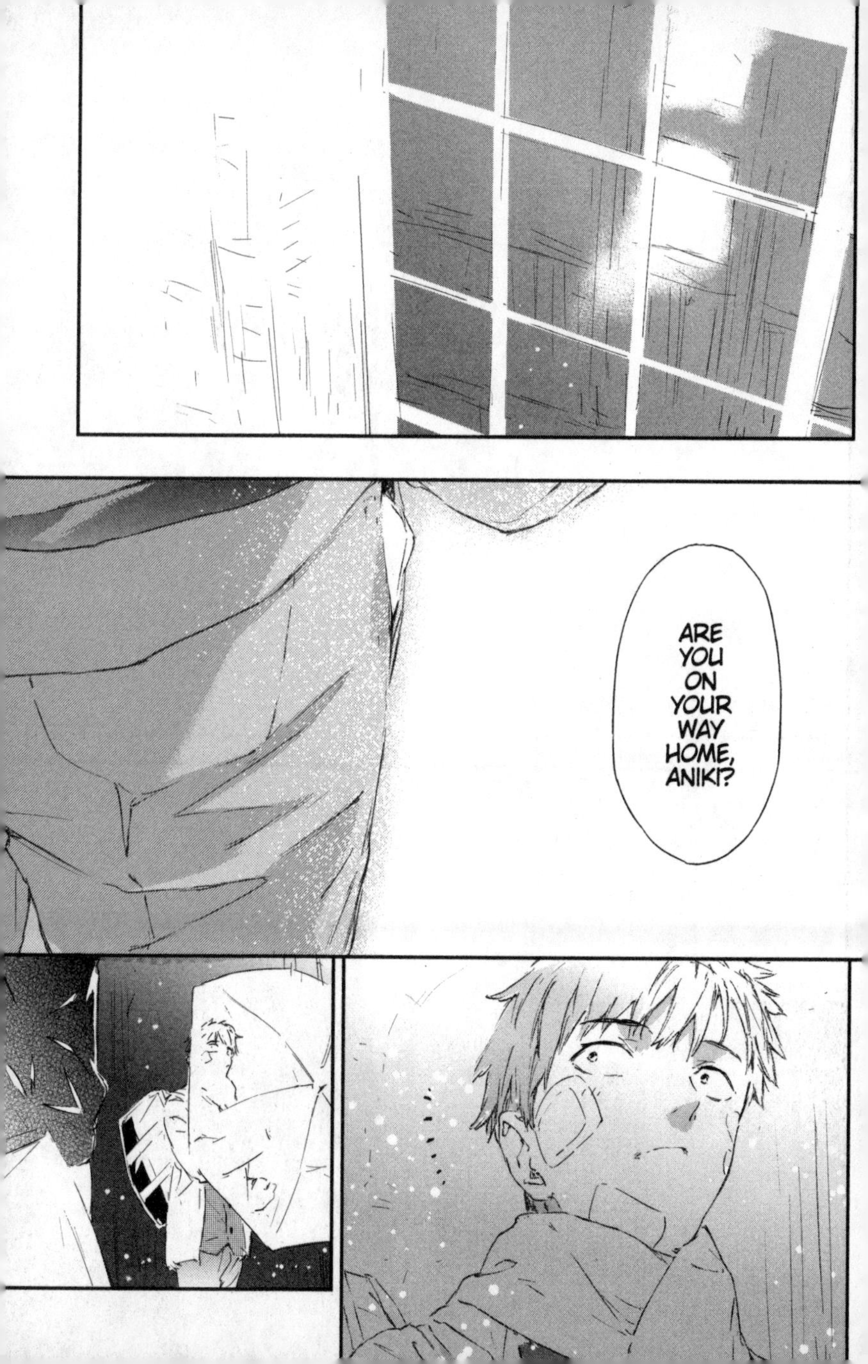
ARE YOU ON YOUR WAY HOME, ANIKI?
...

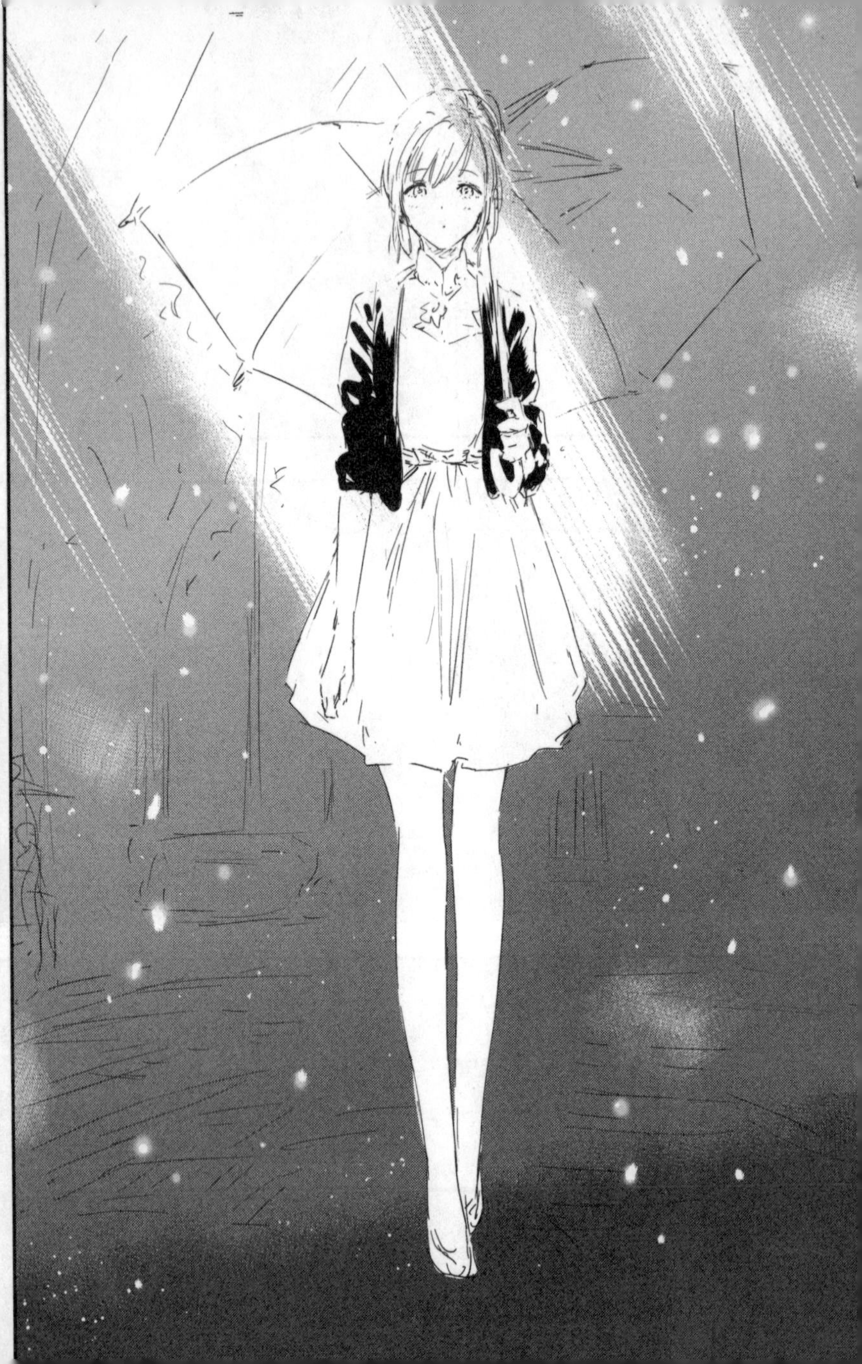

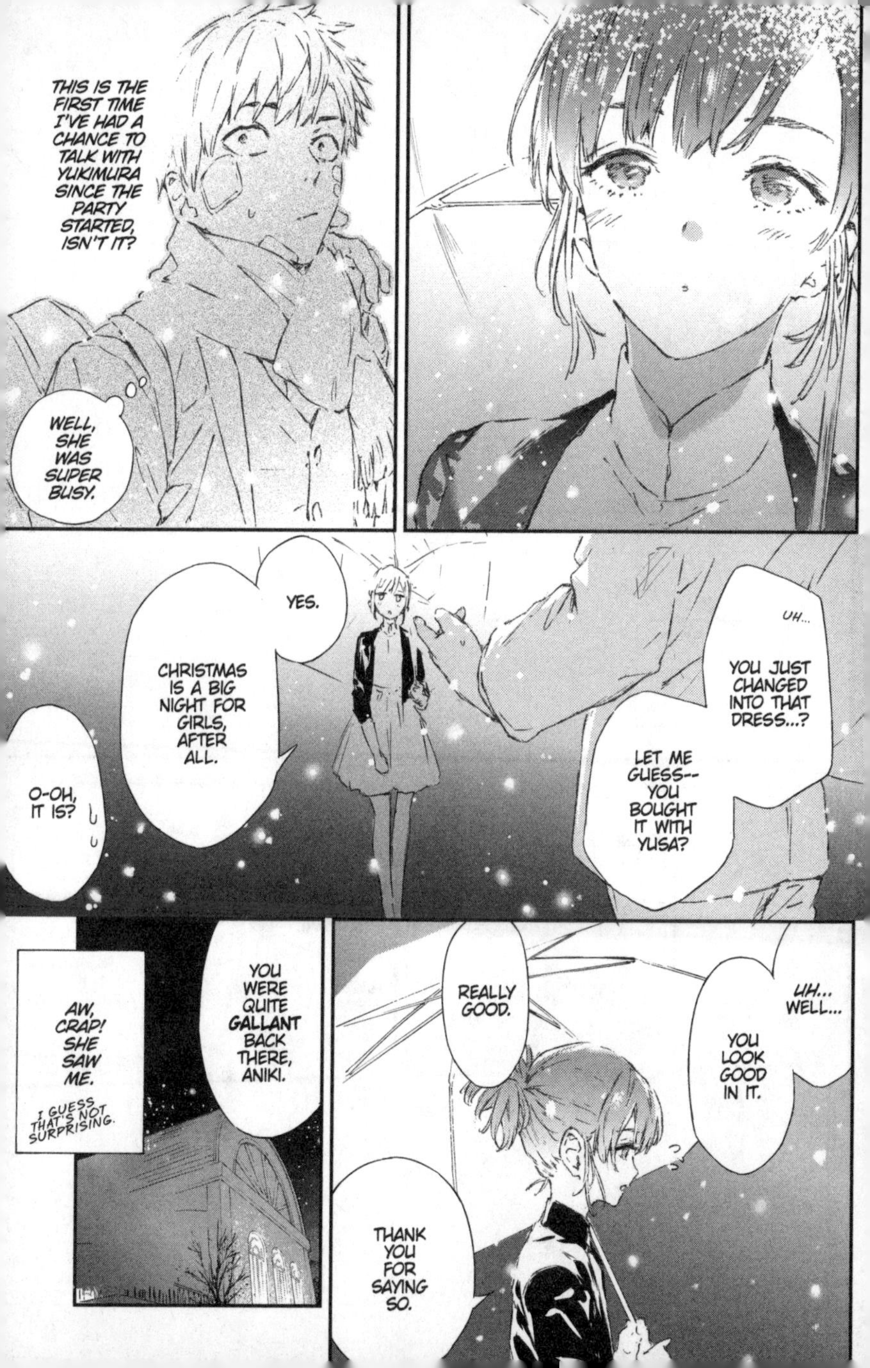
THIS IS THE FIRST TIME I'VE HAD A CHANCE TO TALK WITH YUKIMURA SINCE THE PARTY STARTED, ISN'T IT?
WELL, SHE WAS SUPER BUSY.
UH...
YOU JUST CHANGED INTO THAT DRESS...?
LET ME GUESS-- YOU BOUGHT IT WITH YUSA?
YES.
CHRISTMAS IS A BIG NIGHT FOR GIRLS, AFTER ALL.
O-OH, IT IS?
UH... WELL...
YOU LOOK GOOD IN IT.
REALLY GOOD.
THANK YOU FOR SAYING SO.
YOU WERE QUITE GALLANT BACK THERE, ANIKI.
AW, CRAP! SHE SAW ME.
I GUESS THAT'S NOT SURPRISING.

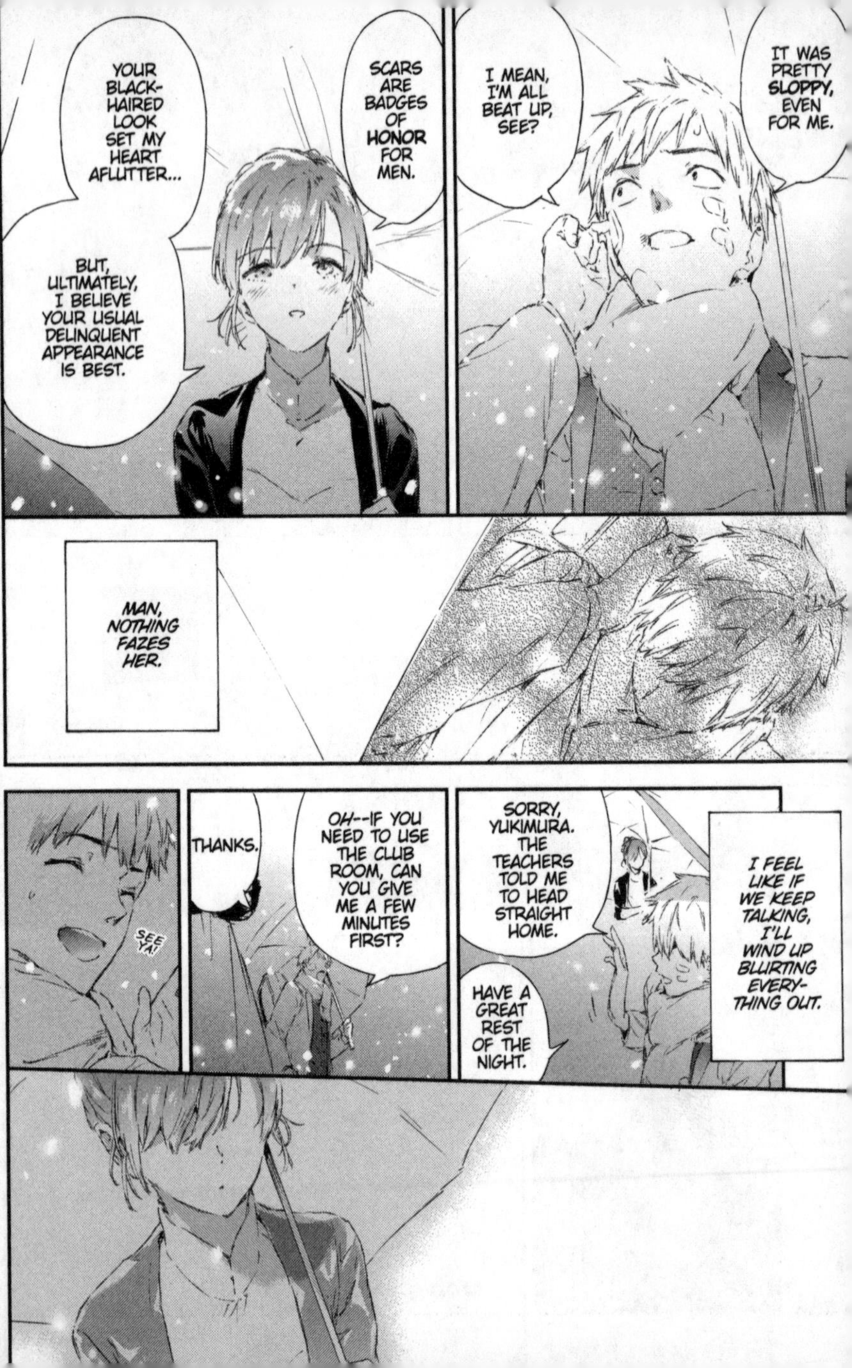
IT WAS PRETTY SLOPPY, EVEN FOR ME.
I MEAN, I'M ALL BEAT UP, SEE?
SCARS ARE BADGES OF HONOR FOR MEN.
YOUR BLACK-HAIRED LOOK SET MY HEART AFLUTTER...
BUT, ULTIMATELY, I BELIEVE YOUR USUAL DELINQUENT APPEARANCE IS BEST.
MAN, NOTHING FAZES HER.
I FEEL LIKE IF WE KEEP TALKING, I'LL WIND UP BLURTING EVERY-THING OUT.
SORRY, YUKIMURA. THE TEACHERS TOLD ME TO HEAD STRAIGHT HOME.
HAVE A GREAT REST OF THE NIGHT.
OH--IF YOU NEED TO USE THE CLUB ROOM, CAN YOU GIVE ME A FEW MINUTES FIRST?
THANKS.
SEE YA!

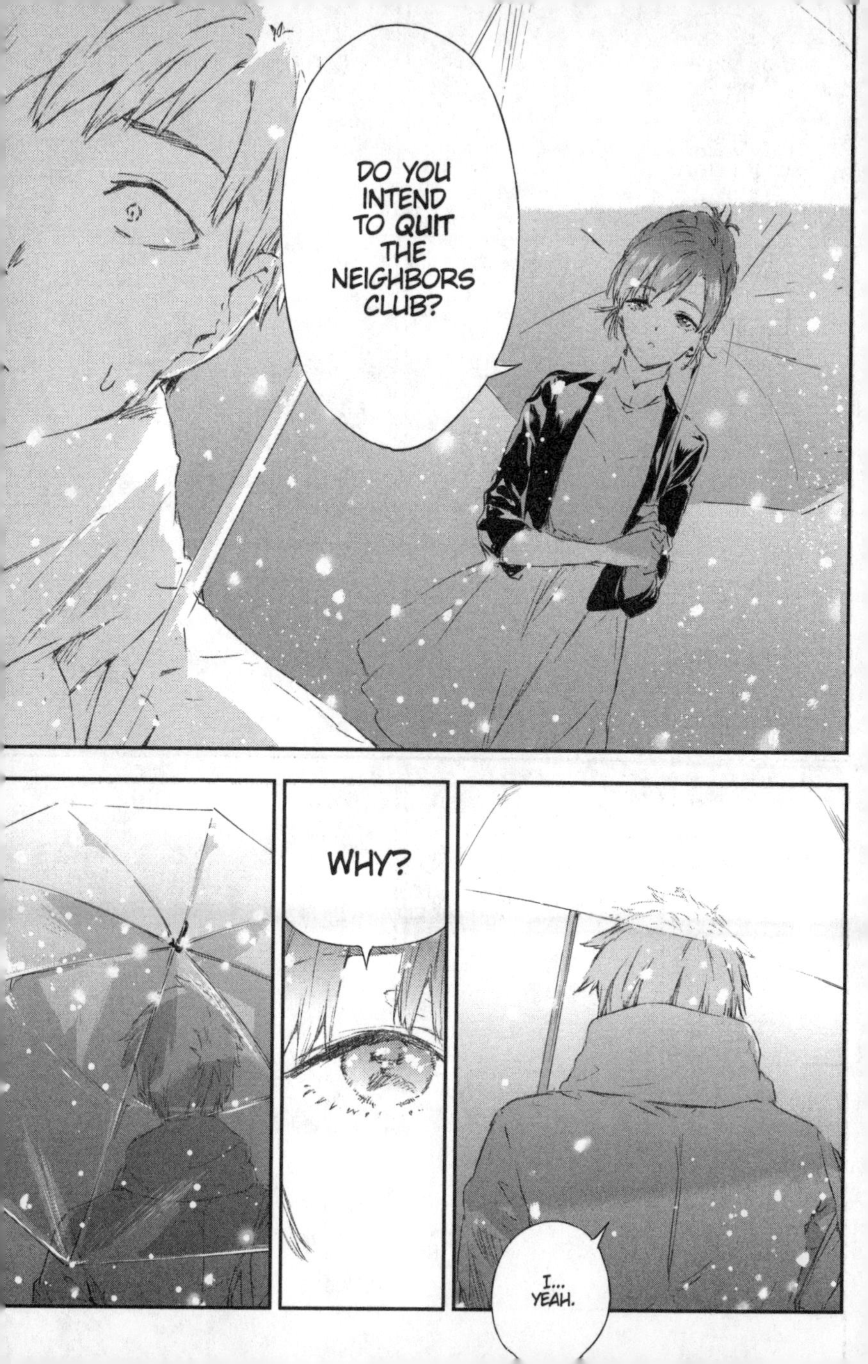
DO YOU INTEND TO QUIT THE NEIGHBORS CLUB?
I... YEAH.
WHY?

SENA AND YOZORA ACKNOWLEDGED EACH OTHER AS FRIENDS BACK THERE.
IF I'M GONE, THERE'LL BE NOTHING LEFT FOR THEM TO FIGHT OVER.
NOTHING LIKE WHAT HAPPENED A FEW DAYS BACK WILL HAPPEN AGAIN.
EVER SINCE SENA TOLD ME SHE LIKED ME ABOUT A MONTH AGO, I'VE BEEN THINKING.
THE NEIGHBORS CLUB IS A HAVEN FOR MISFITS WHERE THEY CAN ACT LIKE THEMSELVES.
IT'S THE PARADISE I ALWAYS DREAMED OF FINDING...
AND YET I'M ALSO ITS BIGGEST DISRUPTIVE ELEMENT.

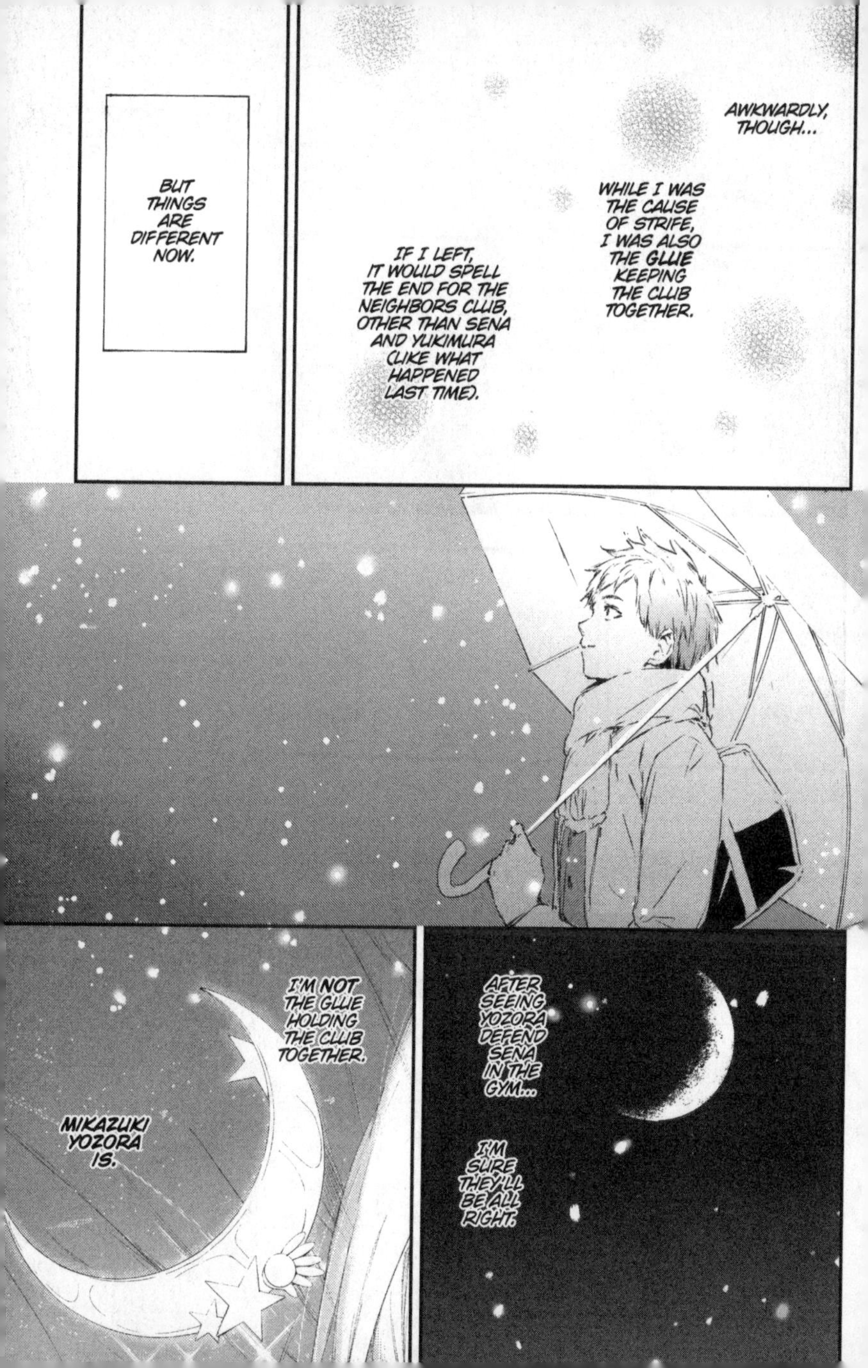
AWKWARDLY, THOUGH...
WHILE I WAS THE CAUSE OF STRIFE, I WAS ALSO THE GLUE KEEPING THE CLUB TOGETHER.
IF I LEFT, IT WOULD SPELL THE END FOR THE NEIGHBORS CLUB, OTHER THAN SENA AND YUKIMURA (LIKE WHAT HAPPENED LAST TIME).
BUT THINGS ARE DIFFERENT NOW.
AFTER SEEING YOZORA DEFEND SENA IN THE GYM...
I'M SURE THEY'LL BE ALL RIGHT.
I'M NOT THE GLUE HOLDING THE CLUB TOGETHER.
MIKAZUKI YOZORA IS.

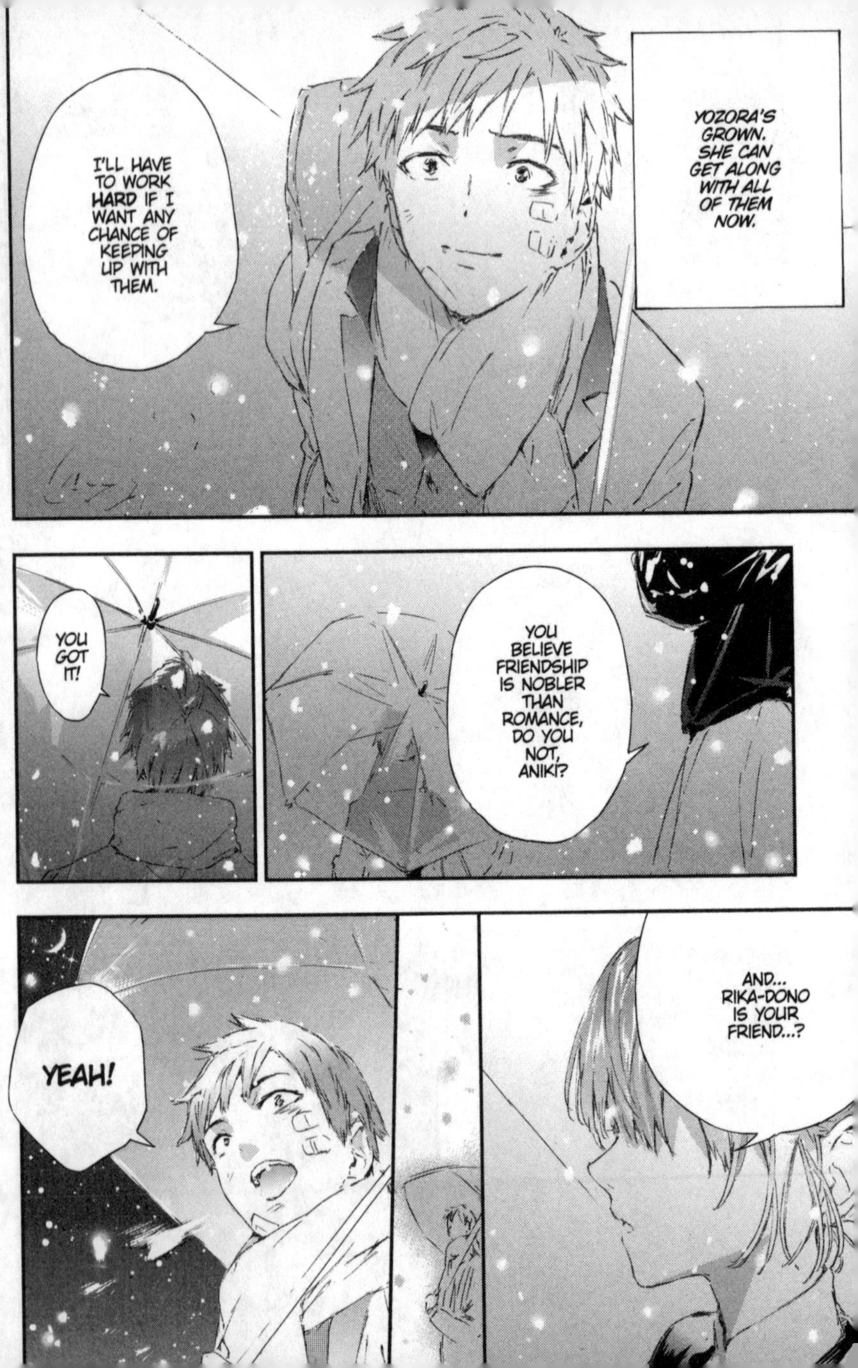
YOZORA'S GROWN. SHE CAN GET ALONG WITH ALL OF THEM NOW.
I'LL HAVE TO WORK **HARD** IF I WANT ANY CHANCE OF KEEPING UP WITH THEM.
YOU BELIEVE FRIENDSHIP IS NOBLER THAN ROMANCE, DO YOU NOT, ANIKI?
YOU GOT IT!
AND... RIKA-DONO IS YOUR FRIEND...?
YEAH!

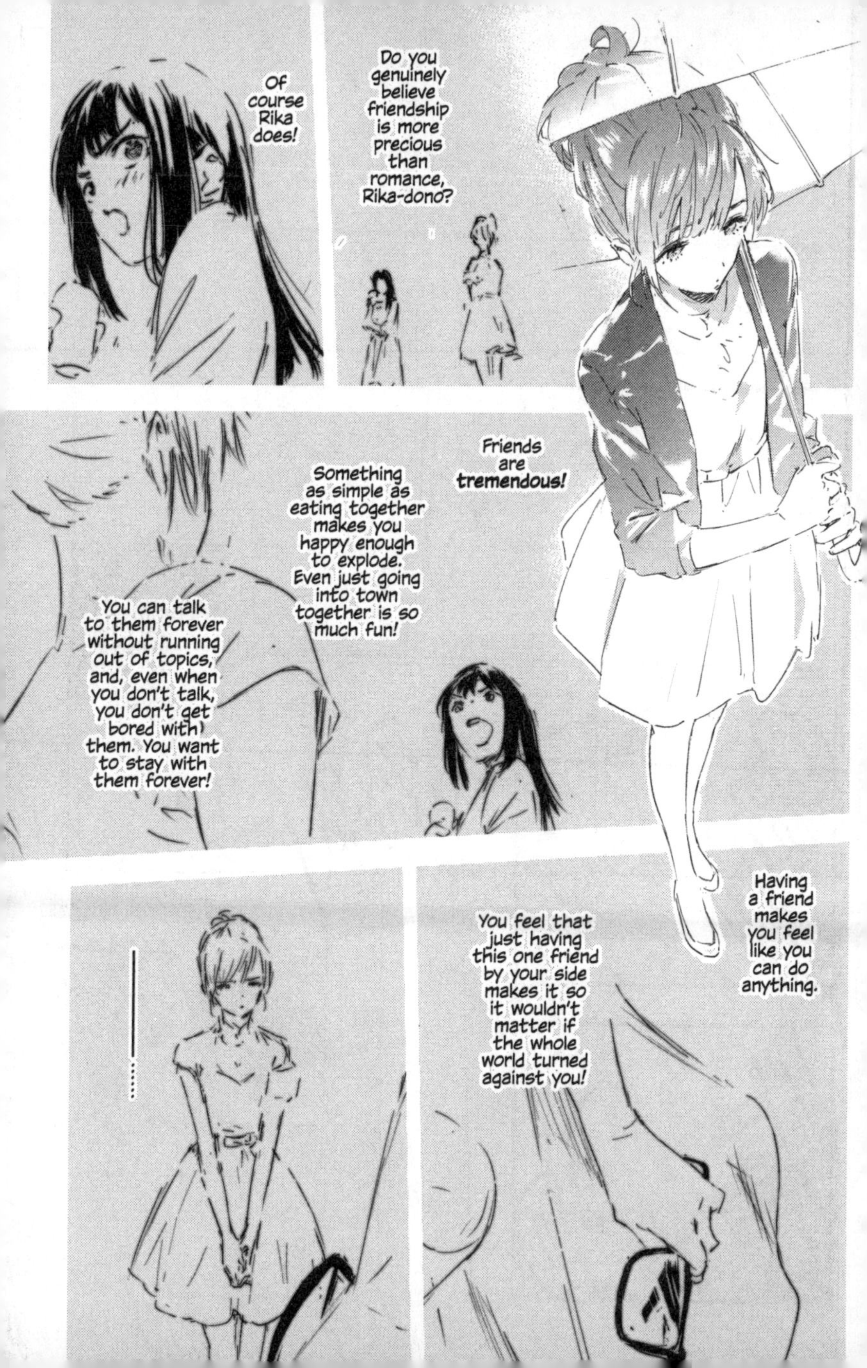

Do you genuinely believe friendship is more precious than romance, Rika-dono?
Of course Rika does!
Friends are **tremendous!**
Something as simple as eating together makes you happy enough to explode. Even just going into town together is so much fun!
You can talk to them forever without running out of topics, and, even when you don't talk, you don't get bored with them. You want to stay with them forever!
Having a friend makes you feel like you can do anything.
You feel that just having this one friend by your side makes it so it wouldn't matter if the whole world turned against you!
——……

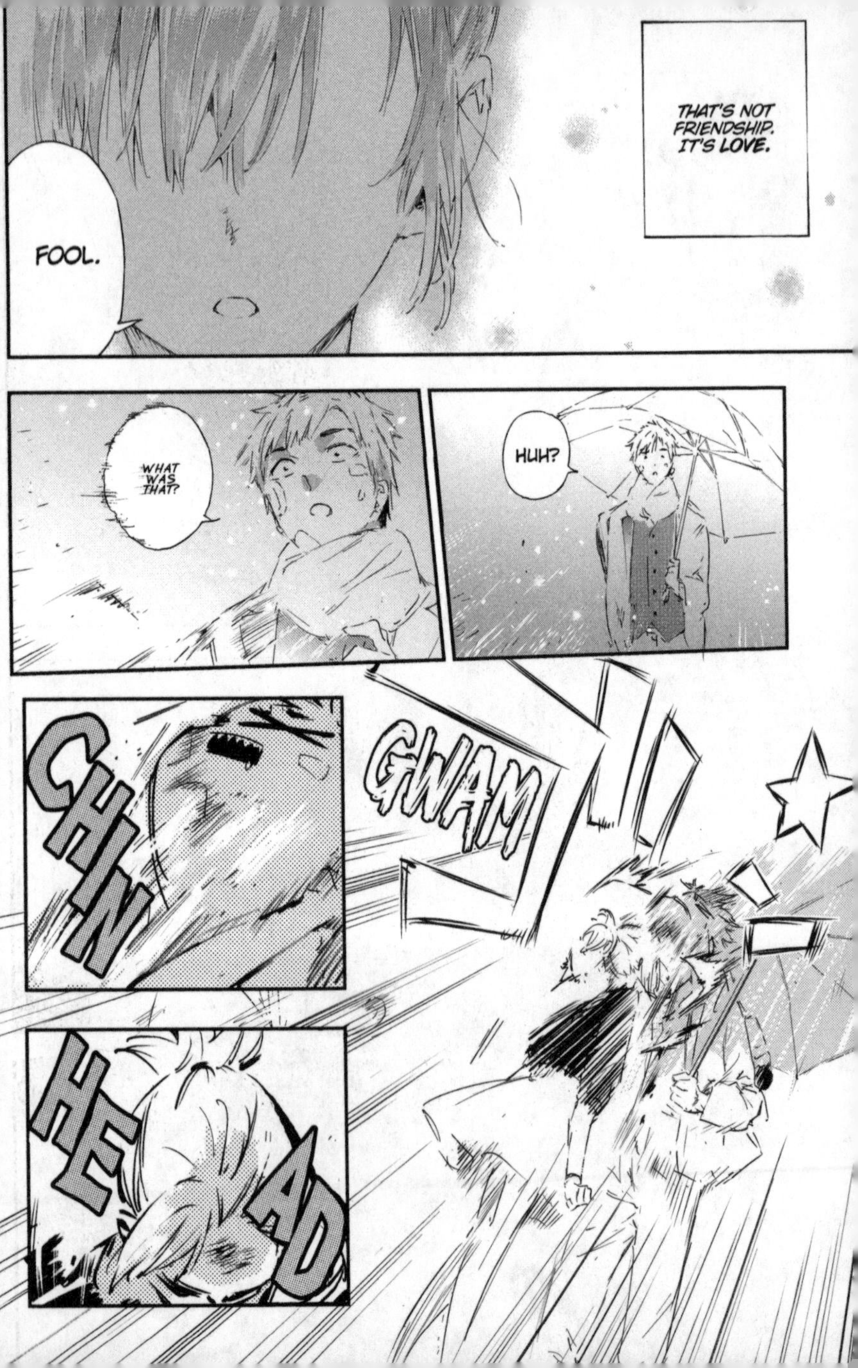
THAT'S NOT FRIENDSHIP. IT'S LOVE.
FOOL.
HUH?
WHAT WAS THAT?
GWAM
CHIN
HEAD

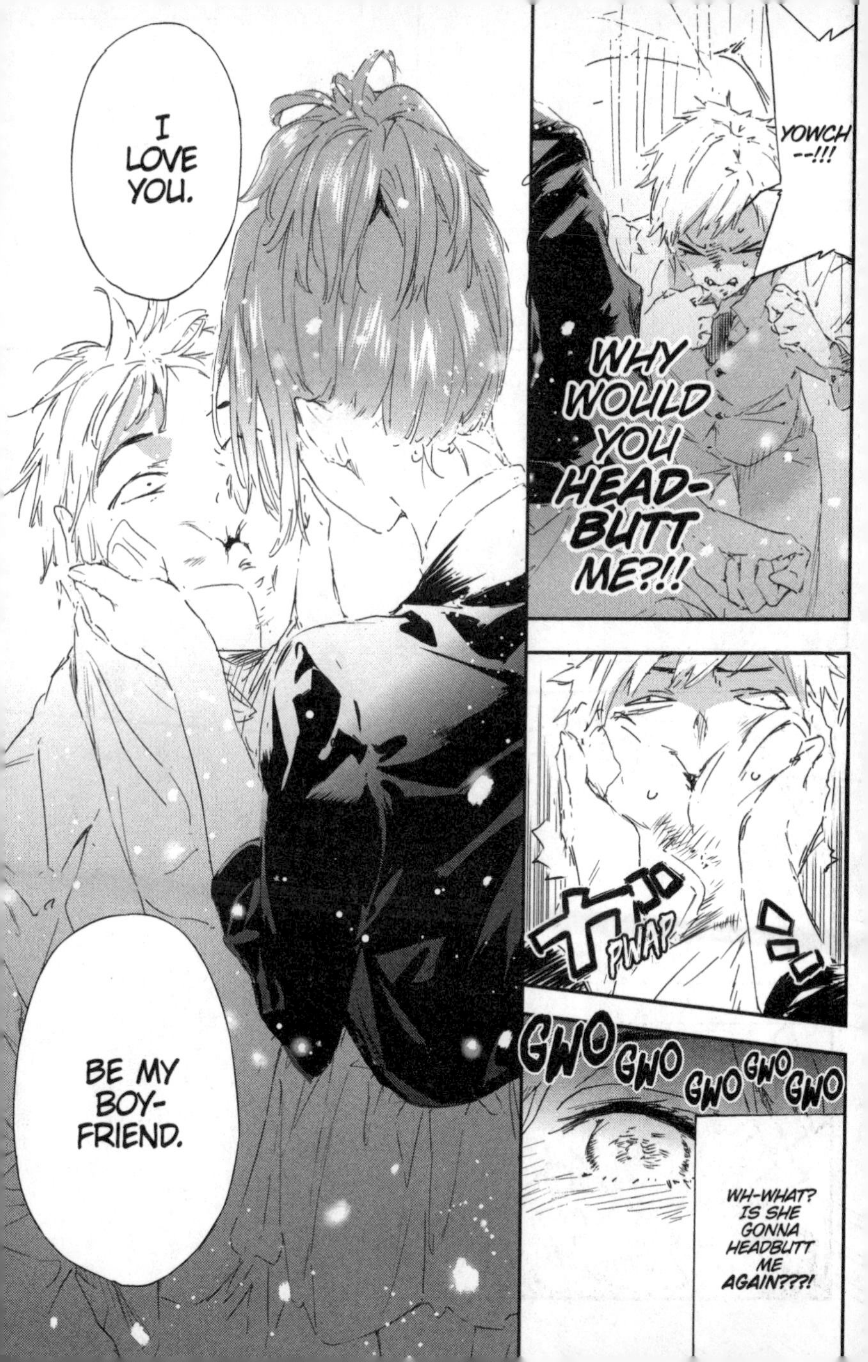
YOWCH--!!!
WHY WOULD YOU HEAD-BUTT ME?!!
PWAP
GWO GWO GWO GWO GWO
WH-WHAT? IS SHE GONNA HEADBUTT ME AGAIN???!
I LOVE YOU.
BE MY BOY-FRIEND.

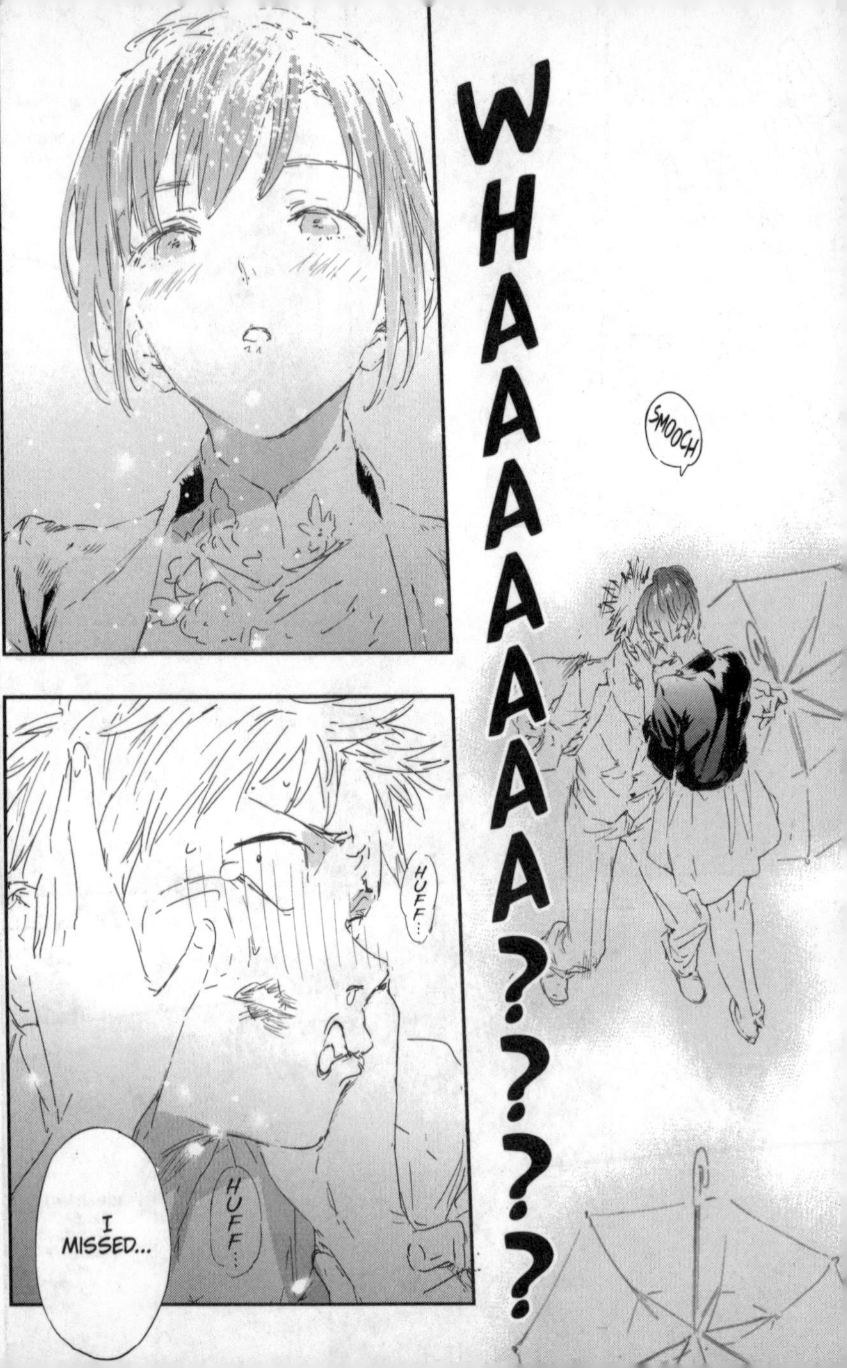
SMOOCH
WHAAAAAAA????
HUFF...
HUFF...
I MISSED...

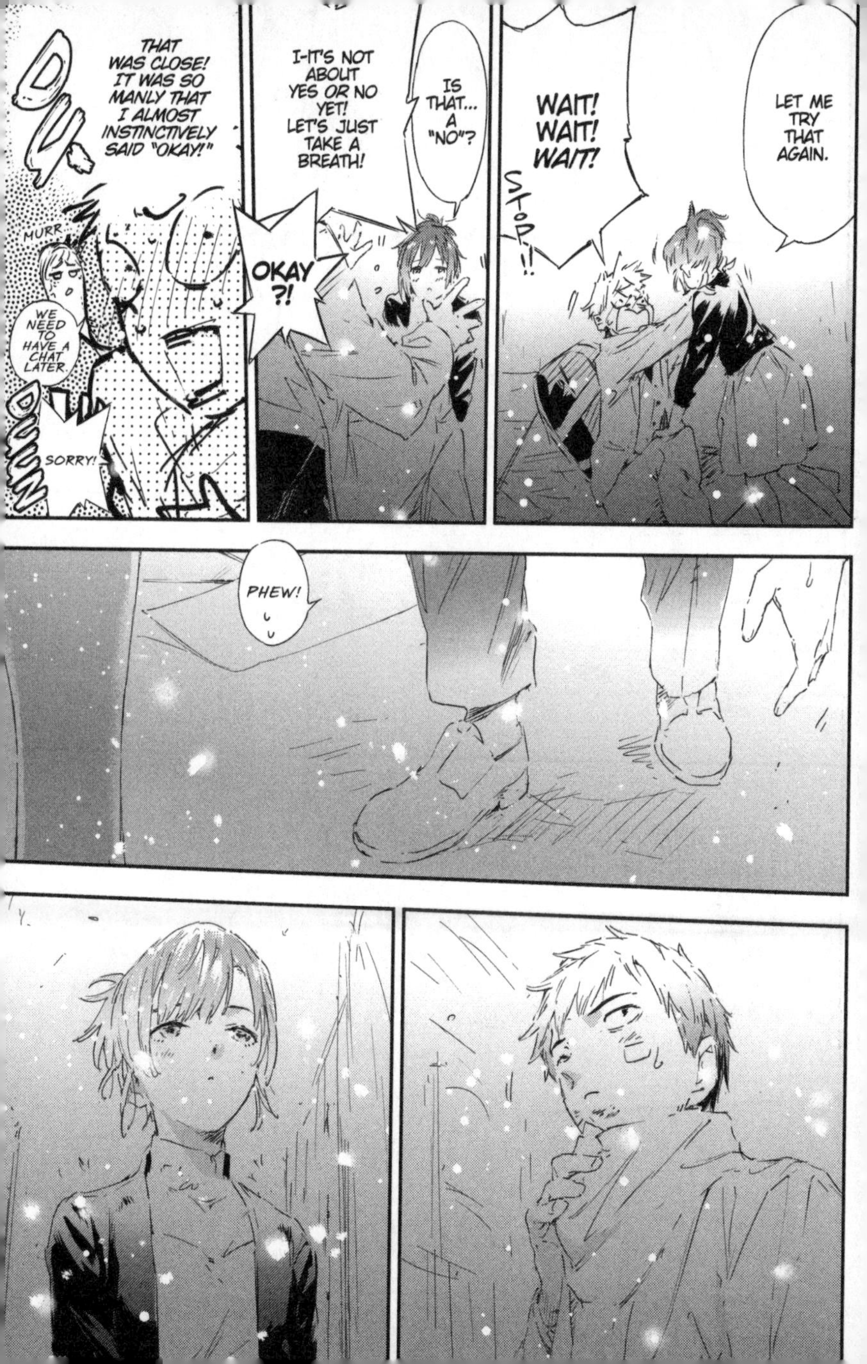
LET ME TRY THAT AGAIN.
WAIT! WAIT! WAIT!
STOP!!
IS THAT... A "NO"?
I-IT'S NOT ABOUT YES OR NO YET! LET'S JUST TAKE A BREATH!
OKAY ?!
THAT WAS CLOSE! IT WAS SO MANLY THAT I ALMOST INSTINCTIVELY SAID "OKAY!"
MURR...
WE NEED TO HAVE A CHAT LATER.
SORRY!
DUUN
PHEW!

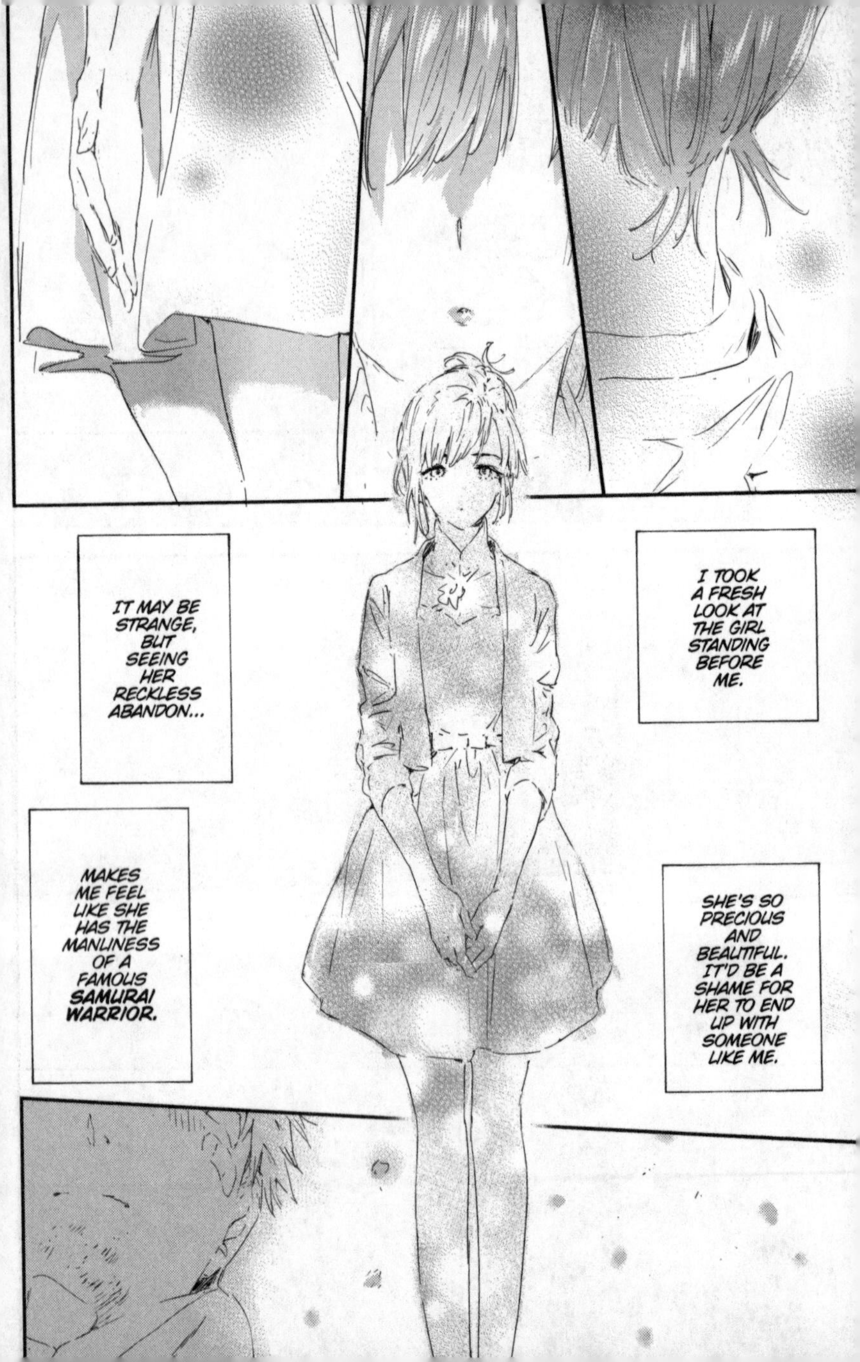
I TOOK A FRESH LOOK AT THE GIRL STANDING BEFORE ME.
IT MAY BE STRANGE, BUT SEEING HER RECKLESS ABANDON...
MAKES ME FEEL LIKE SHE HAS THE MANLINESS OF A FAMOUS SAMURAI WARRIOR.
SHE'S SO PRECIOUS AND BEAUTIFUL. IT'D BE A SHAME FOR HER TO END UP WITH SOMEONE LIKE ME.

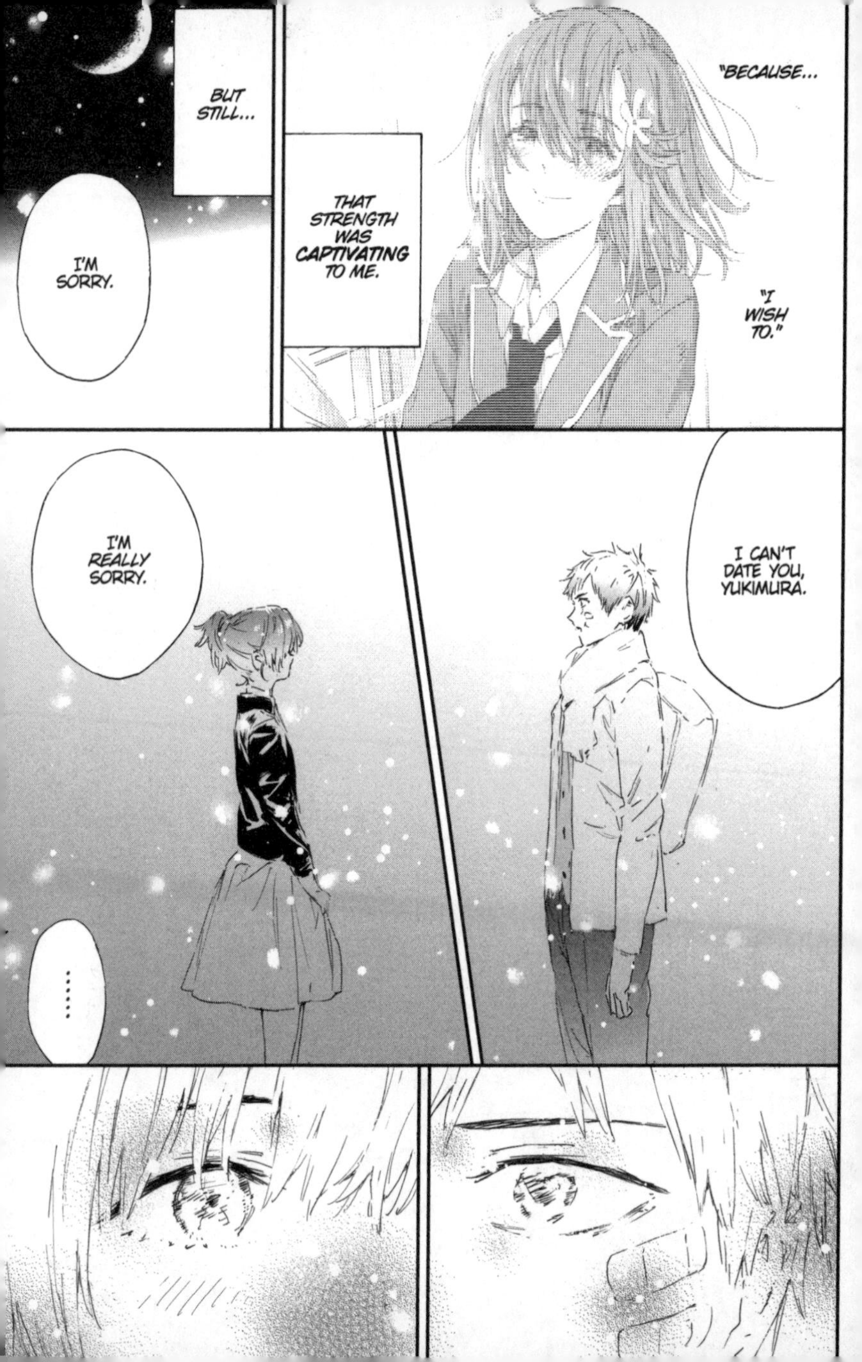
"BECAUSE...
"I WISH TO."
THAT STRENGTH WAS CAPTIVATING TO ME.
BUT STILL...
I'M SORRY.
I CAN'T DATE YOU, YUKIMURA.
I'M REALLY SORRY.
......

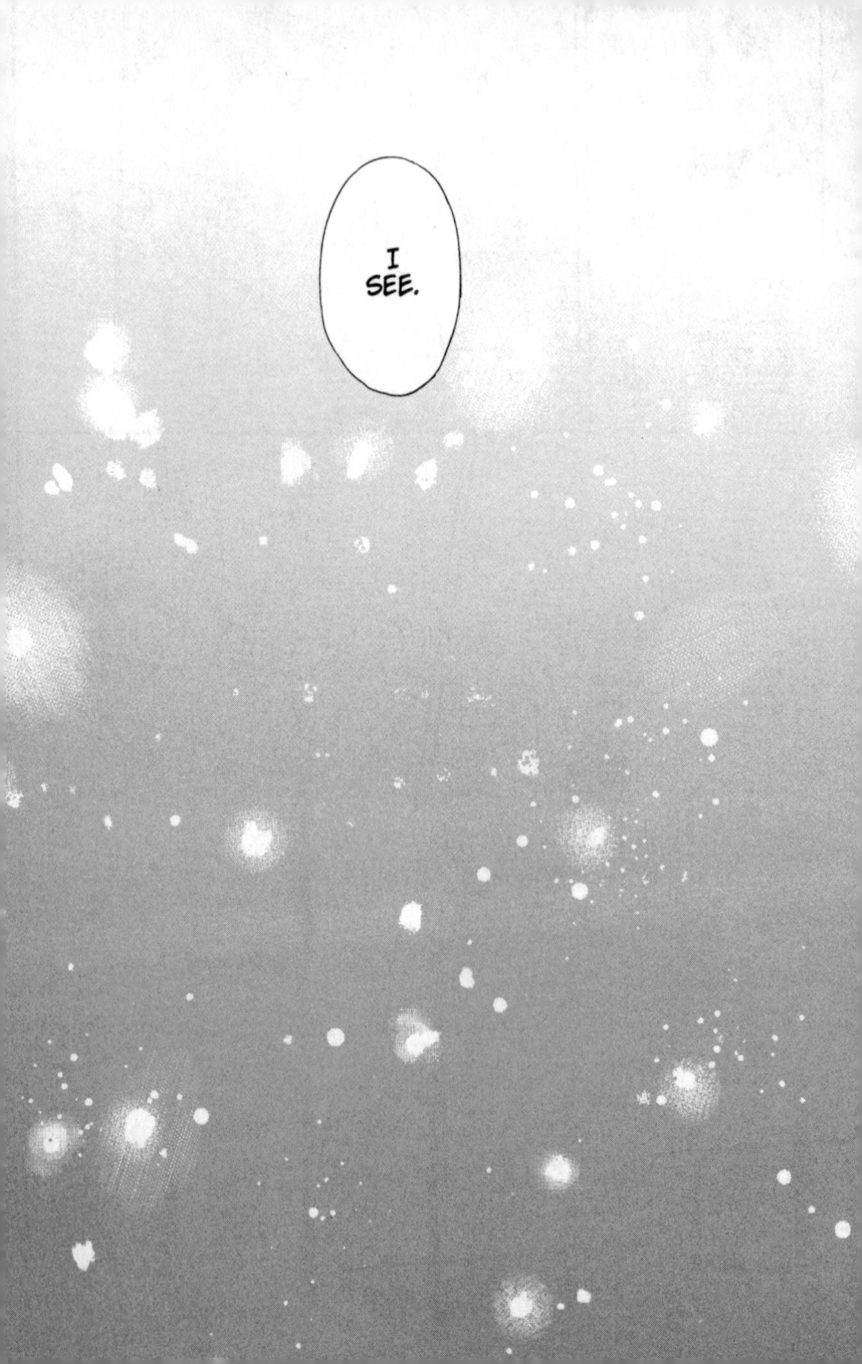
I SEE.

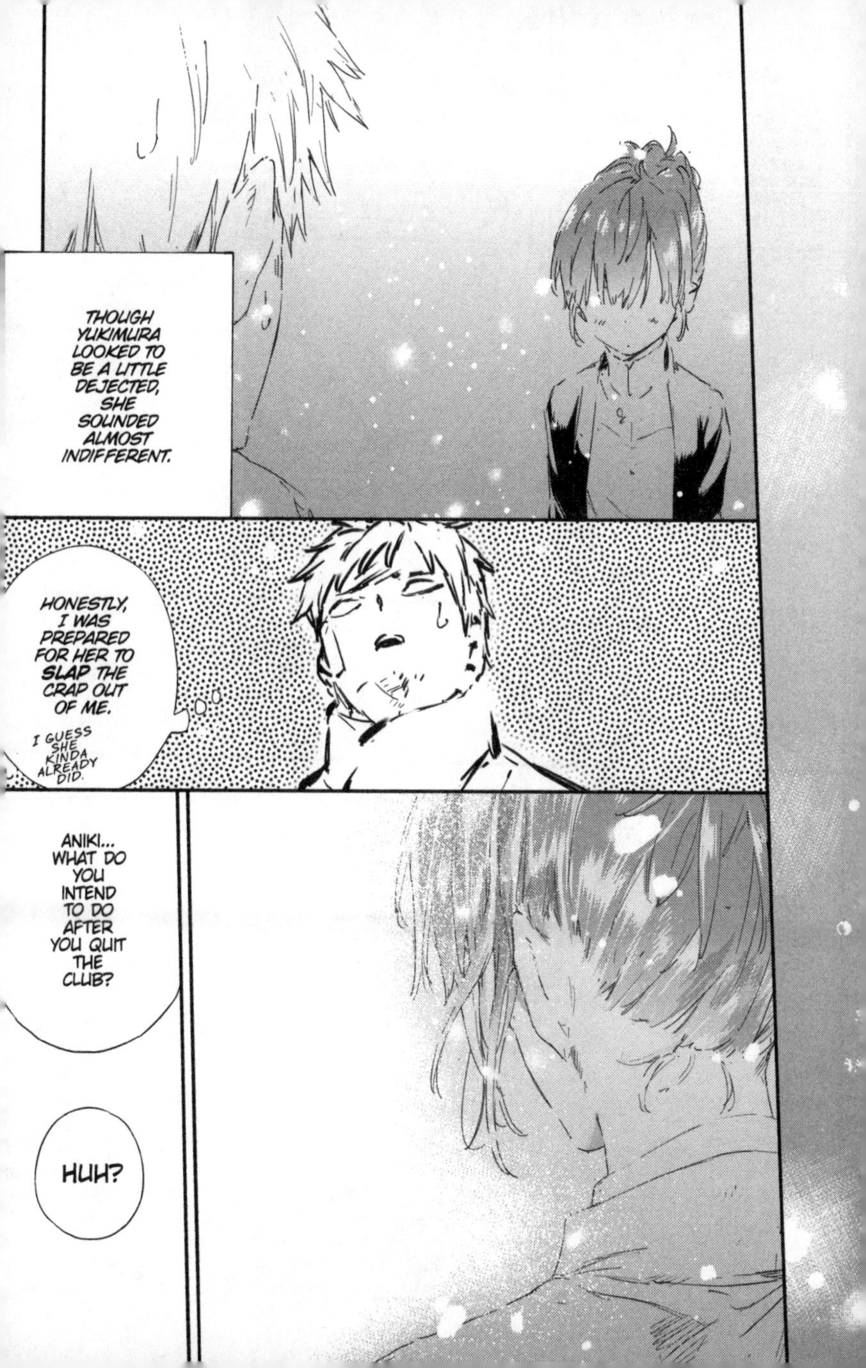
THOUGH YUKIMURA LOOKED TO BE A LITTLE DEJECTED, SHE SOUNDED ALMOST INDIFFERENT.
HONESTLY, I WAS PREPARED FOR HER TO **SLAP** THE CRAP OUT OF ME.
I GUESS SHE KINDA ALREADY DID.
ANIKI... WHAT DO YOU INTEND TO DO AFTER YOU QUIT THE CLUB?
HUH?

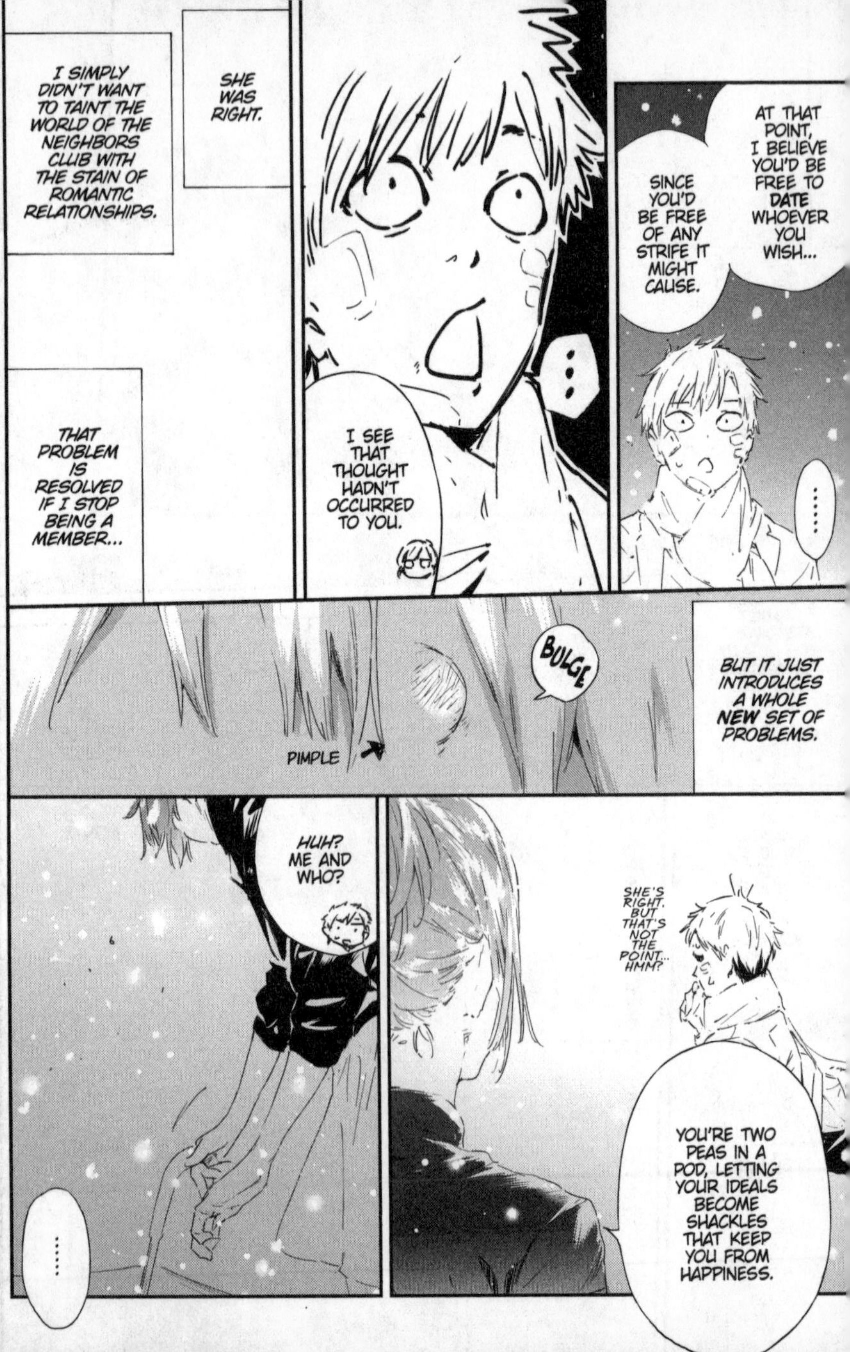
AT THAT POINT, I BELIEVE YOU'D BE FREE TO DATE WHOEVER YOU WISH...
SINCE YOU'D BE FREE OF ANY STRIFE IT MIGHT CAUSE.
......
...
I SEE THAT THOUGHT HADN'T OCCURRED TO YOU.
SHE WAS RIGHT.
I SIMPLY DIDN'T WANT TO TAINT THE WORLD OF THE NEIGHBORS CLUB WITH THE STAIN OF ROMANTIC RELATIONSHIPS.
THAT PROBLEM IS RESOLVED IF I STOP BEING A MEMBER...
BUT IT JUST INTRODUCES A WHOLE NEW SET OF PROBLEMS.
BULGE
PIMPLE
SHE'S RIGHT. BUT THAT'S NOT THE POINT... HMM?
YOU'RE TWO PEAS IN A POD, LETTING YOUR IDEALS BECOME SHACKLES THAT KEEP YOU FROM HAPPINESS.
HUH? ME AND WHO?
......

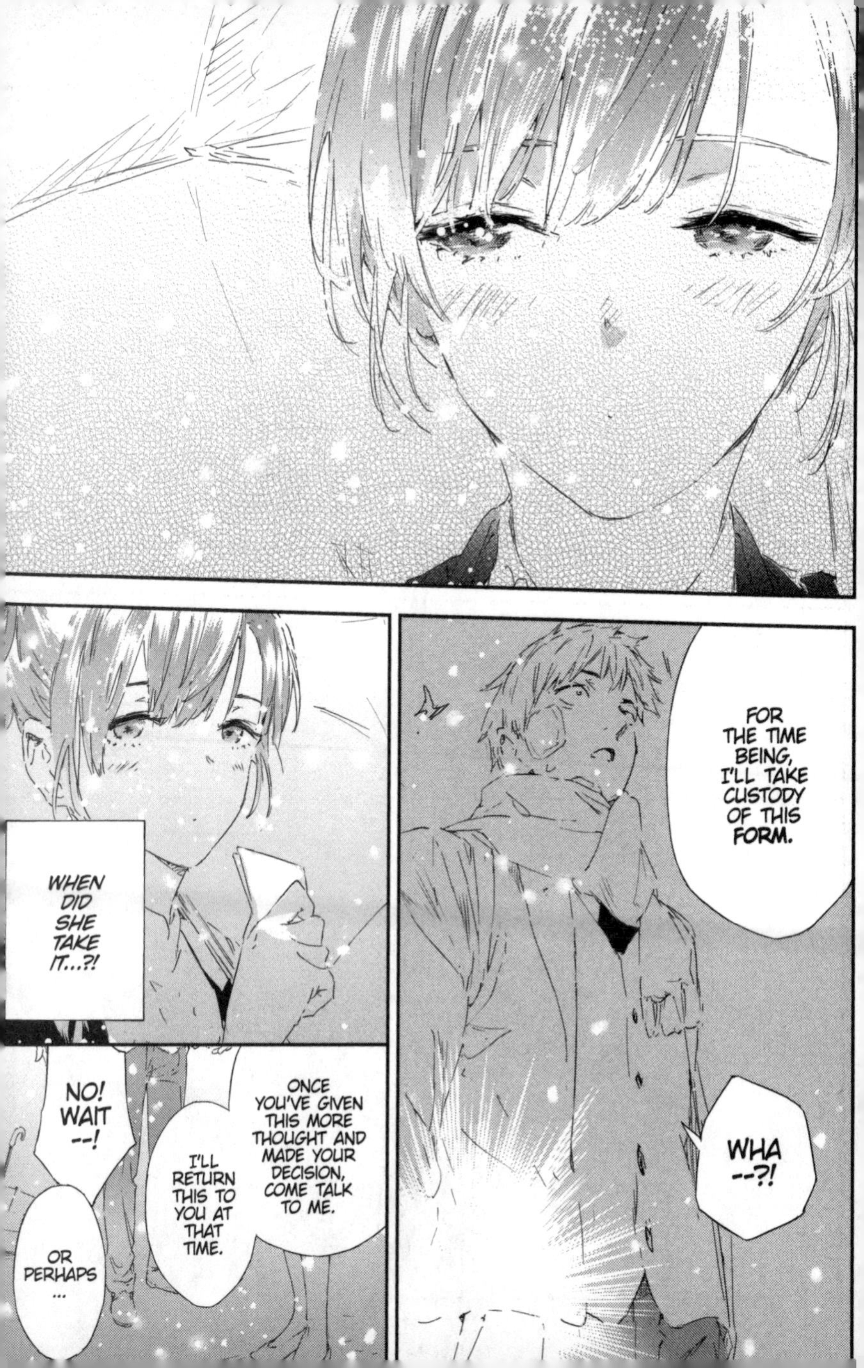
FOR THE TIME BEING, I'LL TAKE CUSTODY OF THIS FORM.
WHA--?!
WHEN DID SHE TAKE IT...?!
ONCE YOU'VE GIVEN THIS MORE THOUGHT AND MADE YOUR DECISION, COME TALK TO ME.
I'LL RETURN THIS TO YOU AT THAT TIME.
NO! WAIT--!
OR PERHAPS...

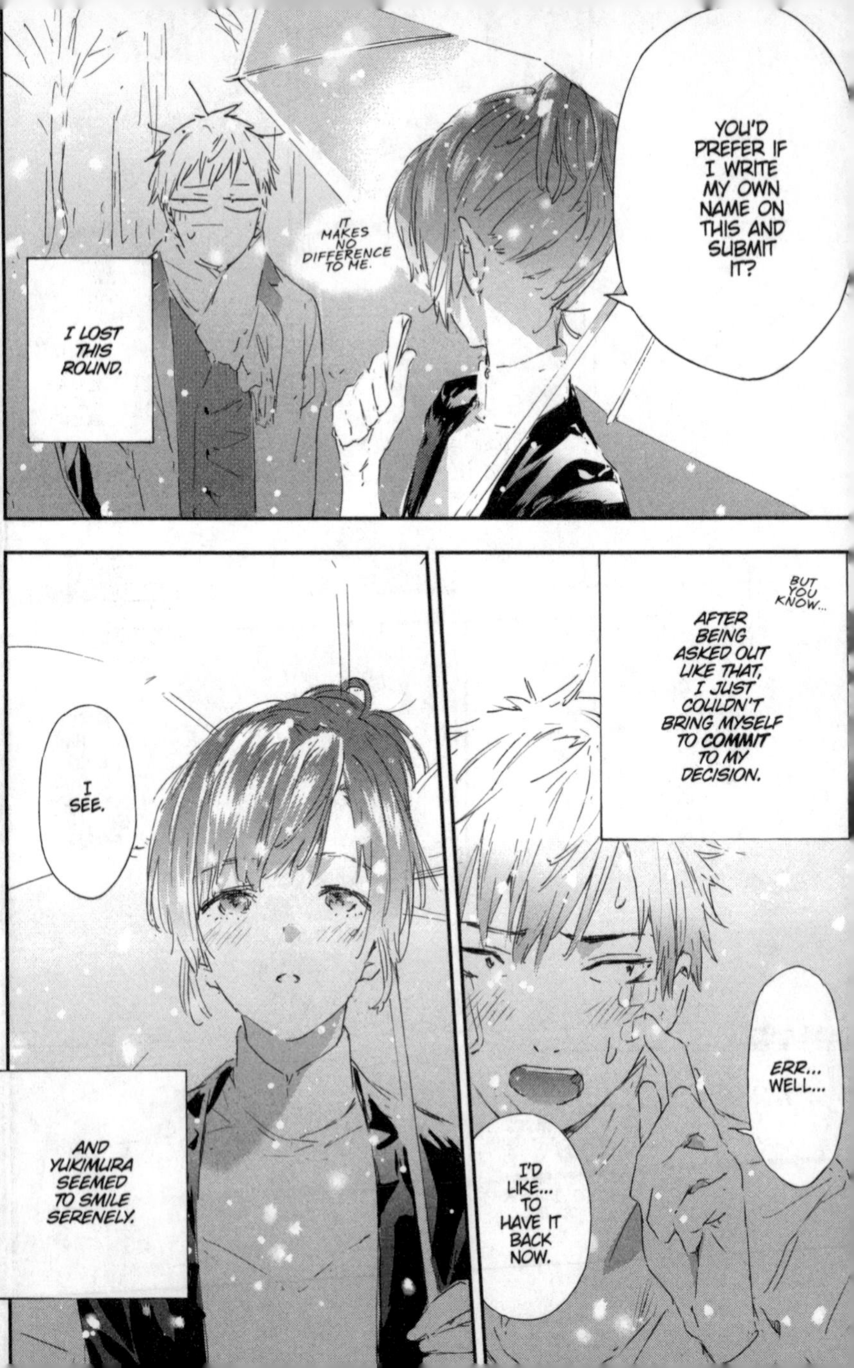
YOU'D PREFER IF I WRITE MY OWN NAME ON THIS AND SUBMIT IT?
IT MAKES NO DIFFERENCE TO ME.
I LOST THIS ROUND.
BUT YOU KNOW...
AFTER BEING ASKED OUT LIKE THAT, I JUST COULDN'T BRING MYSELF TO COMMIT TO MY DECISION.
ERR... WELL...
I'D LIKE... TO HAVE IT BACK NOW.
I SEE.
AND YUKIMURA SEEMED TO SMILE SERENELY.

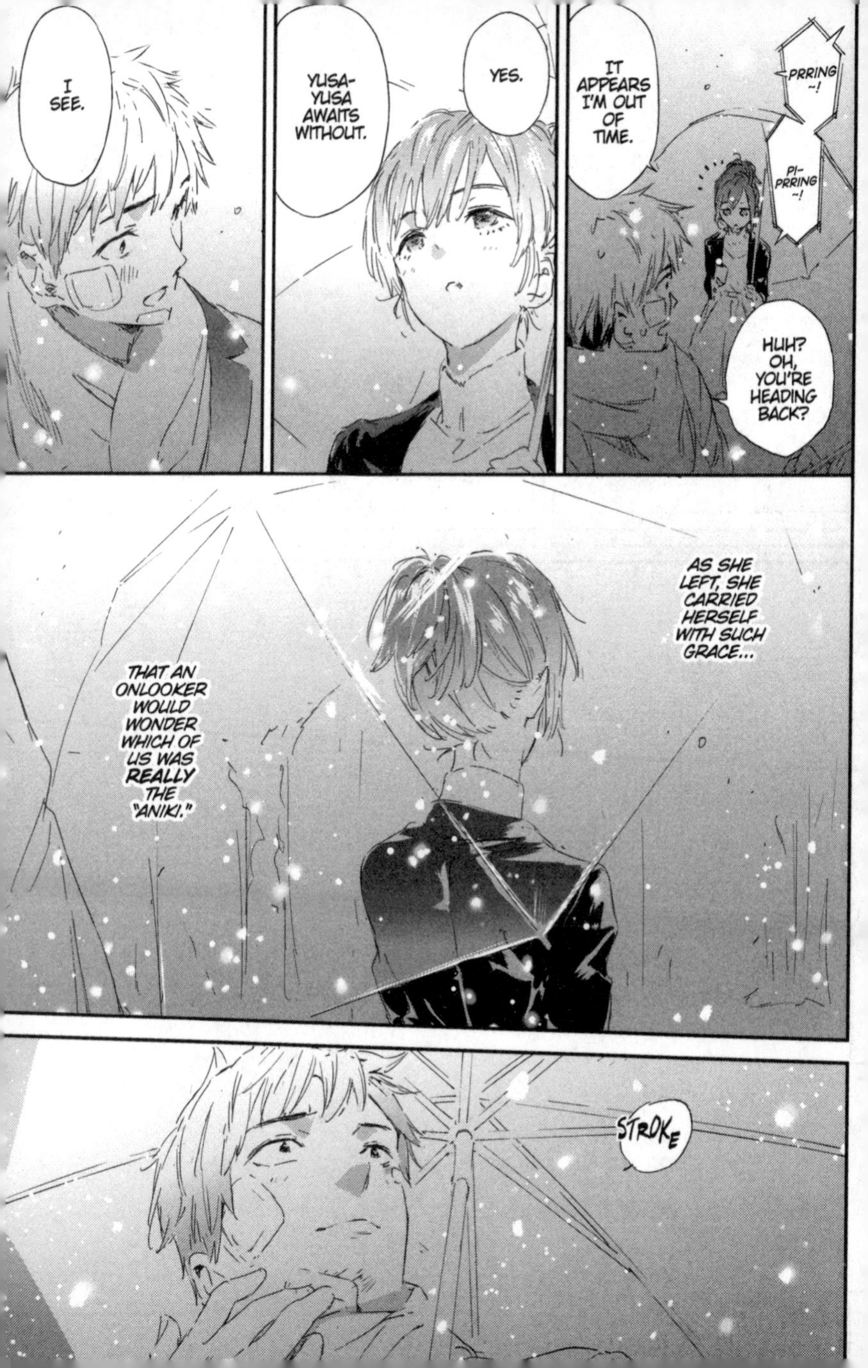
PRRING ~!
IT APPEARS I'M OUT OF TIME.
PI-PRRING ~!
HUH? OH, YOU'RE HEADING BACK?
YES.
YUSA-YUSA AWAITS WITHOUT.
I SEE.
AS SHE LEFT, SHE CARRIED HERSELF WITH SUCH GRACE...
THAT AN ONLOOKER WOULD WONDER WHICH OF US WAS REALLY THE "ANIKI."
STROKE

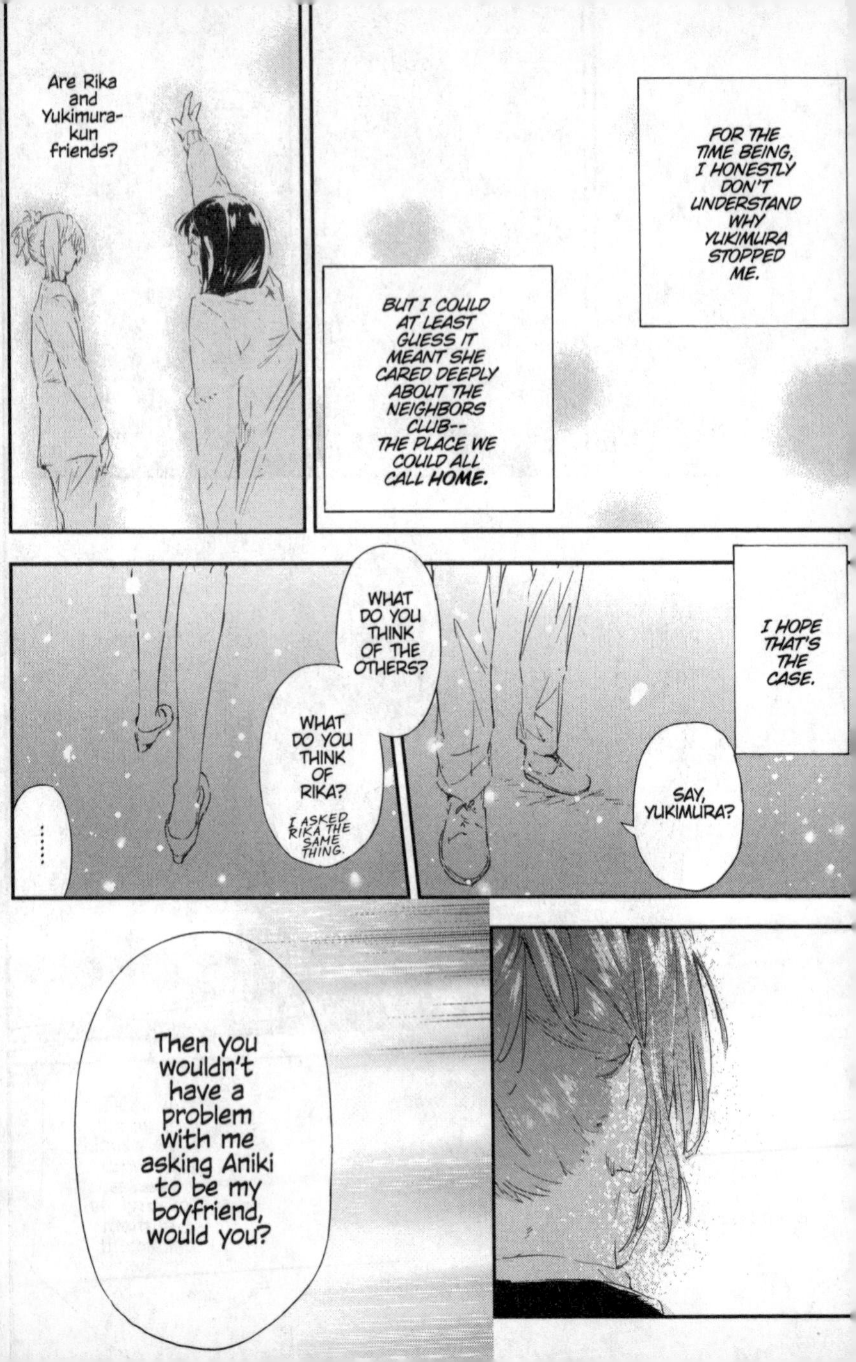
FOR THE TIME BEING, I HONESTLY DON'T UNDERSTAND WHY YUKIMURA STOPPED ME.
BUT I COULD AT LEAST GUESS IT MEANT SHE CARED DEEPLY ABOUT THE NEIGHBORS CLUB-- THE PLACE WE COULD ALL CALL HOME.
Are Rika and Yukimura-kun friends?
I HOPE THAT'S THE CASE.
SAY, YUKIMURA?
WHAT DO YOU THINK OF THE OTHERS?
WHAT DO YOU THINK OF RIKA?
I ASKED RIKA THE SAME THING.
......
Then you wouldn't have a problem with me asking Aniki to be my boyfriend, would you?

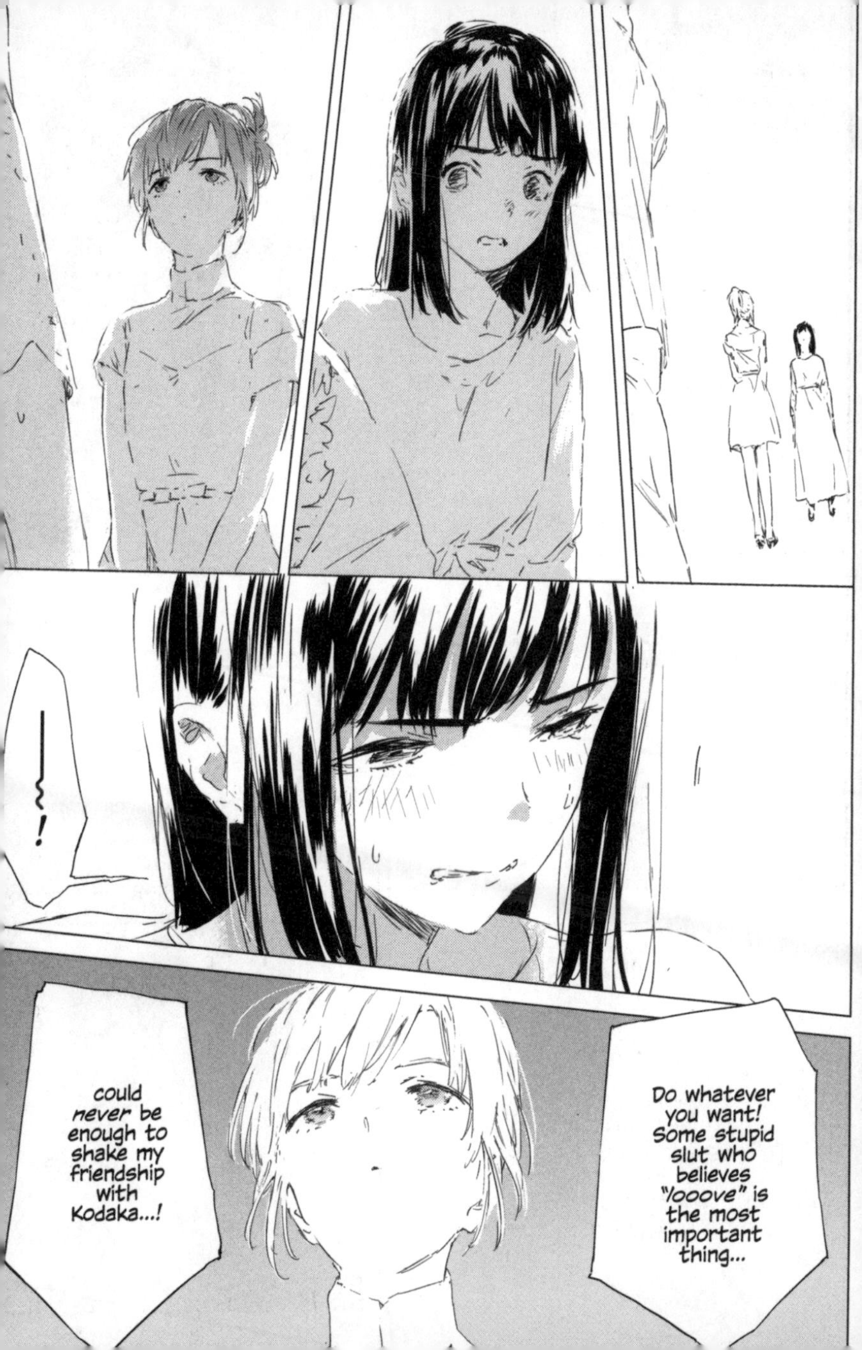
—!
Do whatever you want! Some stupid slut who believes "looove" is the most important thing...
could *never* be enough to shake my friendship with Kodaka...!

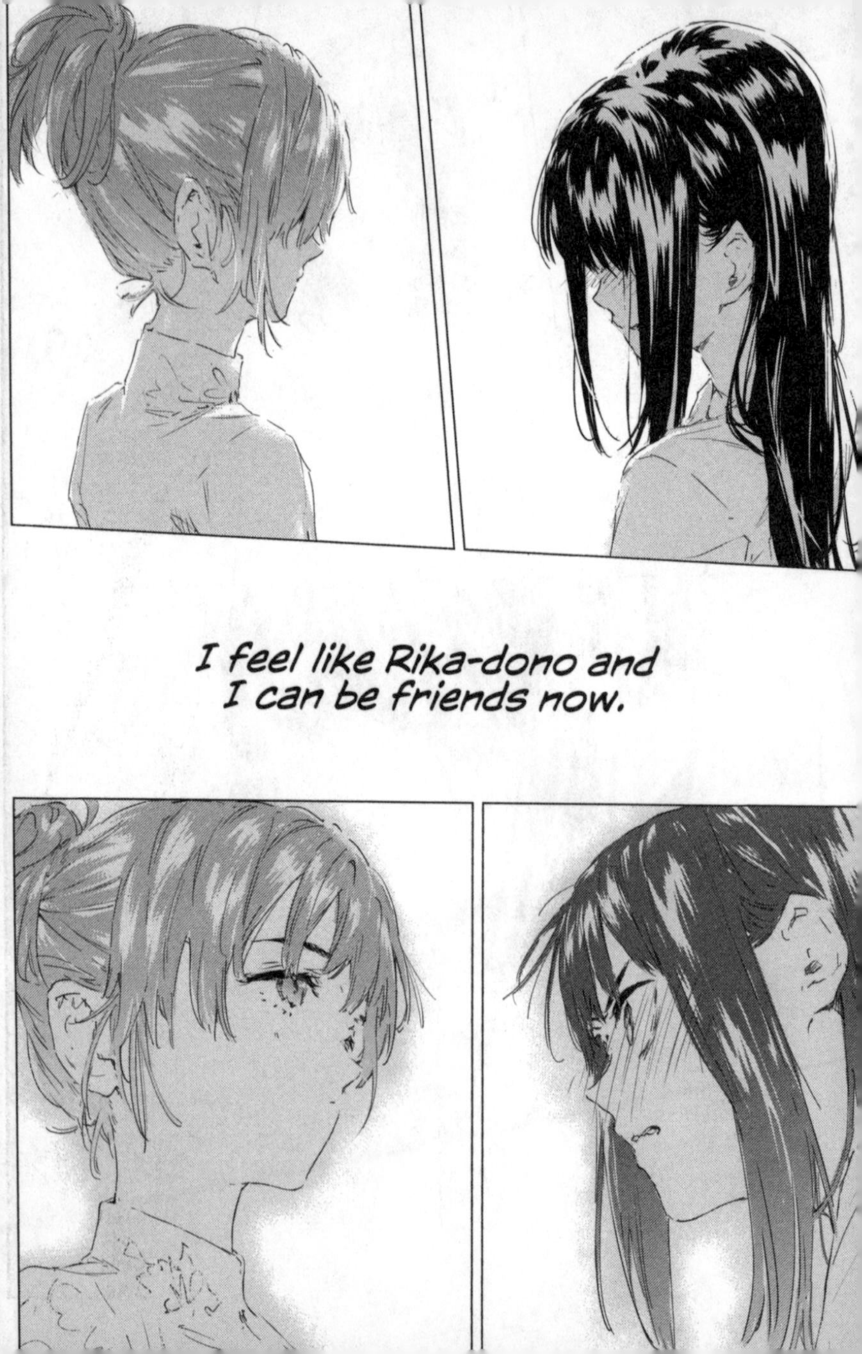
I feel like Rika-dono and I can be friends now.

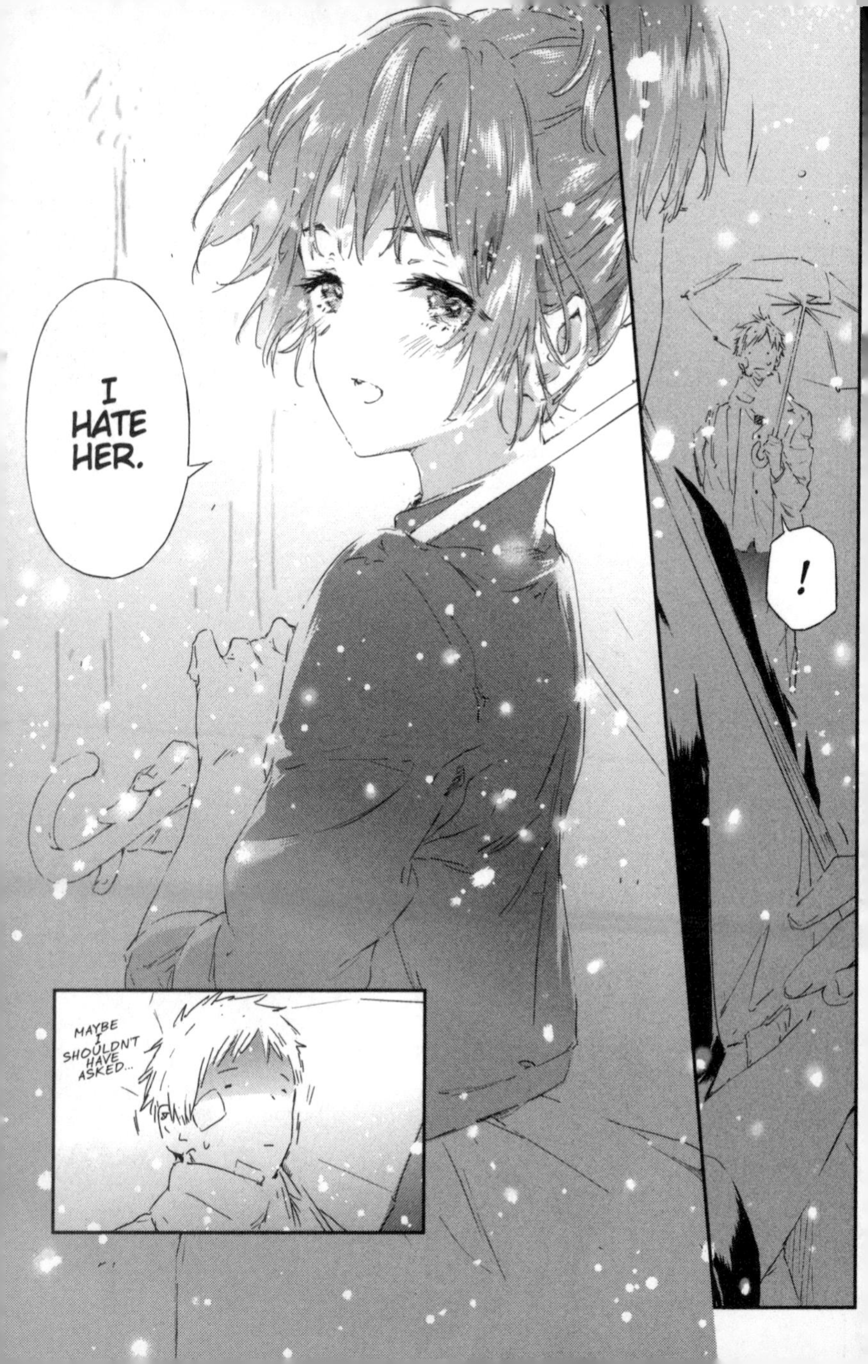
I HATE HER.
!
MAYBE I SHOULDN'T HAVE ASKED...

Haganai I don't have many friends

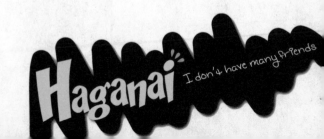

JAPAN WAS
EXPERIENCING
AN
ECONOMIC
BOOM.

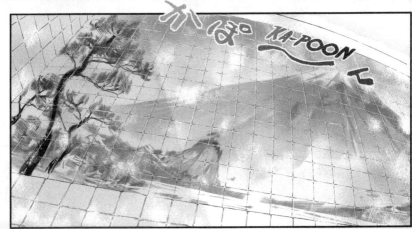

KA-POON

. . . .

I FEEL
LIKE I'VE
SEEN A
TON OF
MANGA
USE THE
"KA-POON"
SOUND
EFFECT IN
BATHING
SCENES
LATELY.

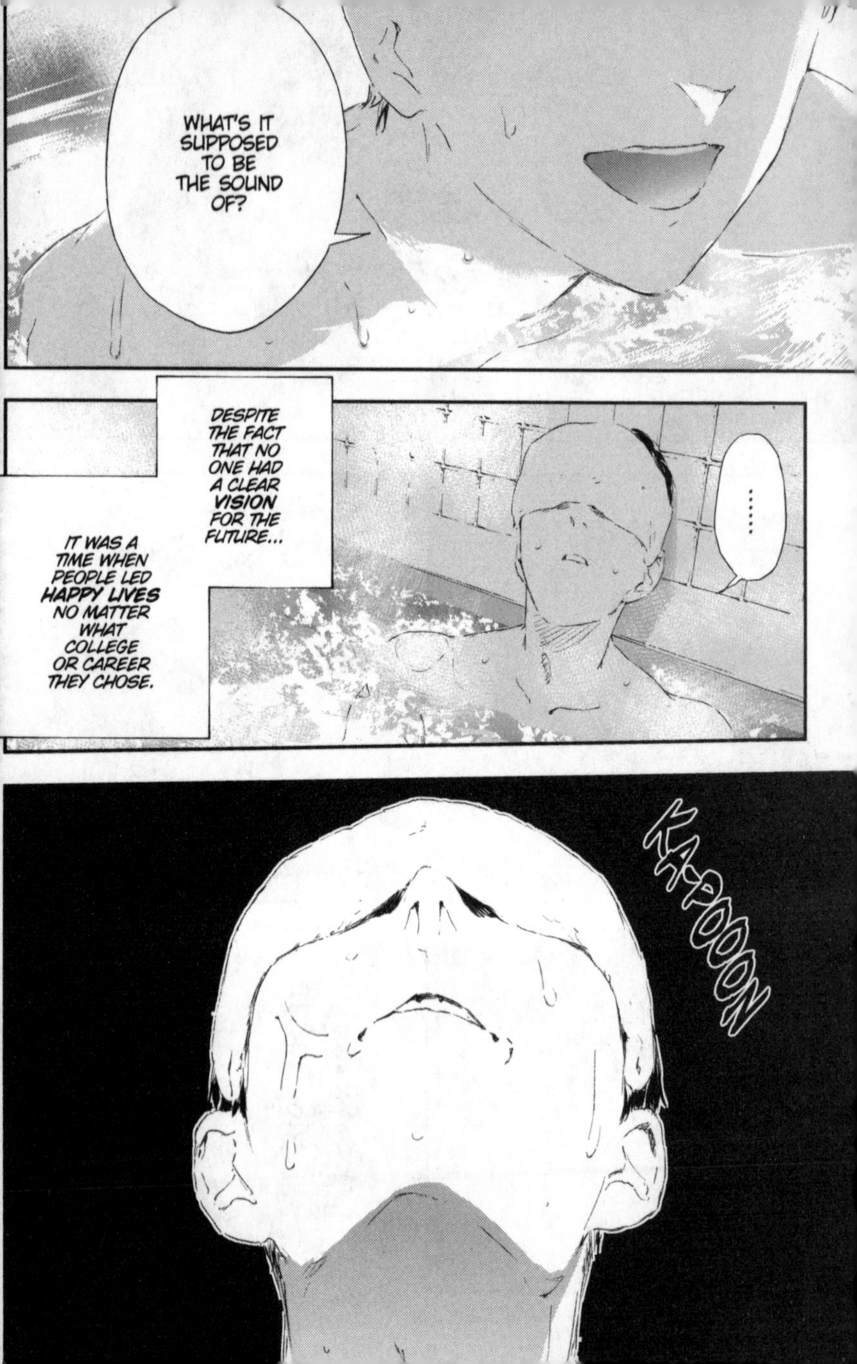
WHAT'S IT SUPPOSED TO BE THE SOUND OF?
......
DESPITE THE FACT THAT NO ONE HAD A CLEAR **VISION** FOR THE FUTURE...
IT WAS A TIME WHEN PEOPLE LED **HAPPY LIVES** NO MATTER WHAT COLLEGE OR CAREER THEY CHOSE.
KA-POOON

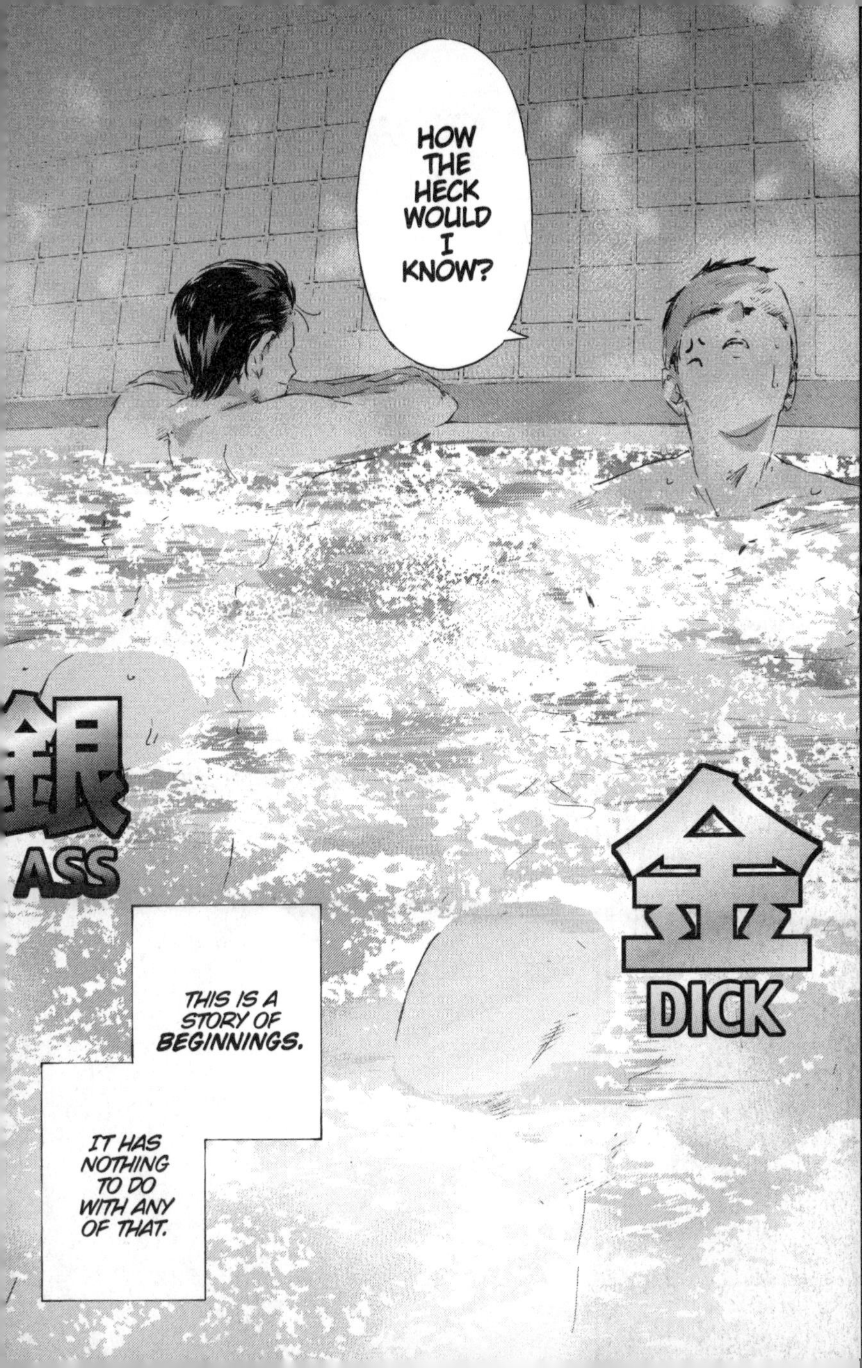
HOW THE HECK WOULD I KNOW?
金
DICK
銀
ASS
THIS IS A STORY OF BEGINNINGS.
IT HAS NOTHING TO DO WITH ANY OF THAT.

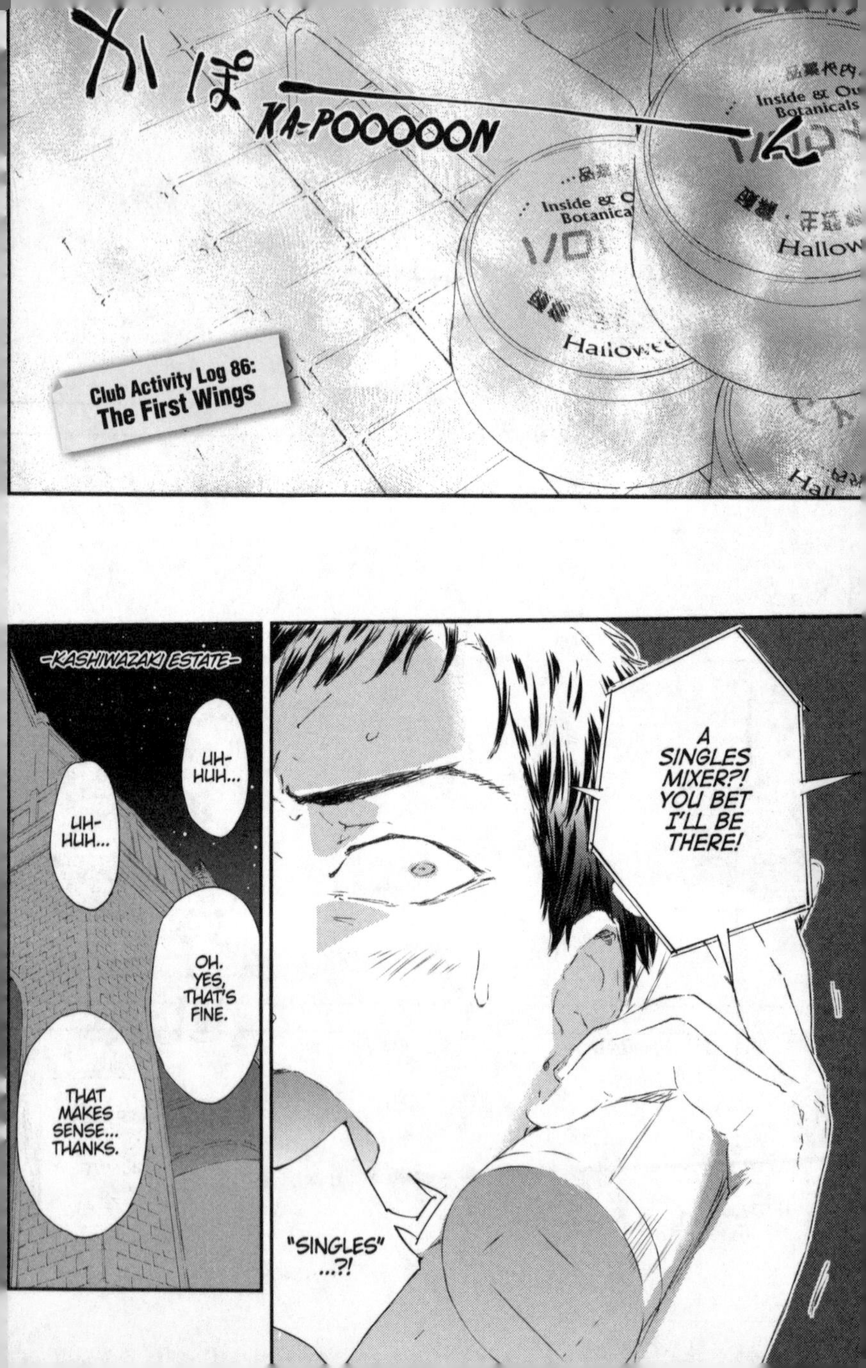
かぽーん
KA-POOOOON
Club Activity Log 86: The First Wings
A SINGLES MIXER?! YOU BET I'LL BE THERE!
"SINGLES" ...?!
-KASHIWAZAKI ESTATE-
UH-HUH...
UH-HUH...
OH. YES, THAT'S FINE.
THAT MAKES SENSE... THANKS.

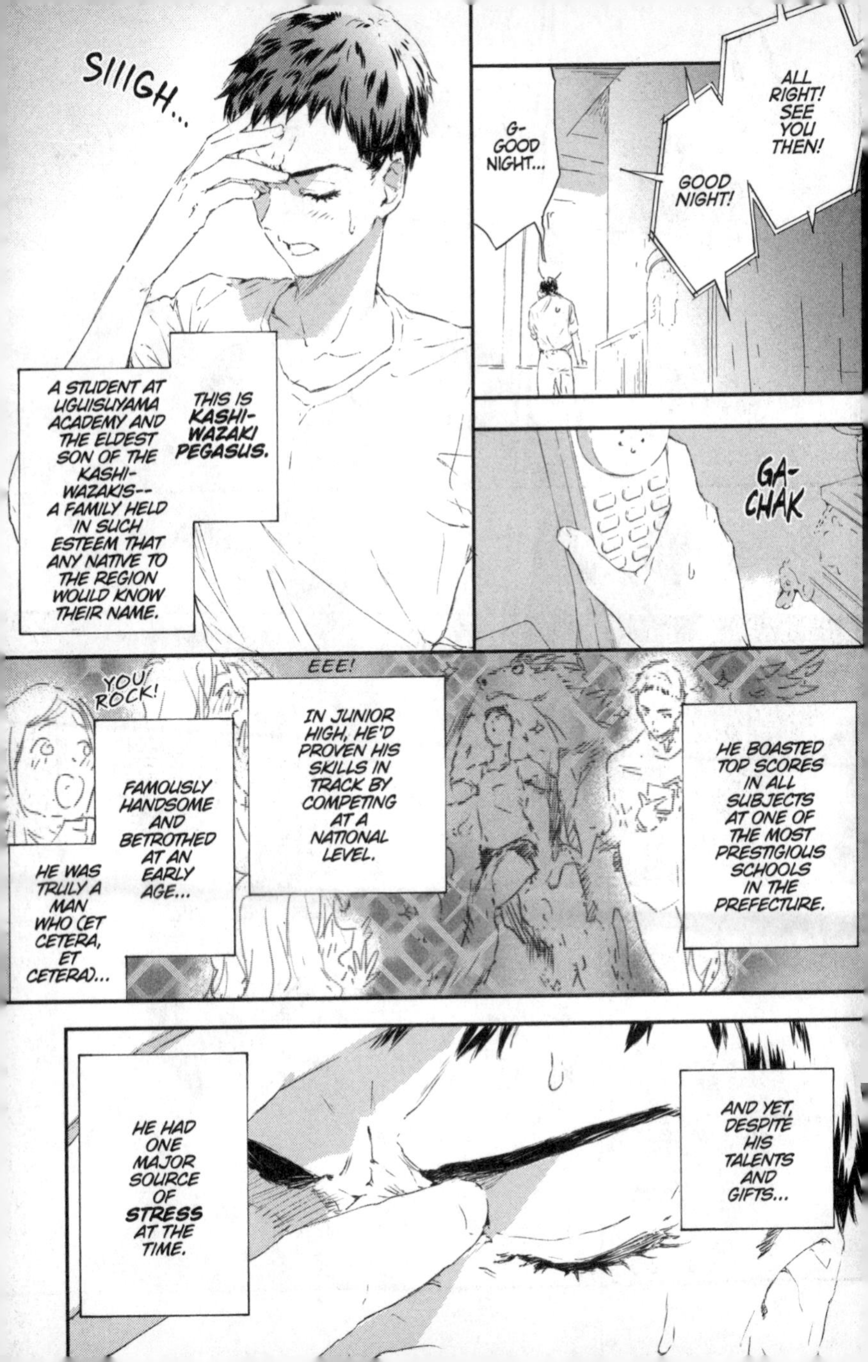
ALL RIGHT! SEE YOU THEN!
GOOD NIGHT!
G-GOOD NIGHT...
GA-CHAK
SIIIGH...
THIS IS KASHI-WAZAKI PEGASUS.
A STUDENT AT UGUISUYAMA ACADEMY AND THE ELDEST SON OF THE KASHI-WAZAKIS-- A FAMILY HELD IN SUCH ESTEEM THAT ANY NATIVE TO THE REGION WOULD KNOW THEIR NAME.
HE BOASTED TOP SCORES IN ALL SUBJECTS AT ONE OF THE MOST PRESTIGIOUS SCHOOLS IN THE PREFECTURE.
IN JUNIOR HIGH, HE'D PROVEN HIS SKILLS IN TRACK BY COMPETING AT A NATIONAL LEVEL.
EEE!
YOU ROCK!
FAMOUSLY HANDSOME AND BETROTHED AT AN EARLY AGE...
HE WAS TRULY A MAN WHO (ET CETERA, ET CETERA)...
AND YET, DESPITE HIS TALENTS AND GIFTS...
HE HAD ONE MAJOR SOURCE OF STRESS AT THE TIME.

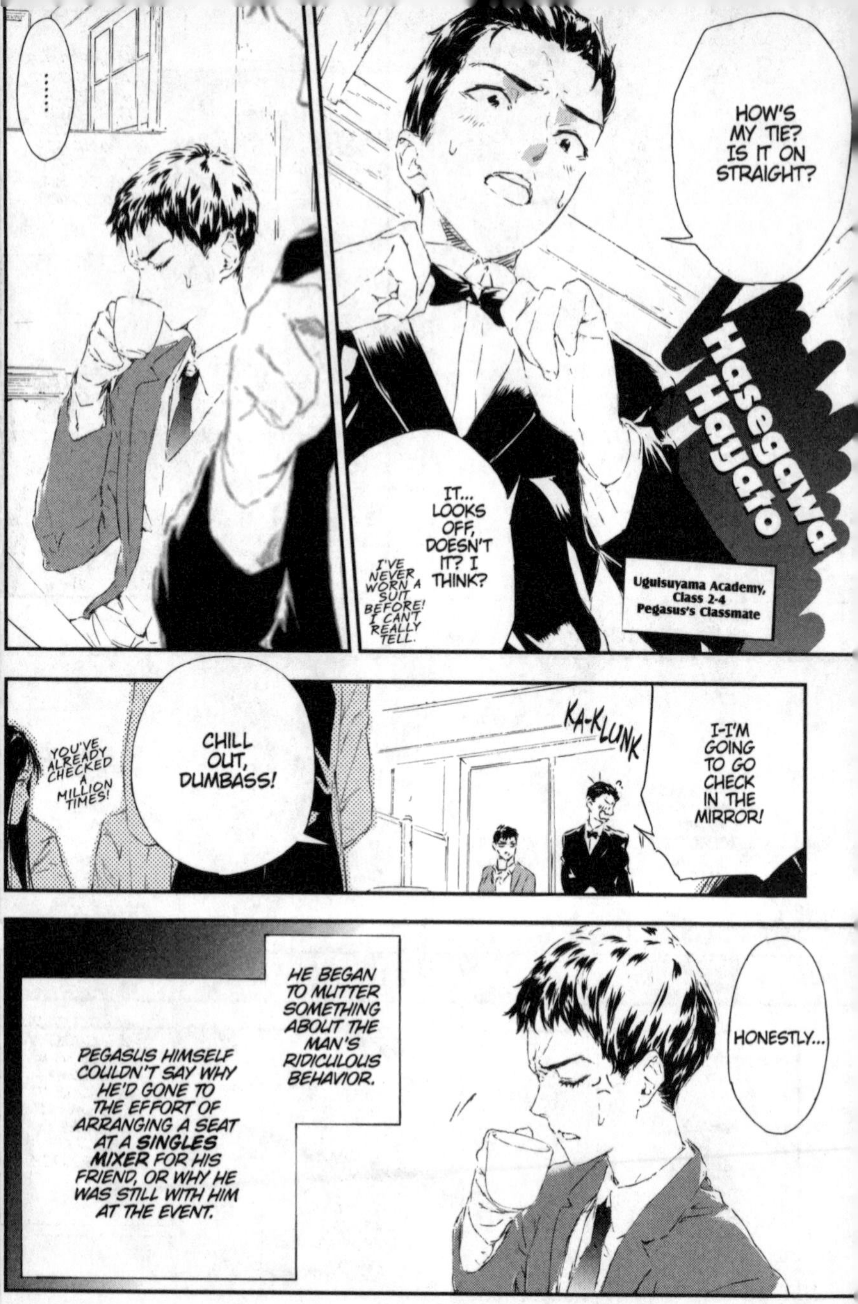

HOW'S MY TIE? IS IT ON STRAIGHT?
Hasegawa Hayato
Uguisuyama Academy, Class 2-4 Pegasus's Classmate
IT... LOOKS OFF, DOESN'T IT? I THINK?
I'VE NEVER WORN A SUIT BEFORE! I CAN'T REALLY TELL.
……
I-I'M GOING TO GO CHECK IN THE MIRROR!
KA-KLUNK
CHILL OUT, DUMBASS!
YOU'VE ALREADY CHECKED A MILLION TIMES!
HONESTLY...
HE BEGAN TO MUTTER SOMETHING ABOUT THE MAN'S RIDICULOUS BEHAVIOR.
PEGASUS HIMSELF COULDN'T SAY WHY HE'D GONE TO THE EFFORT OF ARRANGING A SEAT AT A SINGLES MIXER FOR HIS FRIEND, OR WHY HE WAS STILL WITH HIM AT THE EVENT.

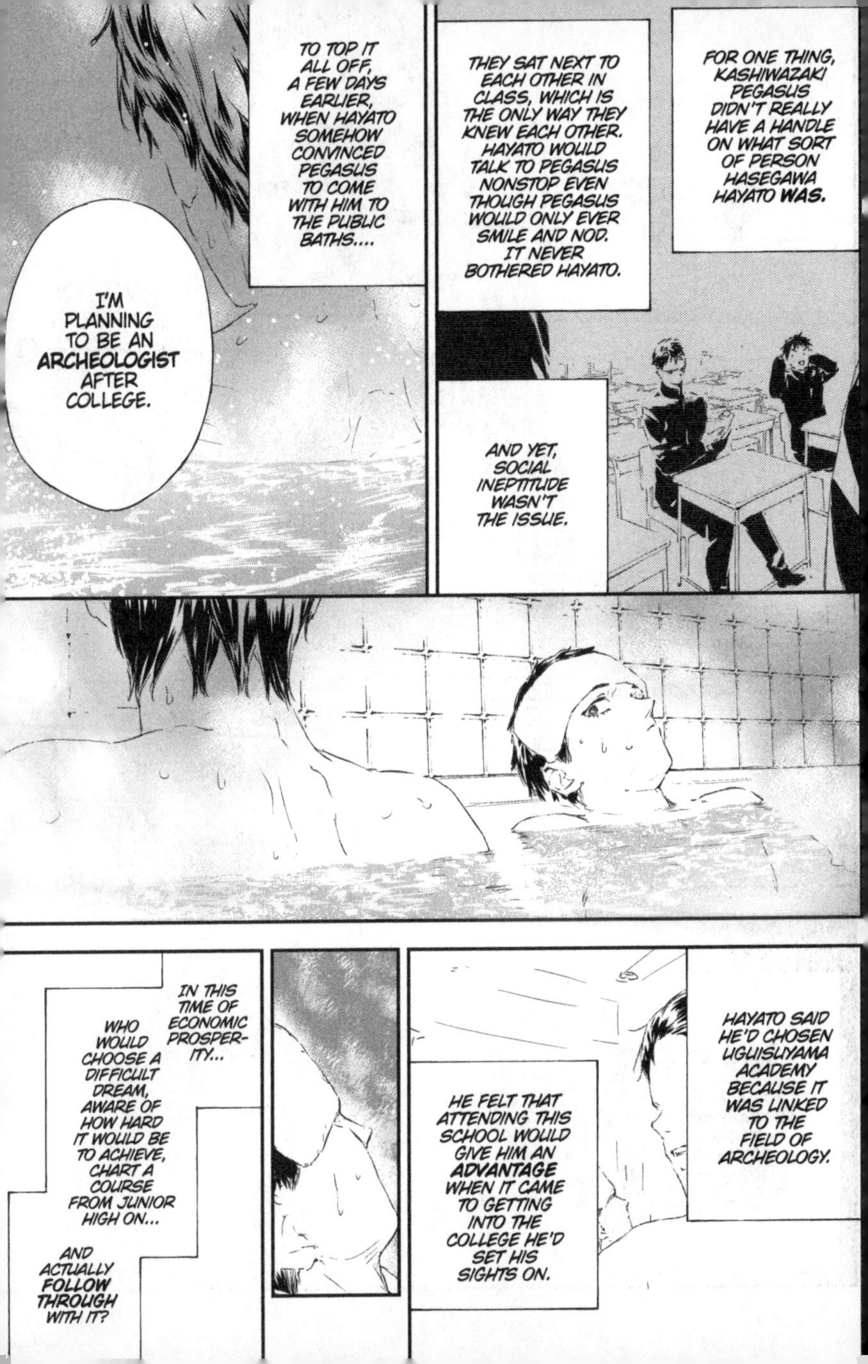

FOR ONE THING, KASHIWAZAKI PEGASUS DIDN'T REALLY HAVE A HANDLE ON WHAT SORT OF PERSON HASEGAWA HAYATO **WAS.**
THEY SAT NEXT TO EACH OTHER IN CLASS, WHICH IS THE ONLY WAY THEY KNEW EACH OTHER. HAYATO WOULD TALK TO PEGASUS NONSTOP EVEN THOUGH PEGASUS WOULD ONLY EVER SMILE AND NOD. IT NEVER BOTHERED HAYATO.
AND YET, SOCIAL INEPTITUDE WASN'T THE ISSUE.
TO TOP IT ALL OFF, A FEW DAYS EARLIER, WHEN HAYATO SOMEHOW CONVINCED PEGASUS TO COME WITH HIM TO THE PUBLIC BATHS....
I'M PLANNING TO BE AN **ARCHEOLOGIST** AFTER COLLEGE.
HAYATO SAID HE'D CHOSEN UGUISUYAMA ACADEMY BECAUSE IT WAS LINKED TO THE FIELD OF ARCHEOLOGY.
HE FELT THAT ATTENDING THIS SCHOOL WOULD GIVE HIM AN **ADVANTAGE** WHEN IT CAME TO GETTING INTO THE COLLEGE HE'D SET HIS SIGHTS ON.
IN THIS TIME OF ECONOMIC PROSPERITY...
WHO WOULD CHOOSE A DIFFICULT DREAM, AWARE OF HOW HARD IT WOULD BE TO ACHIEVE, CHART A COURSE FROM JUNIOR HIGH ON...
AND ACTUALLY **FOLLOW THROUGH** WITH IT?

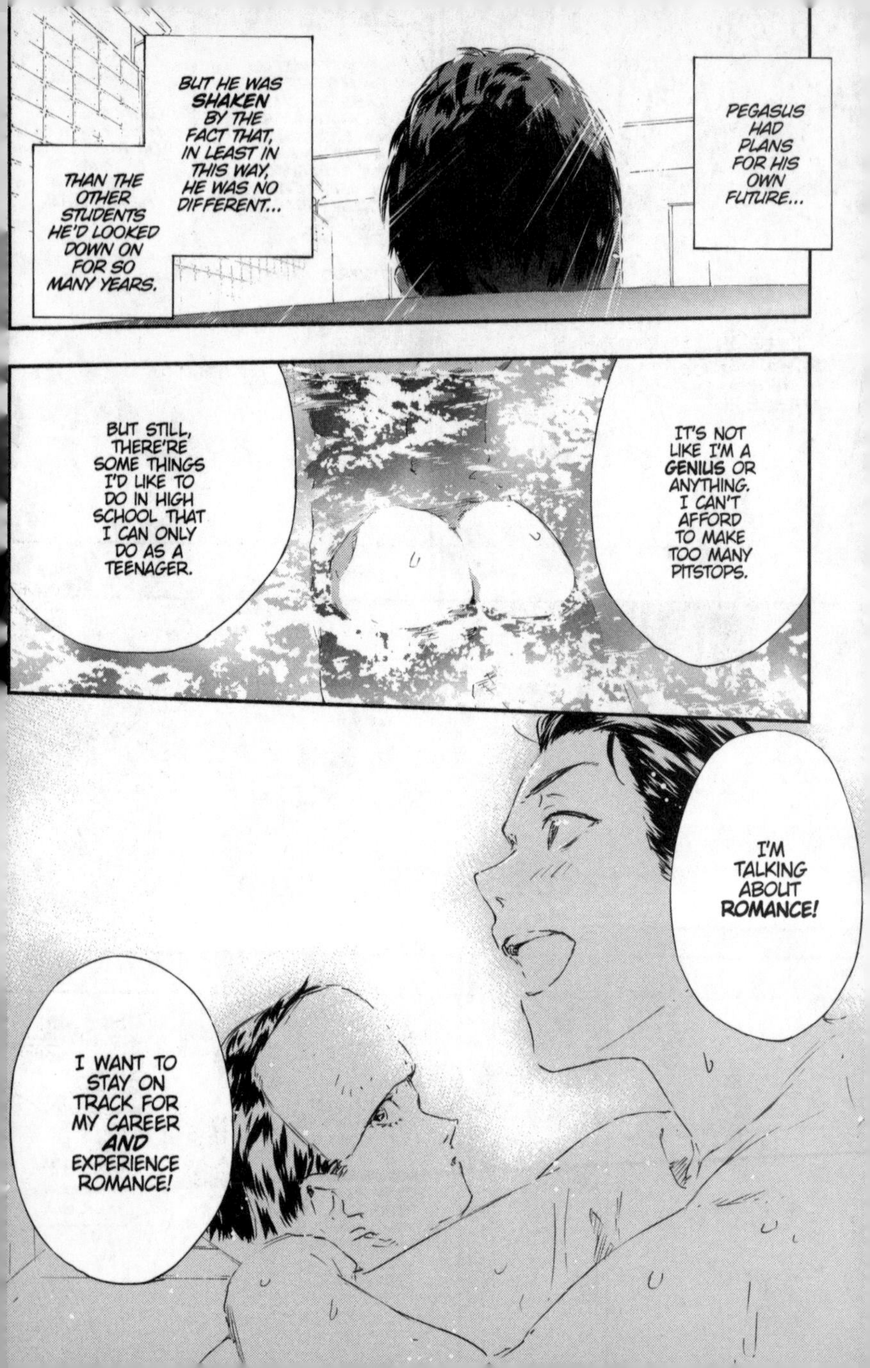
PEGASUS HAD PLANS FOR HIS OWN FUTURE...
BUT HE WAS SHAKEN BY THE FACT THAT, IN LEAST IN THIS WAY, HE WAS NO DIFFERENT...
THAN THE OTHER STUDENTS HE'D LOOKED DOWN ON FOR SO MANY YEARS.
IT'S NOT LIKE I'M A GENIUS OR ANYTHING. I CAN'T AFFORD TO MAKE TOO MANY PITSTOPS.
BUT STILL, THERE'RE SOME THINGS I'D LIKE TO DO IN HIGH SCHOOL THAT I CAN ONLY DO AS A TEENAGER.
I'M TALKING ABOUT ROMANCE!
I WANT TO STAY ON TRACK FOR MY CAREER AND EXPERIENCE ROMANCE!

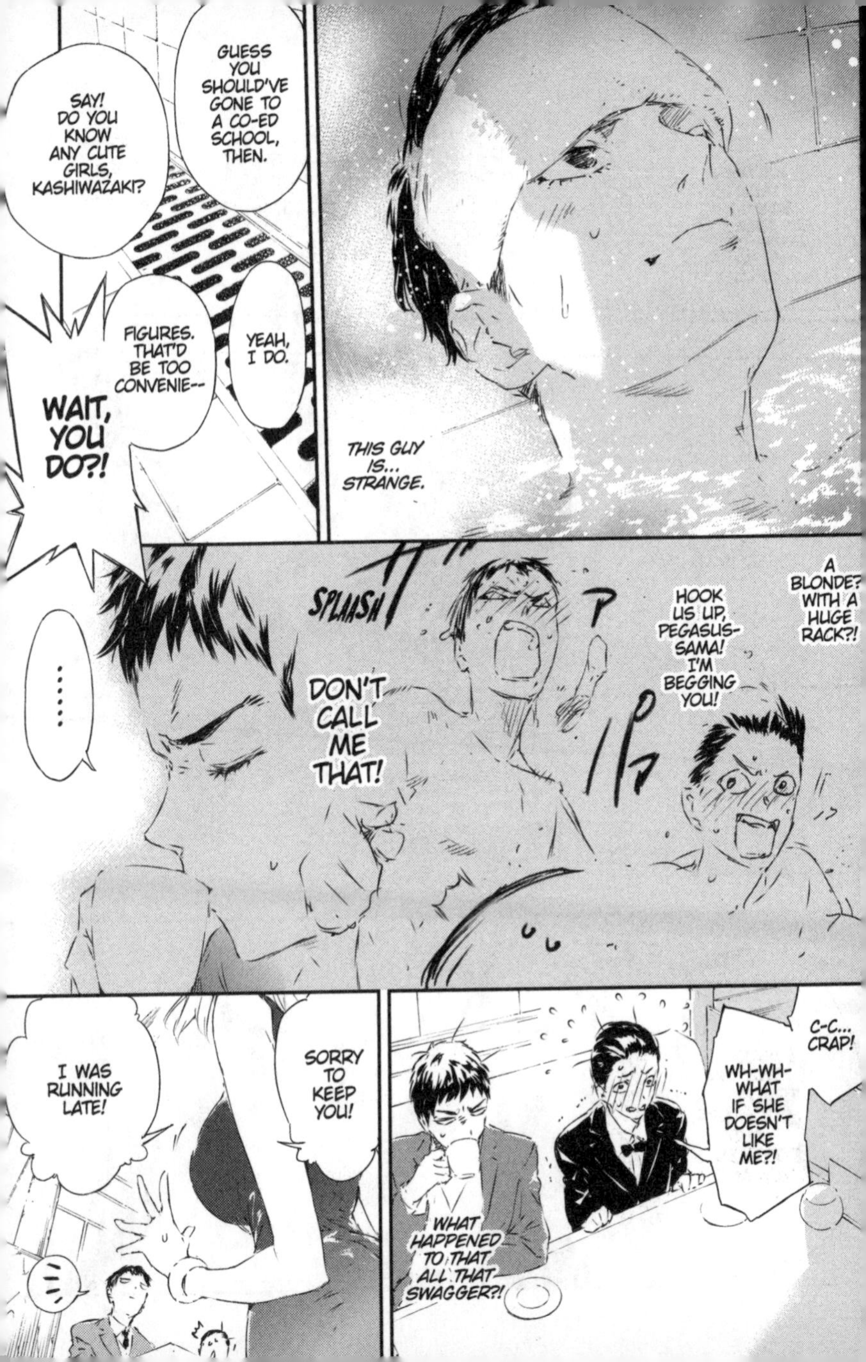
THIS GUY IS... STRANGE.
GUESS YOU SHOULD'VE GONE TO A CO-ED SCHOOL, THEN.
SAY! DO YOU KNOW ANY CUTE GIRLS, KASHIWAZAKI?
YEAH, I DO.
FIGURES. THAT'D BE TOO CONVENIE--
WAIT, YOU DO?!
A BLONDE? WITH A HUGE RACK?!
HOOK US UP, PEGASUS-SAMA! I'M BEGGING YOU!
SPLAASH
DON'T CALL ME THAT!
......
C-C... CRAP!
WH-WH-WHAT IF SHE DOESN'T LIKE ME?!
WHAT HAPPENED TO THAT ALL THAT SWAGGER?!
SORRY TO KEEP YOU!
I WAS RUNNING LATE!
!

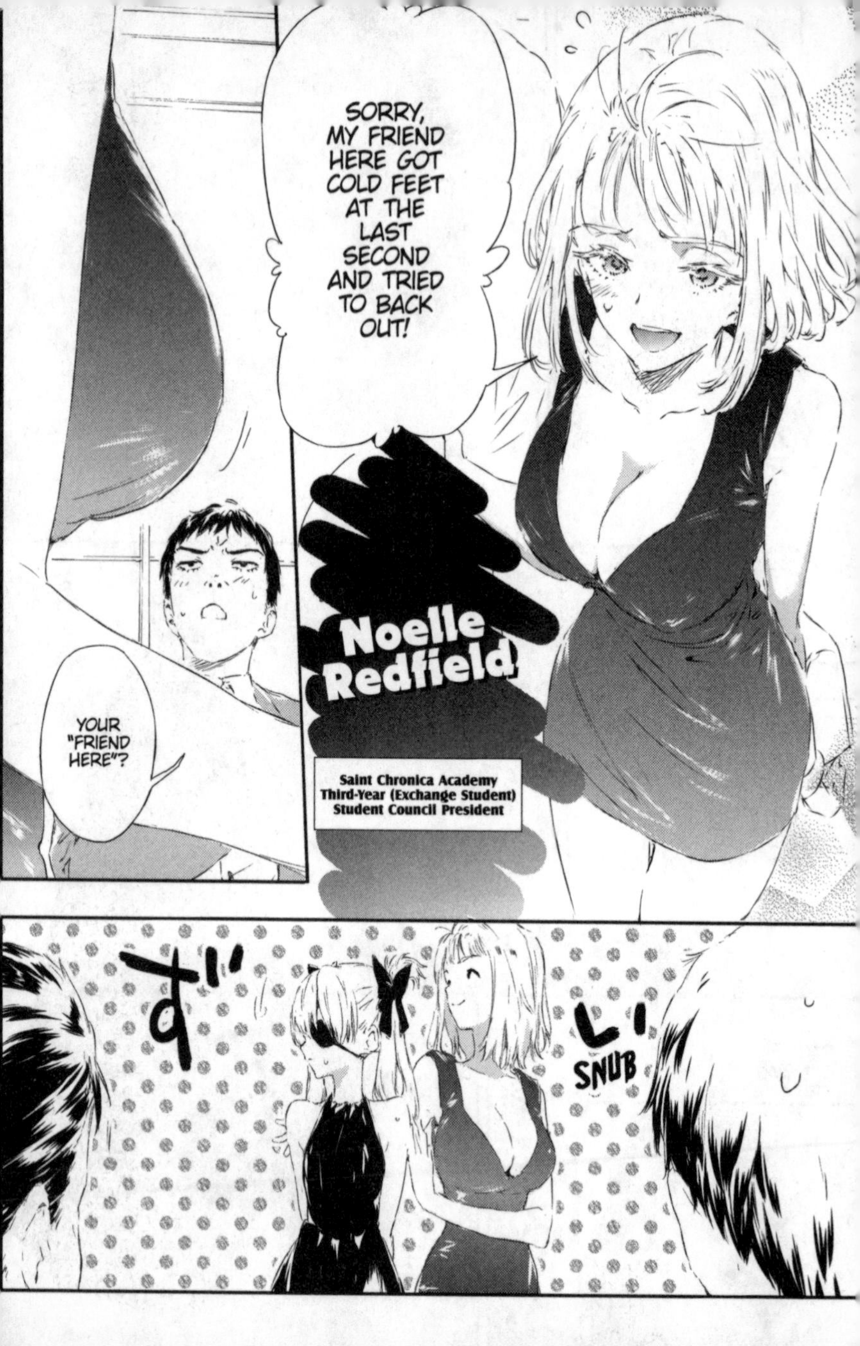
SORRY, MY FRIEND HERE GOT COLD FEET AT THE LAST SECOND AND TRIED TO BACK OUT!
Noelle Redfield
Saint Chronica Academy
Third-Year (Exchange Student)
Student Council President
YOUR "FRIEND HERE"?
ずい
SNUB

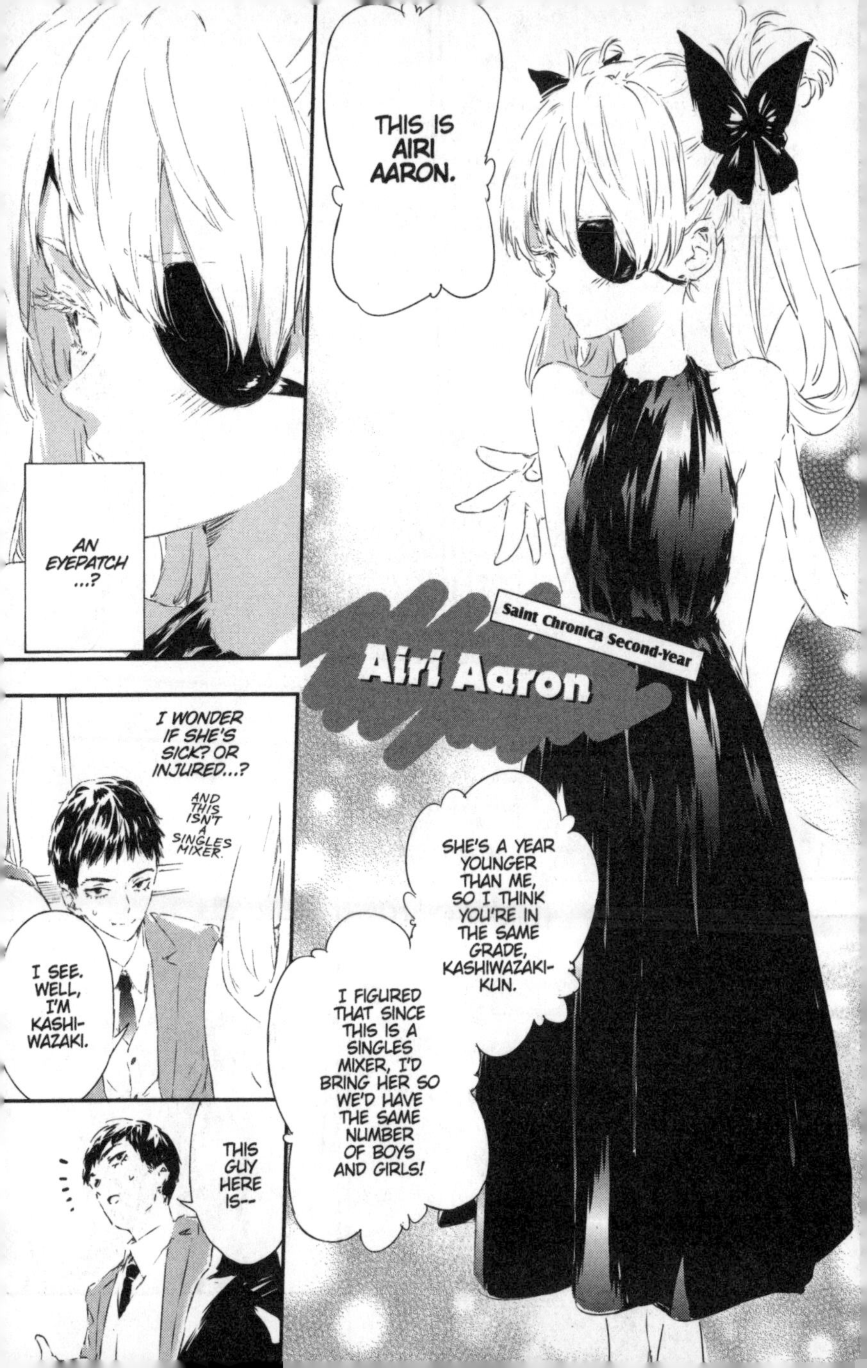
THIS IS AIRI AARON.
Saint Chronica Second-Year
Airi Aaron
SHE'S A YEAR YOUNGER THAN ME, SO I THINK YOU'RE IN THE SAME GRADE, KASHIWAZAKI-KUN.
I FIGURED THAT SINCE THIS IS A SINGLES MIXER, I'D BRING HER SO WE'D HAVE THE SAME NUMBER OF BOYS AND GIRLS!
AN EYEPATCH ...?
I WONDER IF SHE'S SICK? OR INJURED...?
AND THIS ISN'T A SINGLES MIXER.
I SEE. WELL, I'M KASHI-WAZAKI.
THIS GUY HERE IS--

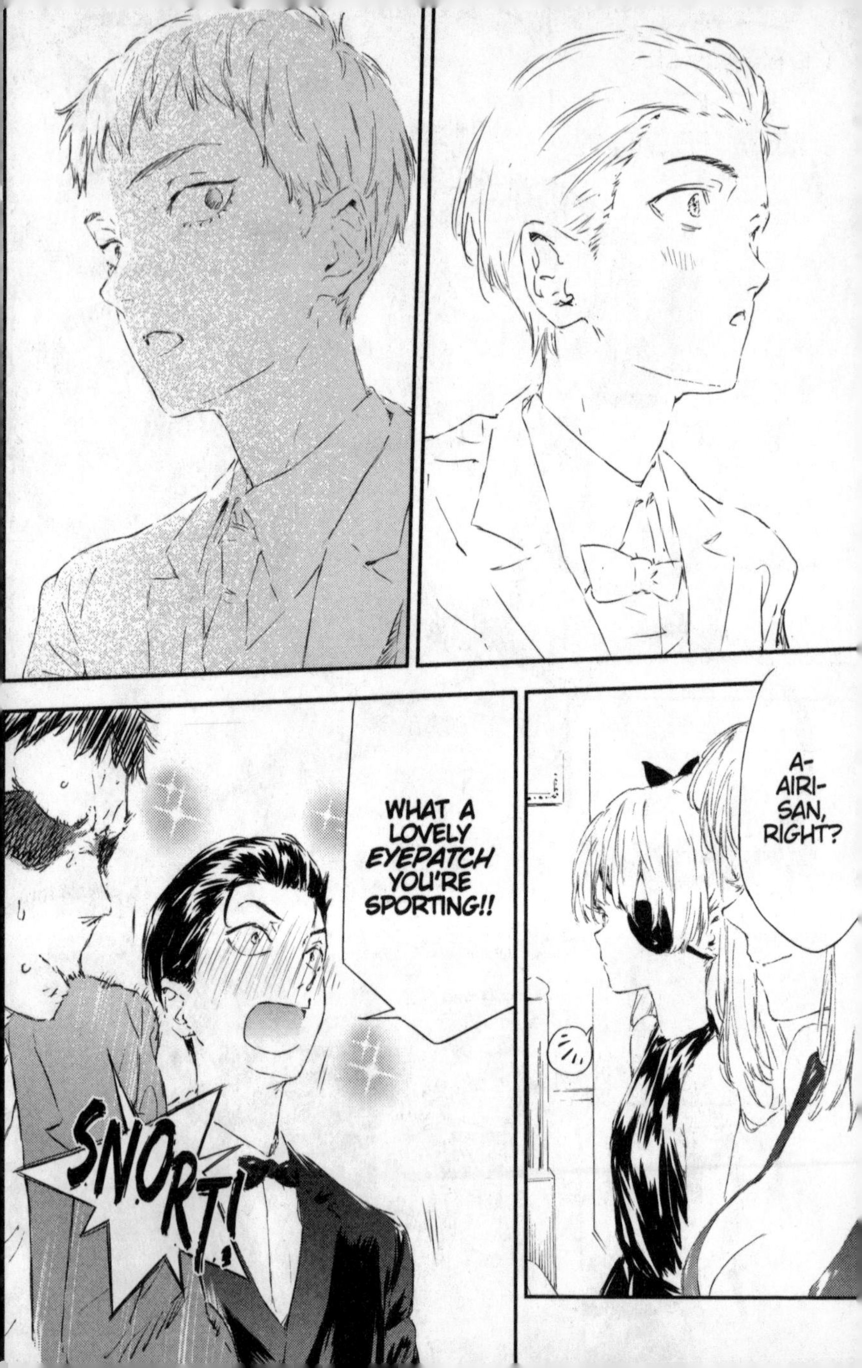
A-AIRI-SAN, RIGHT?
WHAT A LOVELY *EYEPATCH* YOU'RE SPORTING!!
SNORT!

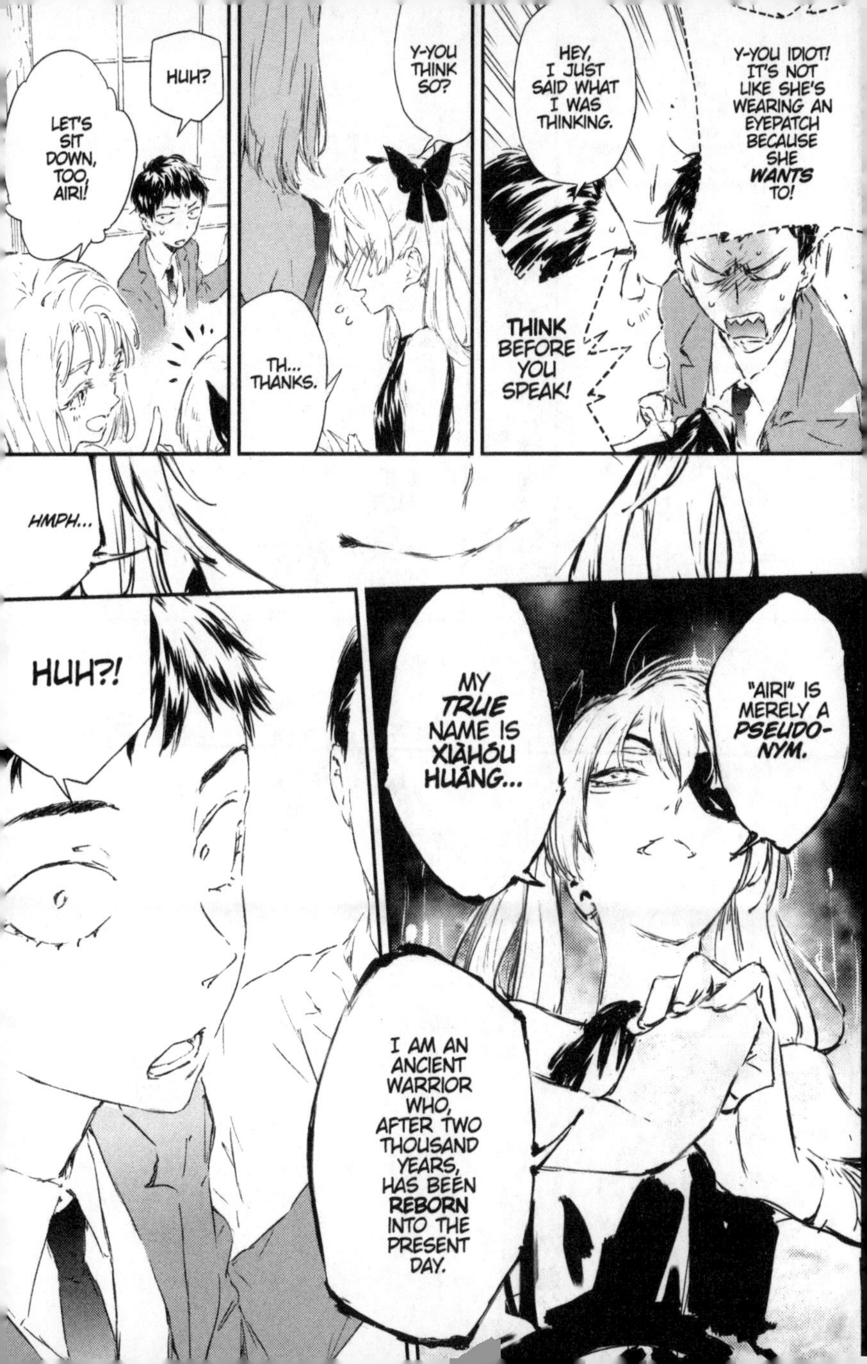
Y-YOU IDIOT! IT'S NOT LIKE SHE'S WEARING AN EYEPATCH BECAUSE SHE *WANTS* TO!
HEY, I JUST SAID WHAT I WAS THINKING.
THINK BEFORE YOU SPEAK!
Y-YOU THINK SO?
TH... THANKS.
HUH?
LET'S SIT DOWN, TOO, AIRI!
HMPH...
"AIRI" IS MERELY A *PSEUDONYM.*
MY *TRUE* NAME IS XIÀHŌU HUĀNG...
I AM AN ANCIENT WARRIOR WHO, AFTER TWO THOUSAND YEARS, HAS BEEN **REBORN** INTO THE PRESENT DAY.
HUH?!

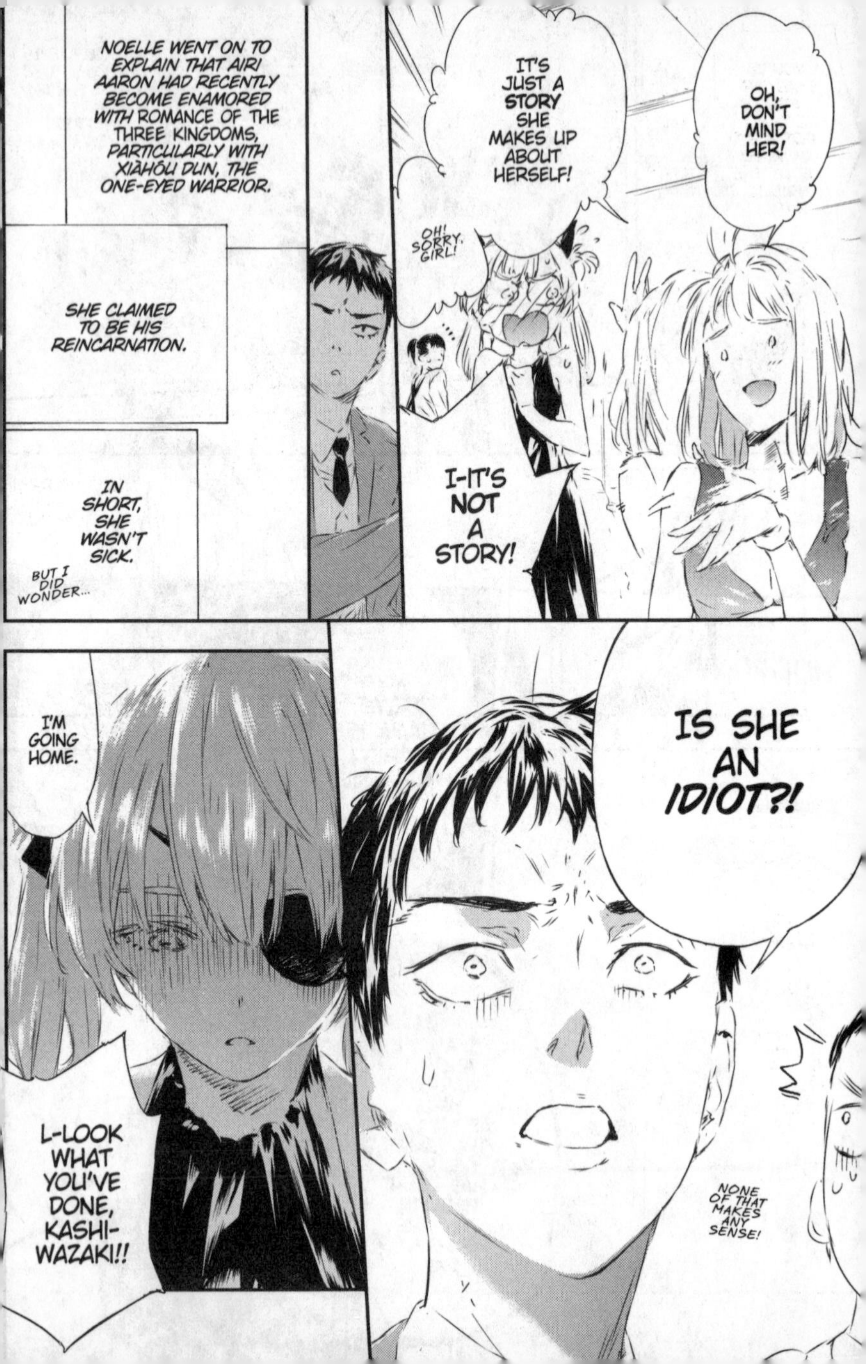
OH, DON'T MIND HER!
IT'S JUST A STORY SHE MAKES UP ABOUT HERSELF!
OH! SORRY, GIRL!
I-IT'S NOT A STORY!
NOELLE WENT ON TO EXPLAIN THAT AIRI AARON HAD RECENTLY BECOME ENAMORED WITH ROMANCE OF THE THREE KINGDOMS, PARTICULARLY WITH XIÀHÓU DUN, THE ONE-EYED WARRIOR.
SHE CLAIMED TO BE HIS REINCARNATION.
IN SHORT, SHE WASN'T SICK.
BUT I DID WONDER...
IS SHE AN IDIOT?!
NONE OF THAT MAKES ANY SENSE!
I'M GOING HOME.
L-LOOK WHAT YOU'VE DONE, KASHI-WAZAKI!!

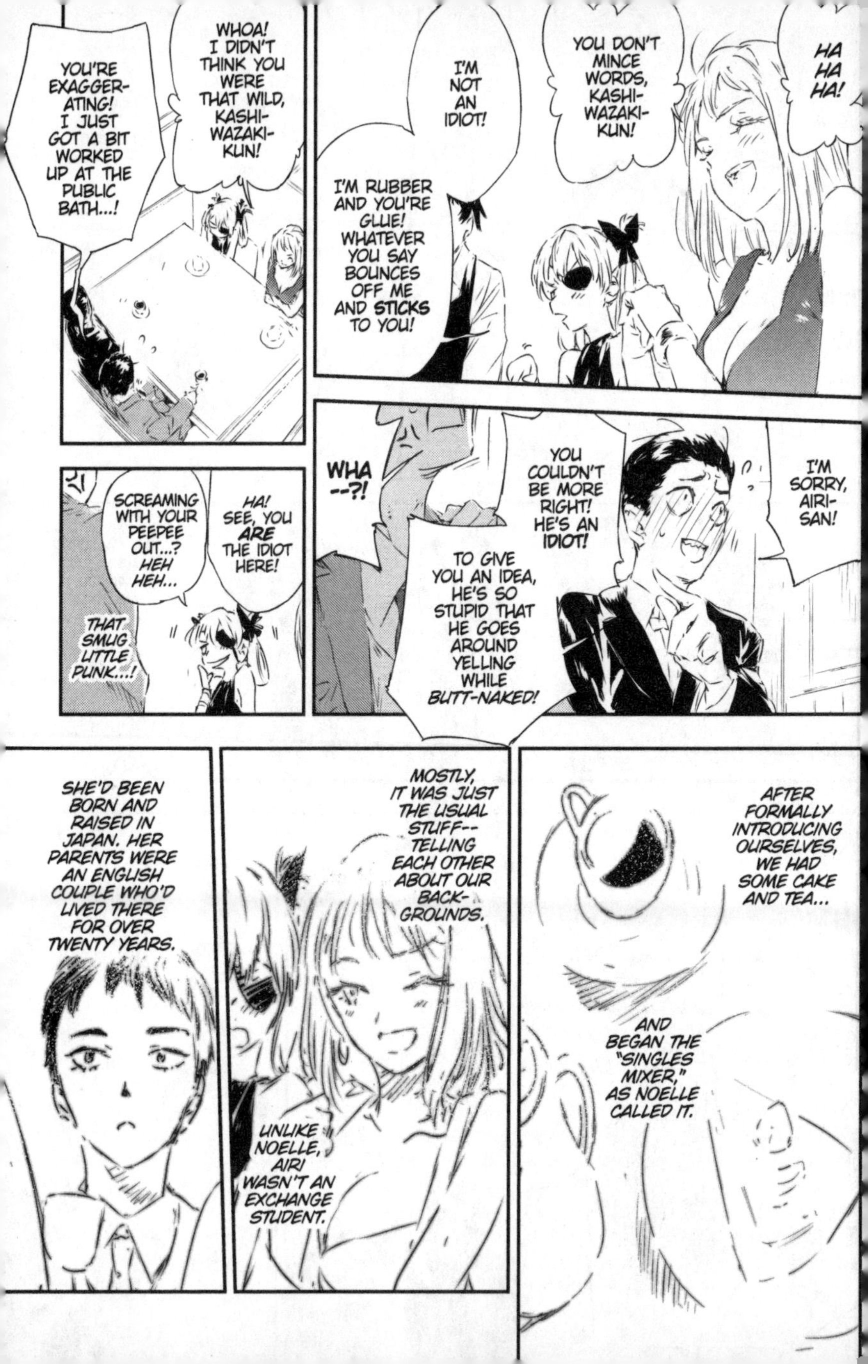
HA HA HA!
YOU DON'T MINCE WORDS, KASHI-WAZAKI-KUN!
I'M NOT AN IDIOT!
I'M RUBBER AND YOU'RE GLUE! WHATEVER YOU SAY BOUNCES OFF ME AND STICKS TO YOU!
WHOA! I DIDN'T THINK YOU WERE THAT WILD, KASHI-WAZAKI-KUN!
YOU'RE EXAGGER-ATING! I JUST GOT A BIT WORKED UP AT THE PUBLIC BATH...!
I'M SORRY, AIRI-SAN!
YOU COULDN'T BE MORE RIGHT! HE'S AN IDIOT!
WHA--?!
TO GIVE YOU AN IDEA, HE'S SO STUPID THAT HE GOES AROUND YELLING WHILE BUTT-NAKED!
HA! SEE, YOU ARE THE IDIOT HERE!
SCREAMING WITH YOUR PEEPEE OUT...? HEH HEH...
THAT SMUG LITTLE PUNK...!
AFTER FORMALLY INTRODUCING OURSELVES, WE HAD SOME CAKE AND TEA...
AND BEGAN THE "SINGLES MIXER," AS NOELLE CALLED IT.
MOSTLY, IT WAS JUST THE USUAL STUFF--TELLING EACH OTHER ABOUT OUR BACK-GROUNDS.
UNLIKE NOELLE, AIRI WASN'T AN EXCHANGE STUDENT.
SHE'D BEEN BORN AND RAISED IN JAPAN. HER PARENTS WERE AN ENGLISH COUPLE WHO'D LIVED THERE FOR OVER TWENTY YEARS.

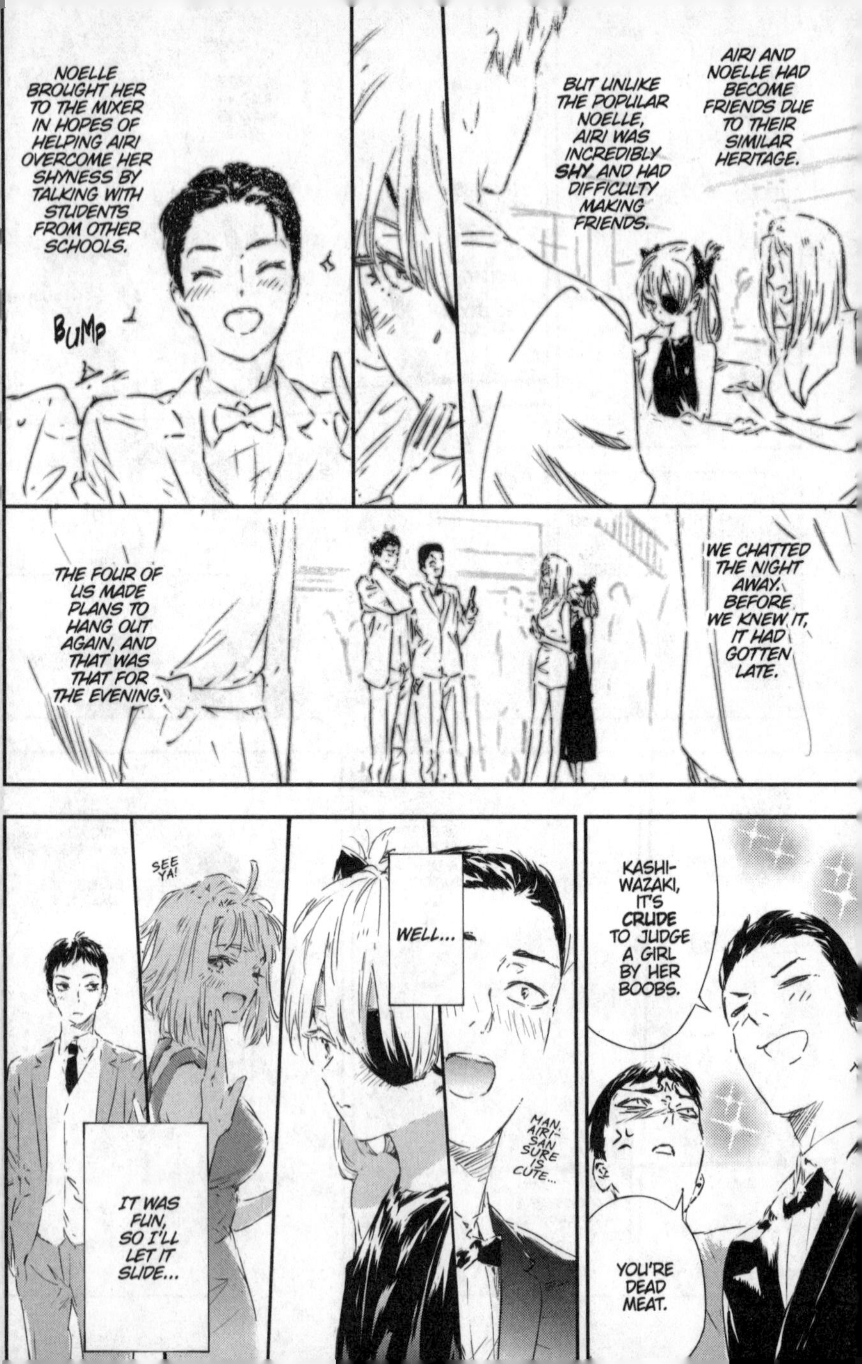
AIRI AND NOELLE HAD BECOME FRIENDS DUE TO THEIR SIMILAR HERITAGE.
BUT UNLIKE THE POPULAR NOELLE, AIRI WAS INCREDIBLY SHY AND HAD DIFFICULTY MAKING FRIENDS.
NOELLE BROUGHT HER TO THE MIXER IN HOPES OF HELPING AIRI OVERCOME HER SHYNESS BY TALKING WITH STUDENTS FROM OTHER SCHOOLS.
BUMP
WE CHATTED THE NIGHT AWAY. BEFORE WE KNEW IT, IT HAD GOTTEN LATE.
THE FOUR OF US MADE PLANS TO HANG OUT AGAIN, AND THAT WAS THAT FOR THE EVENING.
KASHI-WAZAKI, IT'S CRUDE TO JUDGE A GIRL BY HER BOOBS.
YOU'RE DEAD MEAT.
WELL...
MAN, AIRI-SAN SURE IS CUTE...
SEE YA!
IT WAS FUN, SO I'LL LET IT SLIDE...

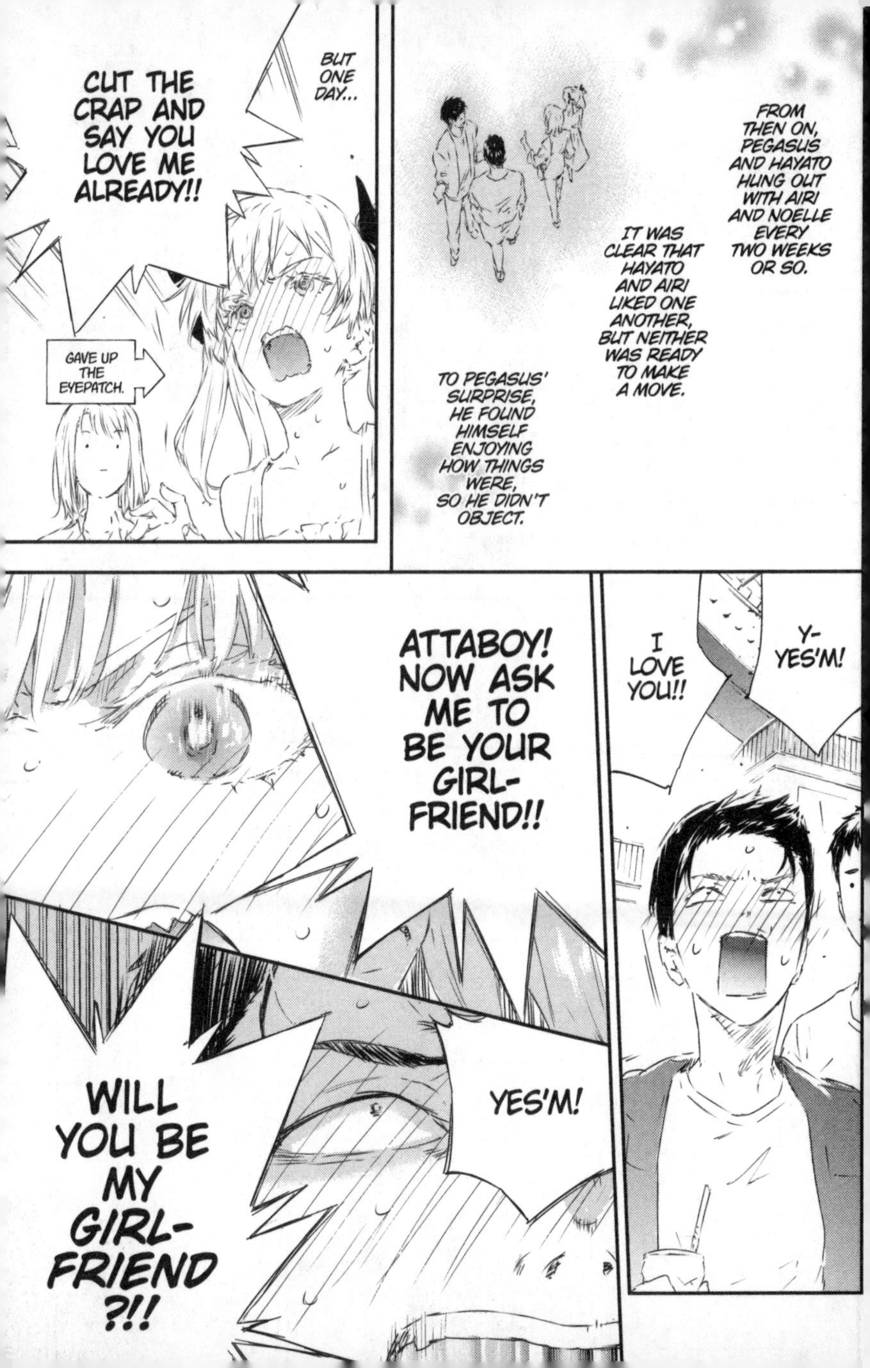
FROM THEN ON, PEGASUS AND HAYATO HUNG OUT WITH AIRI AND NOELLE EVERY TWO WEEKS OR SO.
IT WAS CLEAR THAT HAYATO AND AIRI LIKED ONE ANOTHER, BUT NEITHER WAS READY TO MAKE A MOVE.
TO PEGASUS' SURPRISE, HE FOUND HIMSELF ENJOYING HOW THINGS WERE, SO HE DIDN'T OBJECT.
BUT ONE DAY...
CUT THE CRAP AND SAY YOU LOVE ME ALREADY!!
GAVE UP THE EYEPATCH.
Y-YES'M!
I LOVE YOU!!
ATTABOY! NOW ASK ME TO BE YOUR GIRL-FRIEND!!
YES'M!
WILL YOU BE MY GIRL-FRIEND?!!

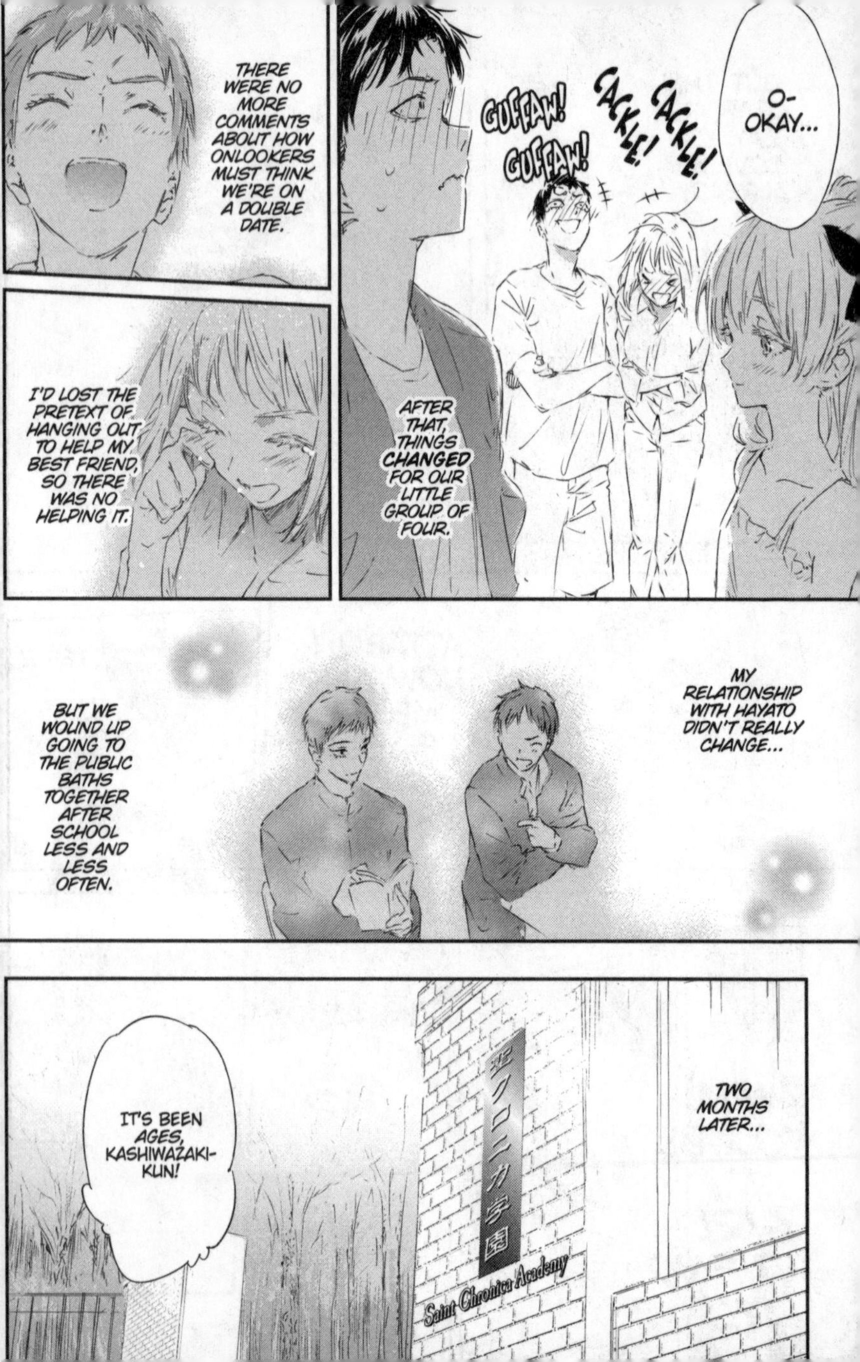
O-OKAY...
CACKLE! CACKLE!
GUFFAW! GUFFAW!
AFTER THAT, THINGS CHANGED FOR OUR LITTLE GROUP OF FOUR.
THERE WERE NO MORE COMMENTS ABOUT HOW ONLOOKERS MUST THINK WE'RE ON A DOUBLE DATE.
I'D LOST THE PRETEXT OF HANGING OUT TO HELP MY BEST FRIEND, SO THERE WAS NO HELPING IT.
MY RELATIONSHIP WITH HAYATO DIDN'T REALLY CHANGE...
BUT WE WOUND UP GOING TO THE PUBLIC BATHS TOGETHER AFTER SCHOOL LESS AND LESS OFTEN.
TWO MONTHS LATER...
聖クロニカ学園
Saint Chronica Academy
IT'S BEEN AGES, KASHIWAZAKI-KUN!

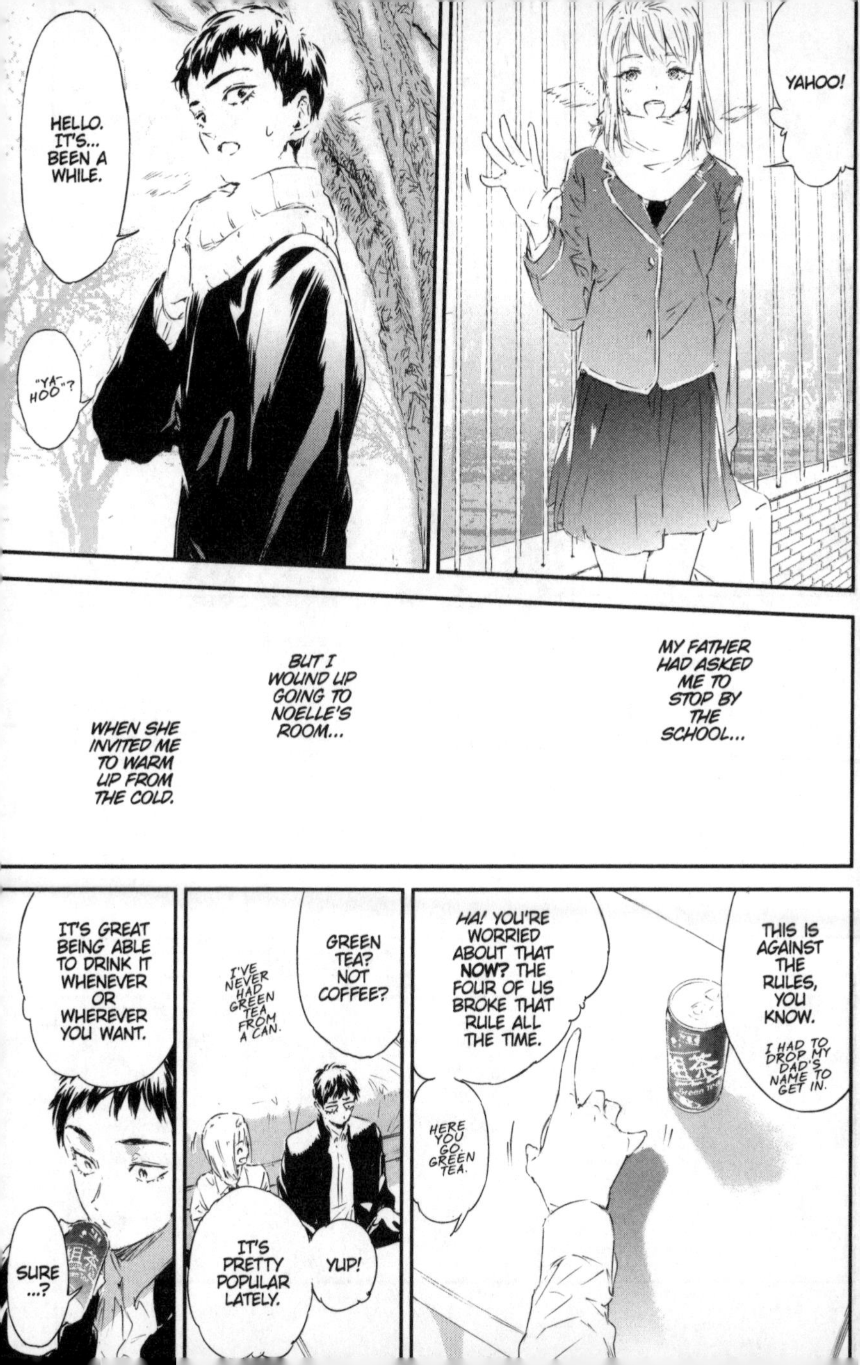
YAHOO!
HELLO. IT'S... BEEN A WHILE.
"YA-HOO"?
MY FATHER HAD ASKED ME TO STOP BY THE SCHOOL...
BUT I WOUND UP GOING TO NOELLE'S ROOM...
WHEN SHE INVITED ME TO WARM UP FROM THE COLD.
THIS IS AGAINST THE RULES, YOU KNOW.
I HAD TO DROP MY DAD'S NAME TO GET IN.
HA! YOU'RE WORRIED ABOUT THAT NOW? THE FOUR OF US BROKE THAT RULE ALL THE TIME.
HERE YOU GO. GREEN TEA.
GREEN TEA? NOT COFFEE?
I'VE NEVER HAD GREEN TEA FROM A CAN.
YUP!
IT'S PRETTY POPULAR LATELY.
IT'S GREAT BEING ABLE TO DRINK IT WHENEVER OR WHEREVER YOU WANT.
SURE ...?

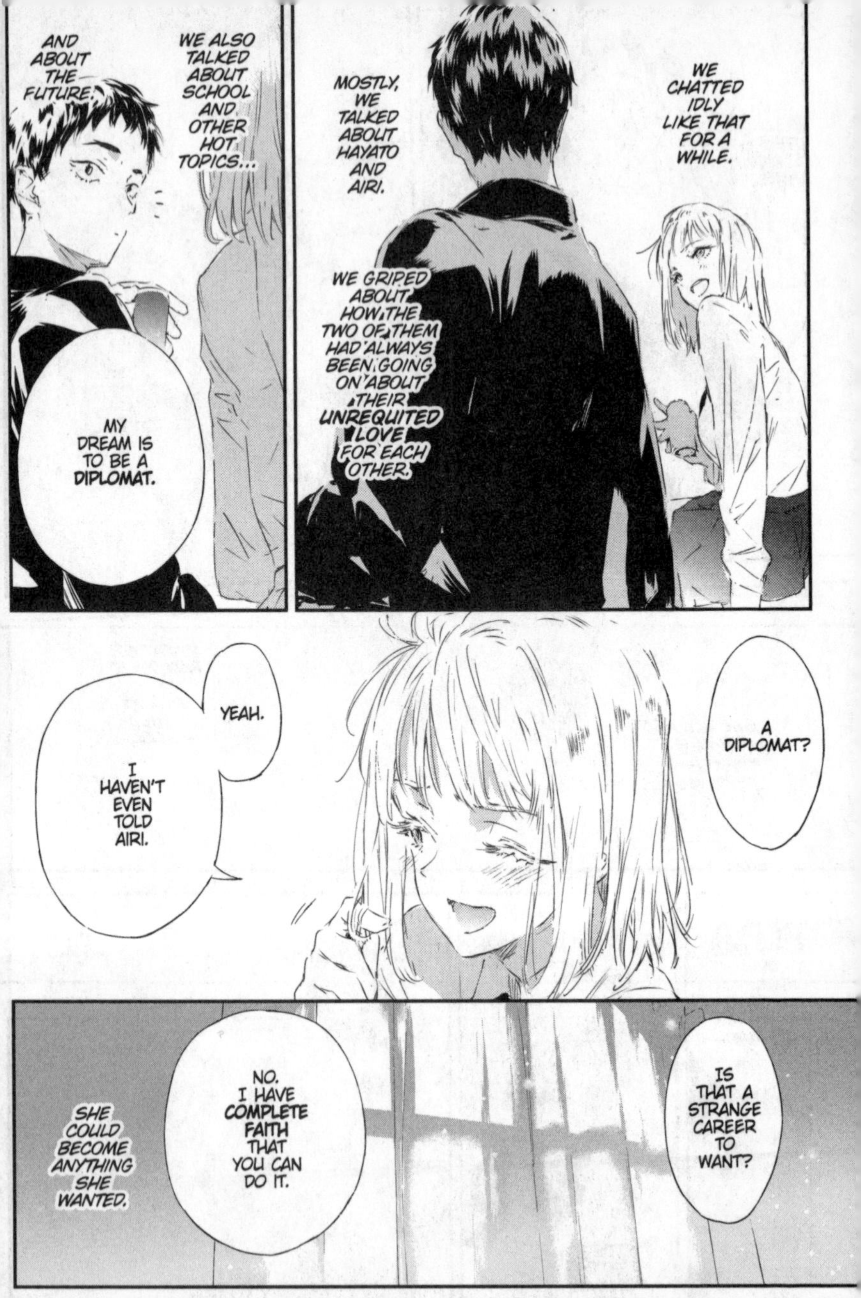
WE CHATTED IDLY LIKE THAT FOR A WHILE.
MOSTLY, WE TALKED ABOUT HAYATO AND AIRI.
WE GRIPED ABOUT HOW THE TWO OF THEM HAD ALWAYS BEEN GOING ON ABOUT THEIR UNREQUITED LOVE FOR EACH OTHER.
WE ALSO TALKED ABOUT SCHOOL AND OTHER HOT TOPICS...
AND ABOUT THE FUTURE.
MY DREAM IS TO BE A DIPLOMAT.
A DIPLOMAT?
YEAH.
I HAVEN'T EVEN TOLD AIRI.
IS THAT A STRANGE CAREER TO WANT?
NO. I HAVE COMPLETE FAITH THAT YOU CAN DO IT.
SHE COULD BECOME ANYTHING SHE WANTED.

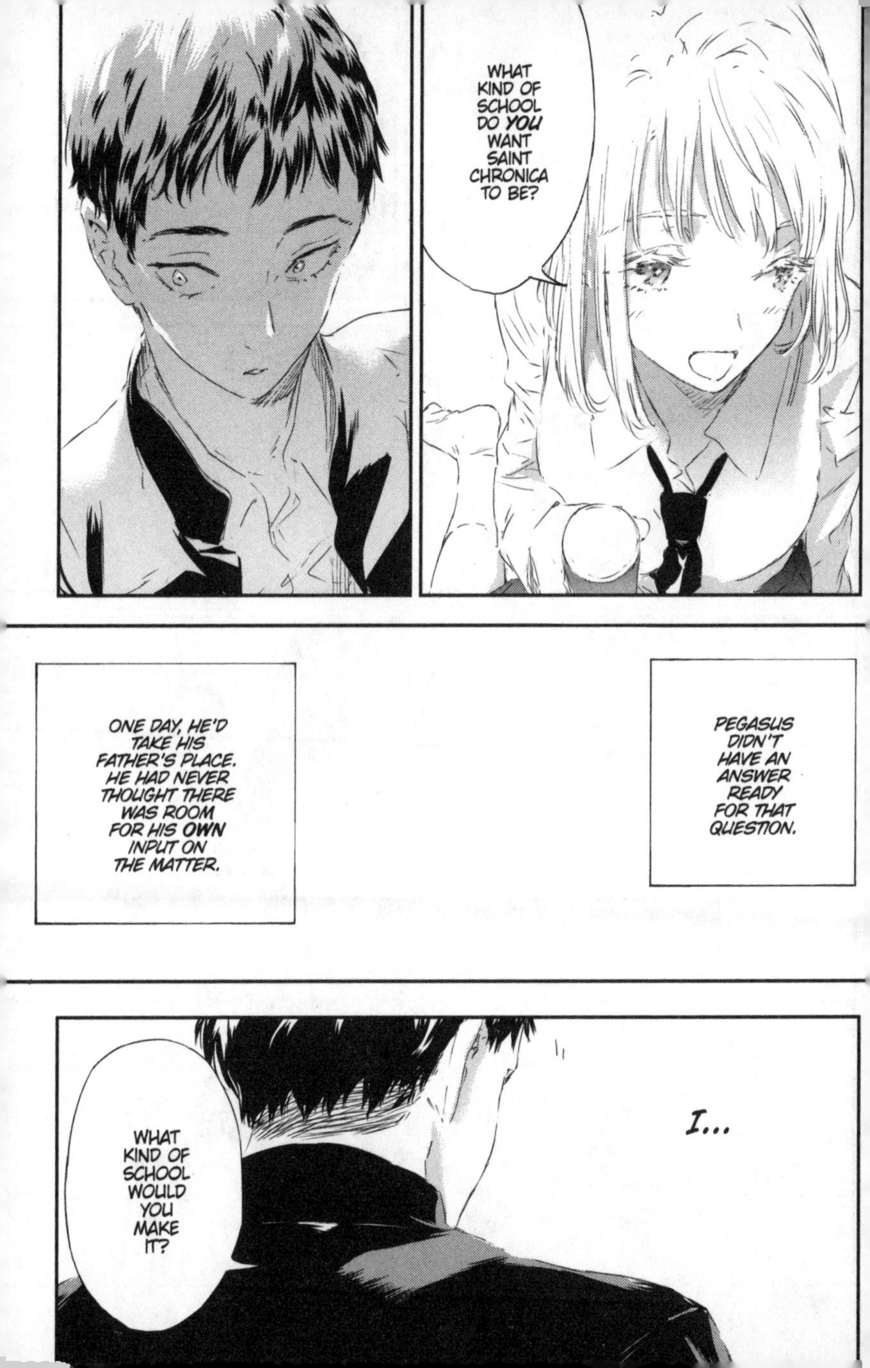
WHAT KIND OF SCHOOL DO *YOU* WANT SAINT CHRONICA TO BE?
PEGASUS DIDN'T HAVE AN ANSWER READY FOR THAT QUESTION.
ONE DAY, HE'D TAKE HIS FATHER'S PLACE. HE HAD NEVER THOUGHT THERE WAS ROOM FOR HIS **OWN** INPUT ON THE MATTER.
I...
WHAT KIND OF SCHOOL WOULD YOU MAKE IT?

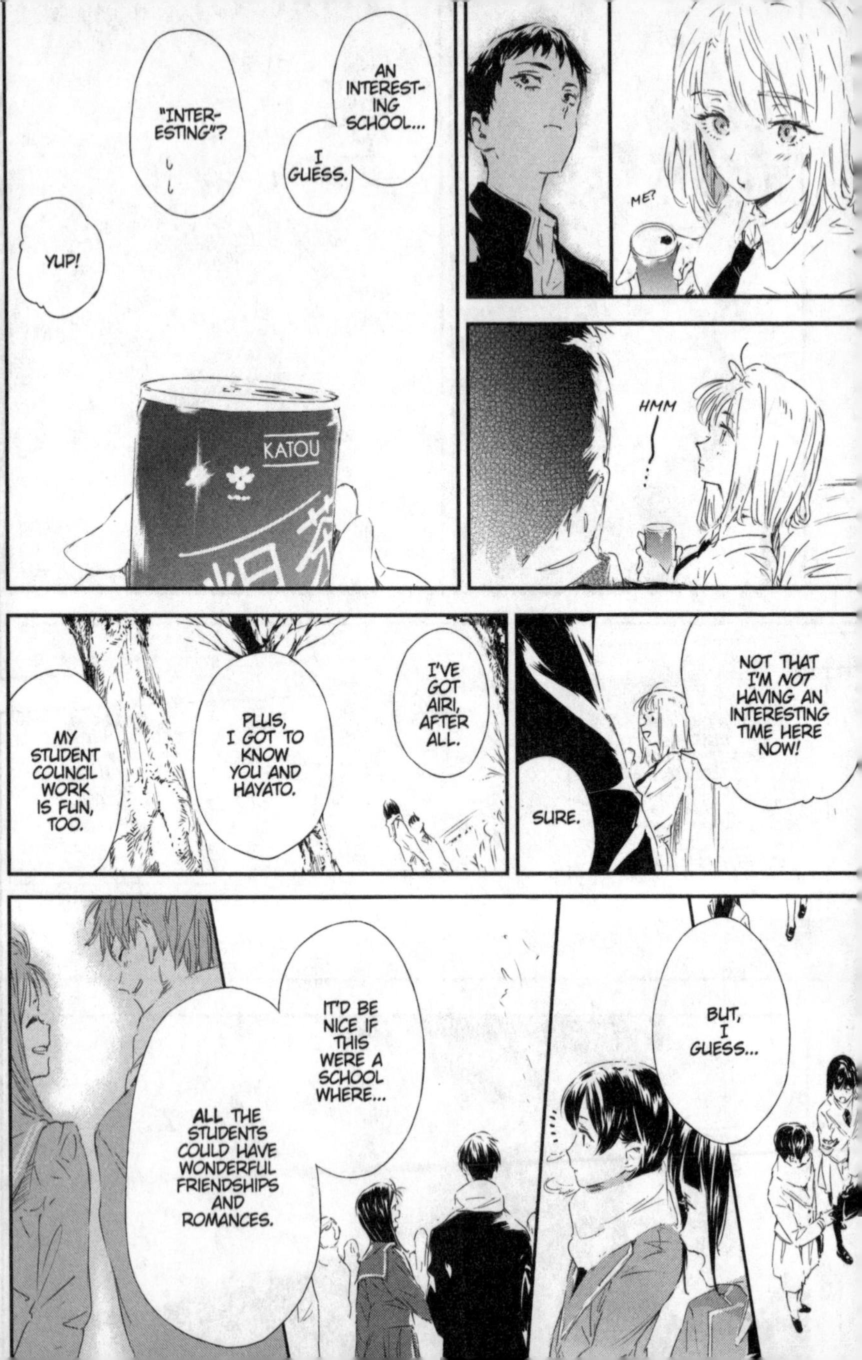

ME?
HMM
AN INTERESTING SCHOOL... I GUESS.
"INTERESTING"?
YUP!
KATOU
NOT THAT I'M *NOT* HAVING AN INTERESTING TIME HERE NOW!
SURE.
I'VE GOT AIRI, AFTER ALL.
PLUS, I GOT TO KNOW YOU AND HAYATO.
MY STUDENT COUNCIL WORK IS FUN, TOO.
BUT, I GUESS...
IT'D BE NICE IF THIS WERE A SCHOOL WHERE...
ALL THE STUDENTS COULD HAVE WONDERFUL FRIENDSHIPS AND ROMANCES.

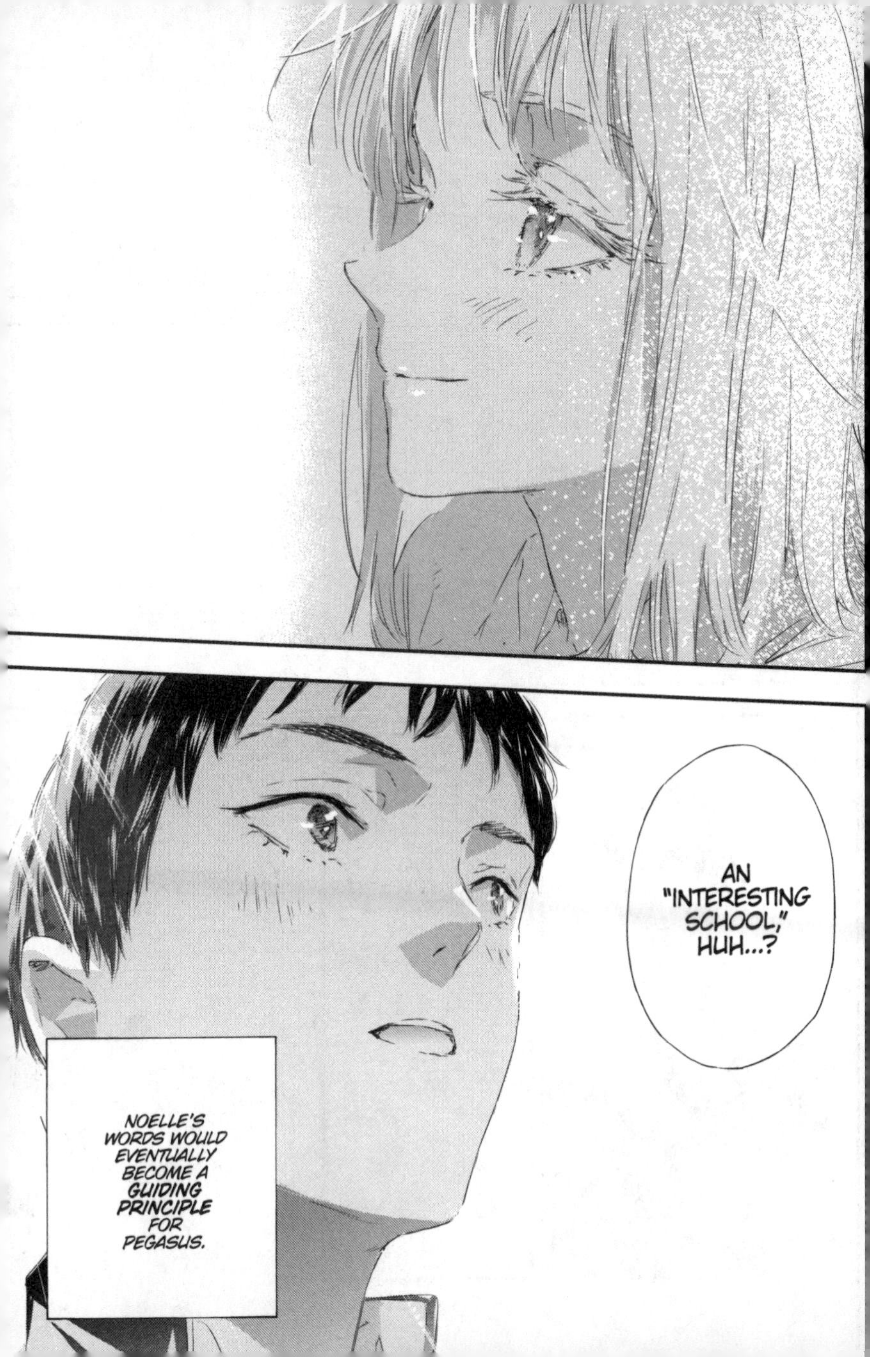
AN "INTERESTING SCHOOL," HUH...?
NOELLE'S WORDS WOULD EVENTUALLY BECOME A **GUIDING PRINCIPLE** FOR PEGASUS.

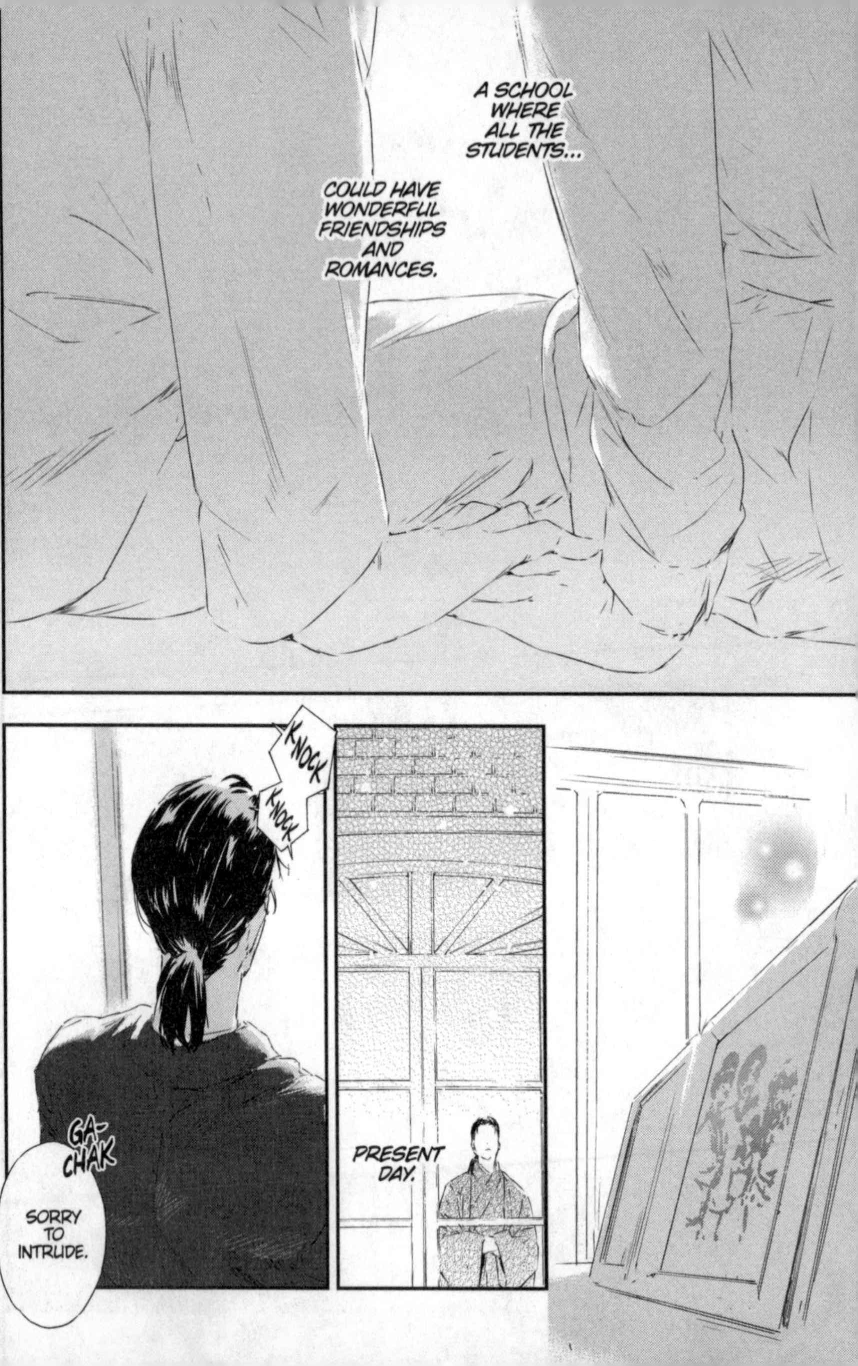
A SCHOOL WHERE ALL THE STUDENTS...
COULD HAVE WONDERFUL FRIENDSHIPS AND ROMANCES.
KNOCK
KNOCK
PRESENT DAY.
GA-CHAK
SORRY TO INTRUDE.

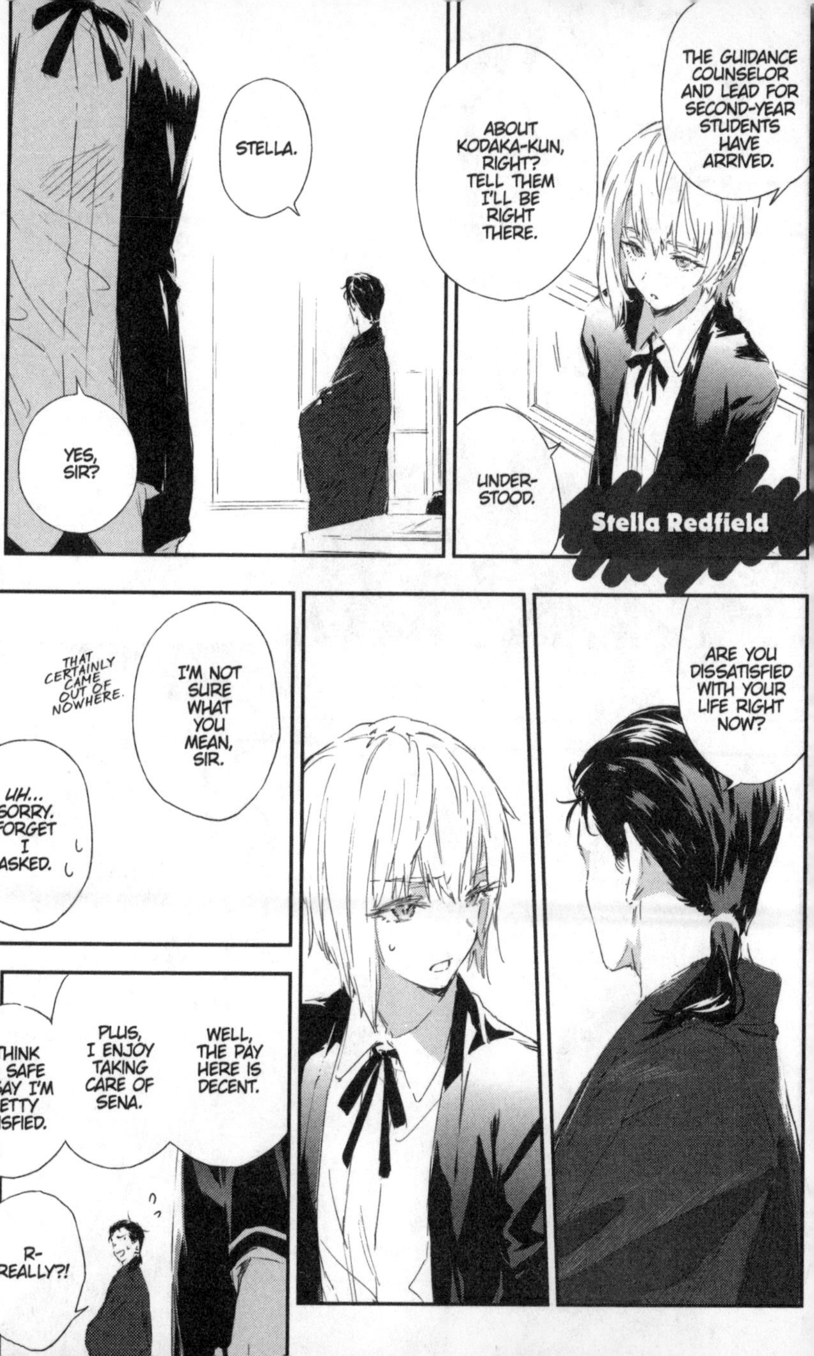
THE GUIDANCE COUNSELOR AND LEAD FOR SECOND-YEAR STUDENTS HAVE ARRIVED.
ABOUT KODAKA-KUN, RIGHT? TELL THEM I'LL BE RIGHT THERE.
UNDER-STOOD.
Stella Redfield
STELLA.
YES, SIR?
ARE YOU DISSATISFIED WITH YOUR LIFE RIGHT NOW?
I'M NOT SURE WHAT YOU MEAN, SIR.
THAT CERTAINLY CAME OUT OF NOWHERE.
UH... SORRY. FORGET I ASKED.
WELL, THE PAY HERE IS DECENT.
PLUS, I ENJOY TAKING CARE OF SENA.
I THINK IT'S SAFE TO SAY I'M PRETTY SATISFIED.
R-REALLY?!

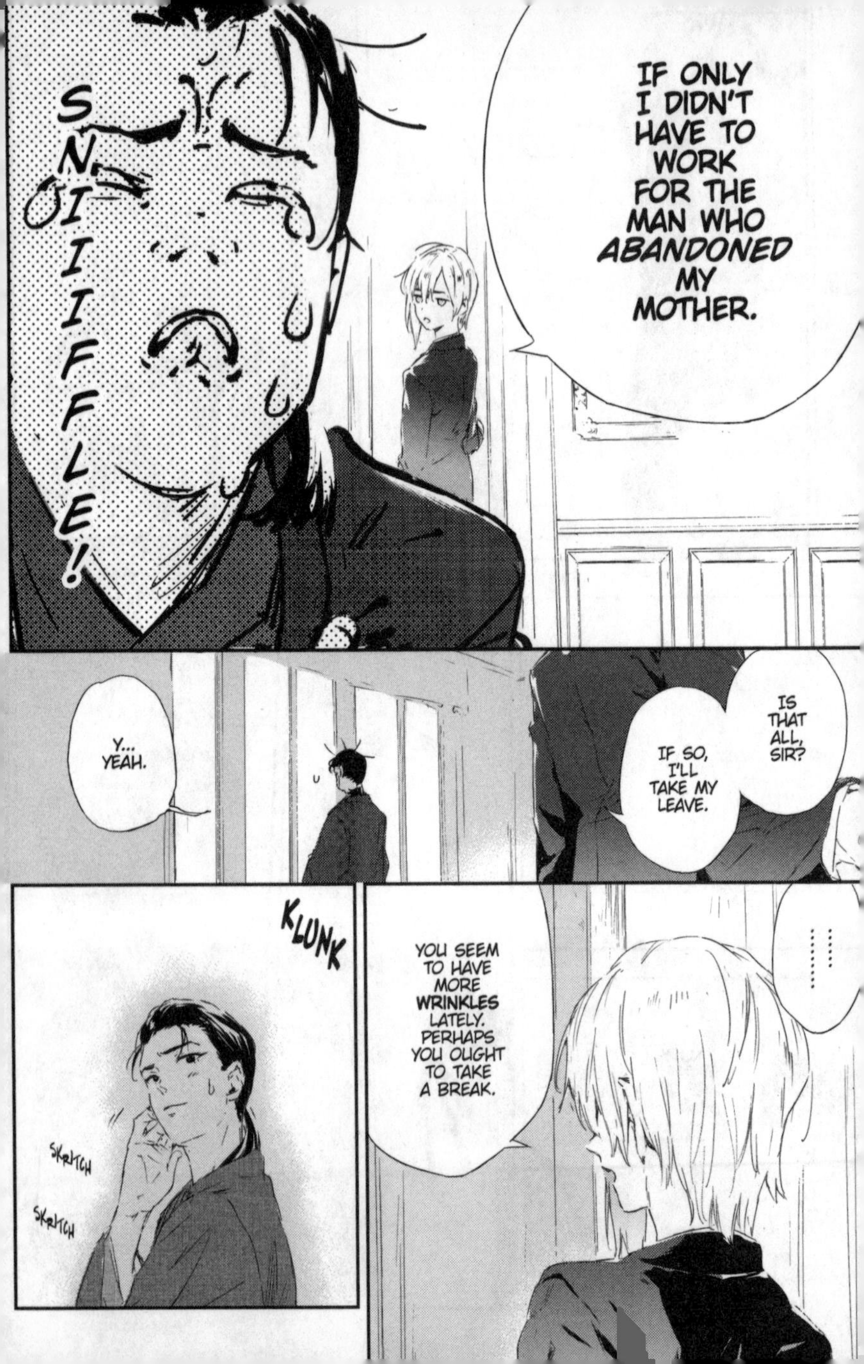
IF ONLY I DIDN'T HAVE TO WORK FOR THE MAN WHO ABANDONED MY MOTHER.
SNIIIFFLE!
IS THAT ALL, SIR?
IF SO, I'LL TAKE MY LEAVE.
Y... YEAH.
......
YOU SEEM TO HAVE MORE WRINKLES LATELY. PERHAPS YOU OUGHT TO TAKE A BREAK.
KLUNK
SKRITCH
SKRITCH

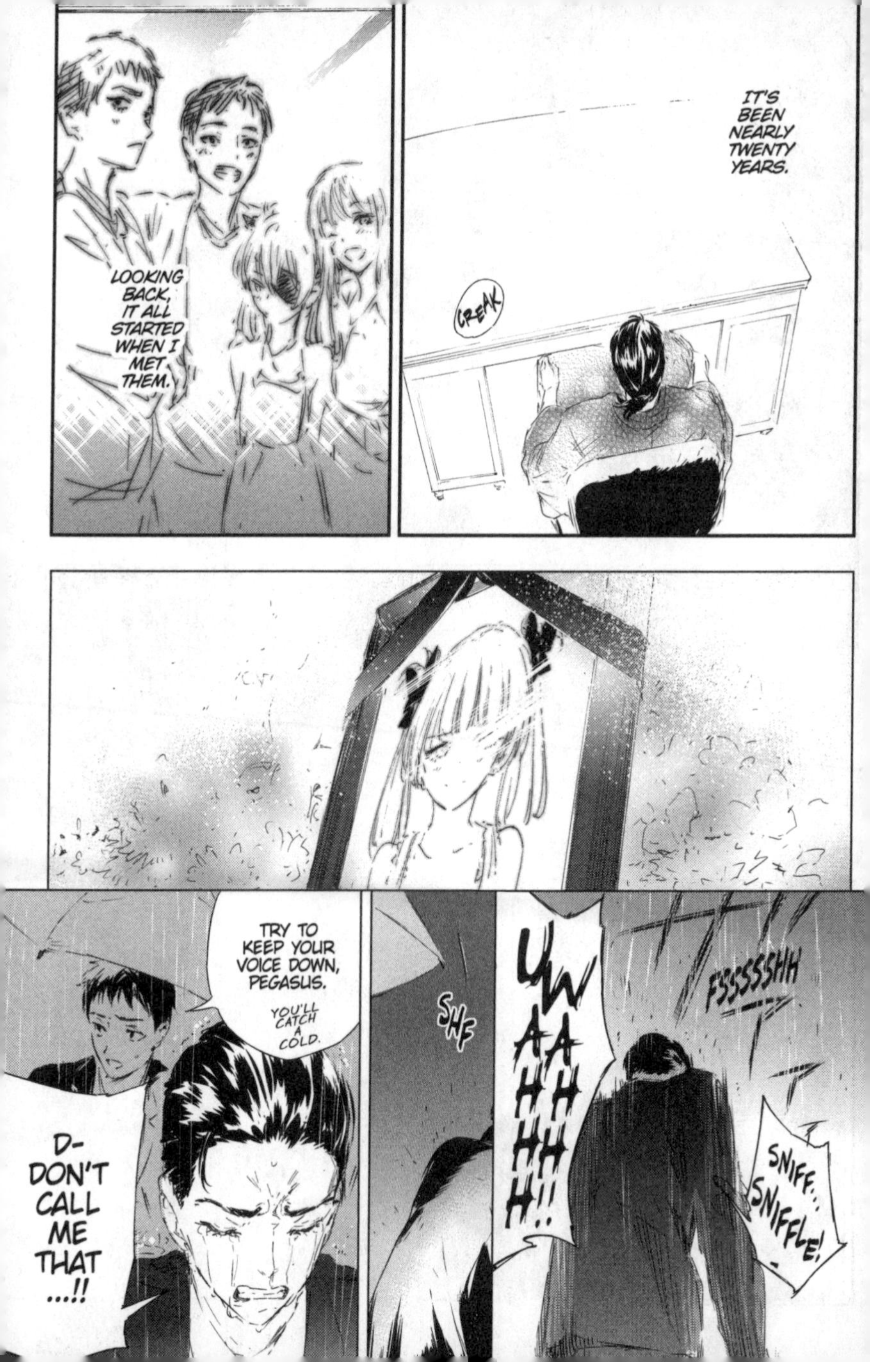
IT'S BEEN NEARLY TWENTY YEARS.
CREAK
LOOKING BACK, IT ALL STARTED WHEN I MET THEM.
FSSSSSSHH
UWAAHHHHHH!!
SNIFF... SNIFF... SNIFFLE!
SHF
TRY TO KEEP YOUR VOICE DOWN, PEGASUS.
YOU'LL CATCH A COLD.
D-DON'T CALL ME THAT...!!

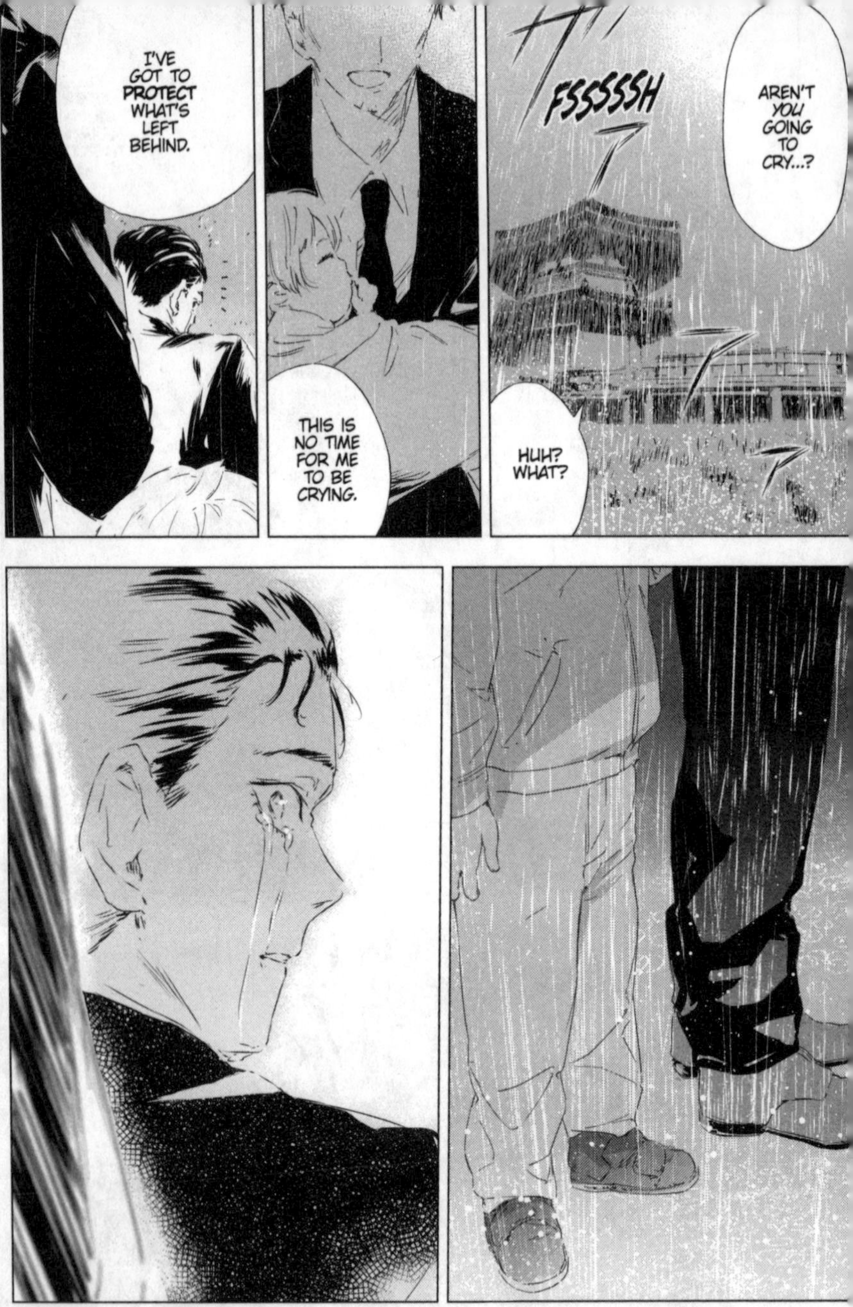
AREN'T YOU GOING TO CRY...?
FSSSSSH
HUH? WHAT?
THIS IS NO TIME FOR ME TO BE CRYING.
I'VE GOT TO PROTECT WHAT'S LEFT BEHIND.

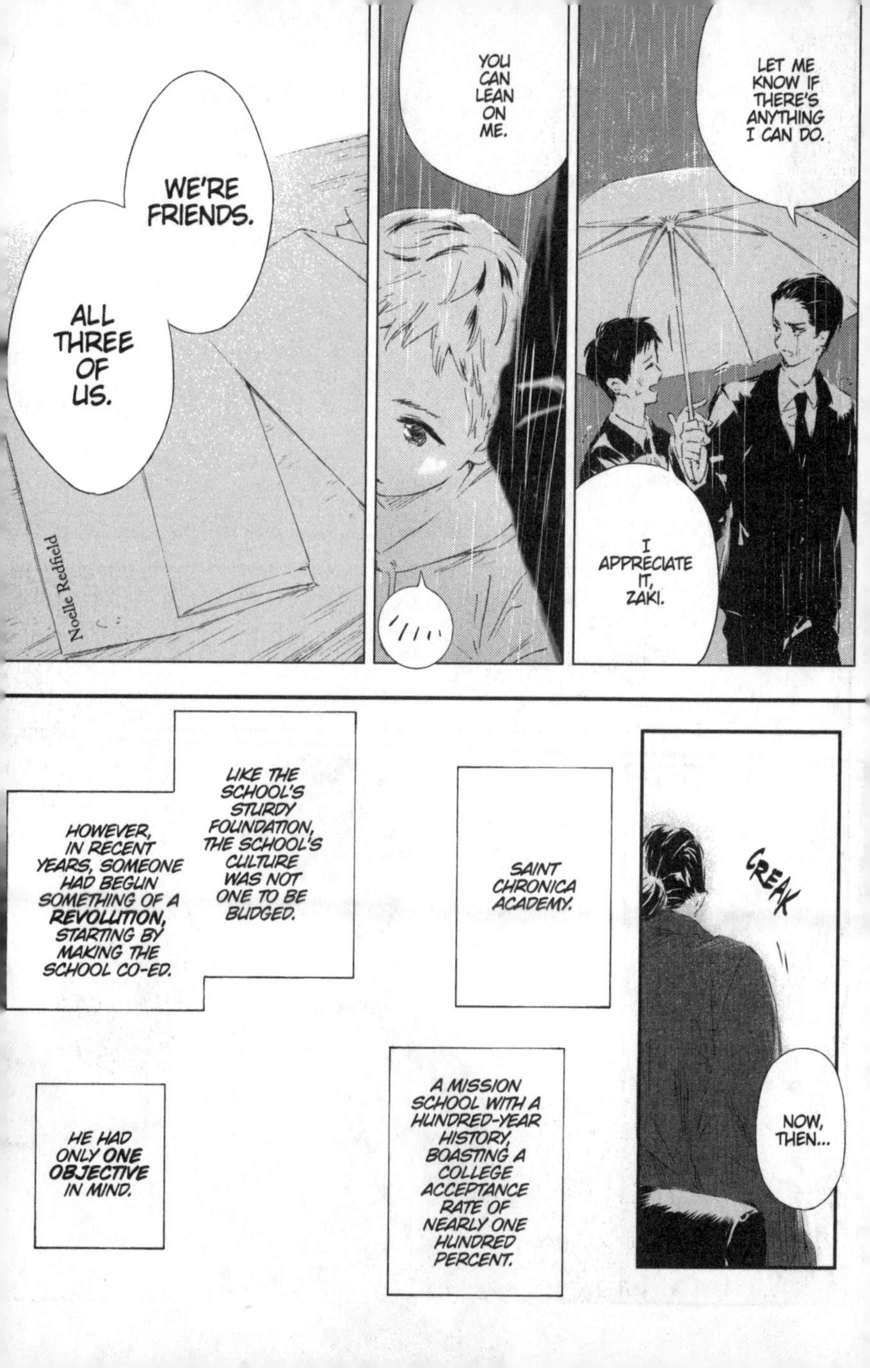
LET ME KNOW IF THERE'S ANYTHING I CAN DO.
I APPRECIATE IT, ZAKI.
YOU CAN LEAN ON ME.
WE'RE FRIENDS.
ALL THREE OF US.
Noelle Redfield
CREAK
NOW, THEN...
SAINT CHRONICA ACADEMY.
A MISSION SCHOOL WITH A HUNDRED-YEAR HISTORY, BOASTING A COLLEGE ACCEPTANCE RATE OF NEARLY ONE HUNDRED PERCENT.
LIKE THE SCHOOL'S STURDY FOUNDATION, THE SCHOOL'S CULTURE WAS NOT ONE TO BE BUDGED.
HOWEVER, IN RECENT YEARS, SOMEONE HAD BEGUN SOMETHING OF A REVOLUTION, STARTING BY MAKING THE SCHOOL CO-ED.
HE HAD ONLY ONE OBJECTIVE IN MIND.

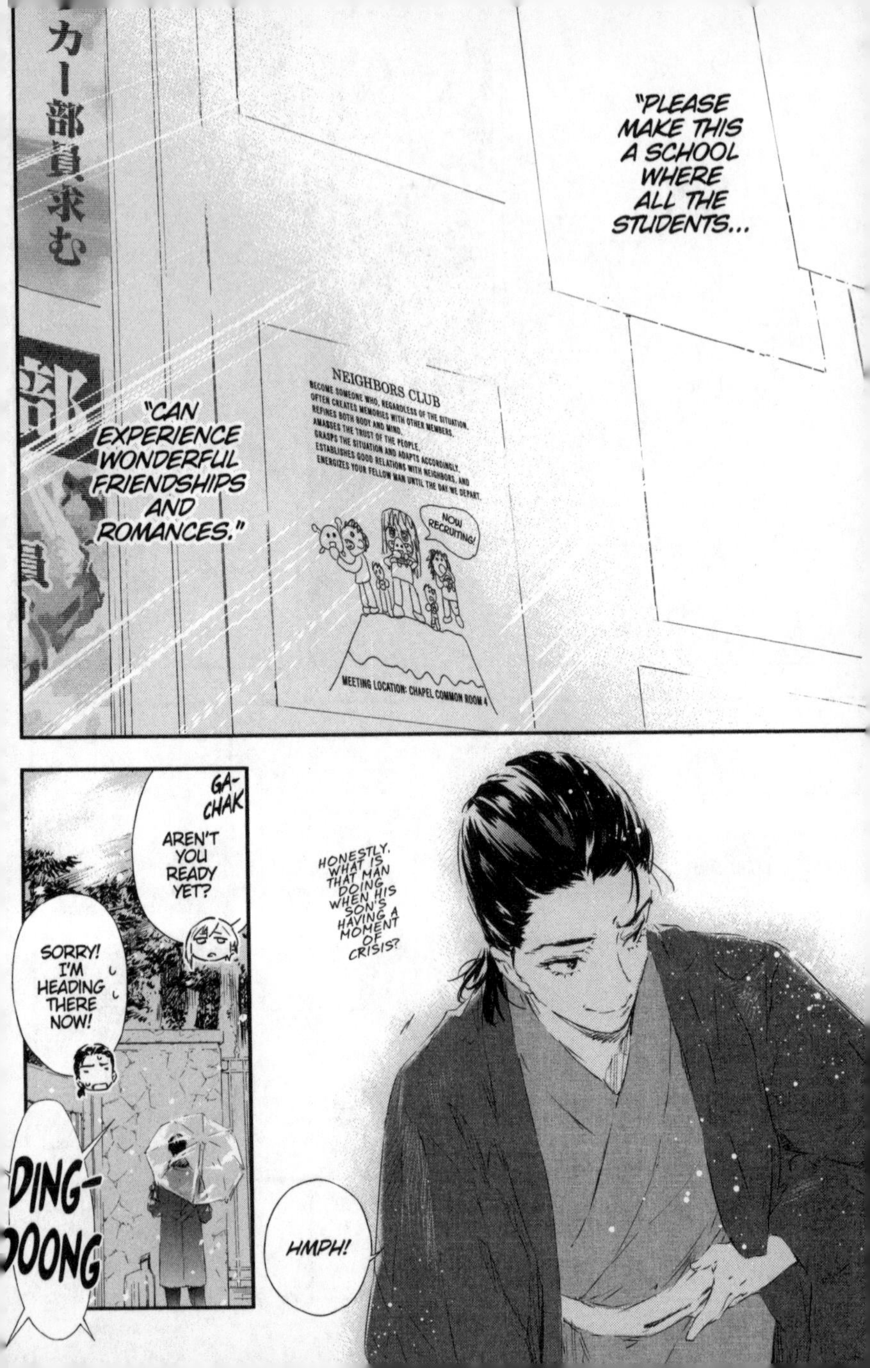
"PLEASE MAKE THIS A SCHOOL WHERE ALL THE STUDENTS...
カー部員求む
"CAN EXPERIENCE WONDERFUL FRIENDSHIPS AND ROMANCES."
NEIGHBORS CLUB
BECOME SOMEONE WHO, REGARDLESS OF THE SITUATION, OFTEN CREATES MEMORIES WITH OTHER MEMBERS, REFINES BOTH BODY AND MIND, AMASSES THE TRUST OF THE PEOPLE, GRASPS THE SITUATION AND ADAPTS ACCORDINGLY, ESTABLISHES GOOD RELATIONS WITH NEIGHBORS, AND ENERGIZES YOUR FELLOW MAN UNTIL THE DAY WE DEPART.
NOW RECRUITING!
MEETING LOCATION: CHAPEL COMMON ROOM 4
HONESTLY, WHAT IS THAT MAN DOING WHEN HIS SON'S HAVING A MOMENT OF CRISIS?
HMPH!
GA-CHAK
AREN'T YOU READY YET?
SORRY! I'M HEADING THERE NOW!
DING-DOONG

I don't have many friends

Haganai
I don't have many friends

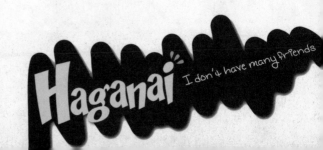

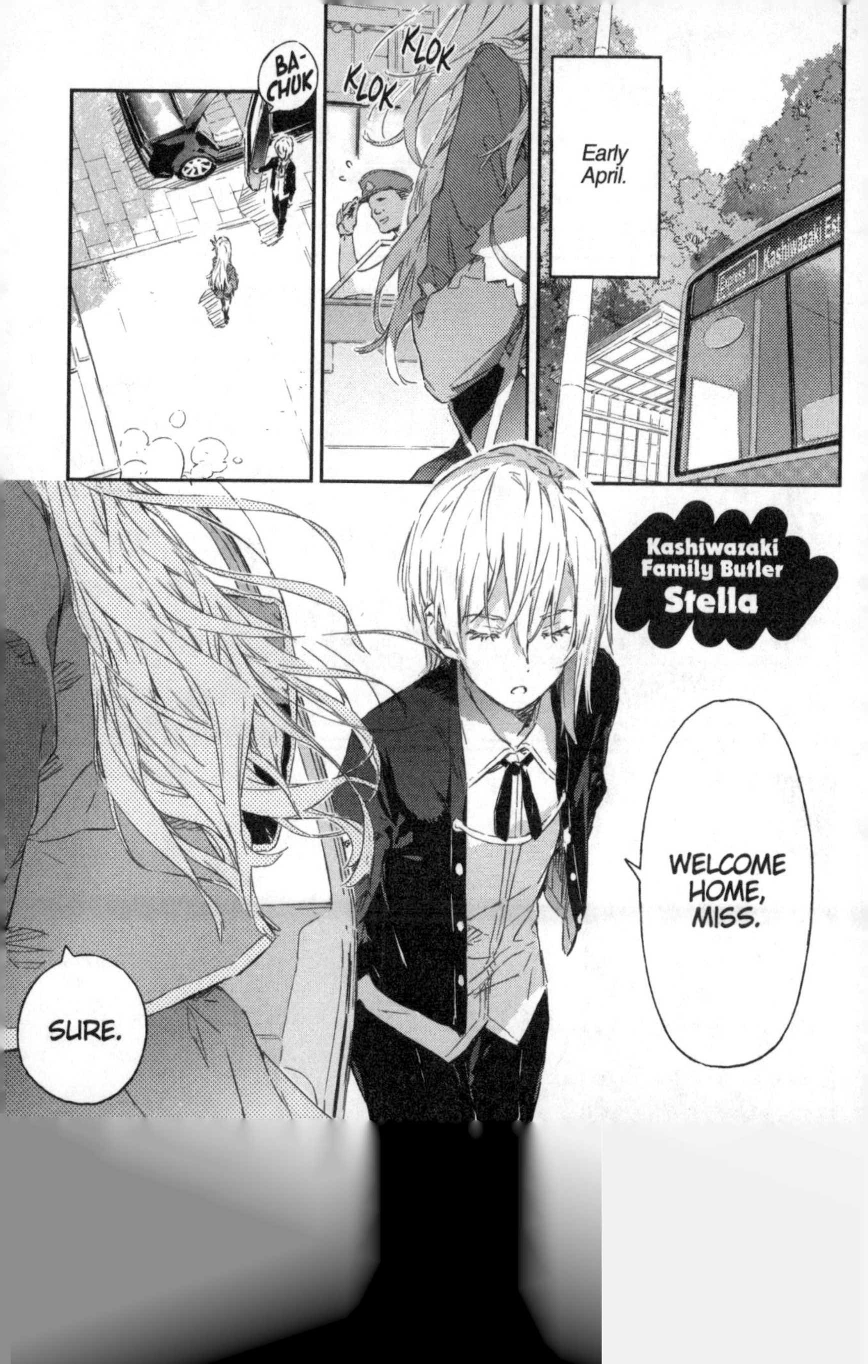
Early April.
KLOK
KLOK
BA-CHUK
Kashiwazaki Family Butler Stella
WELCOME HOME, MISS.
SURE.

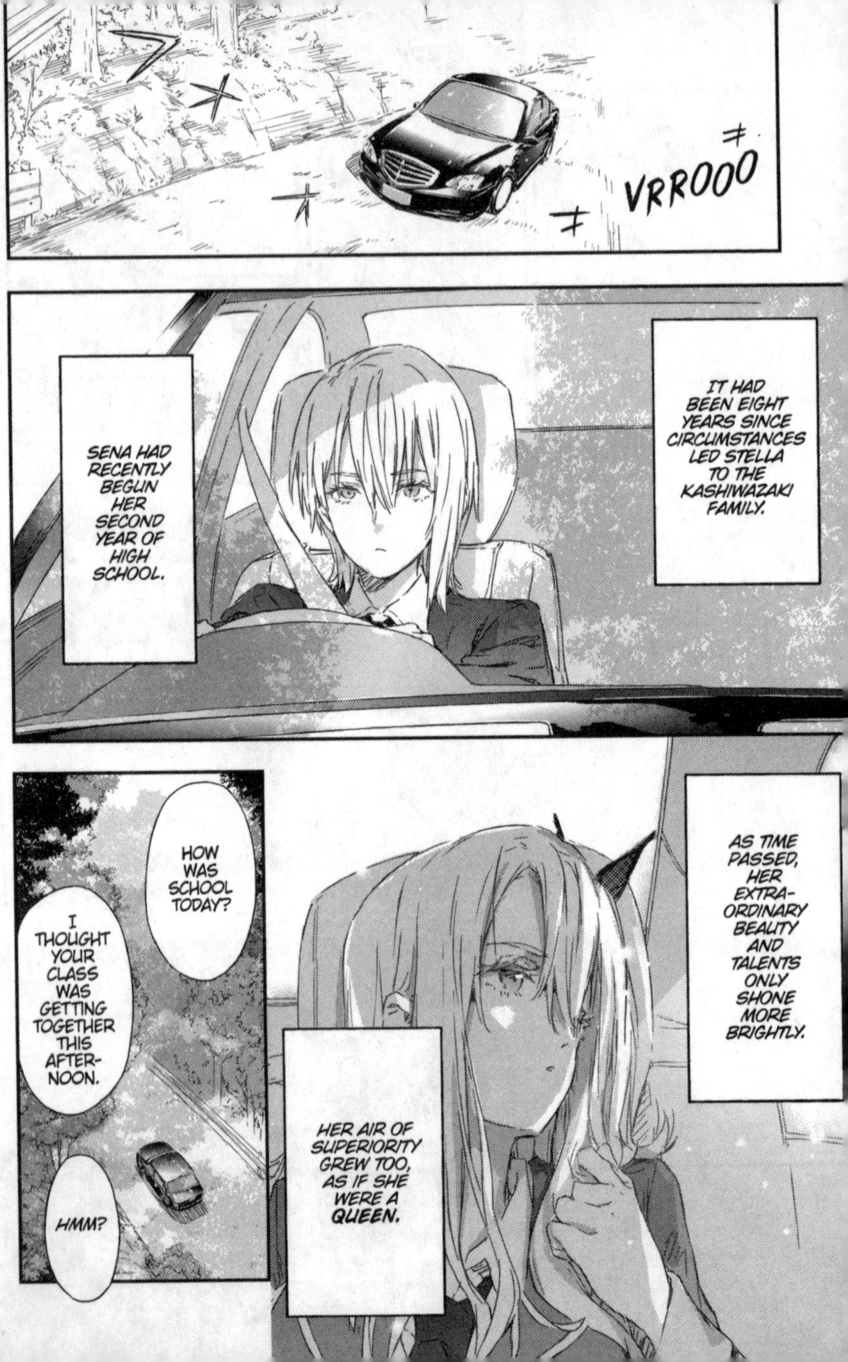
VRROOO
IT HAD BEEN EIGHT YEARS SINCE CIRCUMSTANCES LED STELLA TO THE KASHIWAZAKI FAMILY.
SENA HAD RECENTLY BEGUN HER SECOND YEAR OF HIGH SCHOOL.
AS TIME PASSED, HER EXTRA-ORDINARY BEAUTY AND TALENTS ONLY SHONE MORE BRIGHTLY.
HER AIR OF SUPERIORITY GREW TOO, AS IF SHE WERE A QUEEN.
HOW WAS SCHOOL TODAY?
I THOUGHT YOUR CLASS WAS GETTING TOGETHER THIS AFTER-NOON.
HMM?

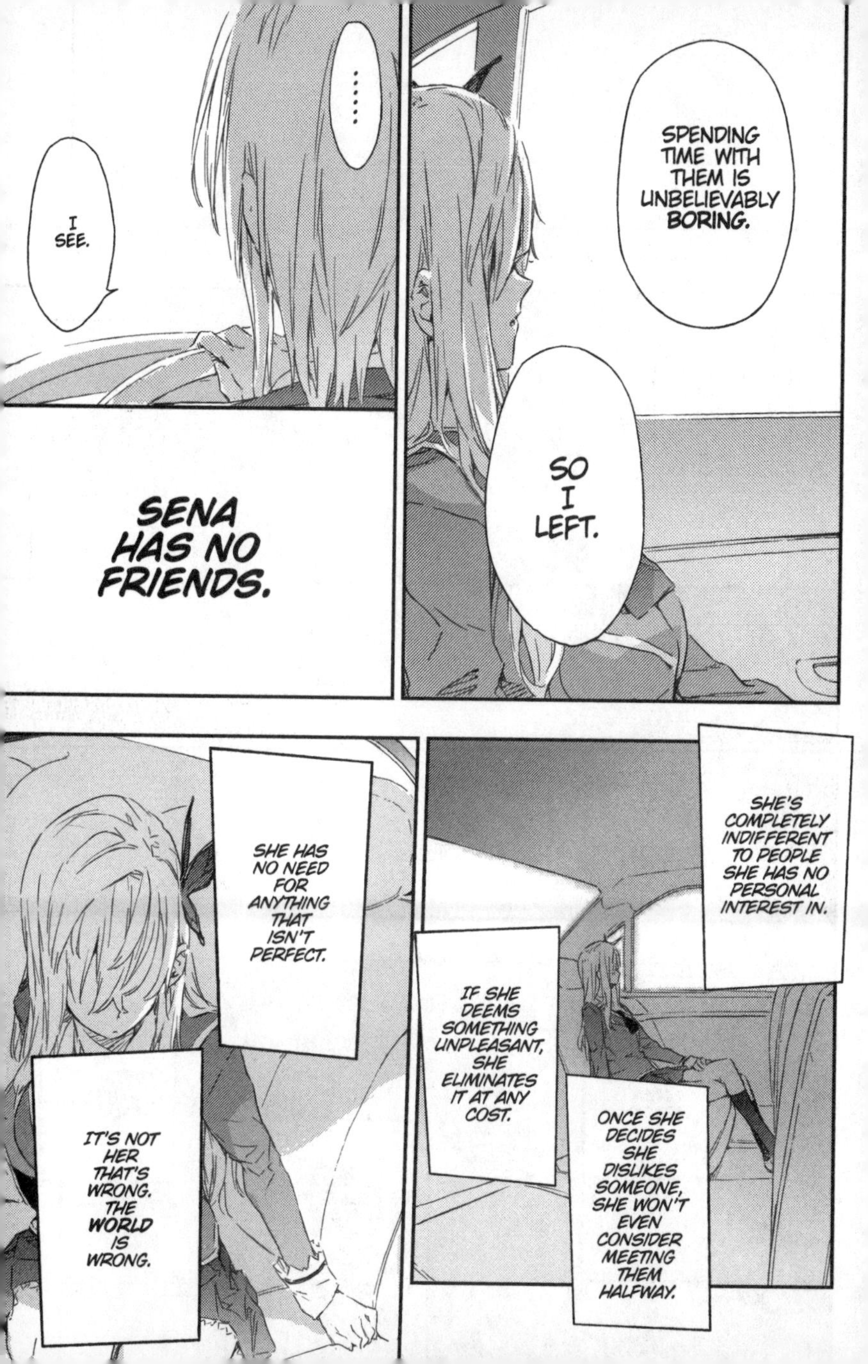
SPENDING TIME WITH THEM IS UNBELIEVABLY BORING.
SO I LEFT.
......
I SEE.
SENA HAS NO FRIENDS.
SHE'S COMPLETELY INDIFFERENT TO PEOPLE SHE HAS NO PERSONAL INTEREST IN.
IF SHE DEEMS SOMETHING UNPLEASANT, SHE ELIMINATES IT AT ANY COST.
ONCE SHE DECIDES SHE DISLIKES SOMEONE, SHE WON'T EVEN CONSIDER MEETING THEM HALFWAY.
SHE HAS NO NEED FOR ANYTHING THAT ISN'T PERFECT.
IT'S NOT HER THAT'S WRONG. THE WORLD IS WRONG.

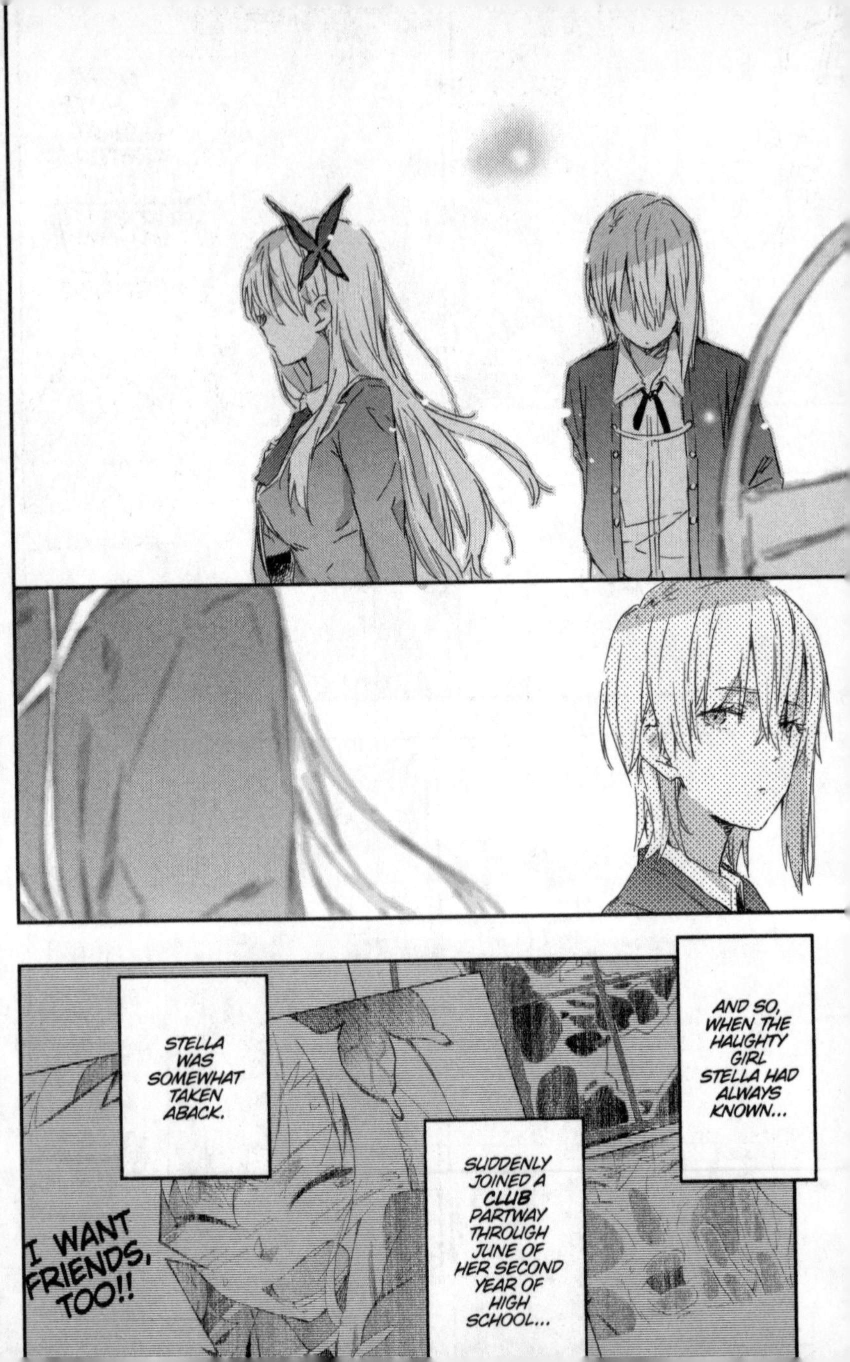

AND SO, WHEN THE HAUGHTY GIRL STELLA HAD ALWAYS KNOWN...
SUDDENLY JOINED A **CLUB** PARTWAY THROUGH JUNE OF HER SECOND YEAR OF HIGH SCHOOL...
STELLA WAS SOMEWHAT TAKEN ABACK.
I WANT FRIENDS, TOO!!

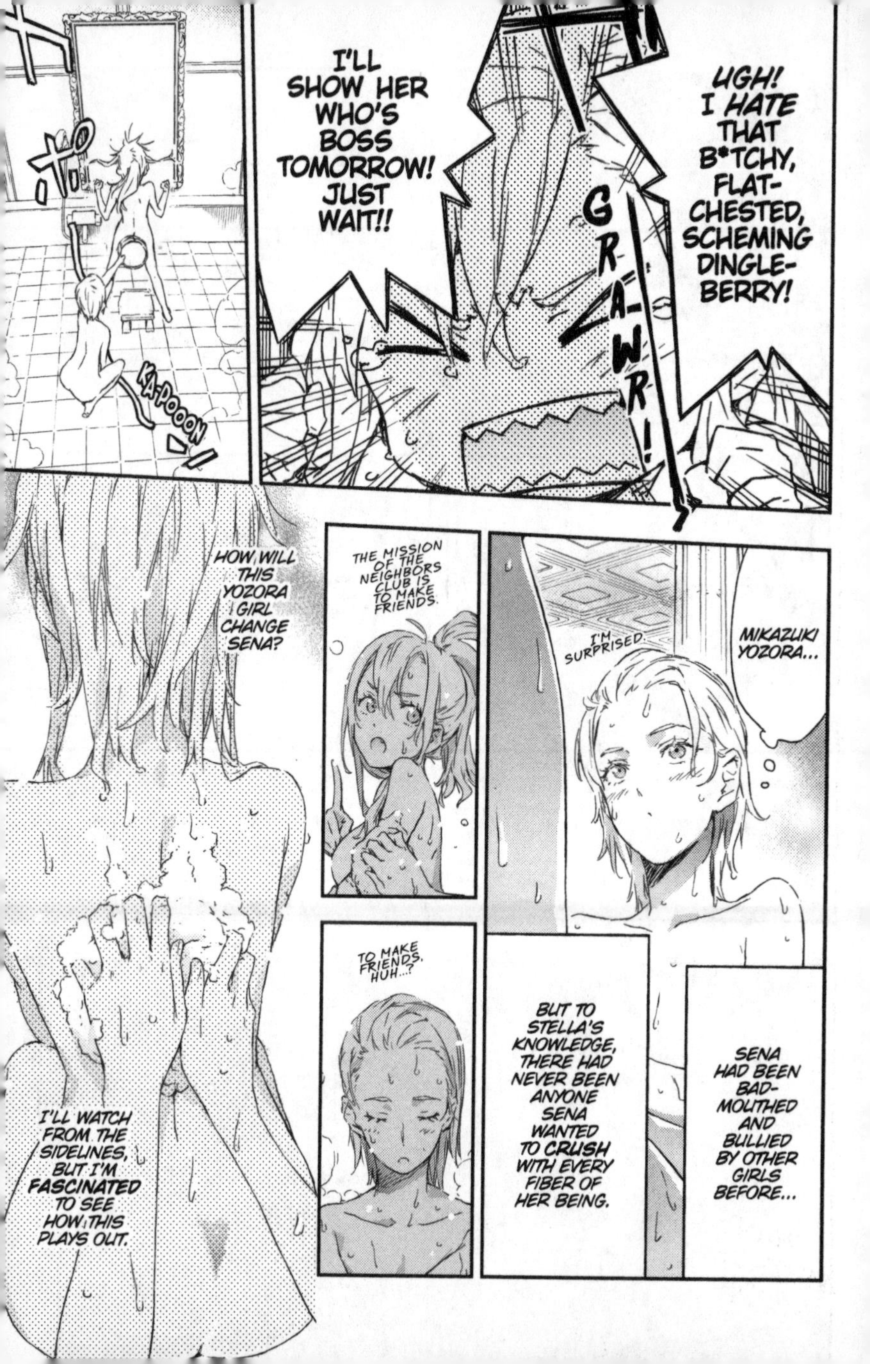
UGH! I HATE THAT B*TCHY, FLAT-CHESTED, SCHEMING DINGLE-BERRY!
GRAWR!
I'LL SHOW HER WHO'S BOSS TOMORROW! JUST WAIT!!
KA-POOON
MIKAZUKI YOZORA...
I'M SURPRISED.
THE MISSION OF THE NEIGHBORS CLUB IS TO MAKE FRIENDS.
SENA HAD BEEN BAD-MOUTHED AND BULLIED BY OTHER GIRLS BEFORE...
BUT TO STELLA'S KNOWLEDGE, THERE HAD NEVER BEEN ANYONE SENA WANTED TO CRUSH WITH EVERY FIBER OF HER BEING.
TO MAKE FRIENDS, HUH...?
HOW WILL THIS YOZORA GIRL CHANGE SENA?
I'LL WATCH FROM THE SIDELINES, BUT I'M FASCINATED TO SEE HOW THIS PLAYS OUT.

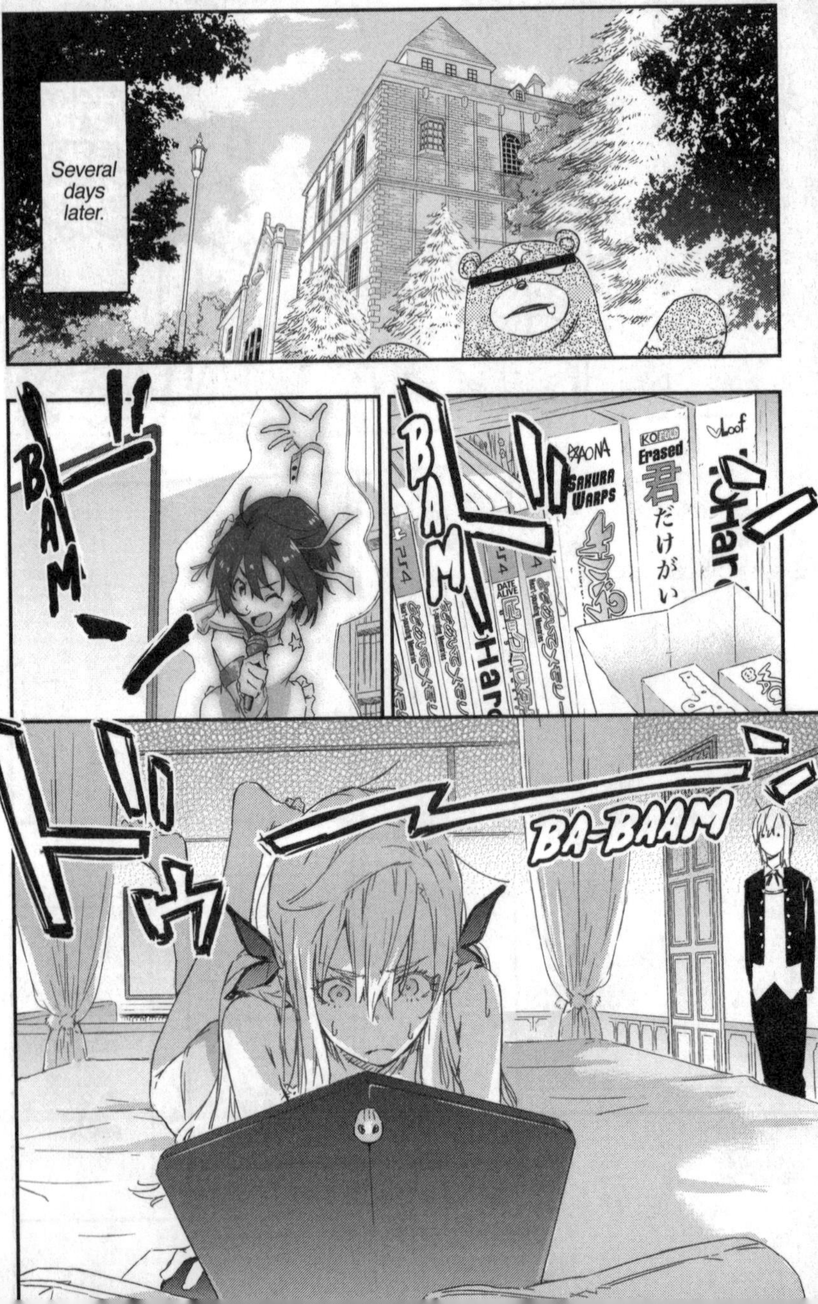
Several days later.
BAM
SAKURA WARPS
Erased
君だけがい
BAM
BA-BAAM

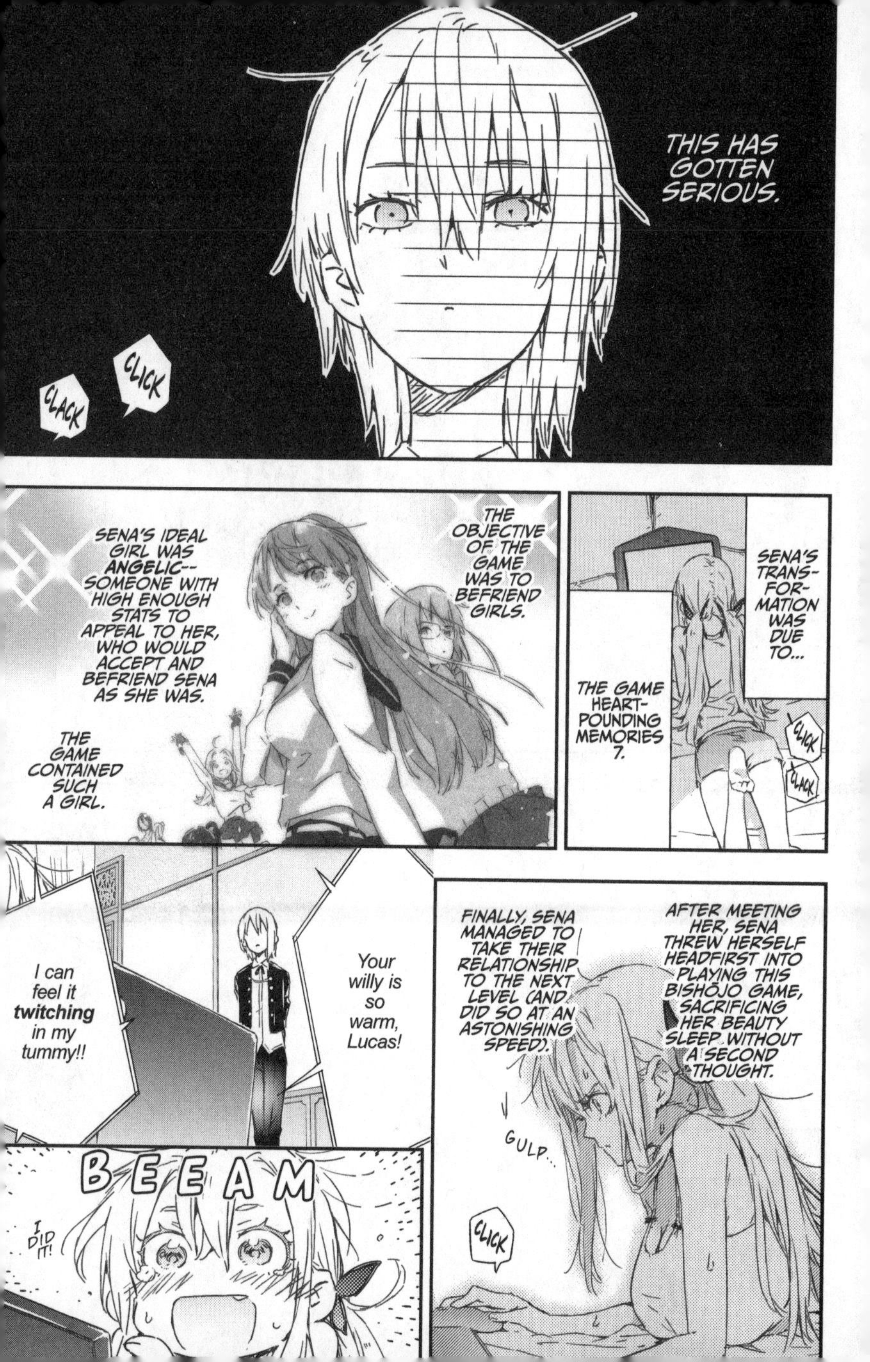
THIS HAS GOTTEN SERIOUS.
CLICK
CLACK
SENA'S TRANS-FOR-MATION WAS DUE TO...
THE GAME HEART-POUNDING MEMORIES 7.
CLICK
CLACK
THE OBJECTIVE OF THE GAME WAS TO BEFRIEND GIRLS.
SENA'S IDEAL GIRL WAS ANGELIC--SOMEONE WITH HIGH ENOUGH STATS TO APPEAL TO HER, WHO WOULD ACCEPT AND BEFRIEND SENA AS SHE WAS.
THE GAME CONTAINED SUCH A GIRL.
AFTER MEETING HER, SENA THREW HERSELF HEADFIRST INTO PLAYING THIS BISHŌJO GAME, SACRIFICING HER BEAUTY SLEEP WITHOUT A SECOND THOUGHT.
FINALLY, SENA MANAGED TO TAKE THEIR RELATIONSHIP TO THE NEXT LEVEL (AND DID SO AT AN ASTONISHING SPEED).
GULP...
CLICK
Your willy is so warm, Lucas!
I can feel it **twitching** in my tummy!!
BEEEAM
I DID IT!

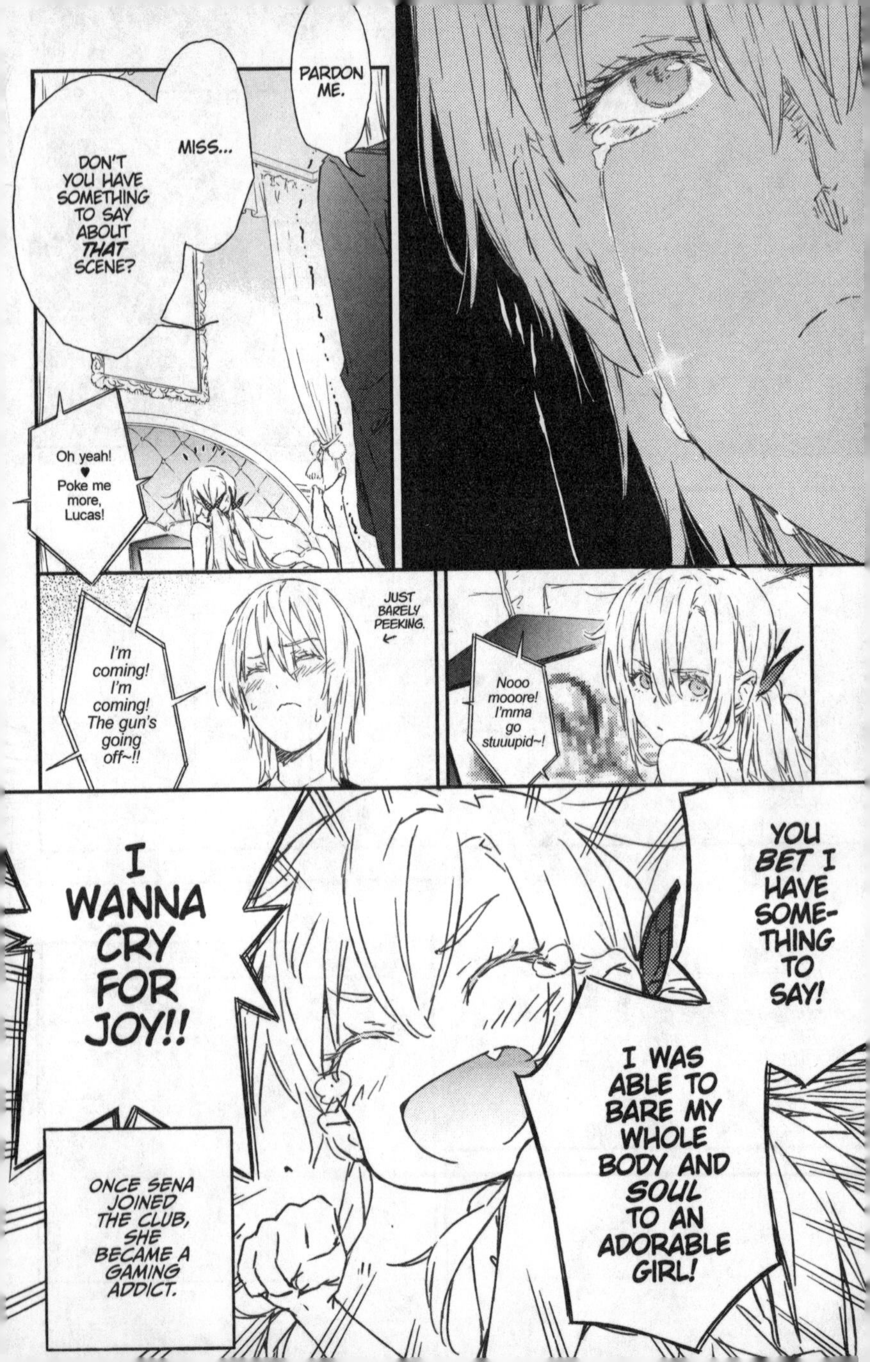
PARDON ME.
MISS...
DON'T YOU HAVE SOMETHING TO SAY ABOUT *THAT* SCENE?
Oh yeah! ♥ Poke me more, Lucas!
Nooo mooore! I'mma go stuuupid~!
JUST BARELY PEEKING.
I'm coming! I'm coming! The gun's going off~!!
YOU *BET* I HAVE SOME-THING TO SAY!
I WANNA CRY FOR JOY!!
I WAS ABLE TO BARE MY WHOLE BODY AND *SOUL* TO AN ADORABLE GIRL!
ONCE SENA JOINED THE CLUB, SHE BECAME A GAMING ADDICT.

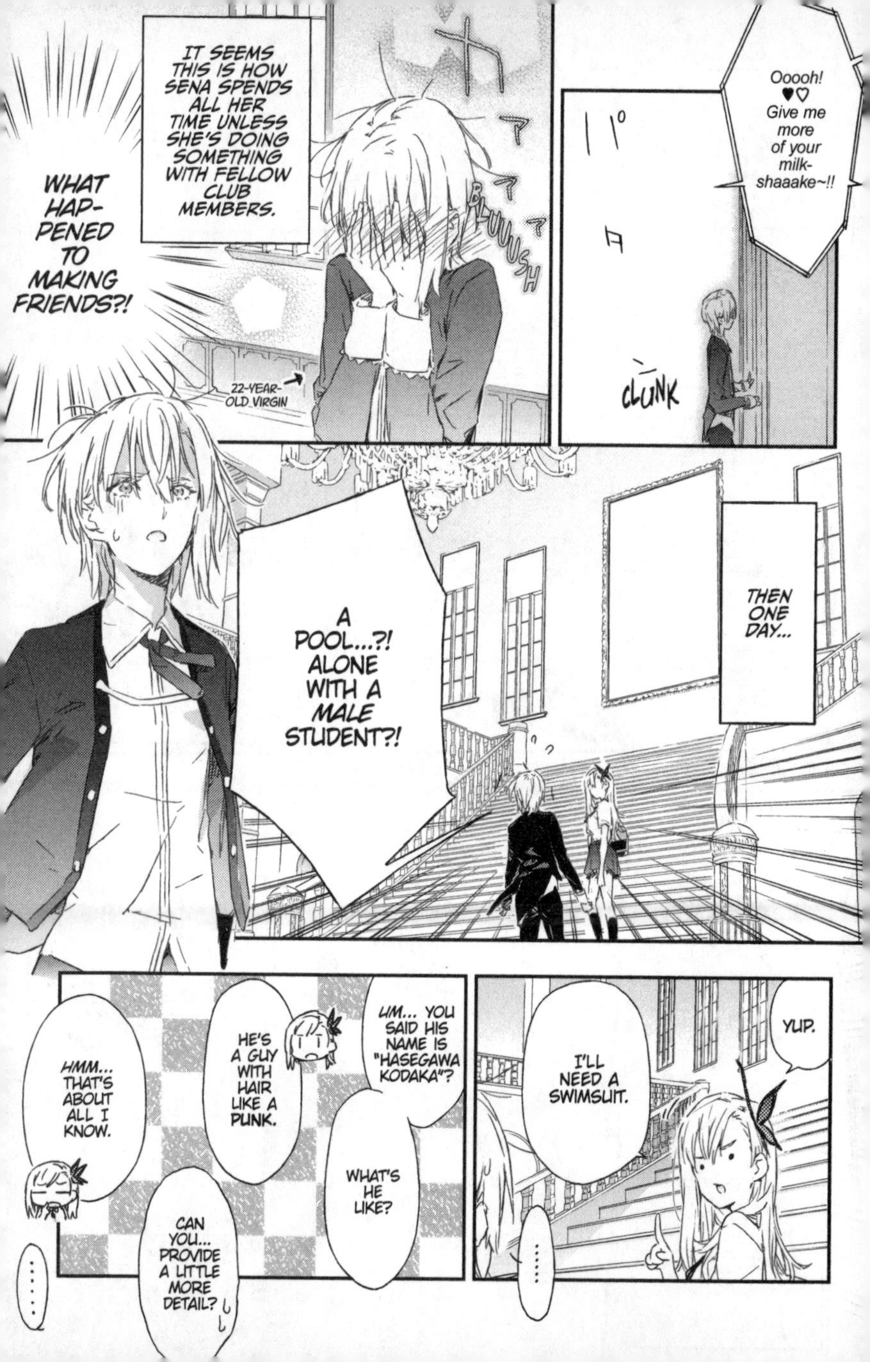
Ooooh! ♥♡ Give me more of your milk-shaaake~!!
CLUNK
IT SEEMS THIS IS HOW SENA SPENDS ALL HER TIME UNLESS SHE'S DOING SOMETHING WITH FELLOW CLUB MEMBERS.
BLUUUSH
22-YEAR-OLD VIRGIN
WHAT HAPPENED TO MAKING FRIENDS?!
THEN ONE DAY...
A POOL...?! ALONE WITH A *MALE* STUDENT?!
YUP.
I'LL NEED A SWIMSUIT.
......
UM... YOU SAID HIS NAME IS "HASEGAWA KODAKA"?
WHAT'S HE LIKE?
HE'S A GUY WITH HAIR LIKE A PUNK.
CAN YOU... PROVIDE A LITTLE MORE DETAIL?
HMM... THAT'S ABOUT ALL I KNOW.
......

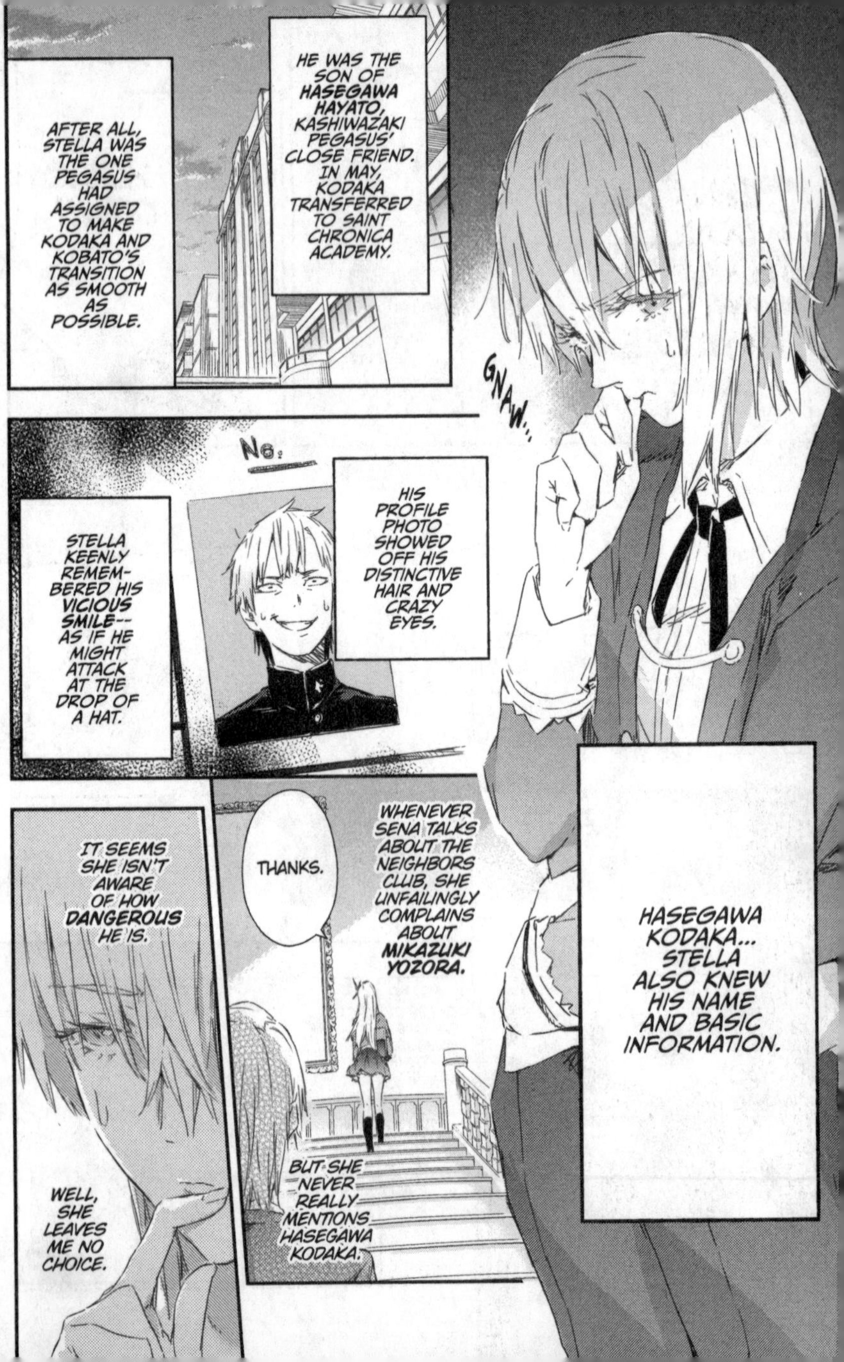
GNAW...
HASEGAWA KODAKA... STELLA ALSO KNEW HIS NAME AND BASIC INFORMATION.
HE WAS THE SON OF HASEGAWA HAYATO, KASHIWAZAKI PEGASUS' CLOSE FRIEND. IN MAY, KODAKA TRANSFERRED TO SAINT CHRONICA ACADEMY.
AFTER ALL, STELLA WAS THE ONE PEGASUS HAD ASSIGNED TO MAKE KODAKA AND KOBATO'S TRANSITION AS SMOOTH AS POSSIBLE.
No.
HIS PROFILE PHOTO SHOWED OFF HIS DISTINCTIVE HAIR AND CRAZY EYES.
STELLA KEENLY REMEMBERED HIS VICIOUS SMILE--AS IF HE MIGHT ATTACK AT THE DROP OF A HAT.
WHENEVER SENA TALKS ABOUT THE NEIGHBORS CLUB, SHE UNFAILINGLY COMPLAINS ABOUT MIKAZUKI YOZORA.
THANKS.
BUT SHE NEVER REALLY MENTIONS HASEGAWA KODAKA.
IT SEEMS SHE ISN'T AWARE OF HOW DANGEROUS HE IS.
WELL, SHE LEAVES ME NO CHOICE.

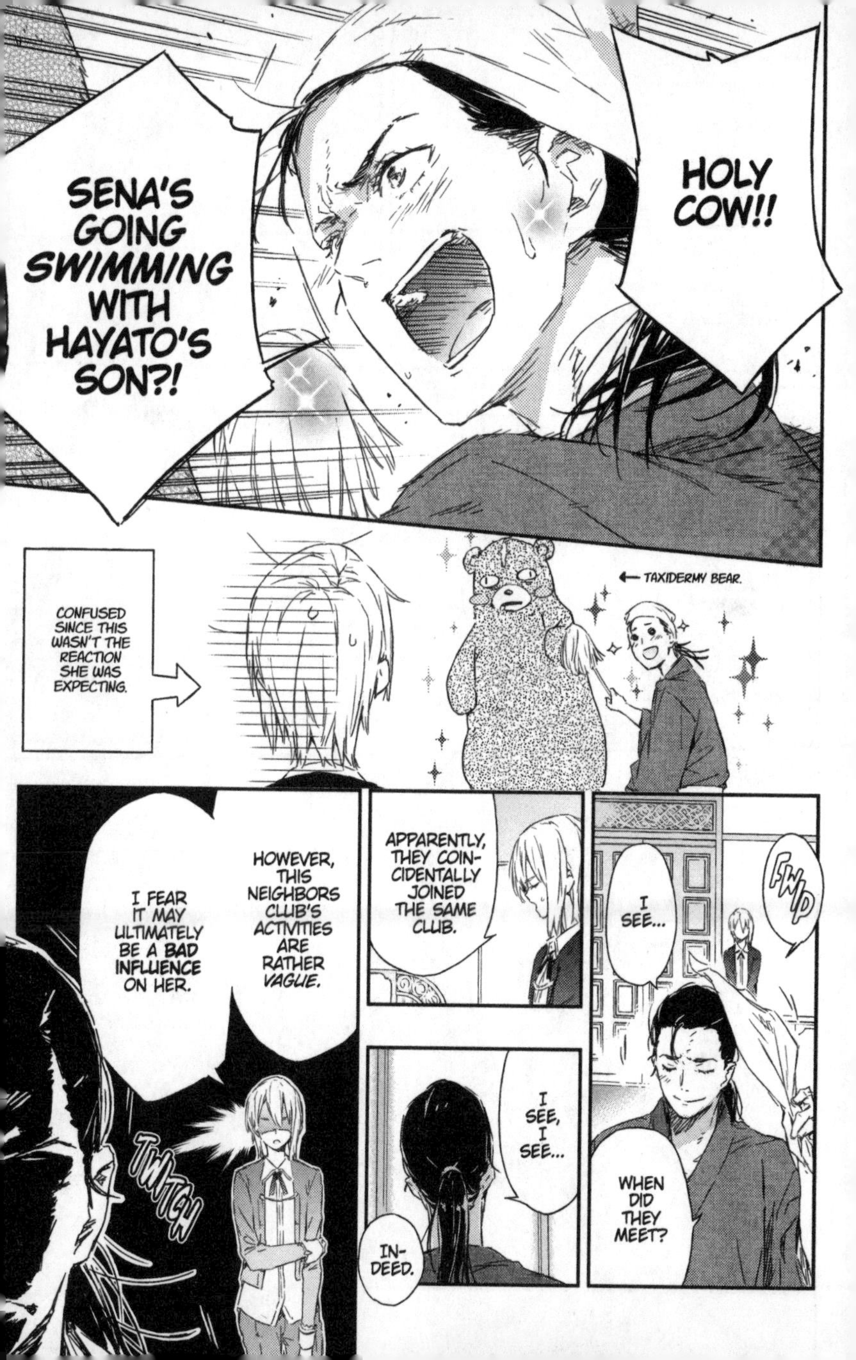
HOLY COW!!
SENA'S GOING SWIMMING WITH HAYATO'S SON?!
← TAXIDERMY BEAR.
CONFUSED SINCE THIS WASN'T THE REACTION SHE WAS EXPECTING.
FWIP
I SEE...
WHEN DID THEY MEET?
APPARENTLY, THEY COIN-CIDENTALLY JOINED THE SAME CLUB.
I SEE, I SEE...
IN-DEED.
HOWEVER, THIS NEIGHBORS CLUB'S ACTIVITIES ARE RATHER VAGUE.
I FEAR IT MAY ULTIMATELY BE A BAD INFLUENCE ON HER.
TWITCH

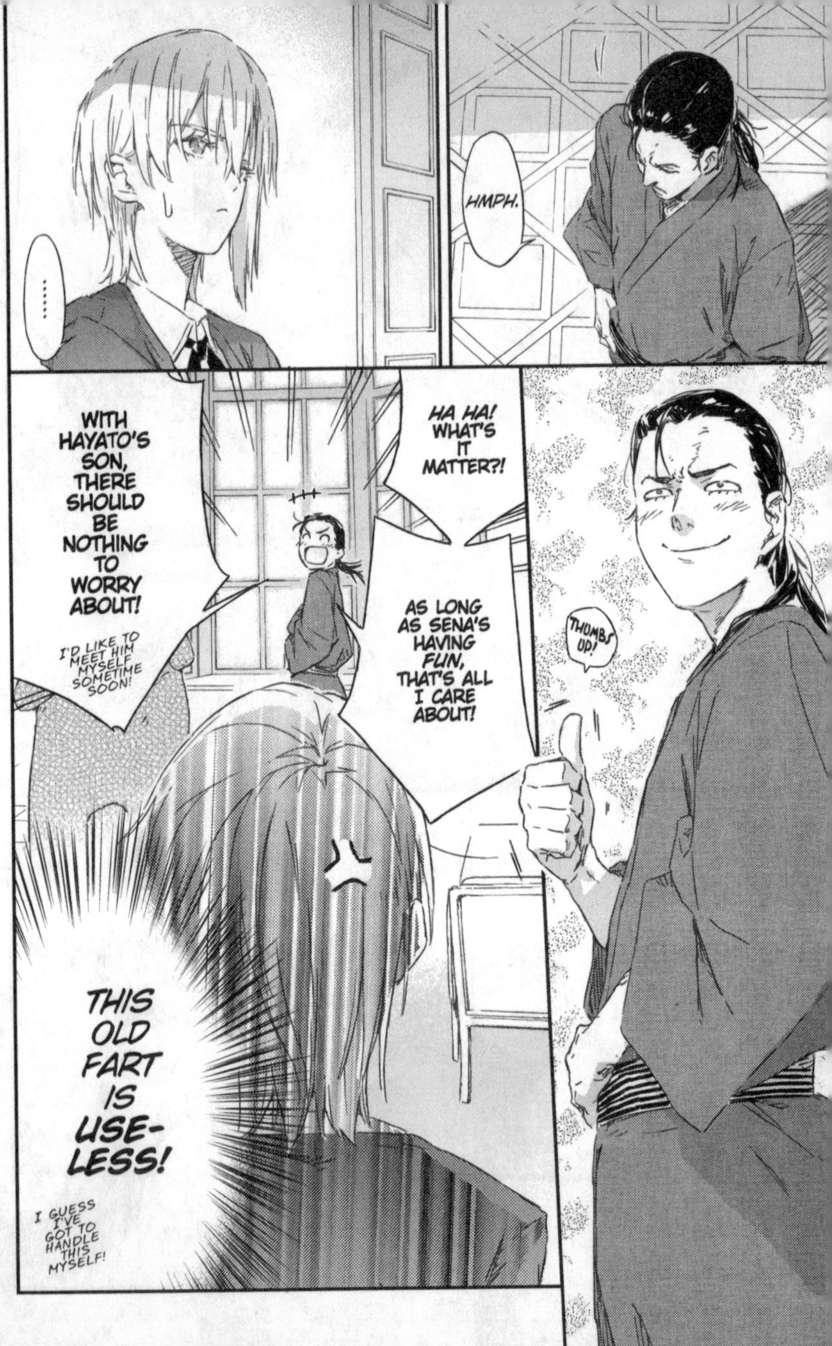
HMPH.
……
HA HA! WHAT'S IT MATTER?!
AS LONG AS SENA'S HAVING *FUN*, THAT'S ALL I CARE ABOUT!
WITH HAYATO'S SON, THERE SHOULD BE NOTHING TO WORRY ABOUT!
I'D LIKE TO MEET HIM MYSELF SOMETIME SOON!
THUMBS UP!
THIS OLD FART IS USE-LESS!
I GUESS I'VE GOT TO HANDLE THIS MYSELF!

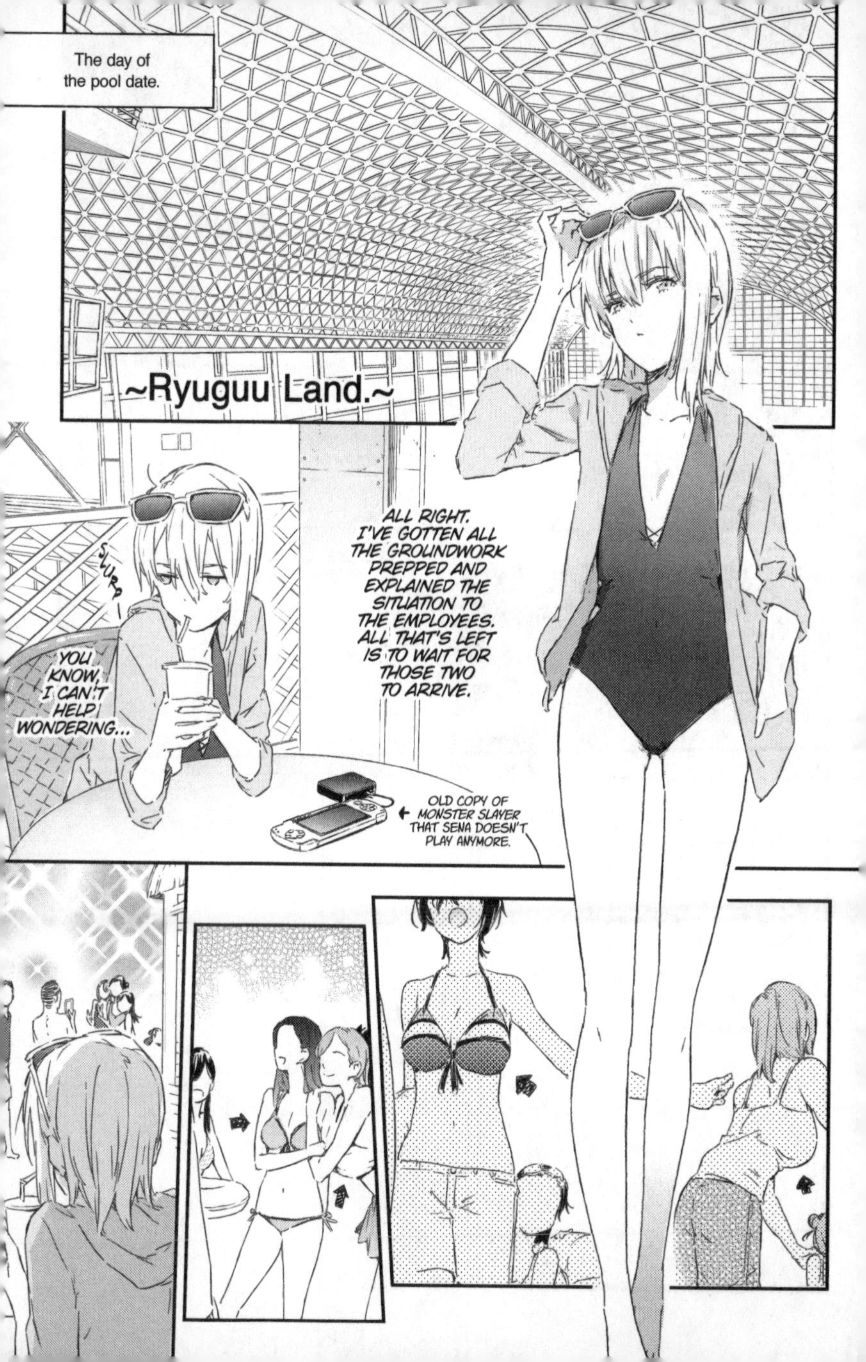
The day of the pool date.
~Ryuguu Land.~
ALL RIGHT. I'VE GOTTEN ALL THE GROUNDWORK PREPPED AND EXPLAINED THE SITUATION TO THE EMPLOYEES. ALL THAT'S LEFT IS TO WAIT FOR THOSE TWO TO ARRIVE.
SLURP
YOU KNOW, I CAN'T HELP WONDERING...
OLD COPY OF MONSTER SLAYER THAT SENA DOESN'T PLAY ANYMORE.

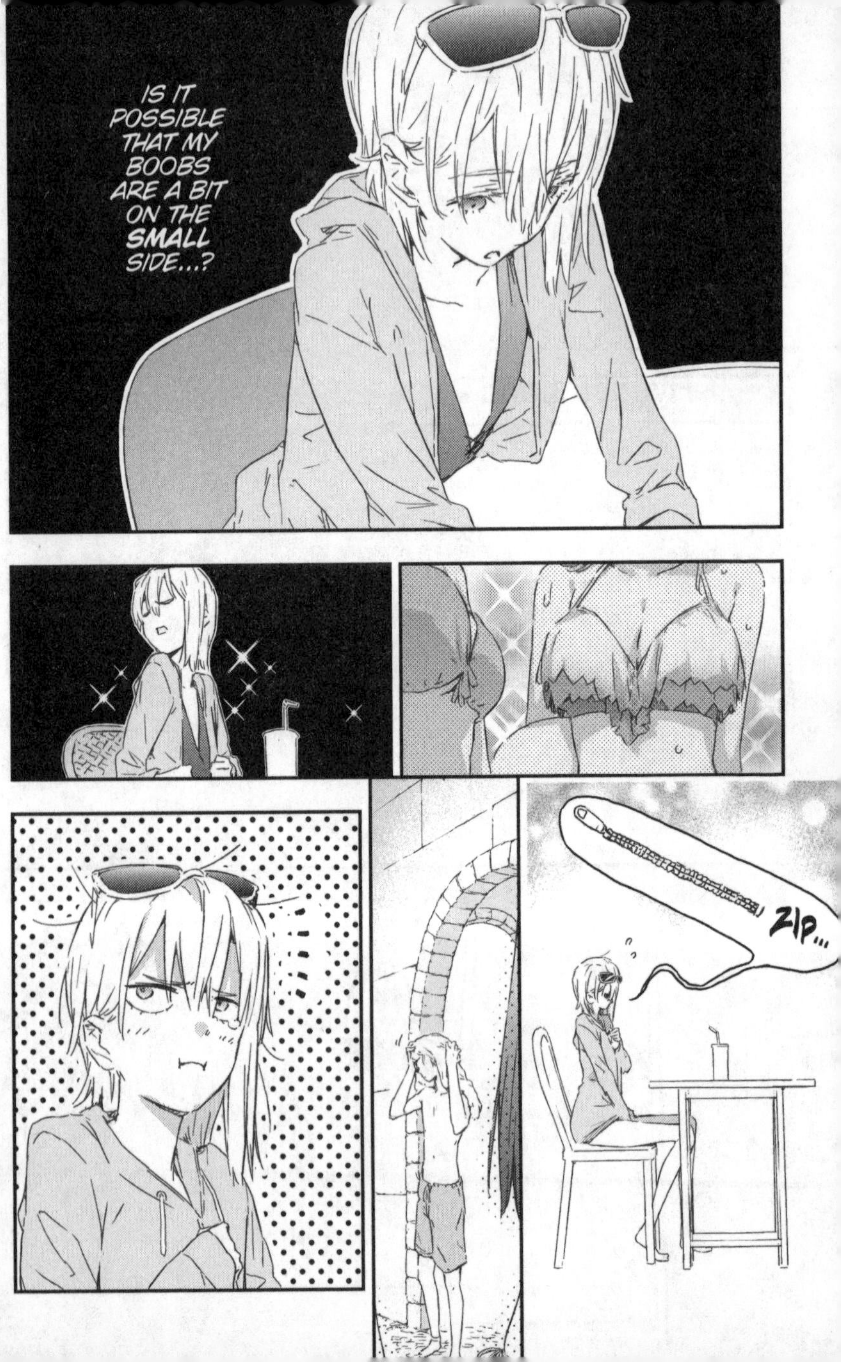
IS IT POSSIBLE THAT MY BOOBS ARE A BIT ON THE **SMALL** SIDE...?
ZIP...

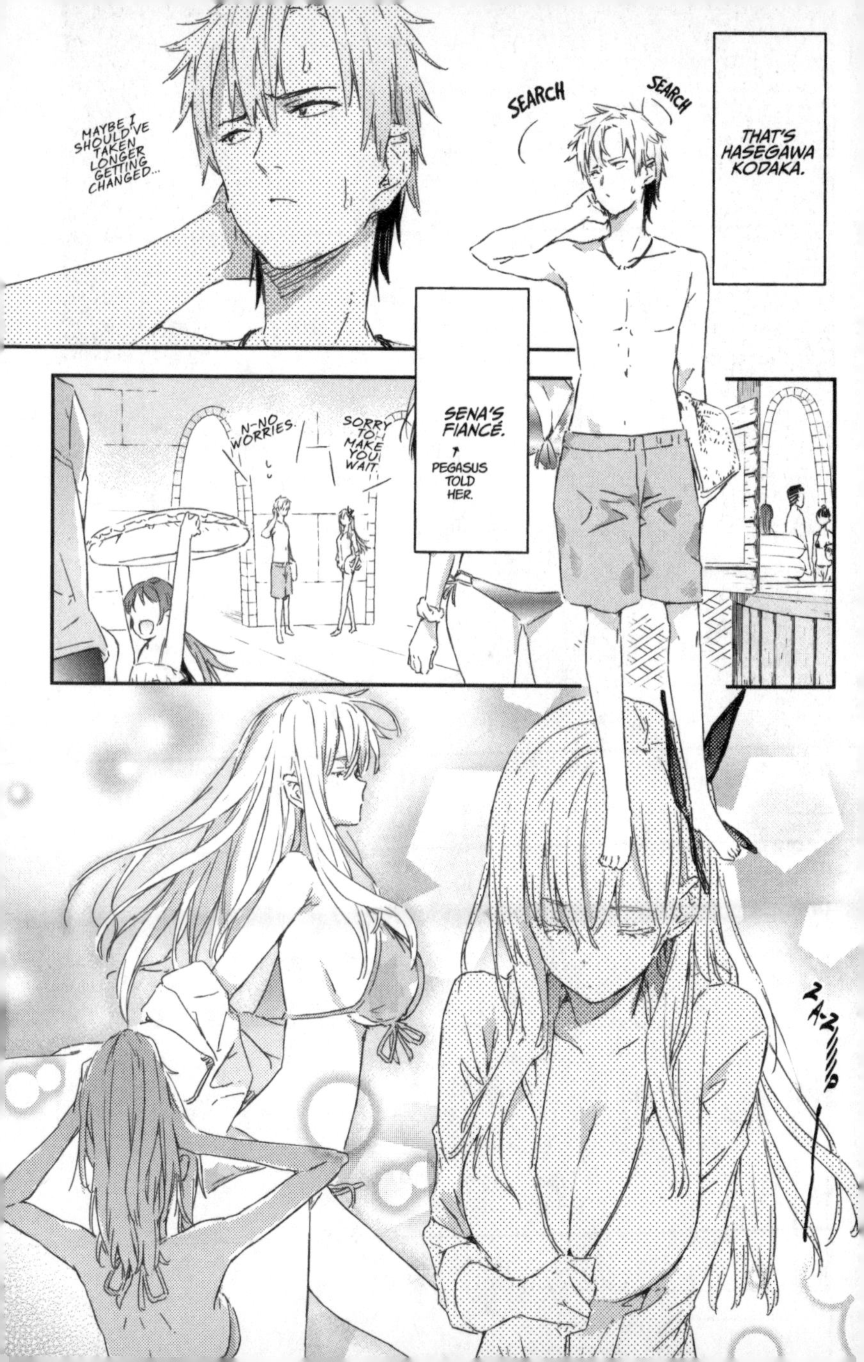
THAT'S HASEGAWA KODAKA.
SEARCH
SEARCH
MAYBE I SHOULD'VE TAKEN LONGER GETTING CHANGED...
SENA'S FIANCÉ.
PEGASUS TOLD HER.
SORRY TO MAKE YOU WAIT.
N-NO WORRIES.
ZA-ZIP

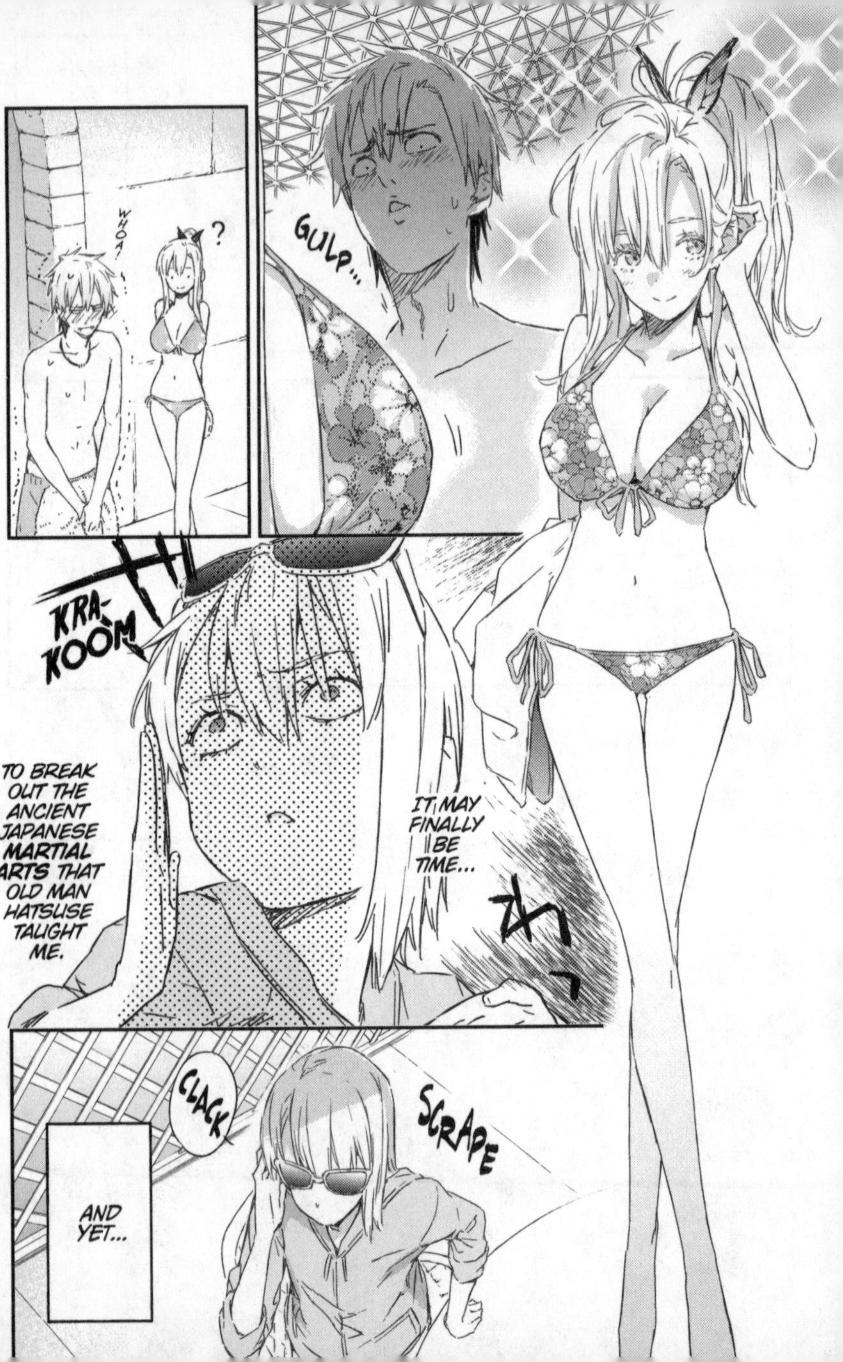
GULP...
WHOA!
?
KRA-KOOM
IT MAY FINALLY BE TIME...
TO BREAK OUT THE ANCIENT JAPANESE MARTIAL ARTS THAT OLD MAN HATSUSE TAUGHT ME.
SCRAPE
CLACK
AND YET...

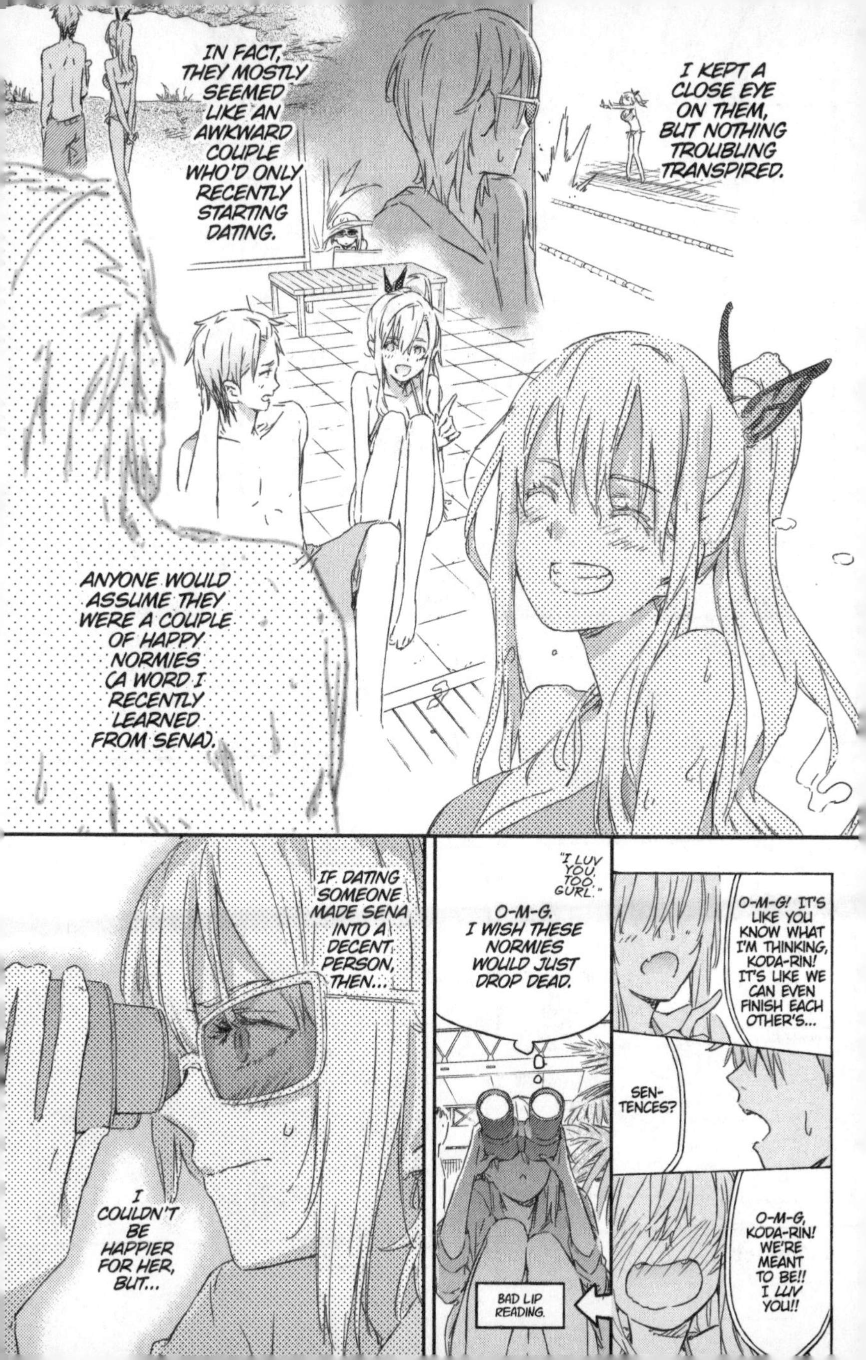
I KEPT A CLOSE EYE ON THEM, BUT NOTHING TROUBLING TRANSPIRED.
IN FACT, THEY MOSTLY SEEMED LIKE AN AWKWARD COUPLE WHO'D ONLY RECENTLY STARTING DATING.
ANYONE WOULD ASSUME THEY WERE A COUPLE OF HAPPY NORMIES (A WORD I RECENTLY LEARNED FROM SENA).
O-M-G! IT'S LIKE YOU KNOW WHAT I'M THINKING, KODA-RIN! IT'S LIKE WE CAN EVEN FINISH EACH OTHER'S...
SEN-TENCES?
O-M-G, KODA-RIN! WE'RE MEANT TO BE!! I LUV YOU!!
"I LUV YOU, TOO, GURL."
O-M-G. I WISH THESE NORMIES WOULD JUST DROP DEAD.
BAD LIP READING.
IF DATING SOMEONE MADE SENA INTO A DECENT PERSON, THEN...
I COULDN'T BE HAPPIER FOR HER, BUT...

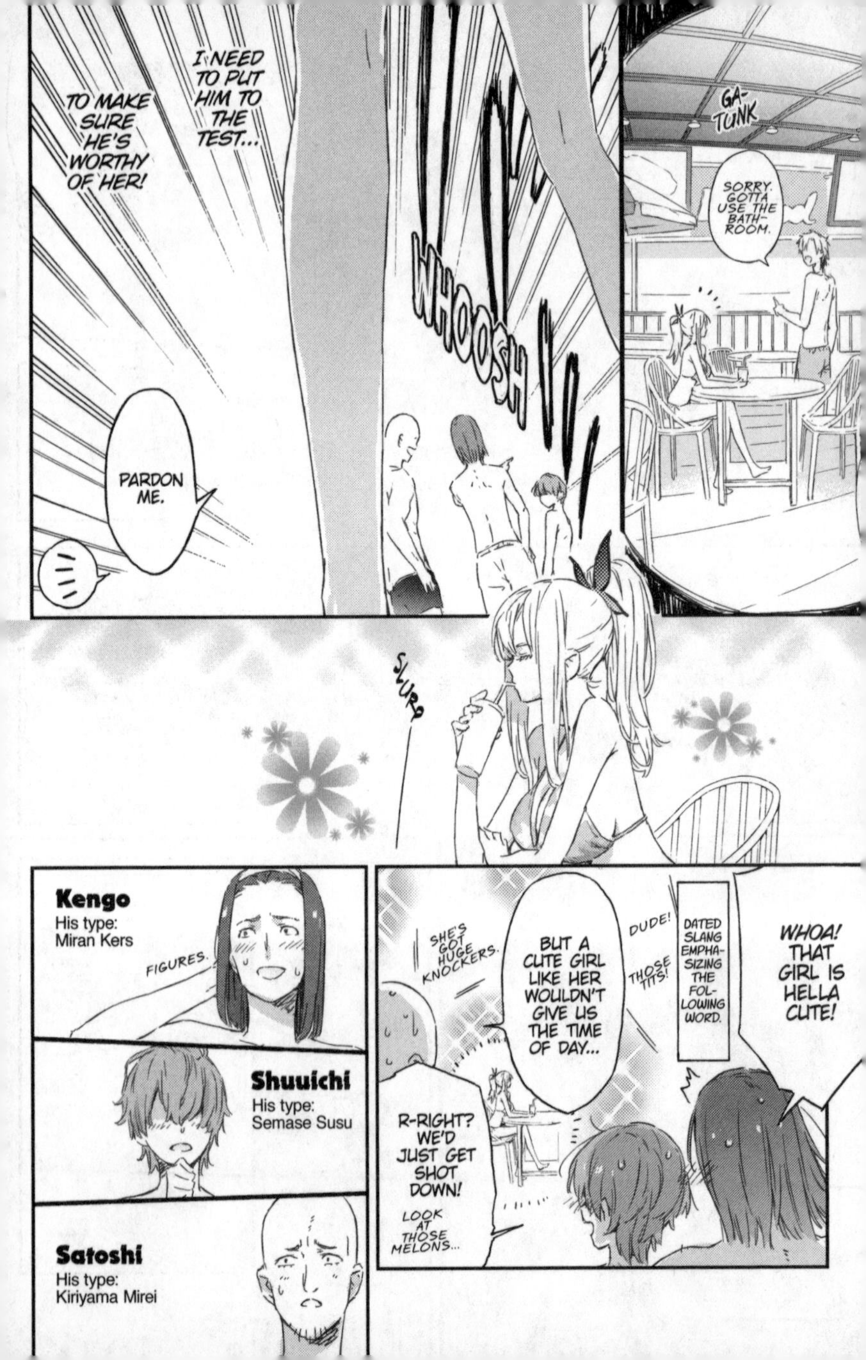
GA-TUNK
SORRY. GOTTA USE THE BATHROOM.
I NEED TO PUT HIM TO THE TEST...
TO MAKE SURE HE'S WORTHY OF HER!
WHOOSH
PARDON ME.
SLURP
WHOA! THAT GIRL IS HELLA CUTE!
DATED SLANG EMPHASIZING THE FOLLOWING WORD.
DUDE!
THOSE TITS!
BUT A CUTE GIRL LIKE HER WOULDN'T GIVE US THE TIME OF DAY...
SHE'S GOT HUGE KNOCKERS.
R-RIGHT? WE'D JUST GET SHOT DOWN!
LOOK AT THOSE MELONS...
Kengo
His type: Miran Kers
FIGURES.
Shuuichi
His type: Semase Susu
Satoshi
His type: Kiriyama Mirei

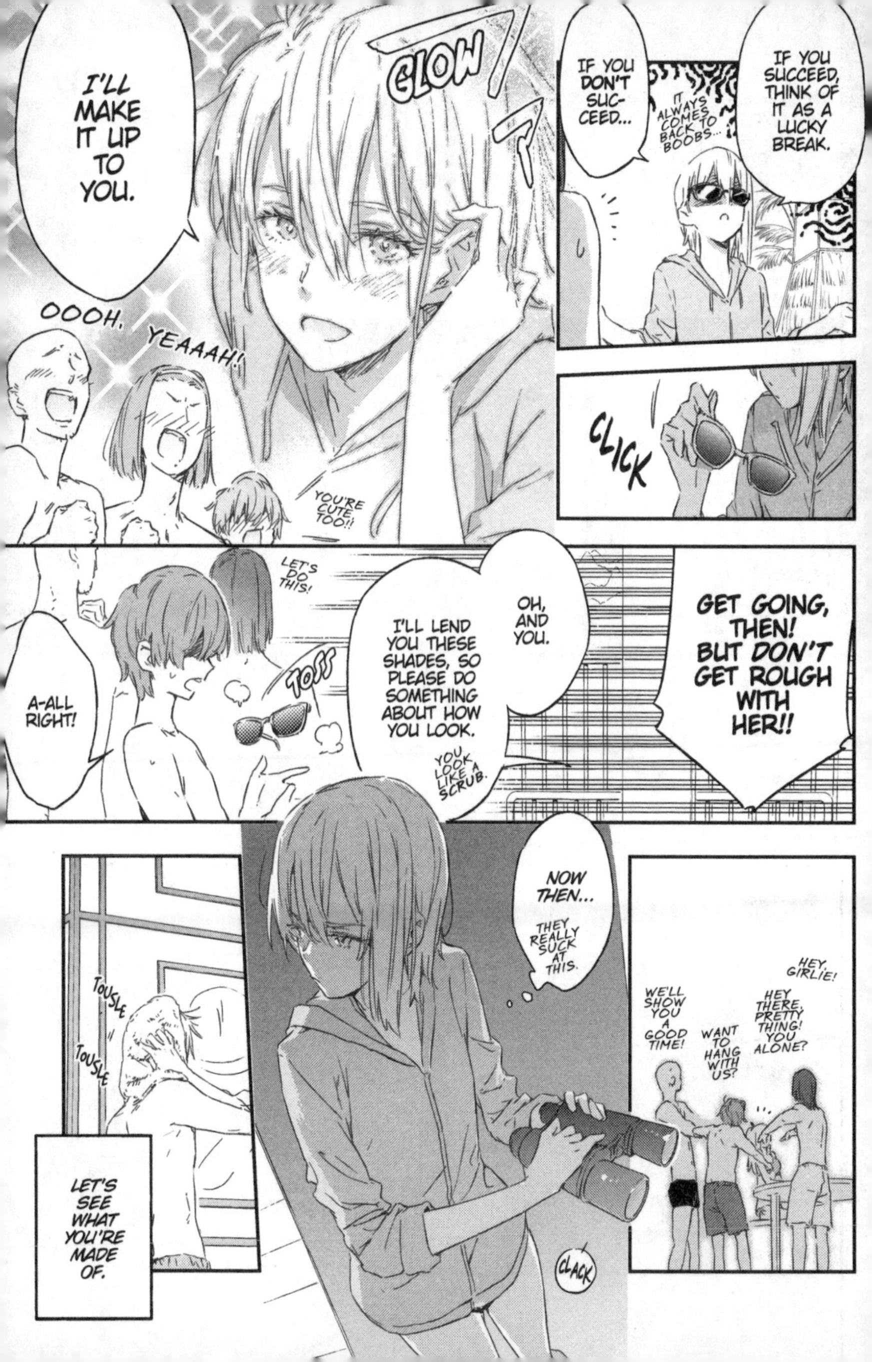
IF YOU SUCCEED, THINK OF IT AS A LUCKY BREAK.
IF YOU DON'T SUC-CEED...
IT ALWAYS COMES BACK TO BOOBS...
CLICK
GLOW
I'LL MAKE IT UP TO YOU.
YEAAAH!
OOOH.
YOU'RE CUTE TOO!!
GET GOING, THEN! BUT DON'T GET ROUGH WITH HER!!
OH, AND YOU.
I'LL LEND YOU THESE SHADES, SO PLEASE DO SOMETHING ABOUT HOW YOU LOOK.
YOU LOOK LIKE A SCRUB.
TOSS
LET'S DO THIS!
A-ALL RIGHT!
HEY, GIRLIE!
HEY THERE, PRETTY THING! YOU ALONE?
WANT TO HANG WITH US?
WE'LL SHOW YOU A GOOD TIME!
NOW THEN...
THEY REALLY SUCK AT THIS.
CLACK
TOUSLE
TOUSLE
LET'S SEE WHAT YOU'RE MADE OF.

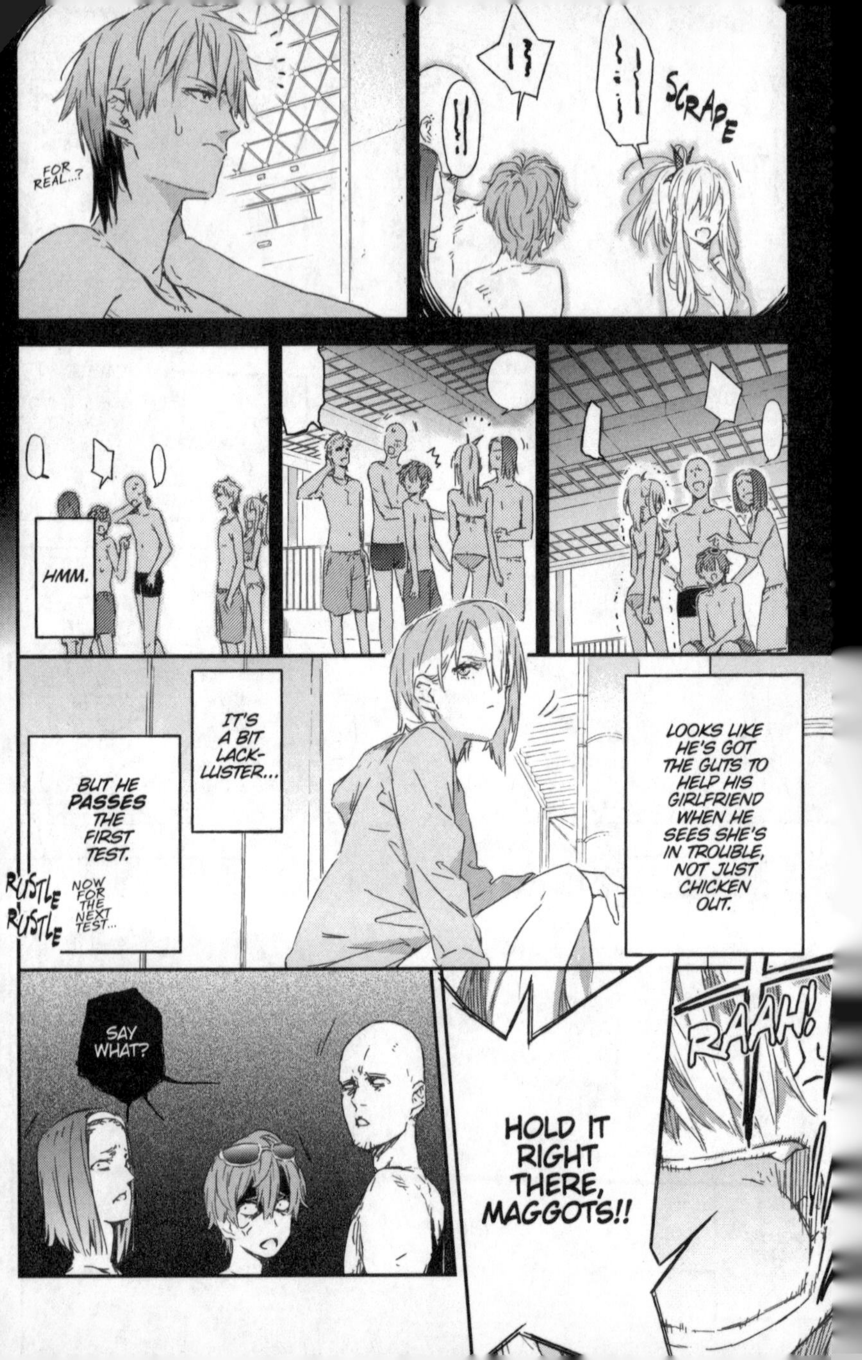
SCRAPE
FOR REAL...?
HMM.
LOOKS LIKE HE'S GOT THE GUTS TO HELP HIS GIRLFRIEND WHEN HE SEES SHE'S IN TROUBLE, NOT JUST CHICKEN OUT.
IT'S A BIT LACK-LUSTER...
BUT HE PASSES THE FIRST TEST.
NOW FOR THE NEXT TEST...
RUSTLE RUSTLE
RAAH!
HOLD IT RIGHT THERE, MAGGOTS!!
SAY WHAT?

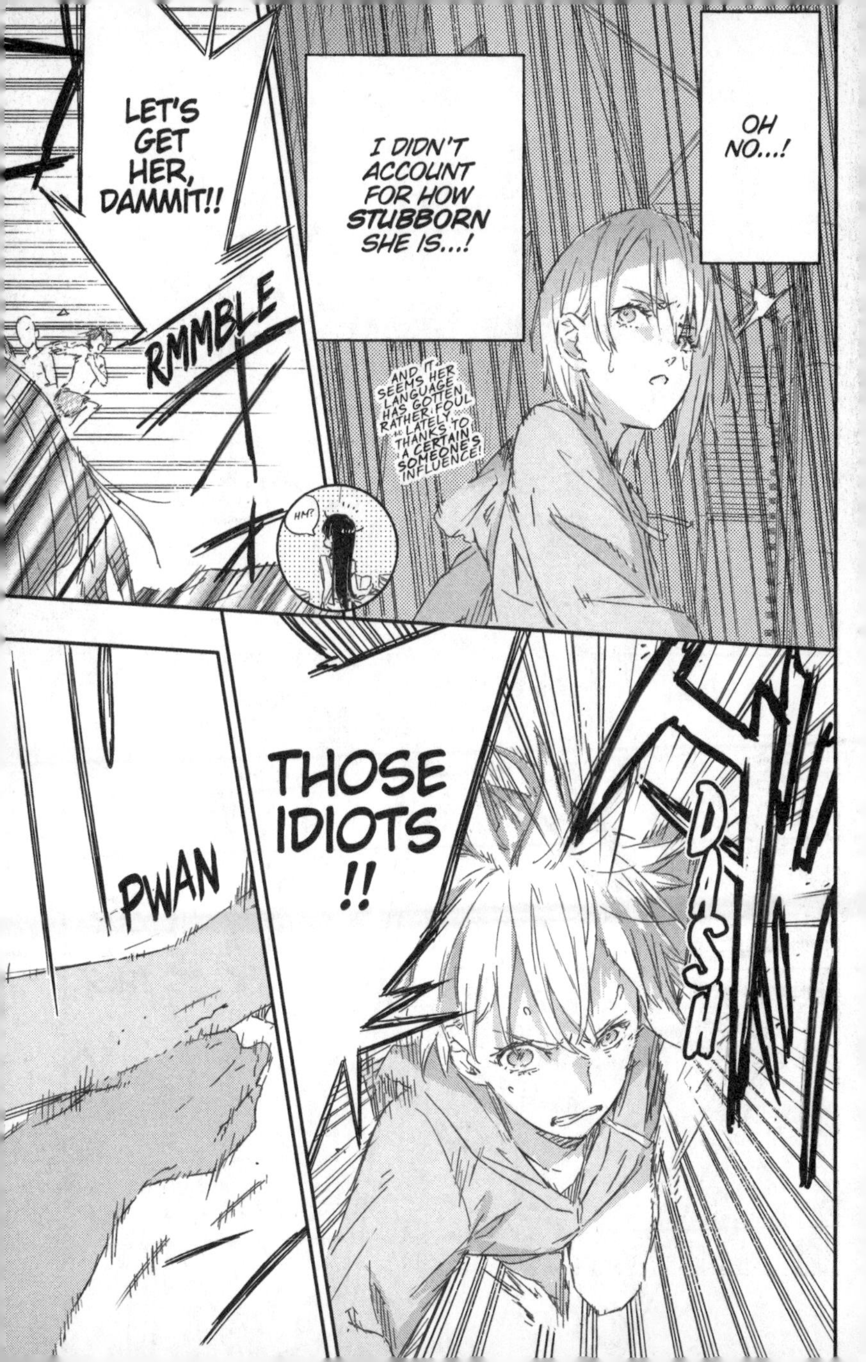
OH NO...!
I DIDN'T ACCOUNT FOR HOW STUBBORN SHE IS...!
AND IT SEEMS HER LANGUAGE HAS GOTTEN RATHER FOUL LATELY THANKS TO A CERTAIN SOMEONE'S INFLUENCE!
HM?
LET'S GET HER, DAMMIT!!
RMMBLE
DASH
THOSE IDIOTS !!
PWAN

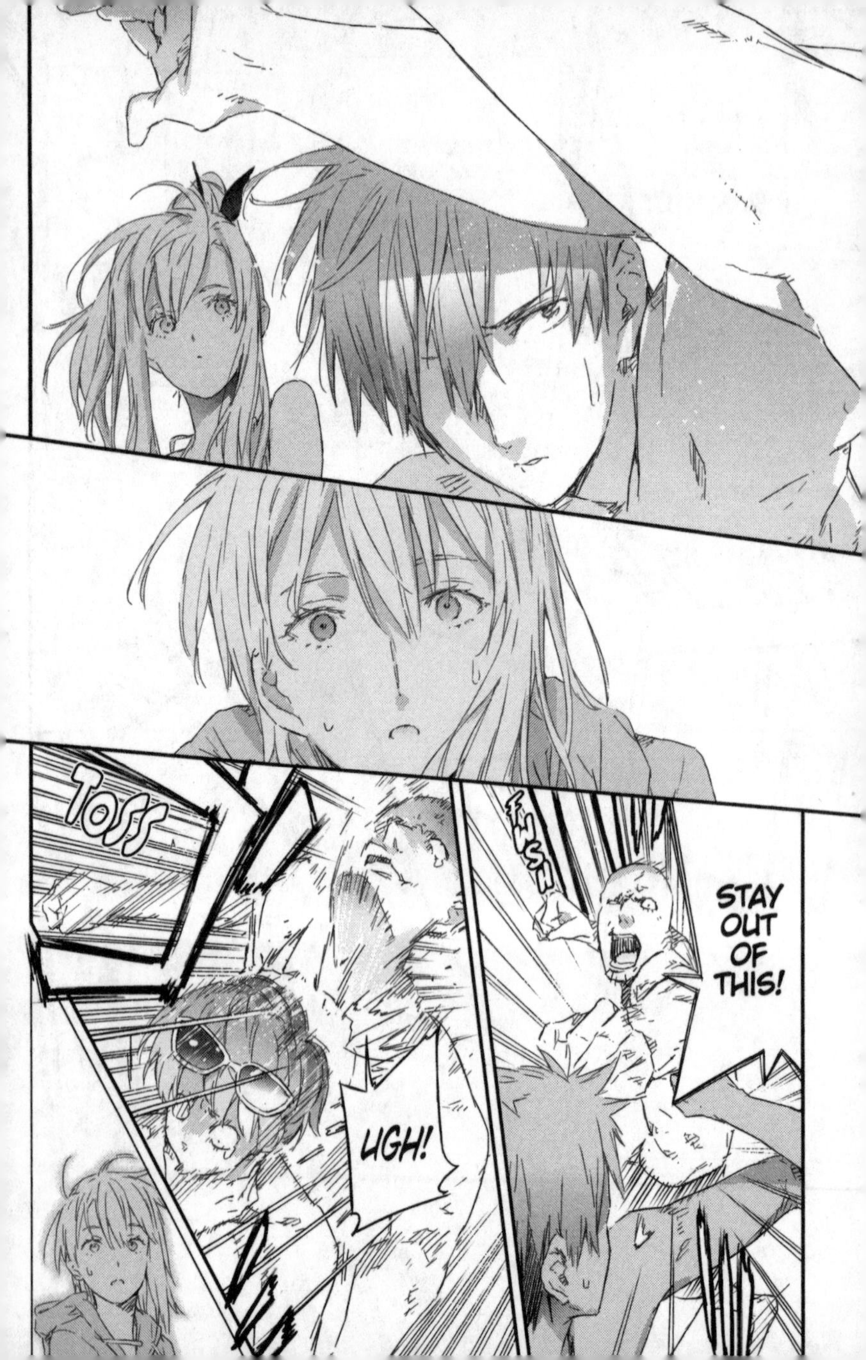
FWSH
STAY OUT OF THIS!
TOSS
UGH!

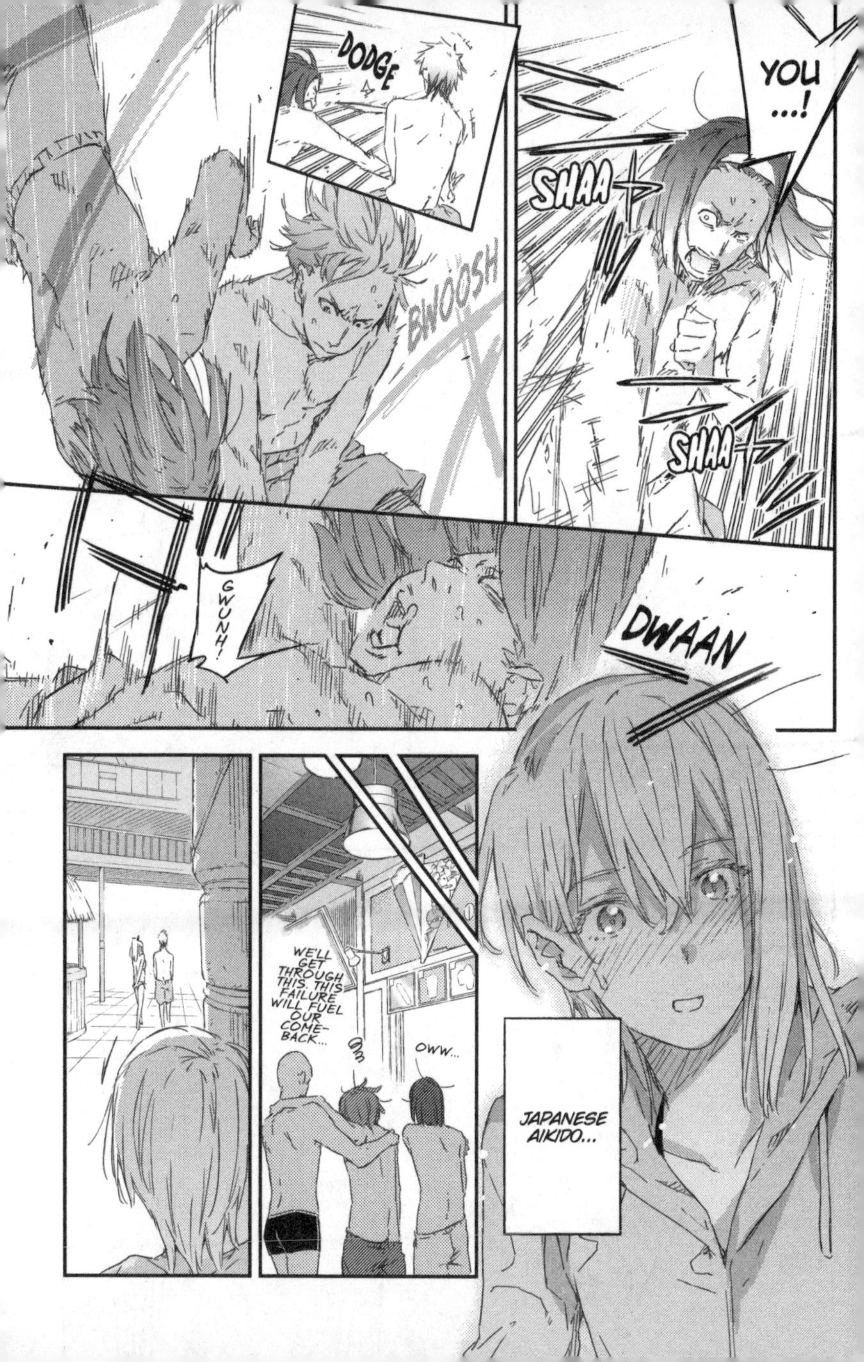
YOU ...!
SHAA
SHAA
DODGE
BWOOSH
DWAAN
GWUNH!
JAPANESE AIKIDO...
WE'LL GET THROUGH THIS. THIS FAILURE WILL FUEL OUR COME-BACK...
OWW...

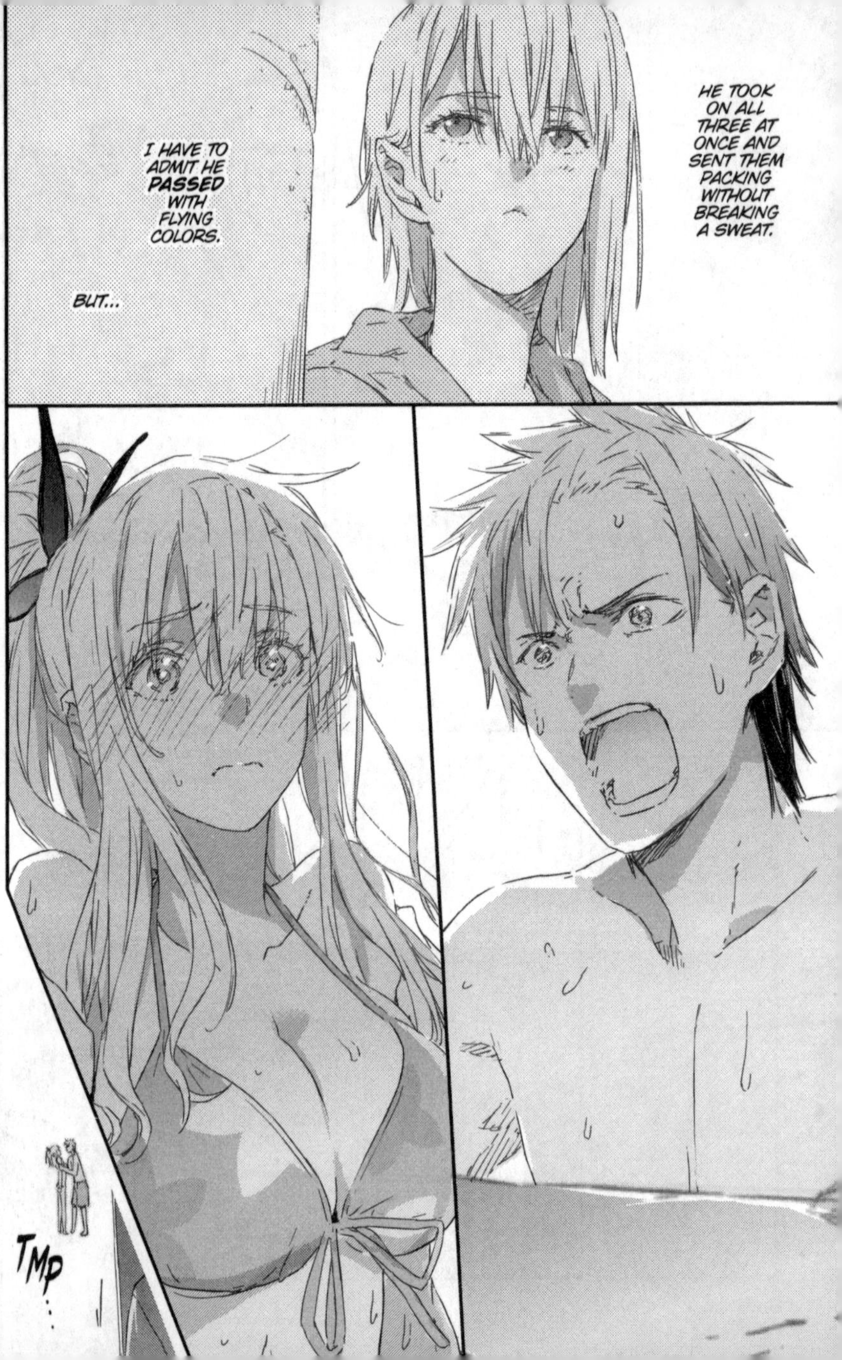
HE TOOK ON ALL THREE AT ONCE AND SENT THEM PACKING WITHOUT BREAKING A SWEAT.
I HAVE TO ADMIT HE **PASSED** WITH FLYING COLORS.
BUT...
TMP...

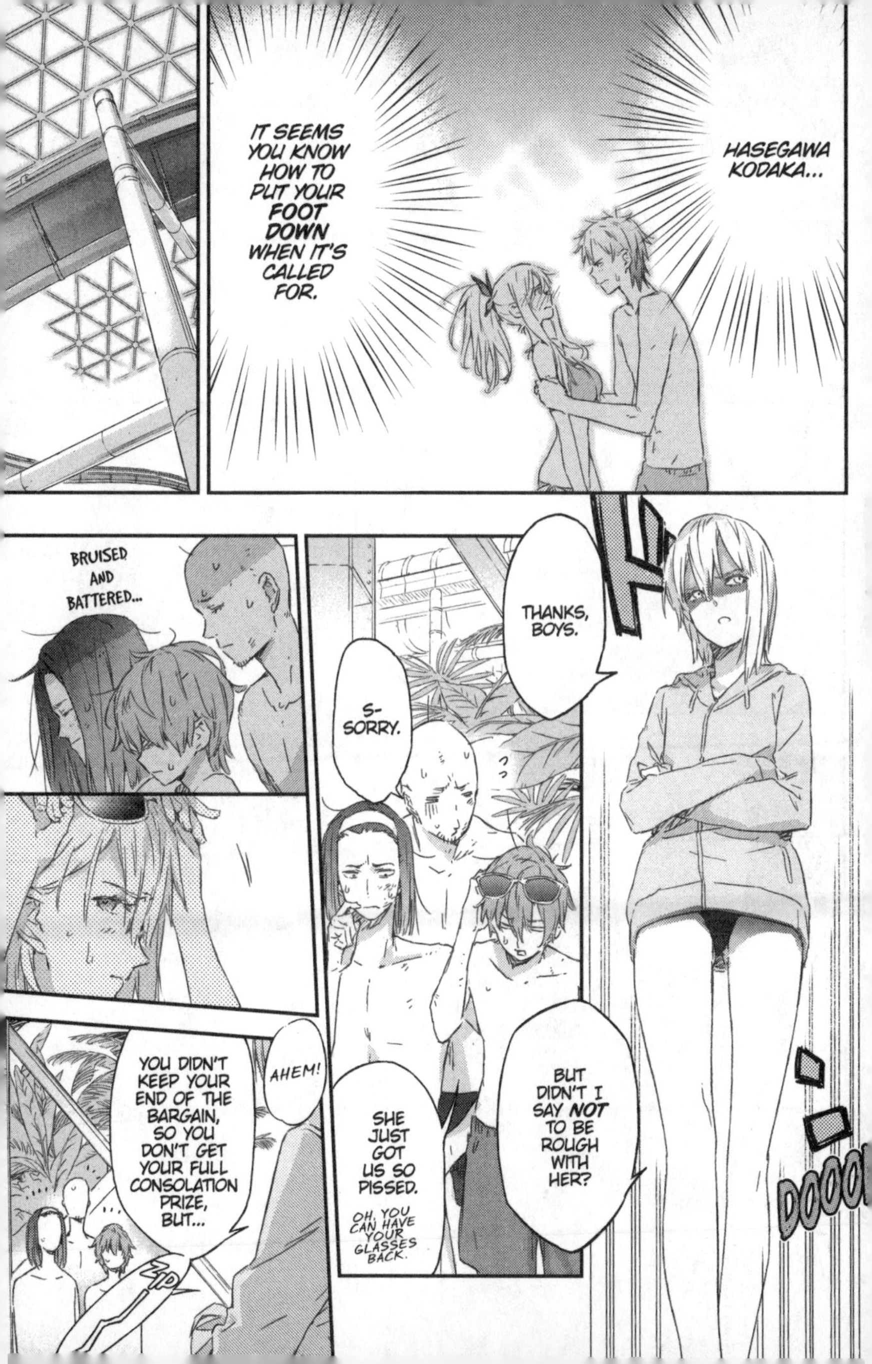
HASEGAWA KODAKA...
IT SEEMS YOU KNOW HOW TO PUT YOUR FOOT DOWN WHEN IT'S CALLED FOR.
THANKS, BOYS.
BUT DIDN'T I SAY NOT TO BE ROUGH WITH HER?
DOOO
S-SORRY.
SHE JUST GOT US SO PISSED.
OH, YOU CAN HAVE YOUR GLASSES BACK.
BRUISED AND BATTERED...
AHEM!
YOU DIDN'T KEEP YOUR END OF THE BARGAIN, SO YOU DON'T GET YOUR FULL CONSOLATION PRIZE, BUT...
ZIP

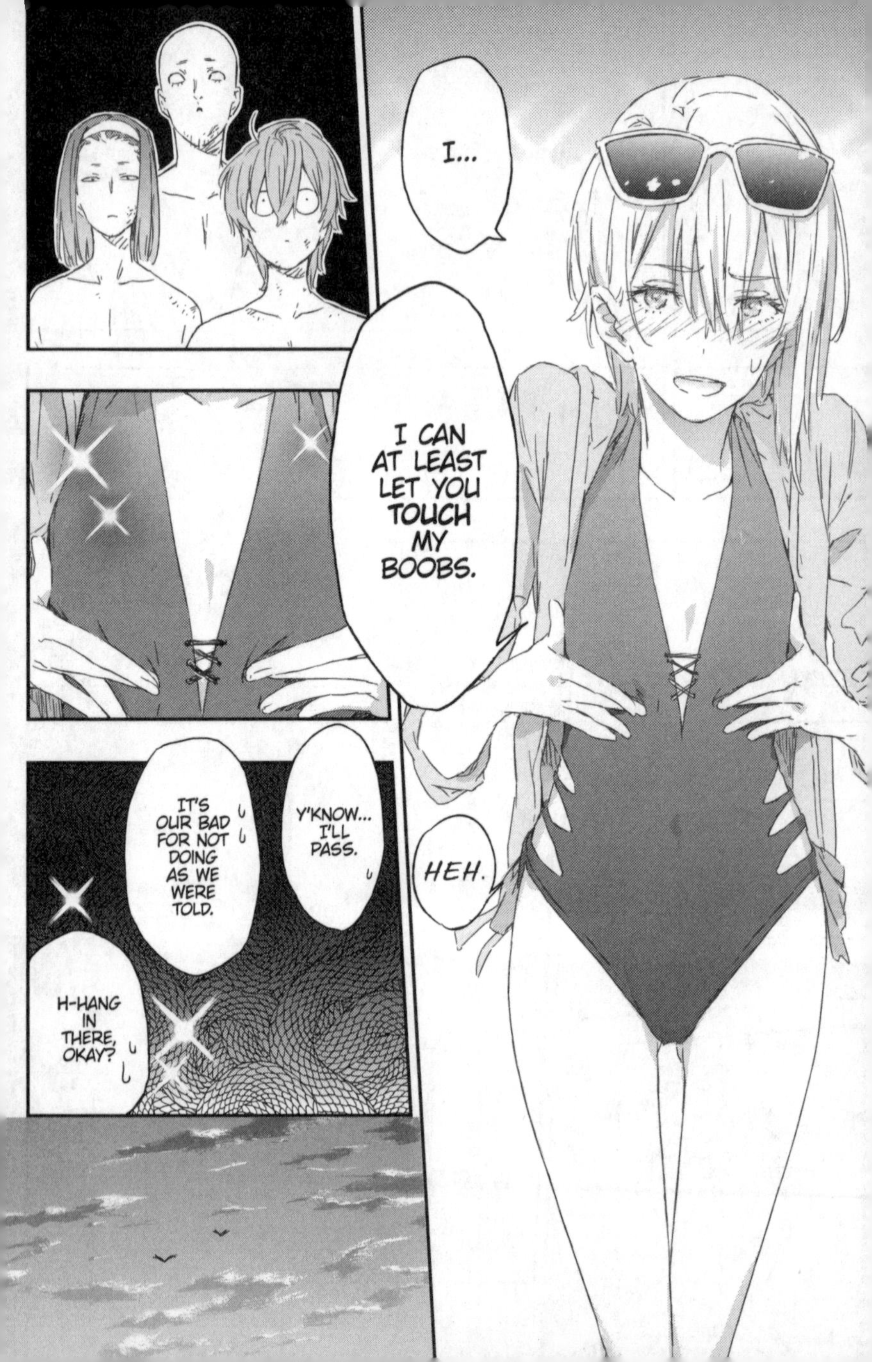
I...
I CAN AT LEAST LET YOU TOUCH MY BOOBS.
HEH.
Y'KNOW... I'LL PASS.
IT'S OUR BAD FOR NOT DOING AS WE WERE TOLD.
H-HANG IN THERE, OKAY?

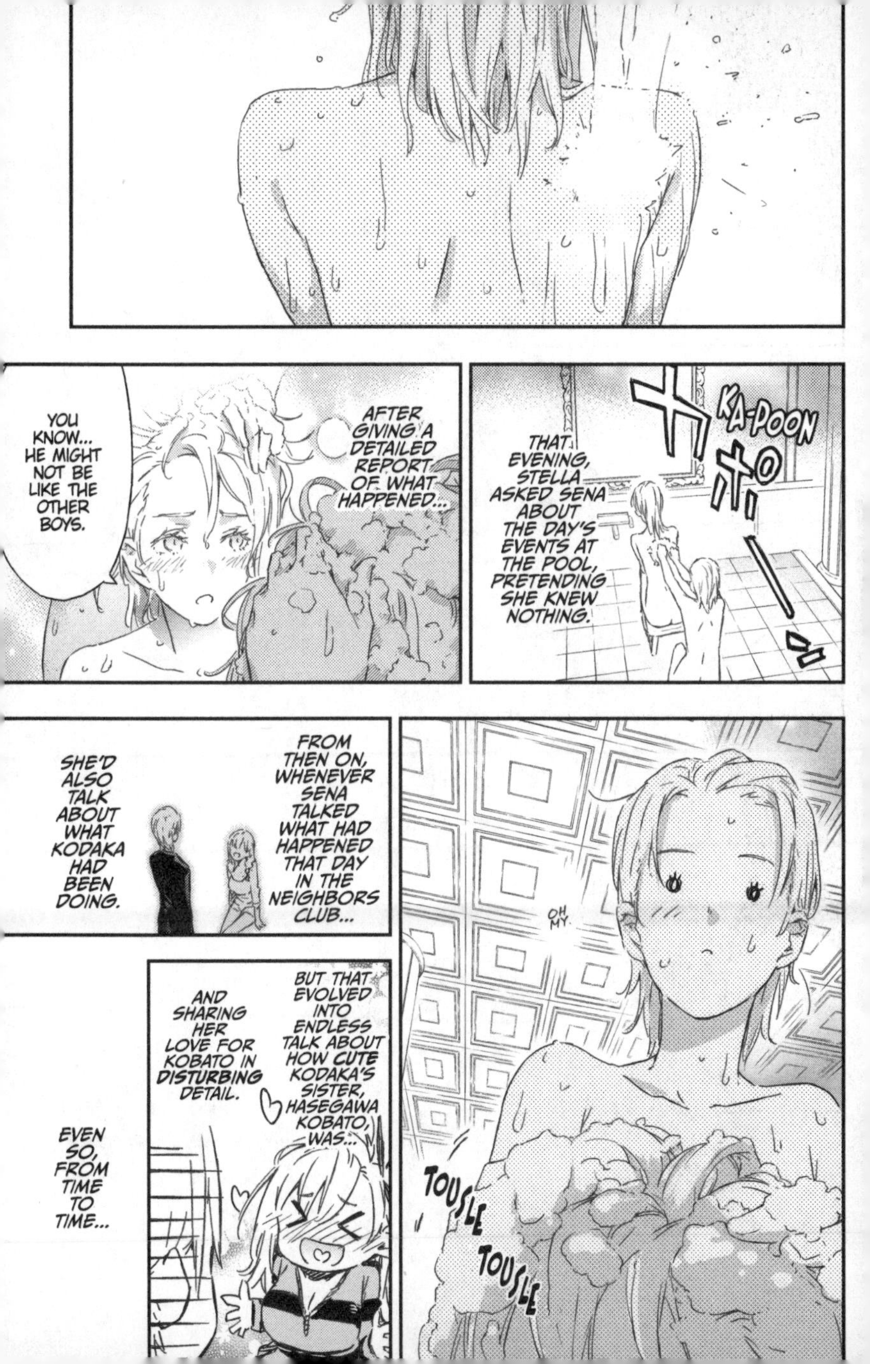
KA-POON
THAT EVENING, STELLA ASKED SENA ABOUT THE DAY'S EVENTS AT THE POOL, PRETENDING SHE KNEW NOTHING.
AFTER GIVING A DETAILED REPORT OF WHAT HAPPENED...
YOU KNOW... HE MIGHT NOT BE LIKE THE OTHER BOYS.
OH MY.
TOUSLE
TOUSLE
FROM THEN ON, WHENEVER SENA TALKED WHAT HAD HAPPENED THAT DAY IN THE NEIGHBORS CLUB...
SHE'D ALSO TALK ABOUT WHAT KODAKA HAD BEEN DOING.
BUT THAT EVOLVED INTO ENDLESS TALK ABOUT HOW CUTE KODAKA'S SISTER, HASEGAWA KOBATO, WAS...
AND SHARING HER LOVE FOR KOBATO IN DISTURBING DETAIL.
EVEN SO, FROM TIME TO TIME...

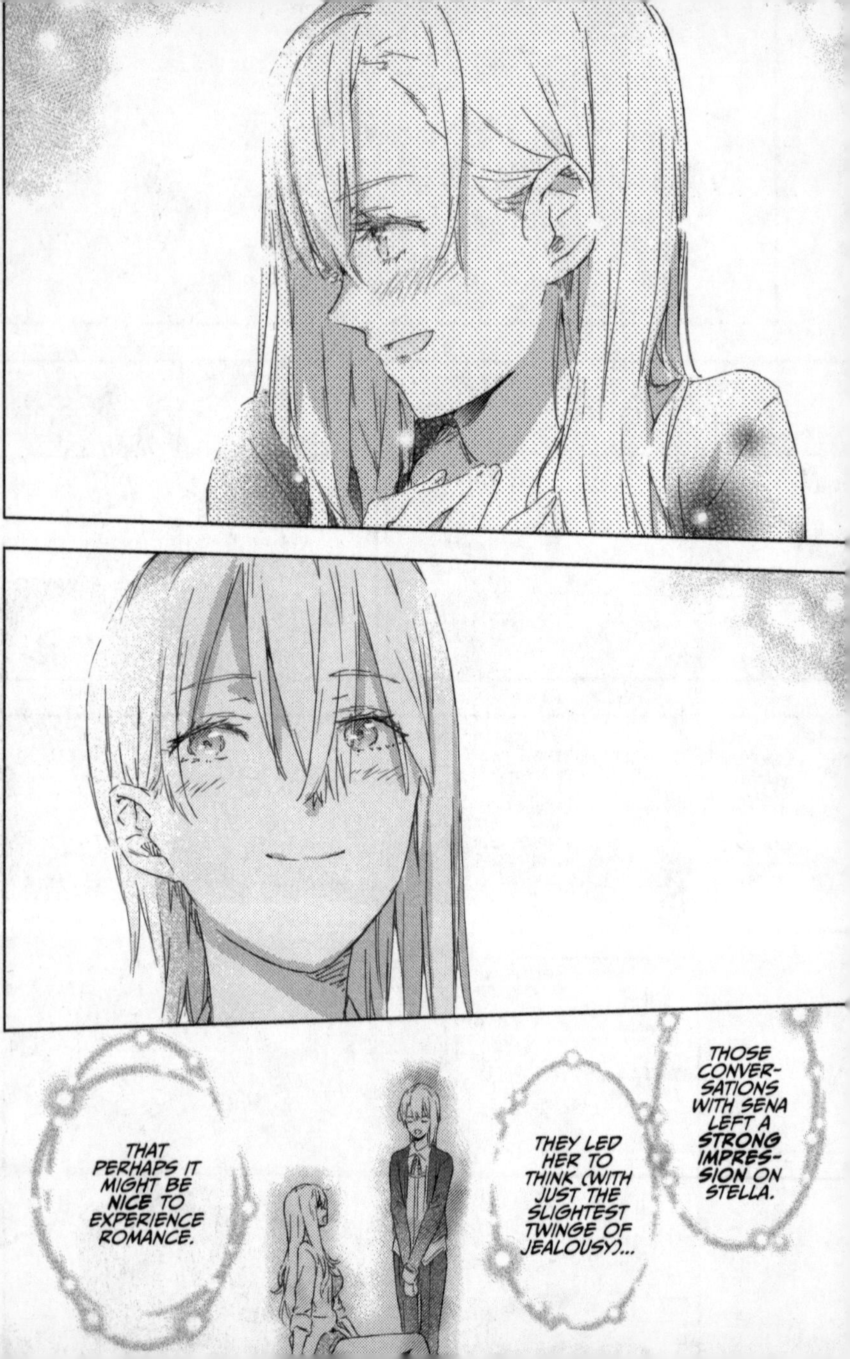
THOSE CONVERSATIONS WITH SENA LEFT A STRONG IMPRESSION ON STELLA.
THEY LED HER TO THINK (WITH JUST THE SLIGHTEST TWINGE OF JEALOUSY)...
THAT PERHAPS IT MIGHT BE NICE TO EXPERIENCE ROMANCE.

I don't have many friends

Haganai

I don't have many friends

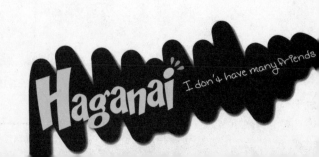

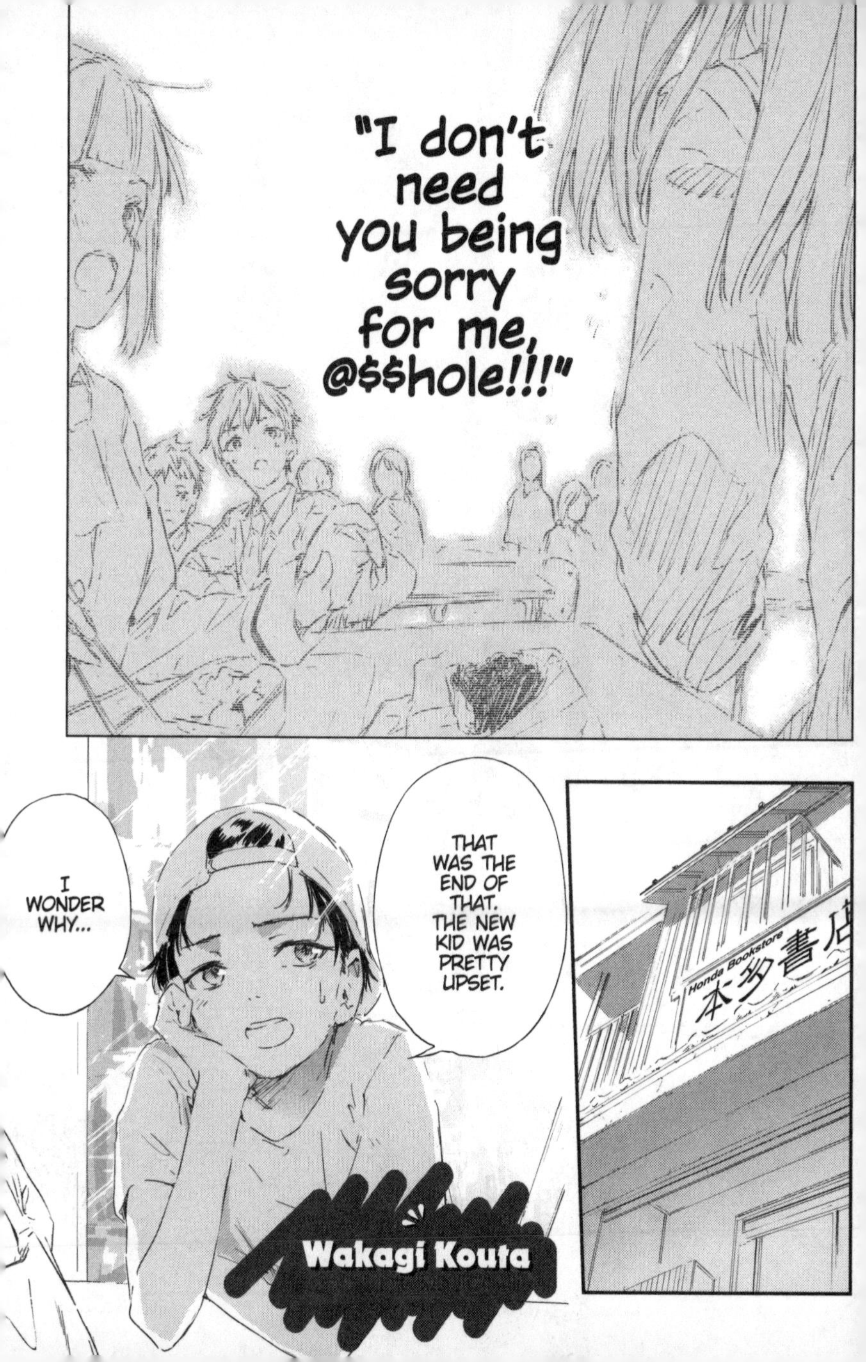
"I don't need you being sorry for me, @$$hole!!!"
Honda Bookstore
本多書店
THAT WAS THE END OF THAT. THE NEW KID WAS PRETTY UPSET.
I WONDER WHY...
Wakagi Kouta

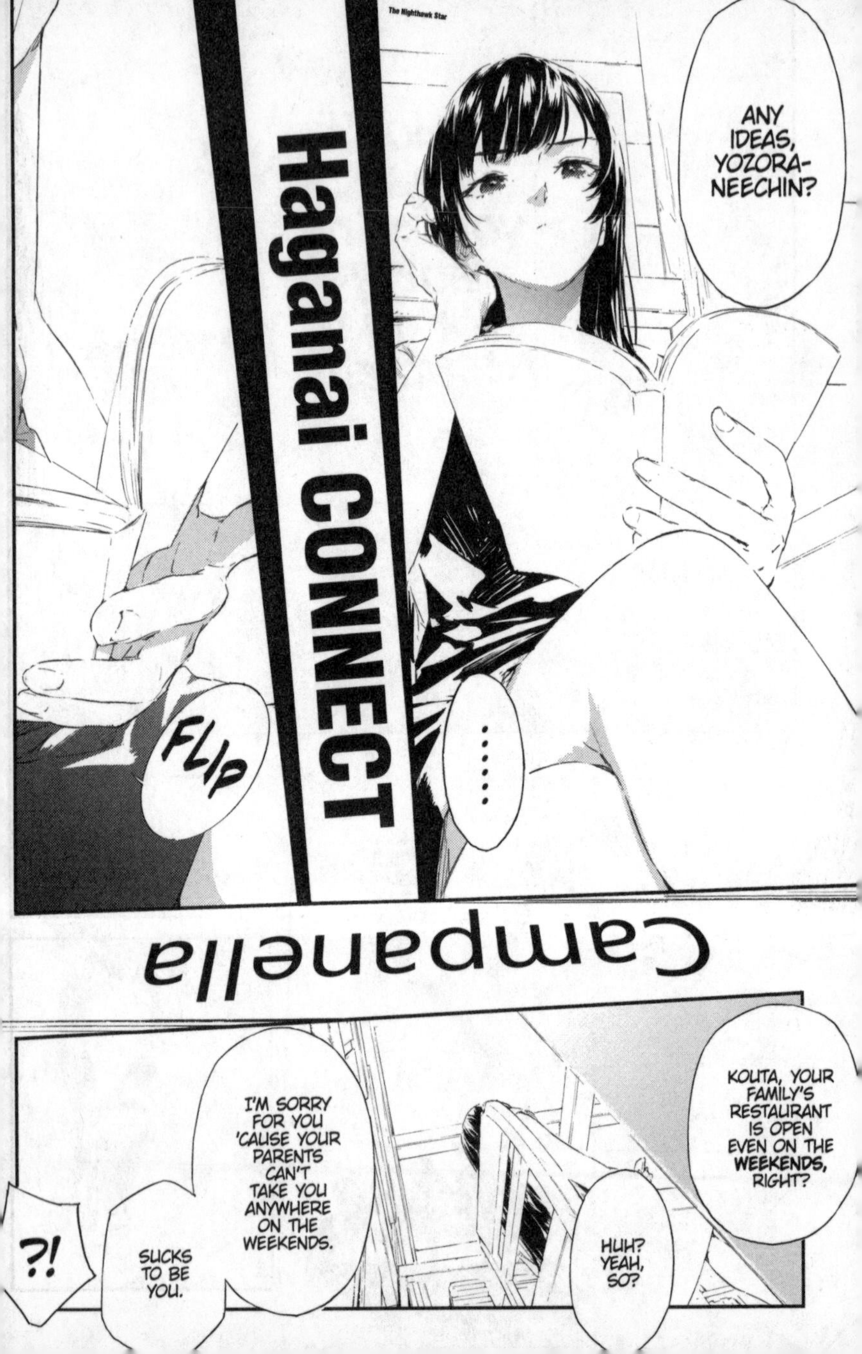
ANY IDEAS, YOZORA-NEECHIN?
......
FLIP
Haganai CONNECT
Campanella
KOUTA, YOUR FAMILY'S RESTAURANT IS OPEN EVEN ON THE WEEKENDS, RIGHT?
HUH? YEAH, SO?
I'M SORRY FOR YOU 'CAUSE YOUR PARENTS CAN'T TAKE YOU ANYWHERE ON THE WEEKENDS.
SUCKS TO BE YOU.
?!

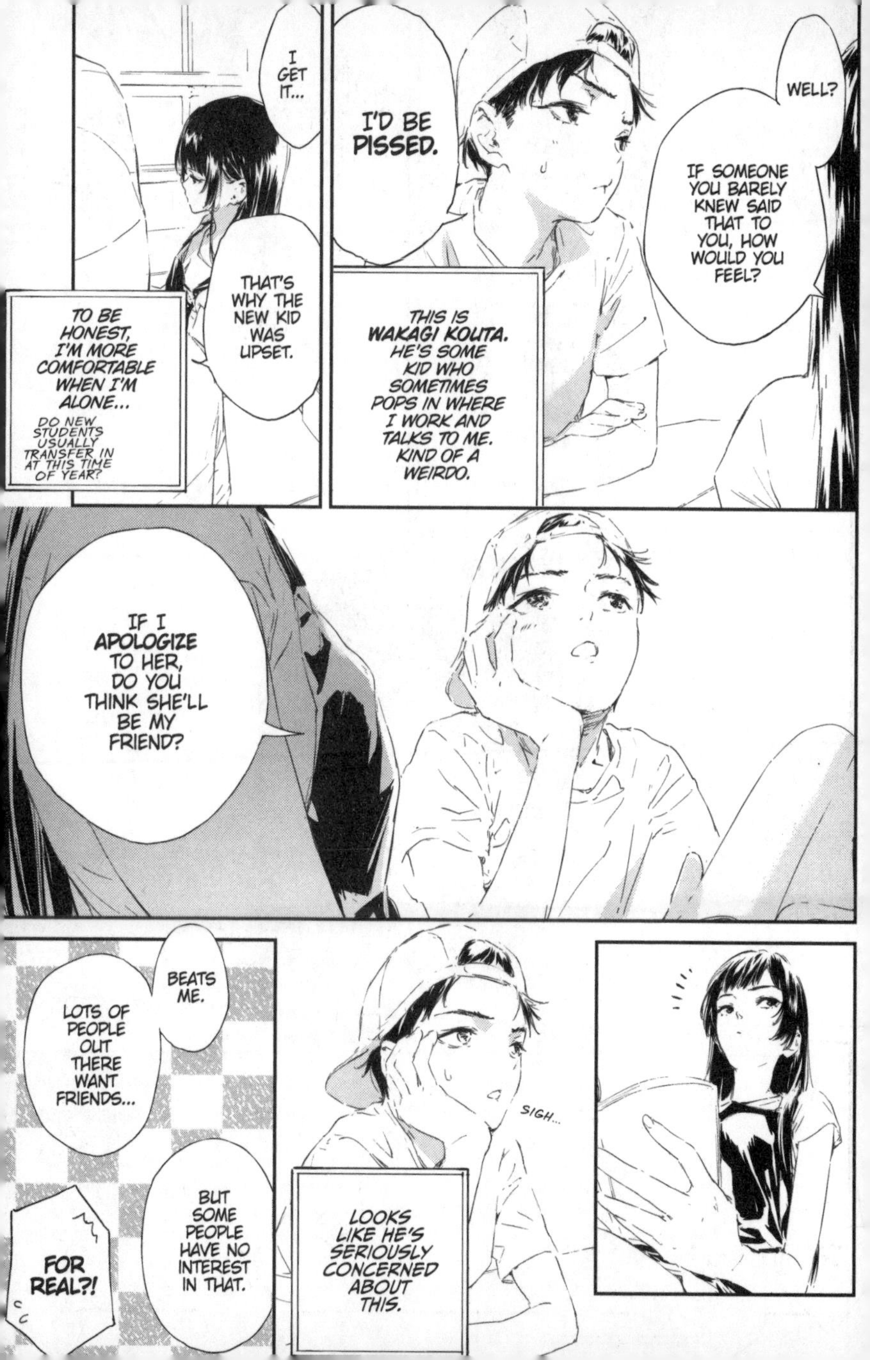
WELL?
IF SOMEONE YOU BARELY KNEW SAID THAT TO YOU, HOW WOULD YOU FEEL?
I'D BE PISSED.
THIS IS WAKAGI KOUTA. HE'S SOME KID WHO SOMETIMES POPS IN WHERE I WORK AND TALKS TO ME. KIND OF A WEIRDO.
I GET IT...
THAT'S WHY THE NEW KID WAS UPSET.
TO BE HONEST, I'M MORE COMFORTABLE WHEN I'M ALONE...
DO NEW STUDENTS USUALLY TRANSFER IN AT THIS TIME OF YEAR?
IF I APOLOGIZE TO HER, DO YOU THINK SHE'LL BE MY FRIEND?
SIGH...
LOOKS LIKE HE'S SERIOUSLY CONCERNED ABOUT THIS.
BEATS ME.
LOTS OF PEOPLE OUT THERE WANT FRIENDS...
BUT SOME PEOPLE HAVE NO INTEREST IN THAT.
FOR REAL?!

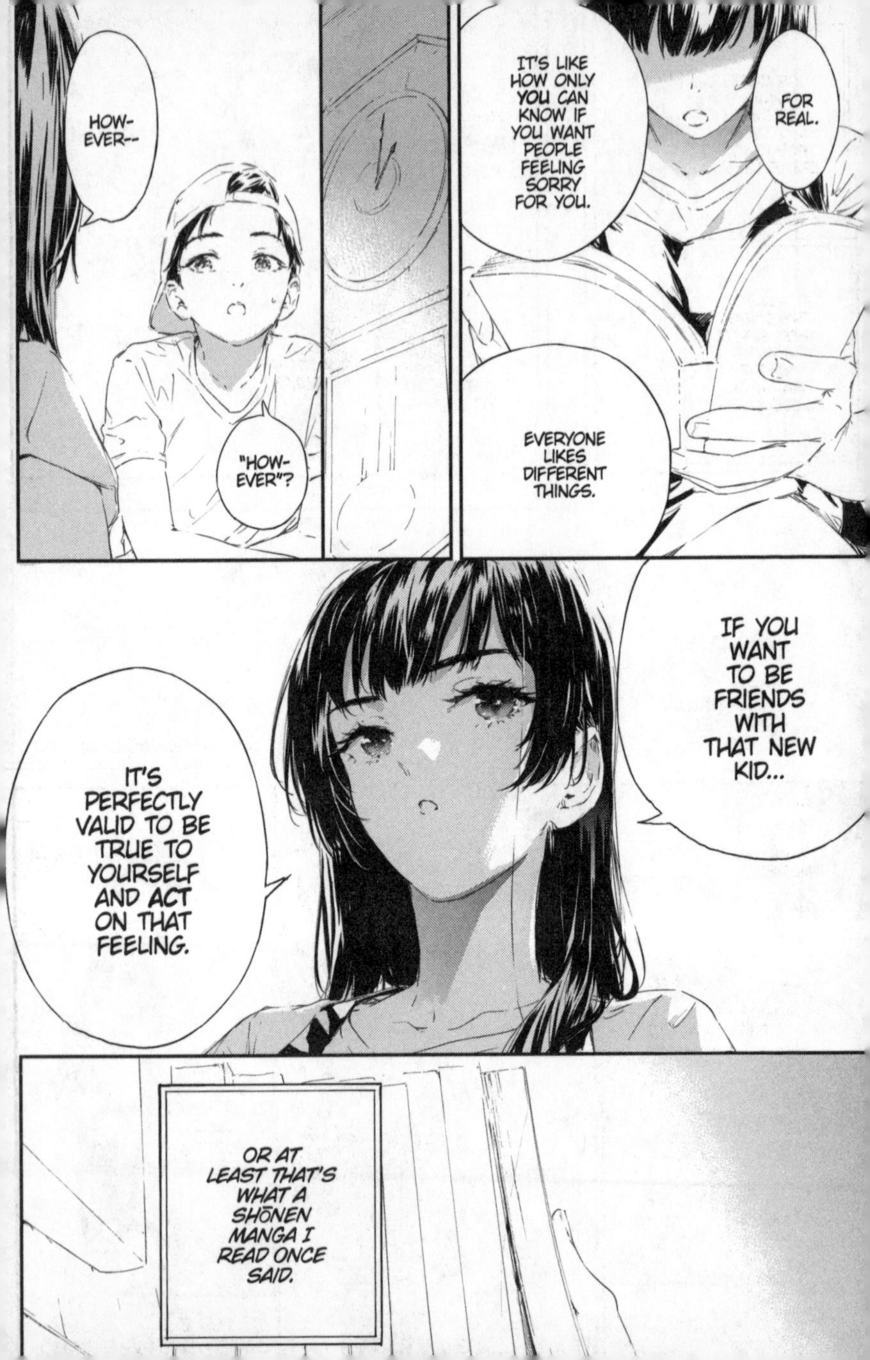
FOR REAL.
IT'S LIKE HOW ONLY YOU CAN KNOW IF YOU WANT PEOPLE FEELING SORRY FOR YOU.
EVERYONE LIKES DIFFERENT THINGS.
HOW-EVER--
"HOW-EVER"?
IF YOU WANT TO BE FRIENDS WITH THAT NEW KID...
IT'S PERFECTLY VALID TO BE TRUE TO YOURSELF AND ACT ON THAT FEELING.
OR AT LEAST THAT'S WHAT A SHŌNEN MANGA I READ ONCE SAID.

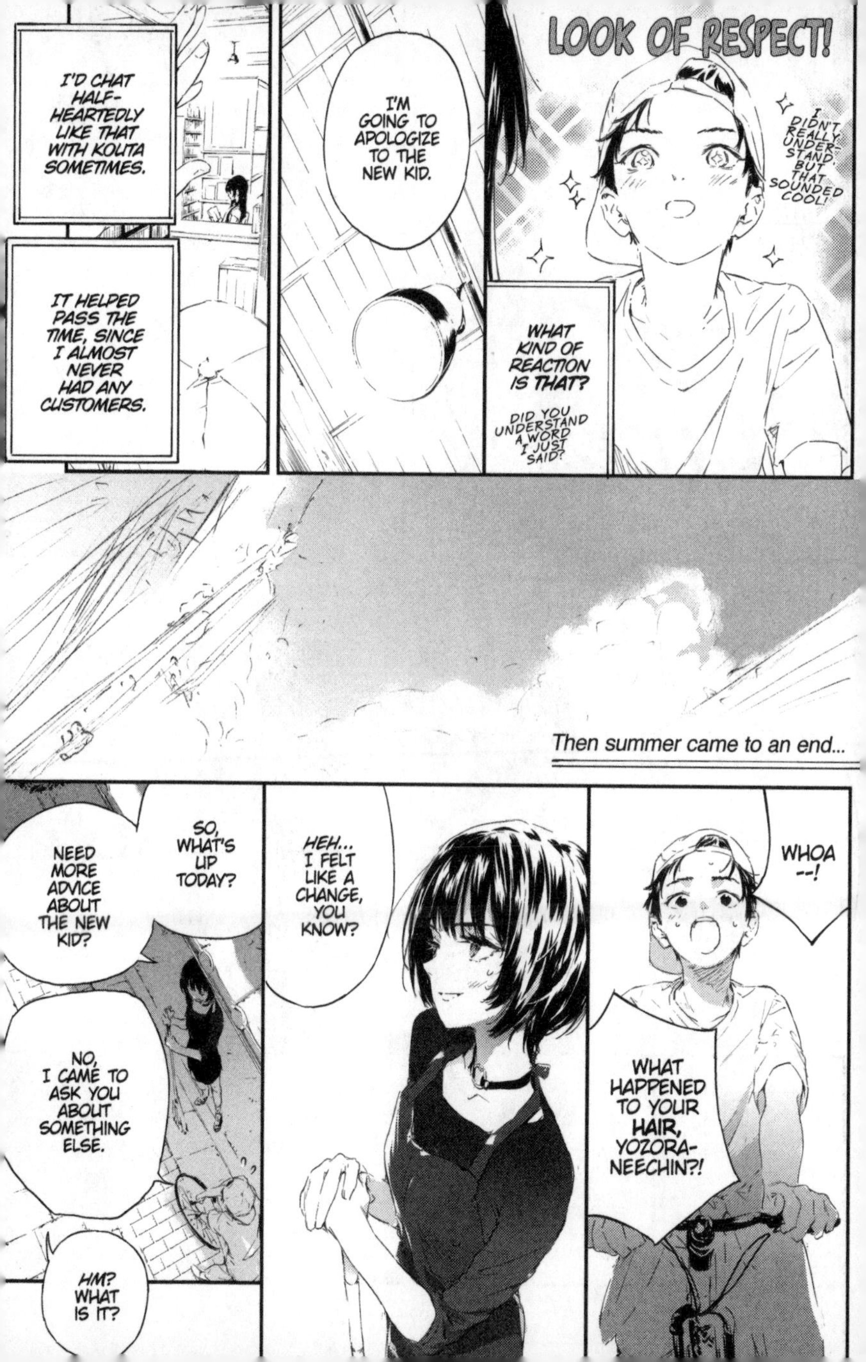
LOOK OF RESPECT!
I DIDN'T REALLY UNDERSTAND, BUT THAT SOUNDED COOL!
WHAT KIND OF REACTION IS THAT?
DID YOU UNDERSTAND A WORD I JUST SAID?
I'M GOING TO APOLOGIZE TO THE NEW KID.
I'D CHAT HALF-HEARTEDLY LIKE THAT WITH KOUTA SOMETIMES.
IT HELPED PASS THE TIME, SINCE I ALMOST NEVER HAD ANY CUSTOMERS.
Then summer came to an end...
WHOA--!
WHAT HAPPENED TO YOUR HAIR, YOZORA-NEECHIN?!
HEH... I FELT LIKE A CHANGE, YOU KNOW?
SO, WHAT'S UP TODAY?
NEED MORE ADVICE ABOUT THE NEW KID?
NO, I CAME TO ASK YOU ABOUT SOMETHING ELSE.
HM? WHAT IS IT?

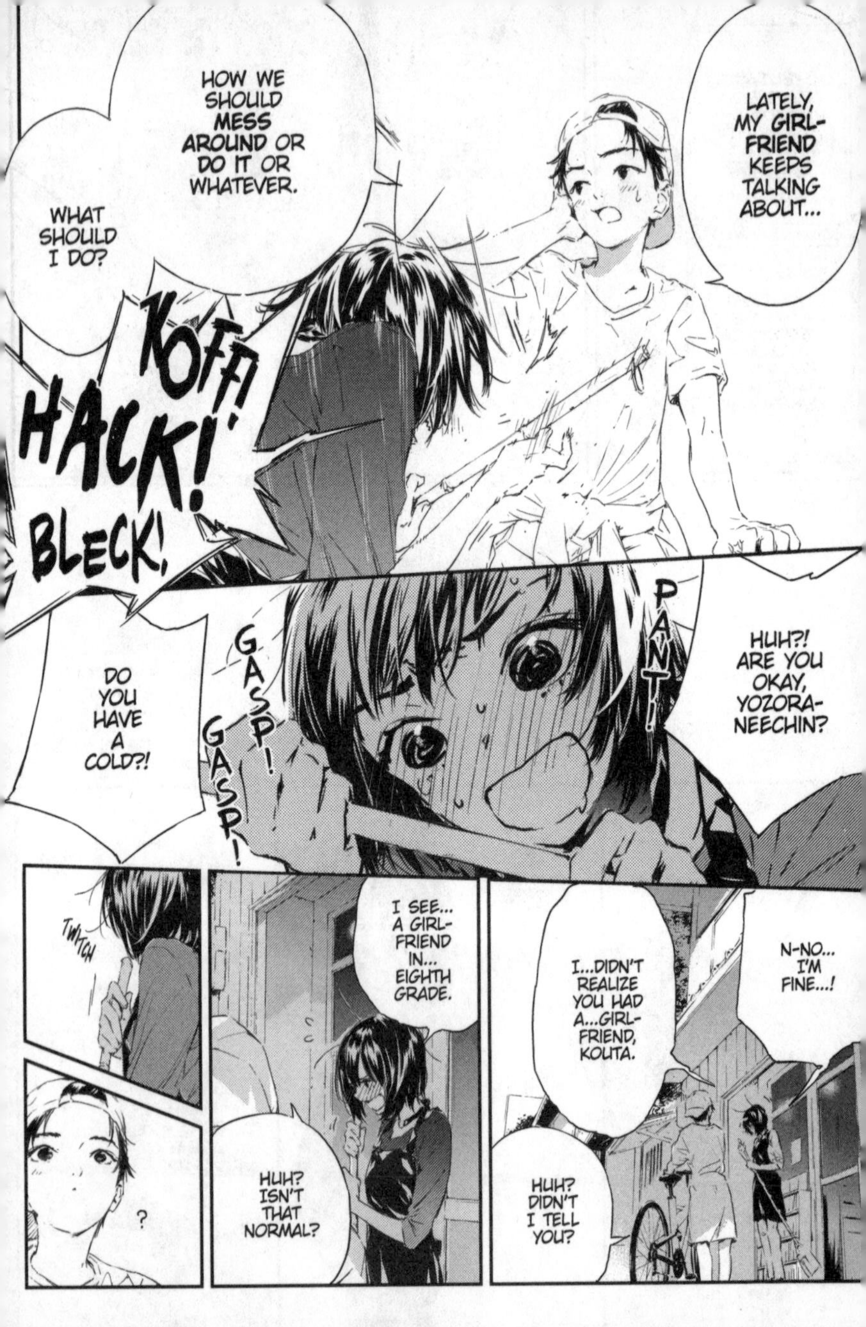
LATELY, MY GIRL-FRIEND KEEPS TALKING ABOUT...
HOW WE SHOULD MESS AROUND OR DO IT OR WHATEVER.
WHAT SHOULD I DO?
KOFF! HACK! BLECK!
HUH?! ARE YOU OKAY, YOZORA-NEECHIN?
PANT!
GASP! GASP!
DO YOU HAVE A COLD?!
N-NO... I'M FINE...!
I...DIDN'T REALIZE YOU HAD A...GIRL-FRIEND, KOUTA.
HUH? DIDN'T I TELL YOU?
I SEE... A GIRL-FRIEND IN... EIGHTH GRADE.
HUH? ISN'T THAT NORMAL?
TWITCH
?

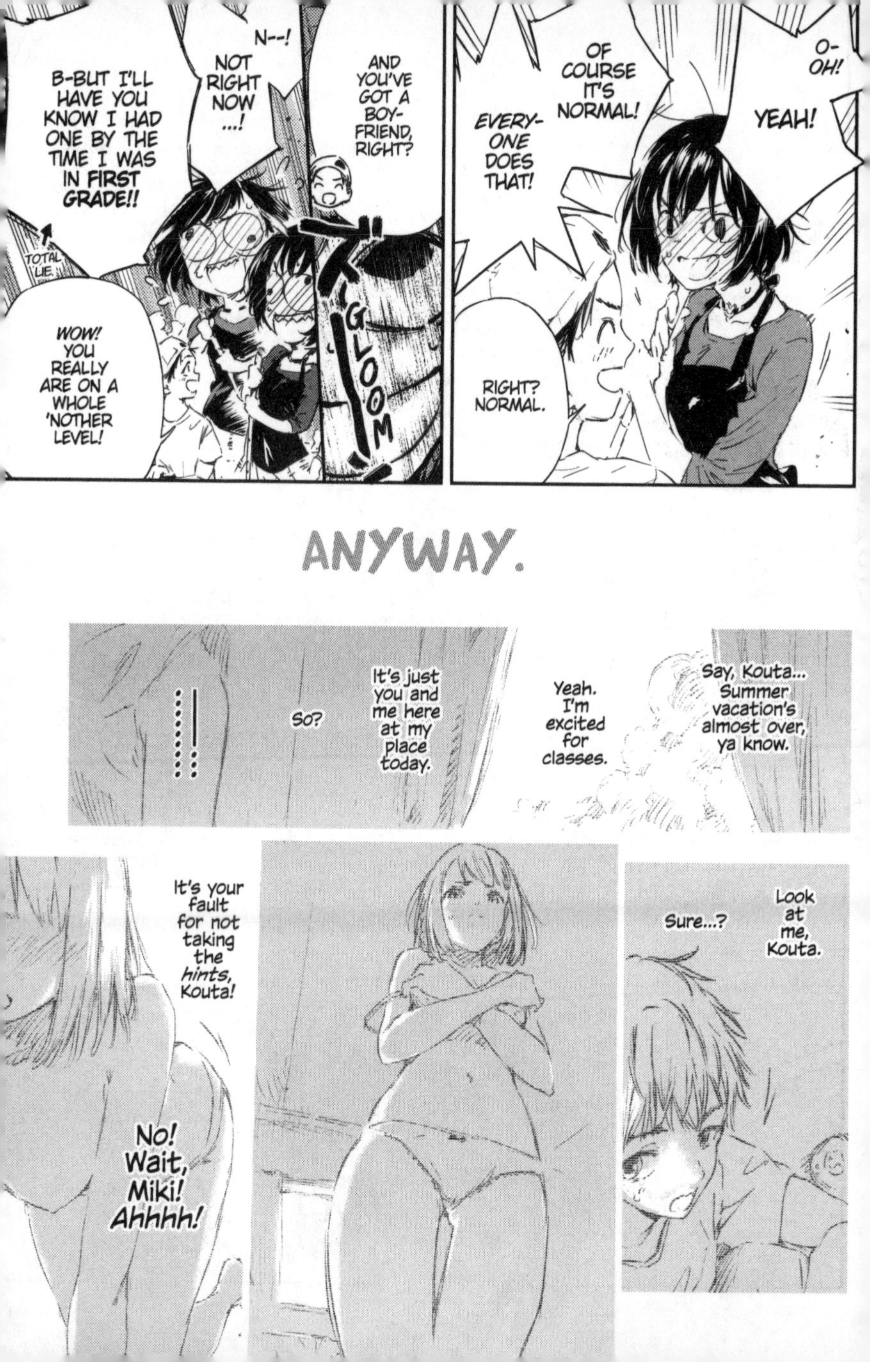
O-OH!
YEAH!
OF COURSE IT'S NORMAL!
EVERY-ONE DOES THAT!
RIGHT? NORMAL.
AND YOU'VE GOT A BOY-FRIEND, RIGHT?
N--!
NOT RIGHT NOW ...!
B-BUT I'LL HAVE YOU KNOW I HAD ONE BY THE TIME I WAS IN FIRST GRADE!!
GLOOM
TOTAL LIE.
WOW! YOU REALLY ARE ON A WHOLE 'NOTHER LEVEL!
ANYWAY.
Say, Kouta... Summer vacation's almost over, ya know.
Yeah. I'm excited for classes.
It's just you and me here at my place today.
So?
......!!
Look at me, Kouta.
Sure...?
It's your fault for not taking the hints, Kouta!
No! Wait, Miki! Ahhhh!

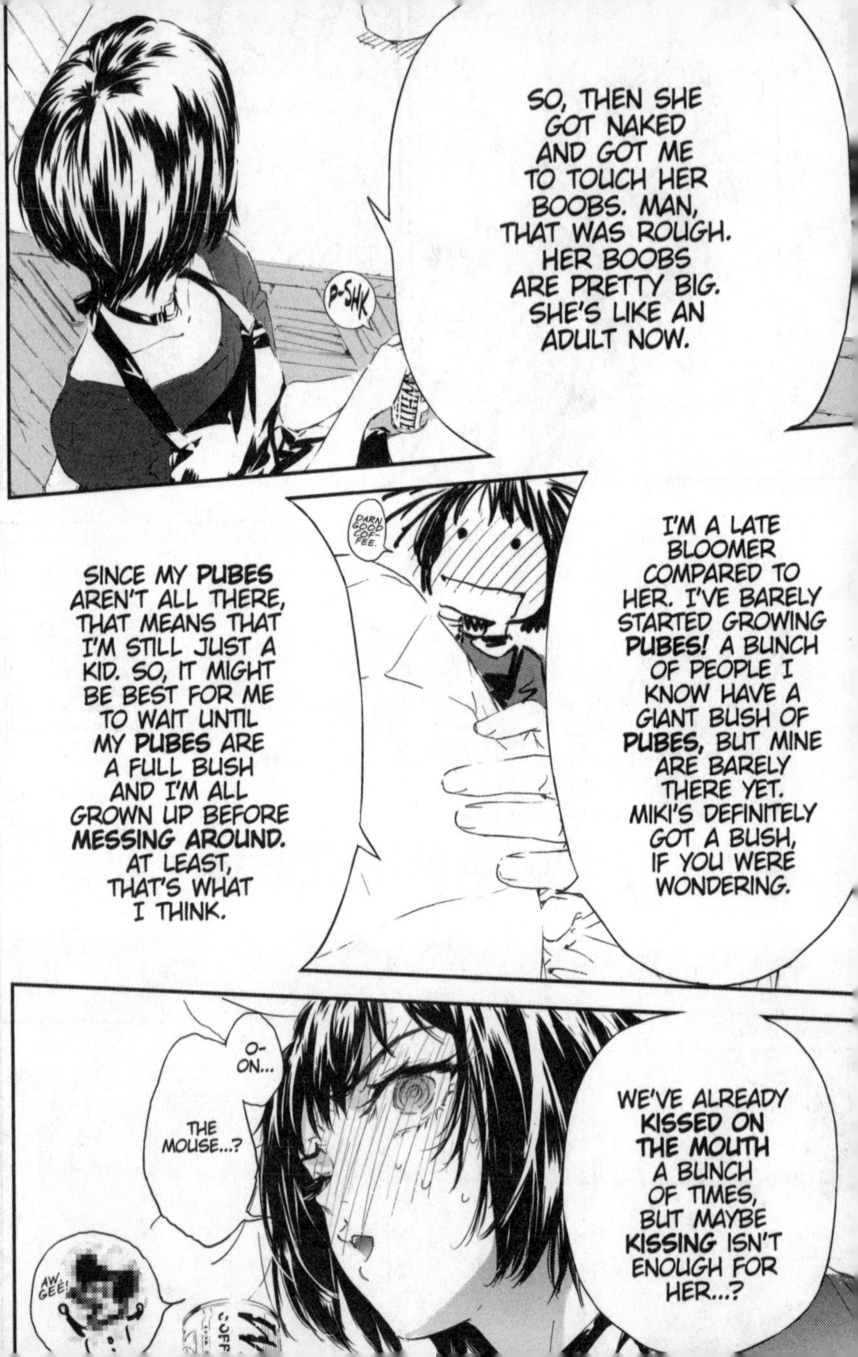
SO, THEN SHE GOT NAKED AND GOT ME TO TOUCH HER BOOBS. MAN, THAT WAS ROUGH. HER BOOBS ARE PRETTY BIG. SHE'S LIKE AN ADULT NOW.
P-SHK
I'M A LATE BLOOMER COMPARED TO HER. I'VE BARELY STARTED GROWING PUBES! A BUNCH OF PEOPLE I KNOW HAVE A GIANT BUSH OF PUBES, BUT MINE ARE BARELY THERE YET. MIKI'S DEFINITELY GOT A BUSH, IF YOU WERE WONDERING.
DARN GOOD COFFEE.
SINCE MY PUBES AREN'T ALL THERE, THAT MEANS THAT I'M STILL JUST A KID. SO, IT MIGHT BE BEST FOR ME TO WAIT UNTIL MY PUBES ARE A FULL BUSH AND I'M ALL GROWN UP BEFORE MESSING AROUND. AT LEAST, THAT'S WHAT I THINK.
WE'VE ALREADY KISSED ON THE MOUTH A BUNCH OF TIMES, BUT MAYBE KISSING ISN'T ENOUGH FOR HER...?
O-ON...
THE MOUSE...?
AW, GEE!

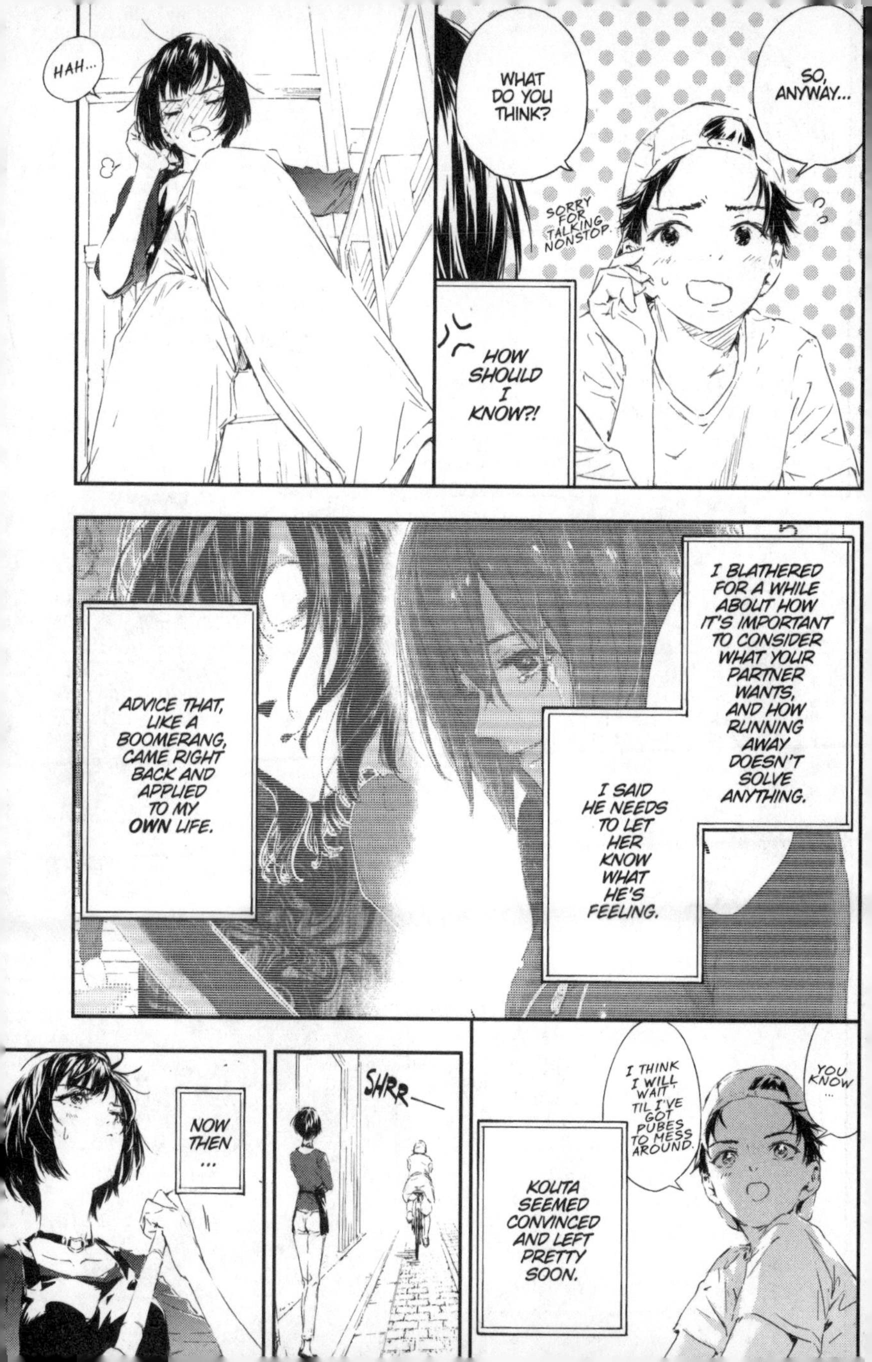
SO, ANYWAY...
SORRY FOR TALKING NONSTOP.
WHAT DO YOU THINK?
HOW SHOULD I KNOW?!
HAH...
I BLATHERED FOR A WHILE ABOUT HOW IT'S IMPORTANT TO CONSIDER WHAT YOUR PARTNER WANTS, AND HOW RUNNING AWAY DOESN'T SOLVE ANYTHING.
I SAID HE NEEDS TO LET HER KNOW WHAT HE'S FEELING.
ADVICE THAT, LIKE A BOOMERANG, CAME RIGHT BACK AND APPLIED TO MY OWN LIFE.
YOU KNOW...
I THINK I WILL WAIT TIL I'VE GOT PUBES TO MESS AROUND.
KOUTA SEEMED CONVINCED AND LEFT PRETTY SOON.
SHRR—
NOW THEN...

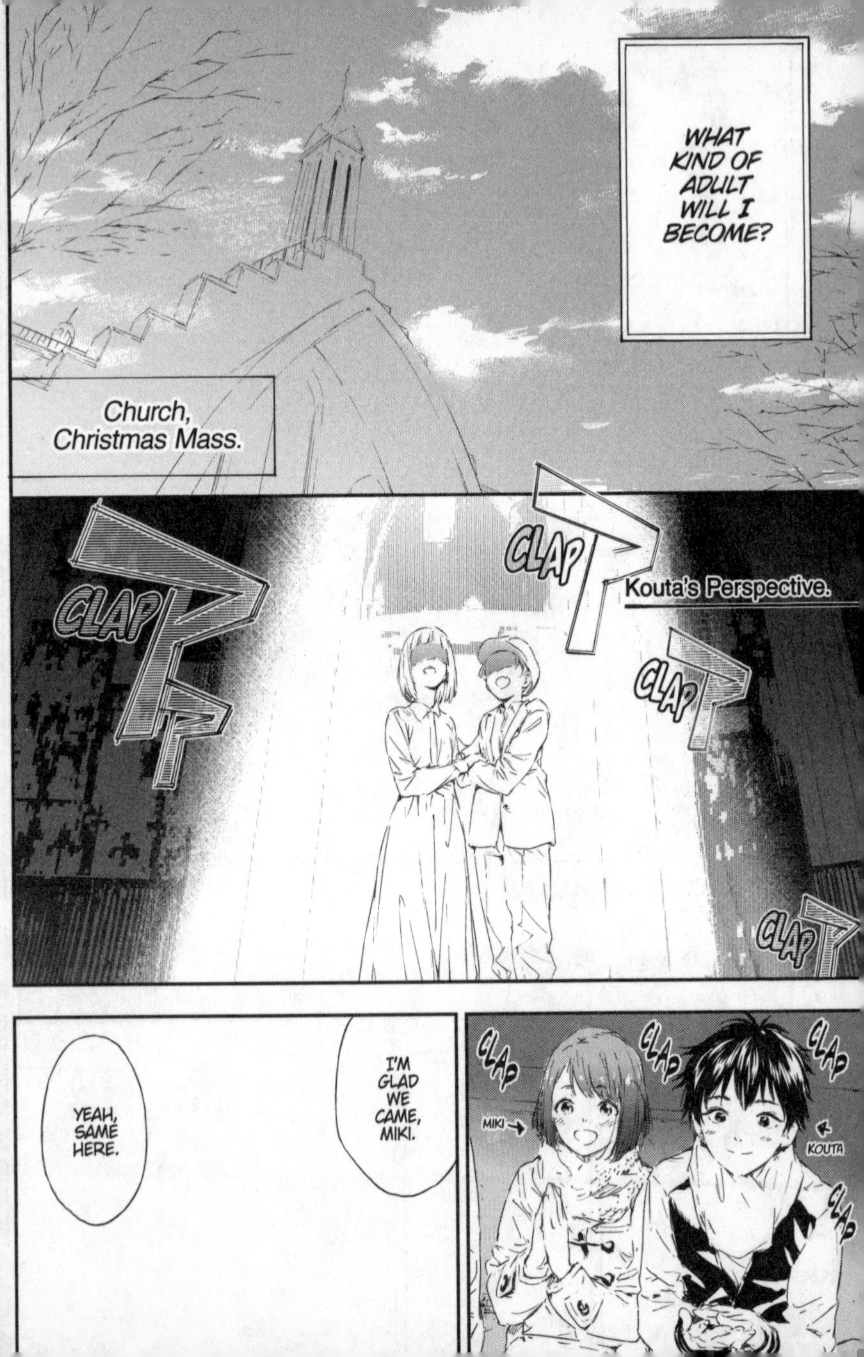
WHAT KIND OF ADULT WILL I BECOME?
Church, Christmas Mass.
CLAP
Kouta's Perspective.
CLAP
CLAP
CLAP
CLAP
CLAP
CLAP
CLAP
KOUTA
MIKI
I'M GLAD WE CAME, MIKI.
YEAH, SAME HERE.

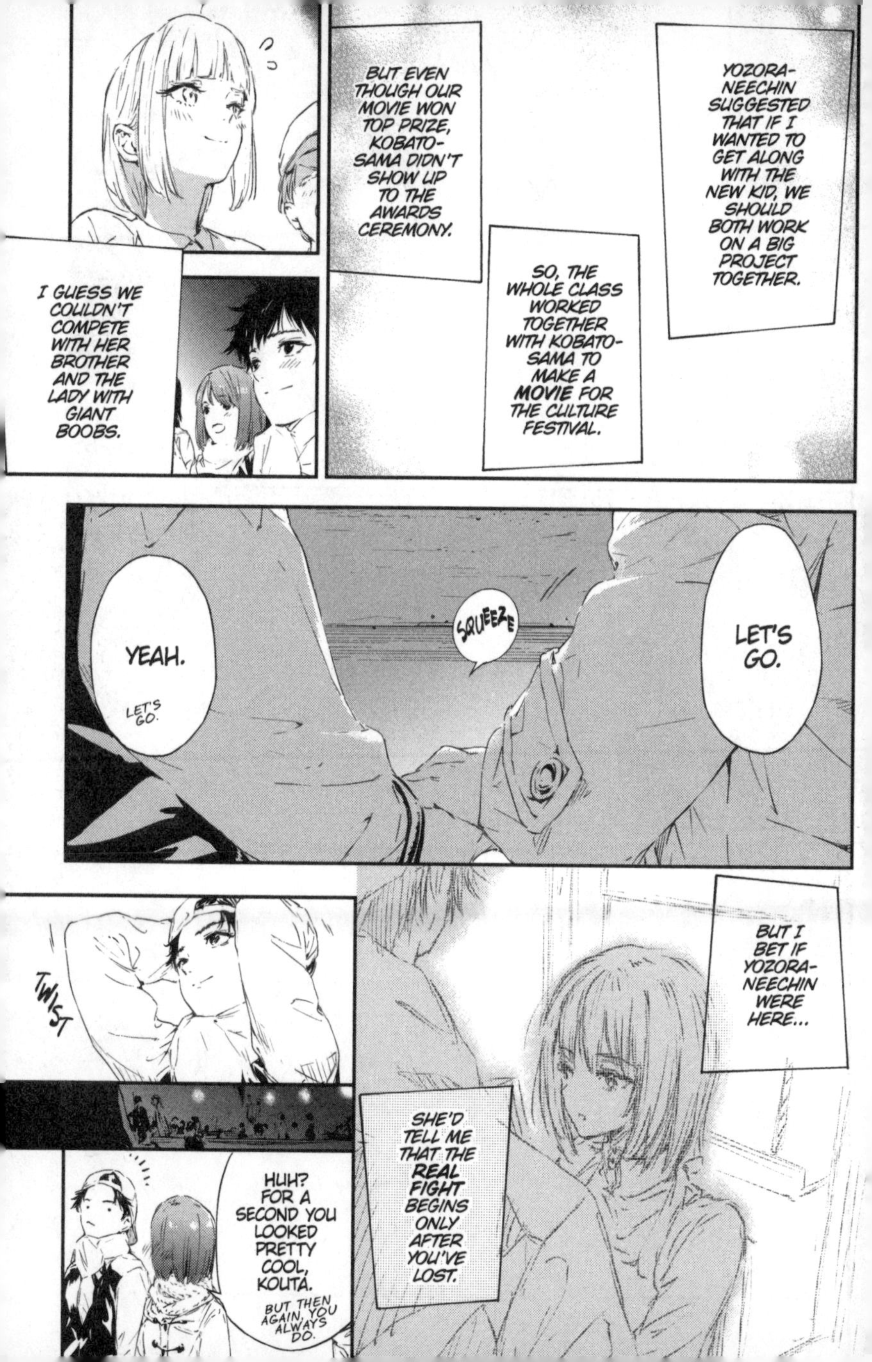
YOZORA-NEECHIN SUGGESTED THAT IF I WANTED TO GET ALONG WITH THE NEW KID, WE SHOULD BOTH WORK ON A BIG PROJECT TOGETHER.
SO, THE WHOLE CLASS WORKED TOGETHER WITH KOBATO-SAMA TO MAKE A **MOVIE** FOR THE CULTURE FESTIVAL.
BUT EVEN THOUGH OUR MOVIE WON TOP PRIZE, KOBATO-SAMA DIDN'T SHOW UP TO THE AWARDS CEREMONY.
I GUESS WE COULDN'T COMPETE WITH HER BROTHER AND THE LADY WITH GIANT BOOBS.
LET'S GO.
SQUEEZE
YEAH.
LET'S GO.
BUT I BET IF YOZORA-NEECHIN WERE HERE...
SHE'D TELL ME THAT THE **REAL FIGHT** BEGINS ONLY AFTER YOU'VE LOST.
TWIST
HUH? FOR A SECOND YOU LOOKED PRETTY COOL, KOUTA.
BUT THEN AGAIN, YOU ALWAYS DO.

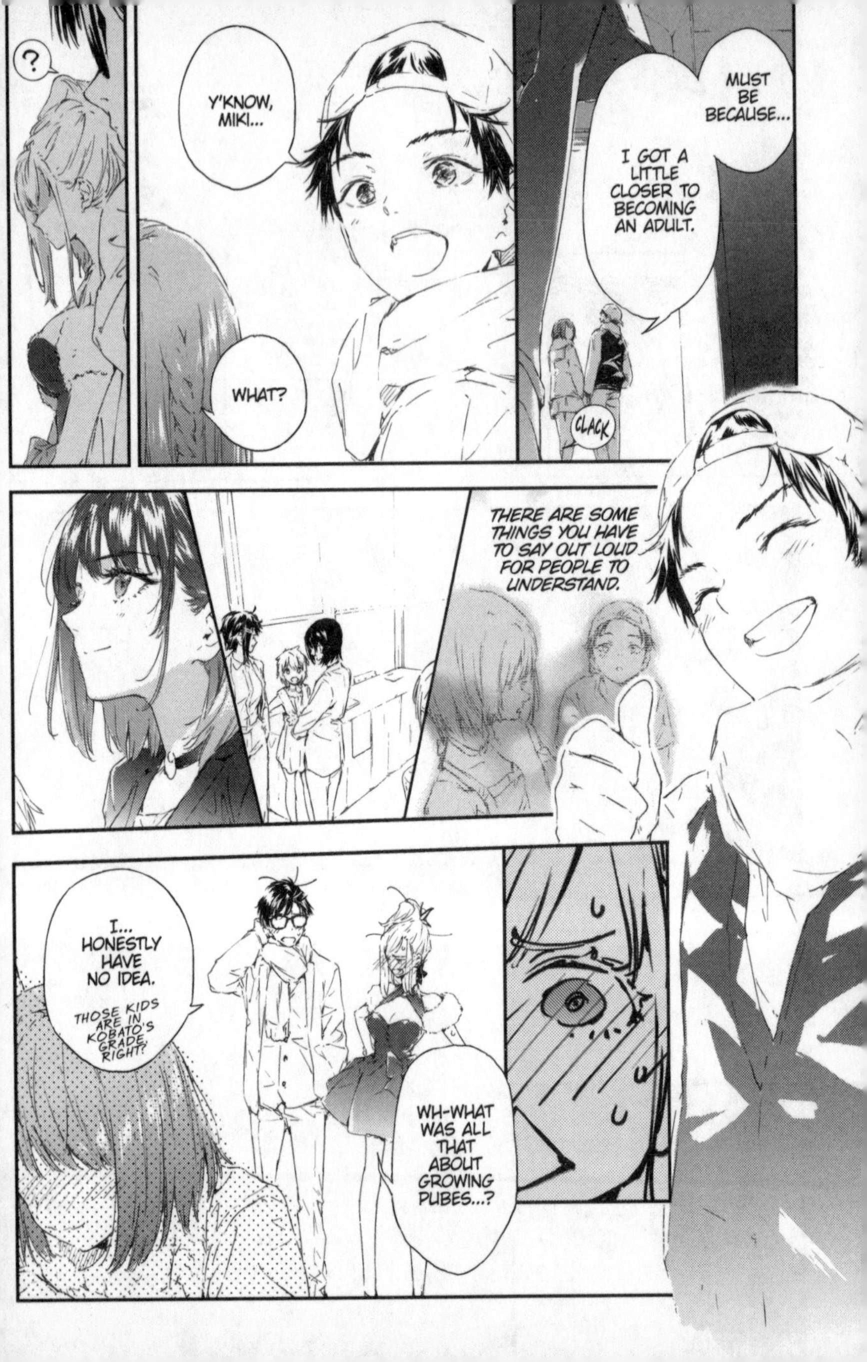
MUST BE BECAUSE...
I GOT A LITTLE CLOSER TO BECOMING AN ADULT.
CLACK
Y'KNOW, MIKI...
WHAT?
?
THERE ARE SOME THINGS YOU HAVE TO SAY OUT LOUD FOR PEOPLE TO UNDERSTAND.
WH-WHAT WAS ALL THAT ABOUT GROWING PUBES...?
I... HONESTLY HAVE NO IDEA.
THOSE KIDS ARE IN KOBATO'S GRADE RIGHT?

I don't have many friends

Haganai

I don't have many friends

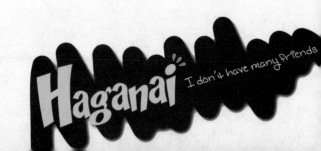

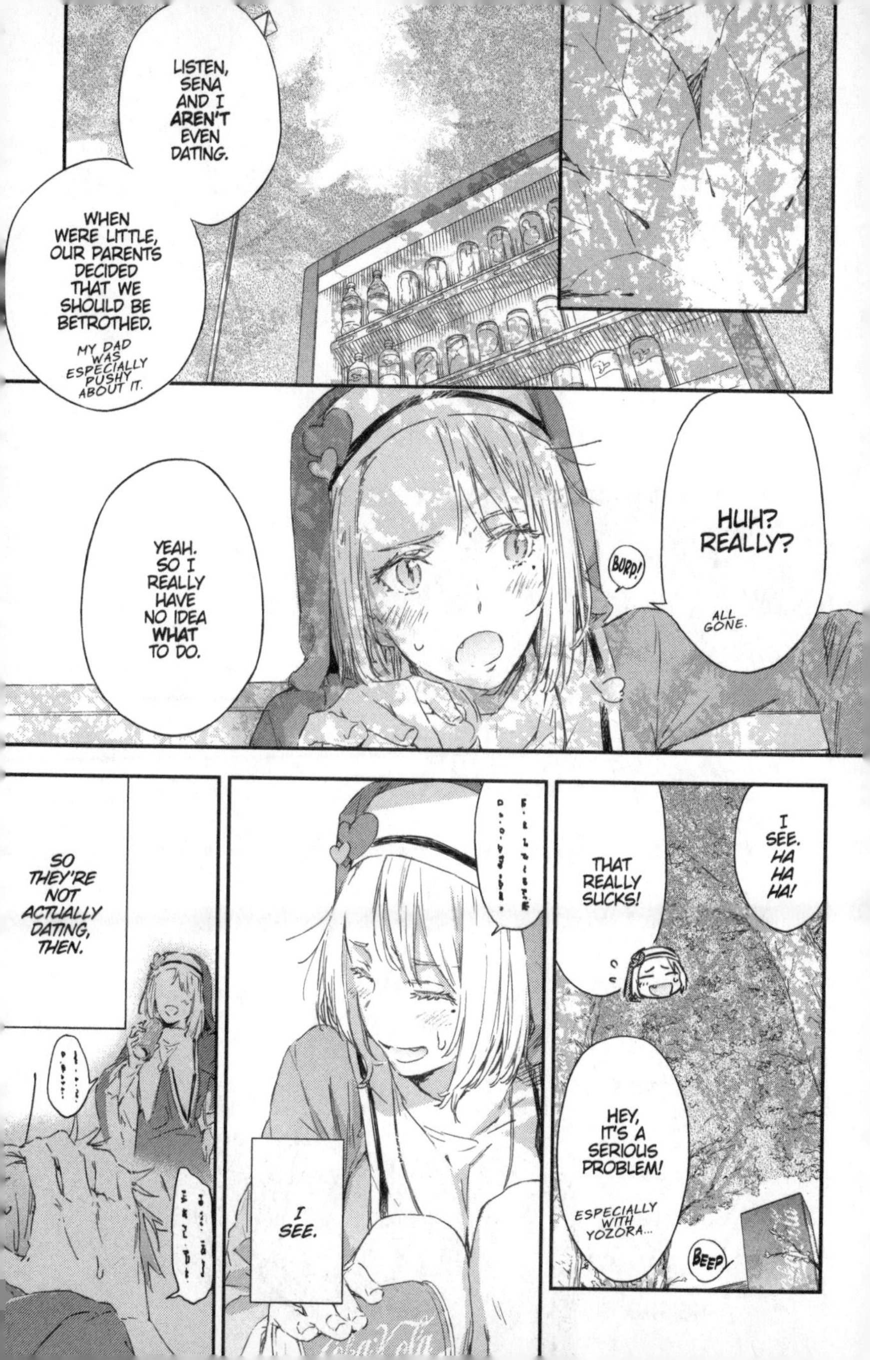
LISTEN, SENA AND I AREN'T EVEN DATING.
WHEN WERE LITTLE, OUR PARENTS DECIDED THAT WE SHOULD BE BETROTHED.
MY DAD WAS ESPECIALLY PUSHY ABOUT IT.
HUH? REALLY?
ALL GONE.
BURP!
YEAH. SO I REALLY HAVE NO IDEA WHAT TO DO.
I SEE. HA HA HA!
THAT REALLY SUCKS!
HEY, IT'S A SERIOUS PROBLEM!
ESPECIALLY WITH YOZORA...
BEEP
I SEE.
SO THEY'RE NOT ACTUALLY DATING, THEN.

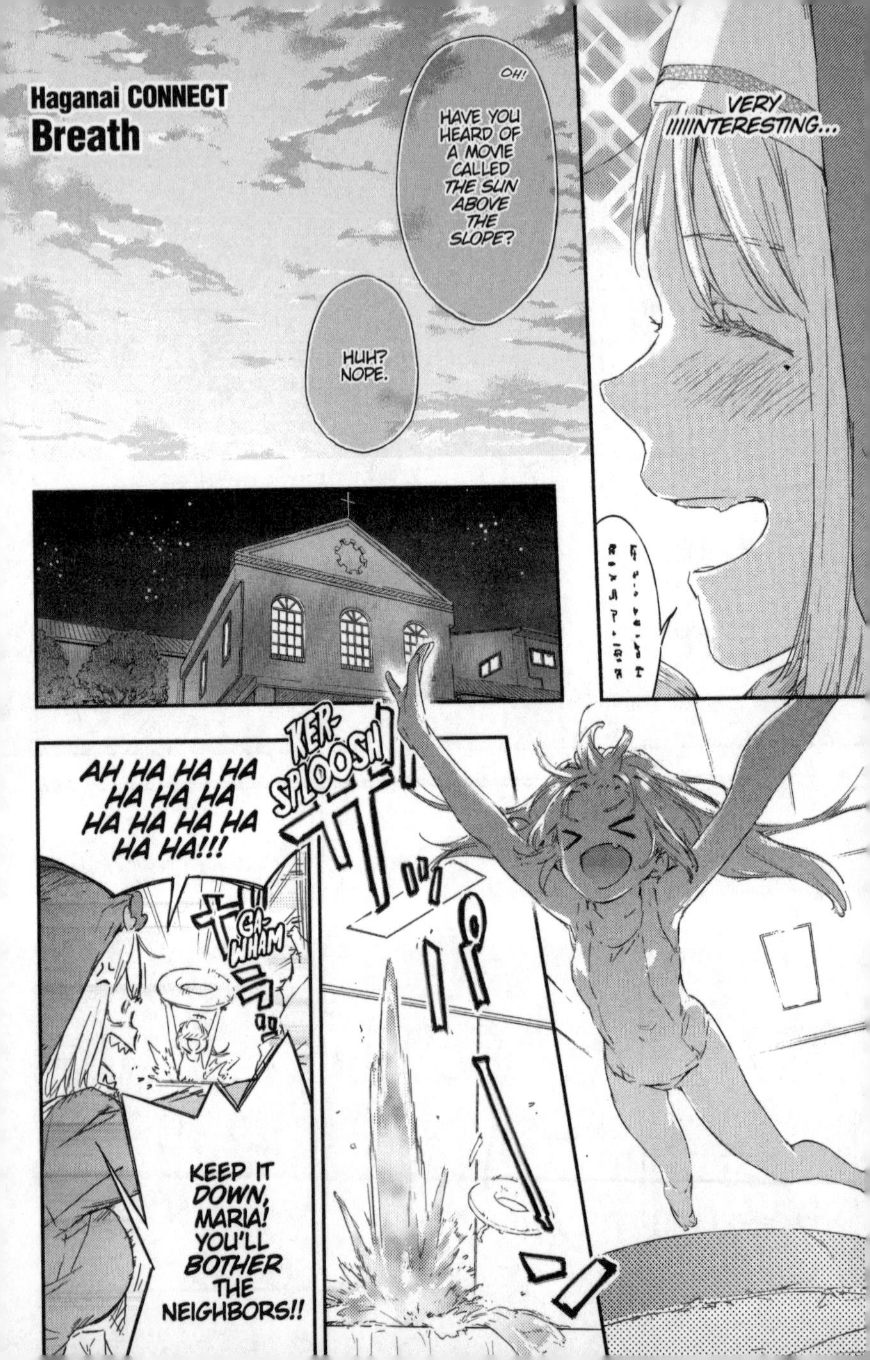
Haganai CONNECT
Breath
VERY IIIIIINTERESTING...
OH!
HAVE YOU HEARD OF A MOVIE CALLED THE SUN ABOVE THE SLOPE?
HUH? NOPE.
KER-SPLOOSH!
AH HA HA HA HA HA HA HA HA HA HA HA HA!!!
CA-WHAM
KEEP IT DOWN, MARIA! YOU'LL BOTHER THE NEIGHBORS!!

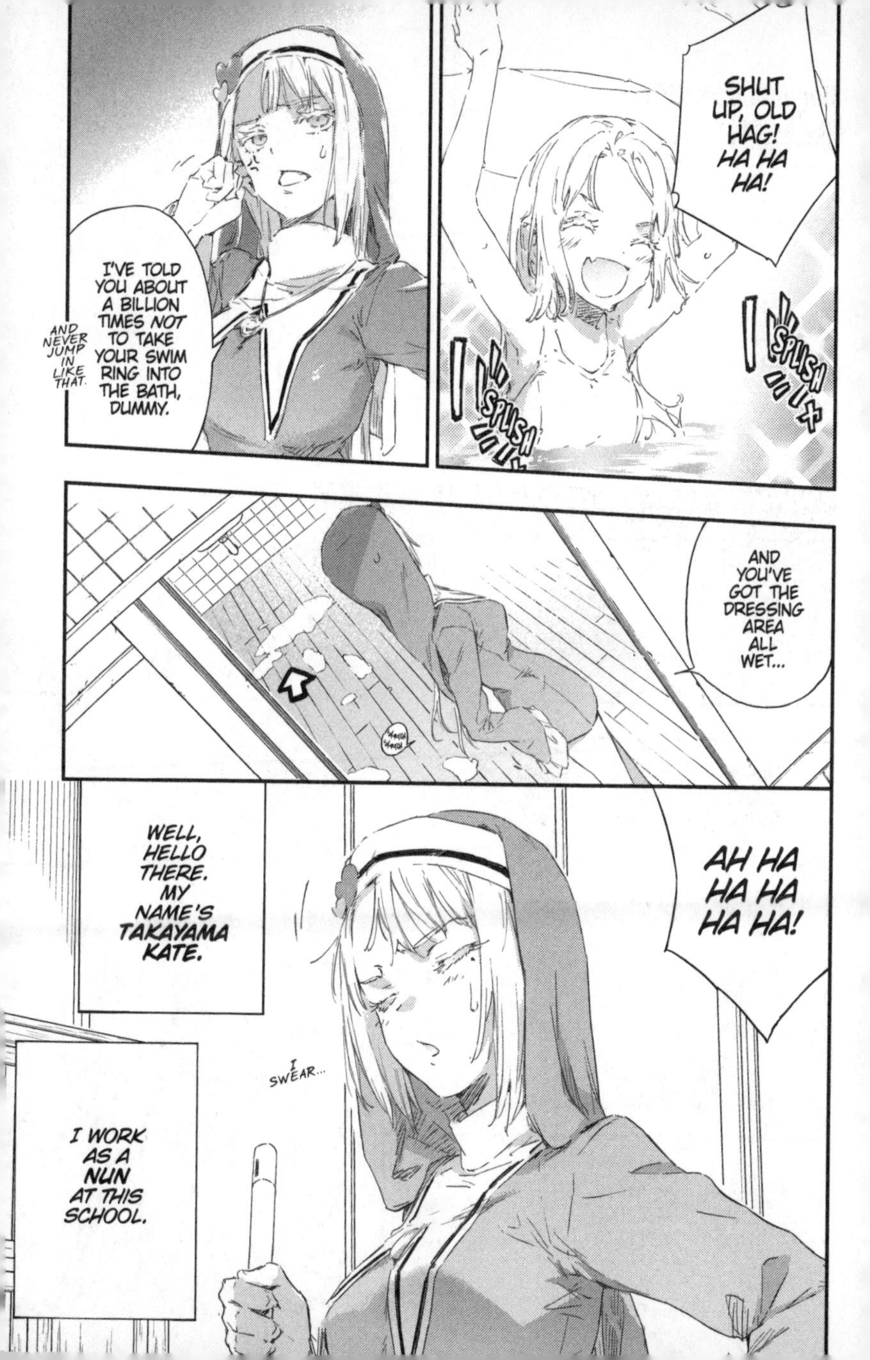
SHUT UP, OLD HAG! HA HA HA!
SPLISH
SPLISH
I'VE TOLD YOU ABOUT A BILLION TIMES NOT TO TAKE YOUR SWIM RING INTO THE BATH, DUMMY.
AND NEVER JUMP IN LIKE THAT.
AND YOU'VE GOT THE DRESSING AREA ALL WET...
AH HA HA HA HA HA!
WELL, HELLO THERE. MY NAME'S TAKAYAMA KATE.
I SWEAR...
I WORK AS A NUN AT THIS SCHOOL.

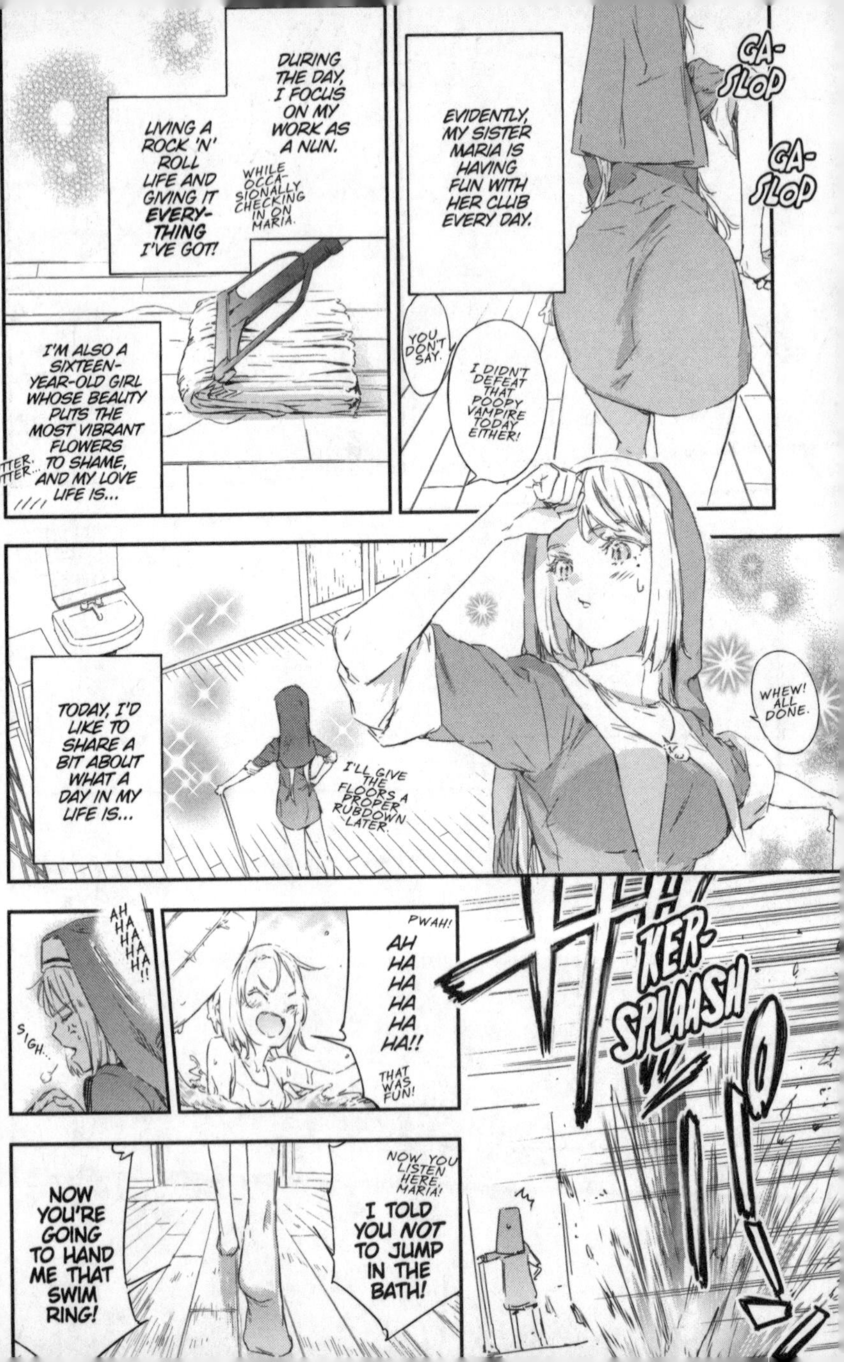
GA-SLOP
GA-SLOP
EVIDENTLY, MY SISTER MARIA IS HAVING FUN WITH HER CLUB EVERY DAY.
I DIDN'T DEFEAT THAT POOPY VAMPIRE TODAY EITHER!
YOU DON'T SAY.
DURING THE DAY, I FOCUS ON MY WORK AS A NUN.
WHILE OCCASIONALLY CHECKING IN ON MARIA.
LIVING A ROCK 'N' ROLL LIFE AND GIVING IT EVERYTHING I'VE GOT!
I'M ALSO A SIXTEEN-YEAR-OLD GIRL WHOSE BEAUTY PUTS THE MOST VIBRANT FLOWERS TO SHAME, AND MY LOVE LIFE IS...
MUTTER MUTTER...
WHEW! ALL DONE.
I'LL GIVE THE FLOORS A PROPER RUBDOWN LATER.
TODAY, I'D LIKE TO SHARE A BIT ABOUT WHAT A DAY IN MY LIFE IS...
KER-SPLAASH
PWAH!
AH HA HA HA HA HA!!
THAT WAS FUN!
AH HA HA HA HA!!
SIGH...
NOW YOU LISTEN HERE, MARIA!
I TOLD YOU NOT TO JUMP IN THE BATH!
NOW YOU'RE GOING TO HAND ME THAT SWIM RING!

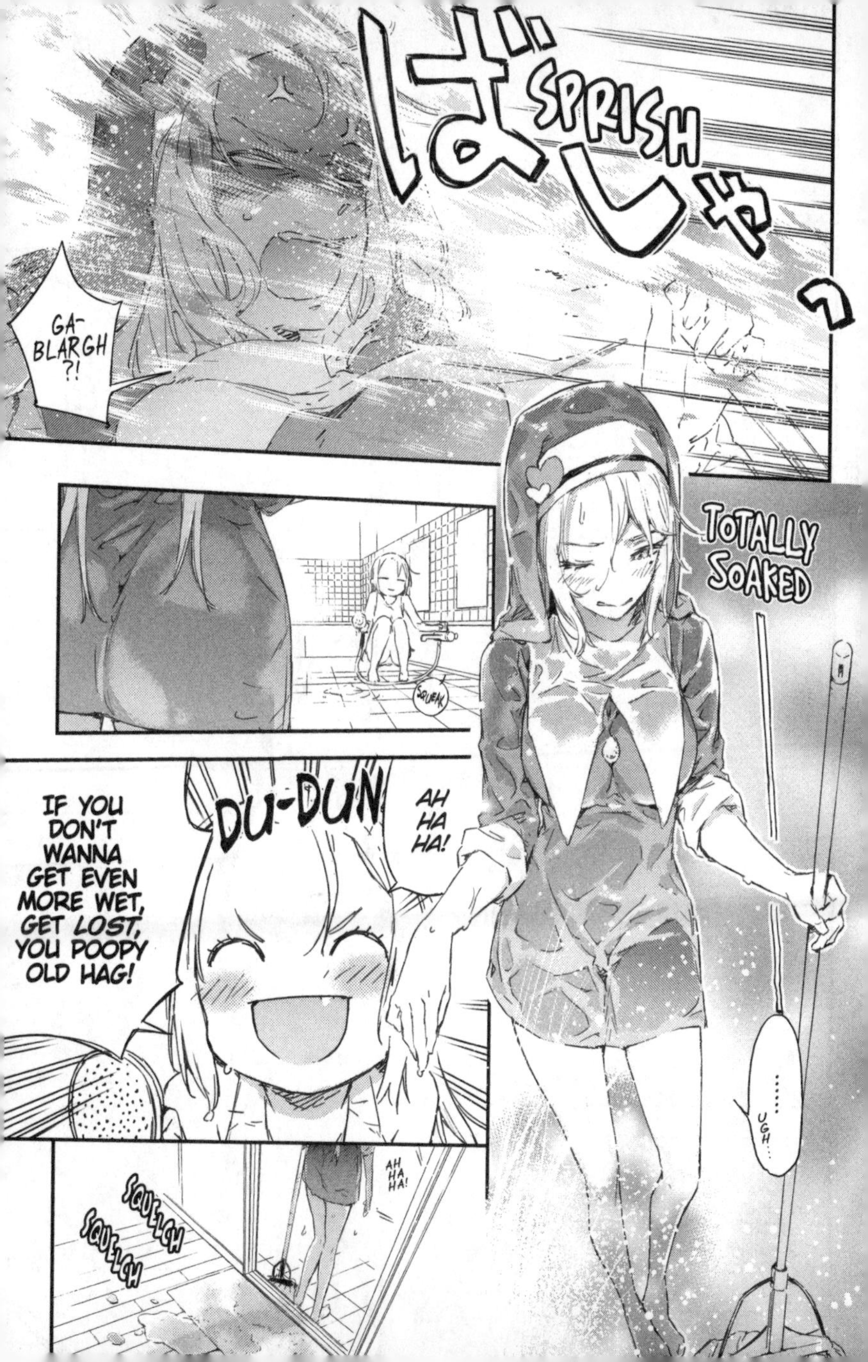

ばしゃっ
SPRISH
GA-BLARGH?!
TOTALLY SOAKED
...... UGH...
SQUEAK
DU-DUN
AH HA HA!
IF YOU DON'T WANNA GET EVEN MORE WET, GET LOST, YOU POOPY OLD HAG!
AH HA HA!
SQUELCH
SQUELCH

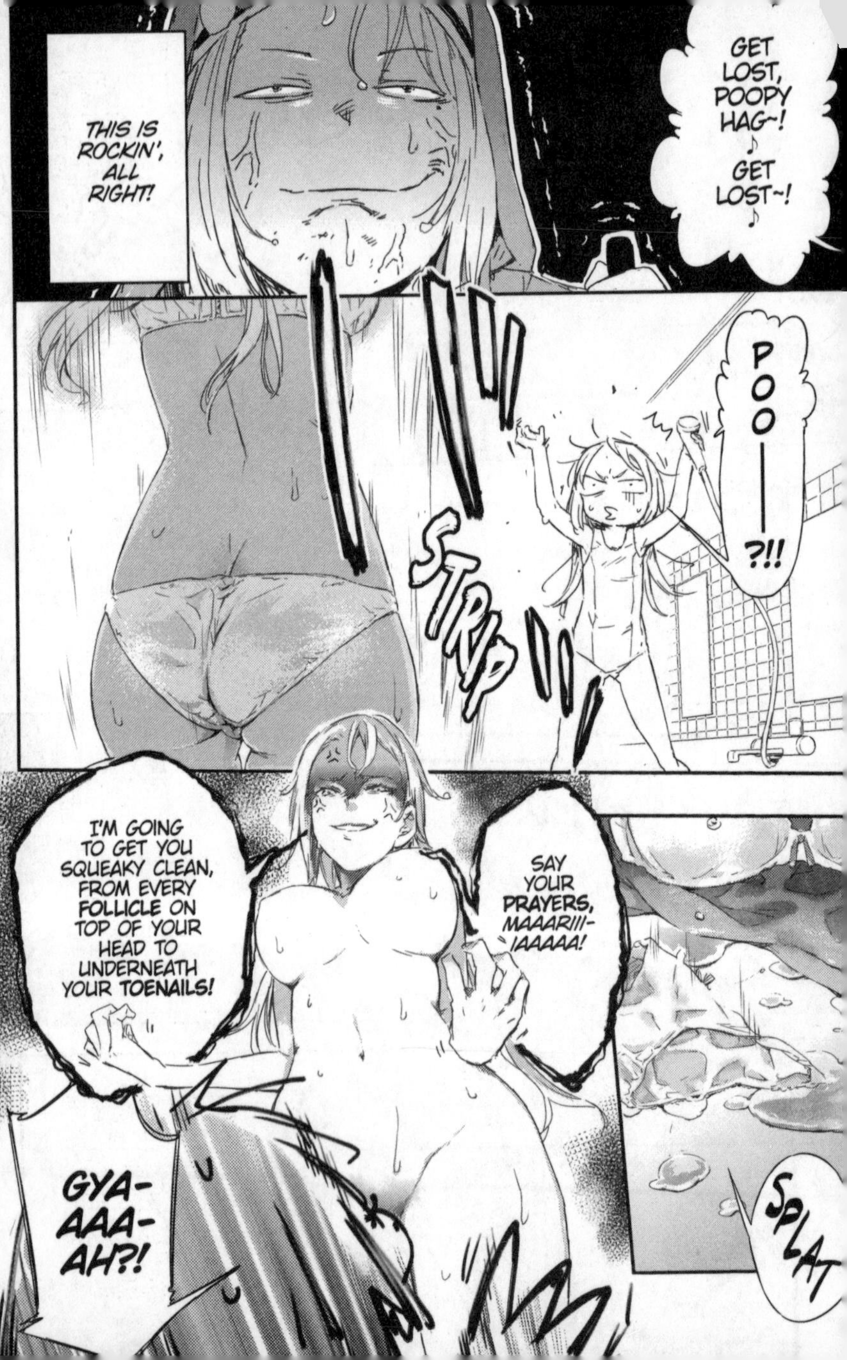
GET LOST, POOPY HAG~! ♪ GET LOST~! ♪
THIS IS ROCKIN', ALL RIGHT!
POO——?!!
STRIP
SPLAT
SAY YOUR PRAYERS, MAAARIII-IAAAAA!
I'M GOING TO GET YOU SQUEAKY CLEAN, FROM EVERY FOLLICLE ON TOP OF YOUR HEAD TO UNDERNEATH YOUR TOENAILS!
GYA-AAAA-AH?!

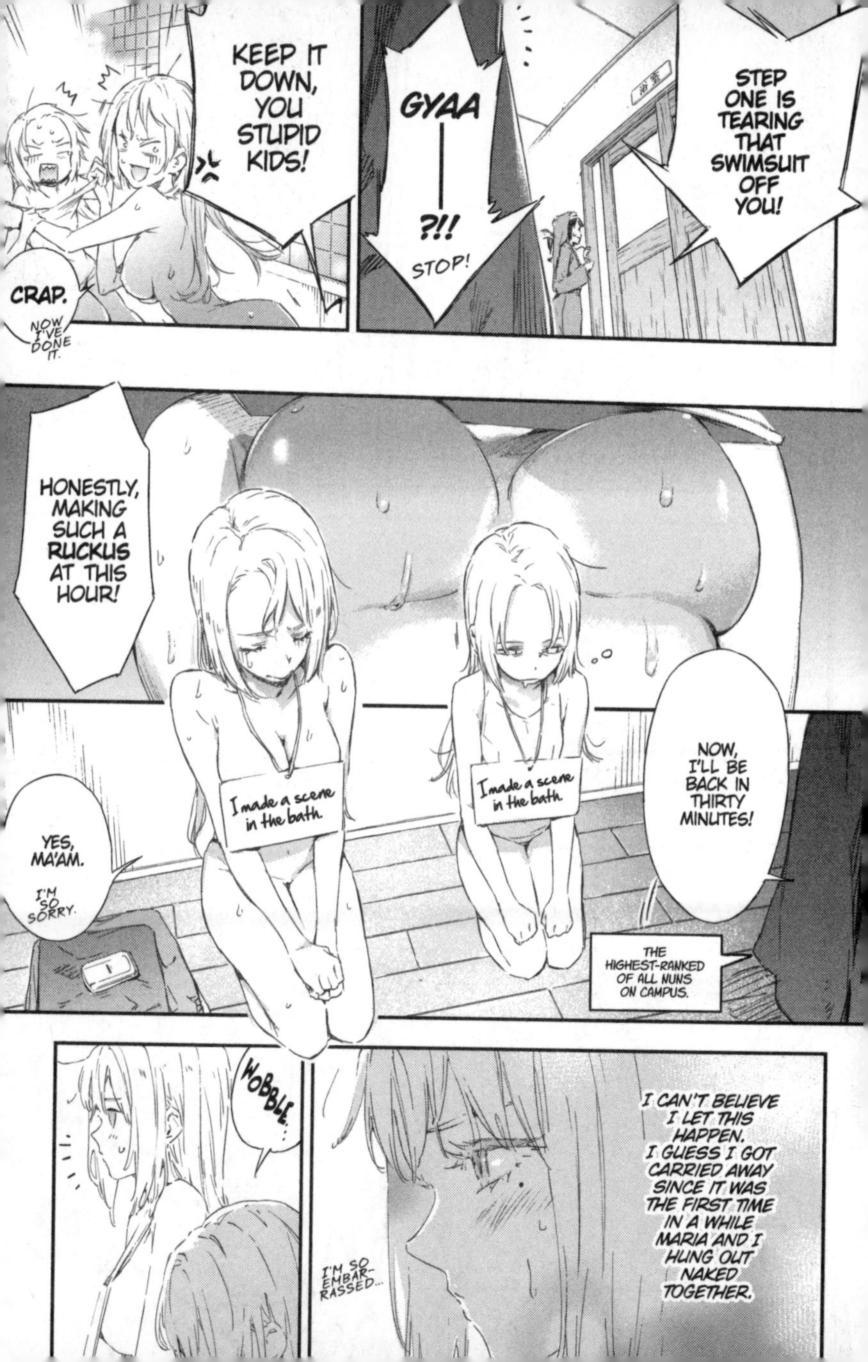
STEP ONE IS TEARING THAT SWIMSUIT OFF YOU!
GYAA—?!!
STOP!
KEEP IT DOWN, YOU STUPID KIDS!
CRAP.
NOW I'VE DONE IT.
HONESTLY, MAKING SUCH A RUCKUS AT THIS HOUR!
NOW, I'LL BE BACK IN THIRTY MINUTES!
THE HIGHEST-RANKED OF ALL NUNS ON CAMPUS.
I made a scene in the bath.
I made a scene in the bath.
YES, MA'AM.
I'M SO SORRY.
I CAN'T BELIEVE I LET THIS HAPPEN. I GUESS I GOT CARRIED AWAY SINCE IT WAS THE FIRST TIME IN A WHILE MARIA AND I HUNG OUT NAKED TOGETHER.
I'M SO EMBARRASSED...
WOBBLE...

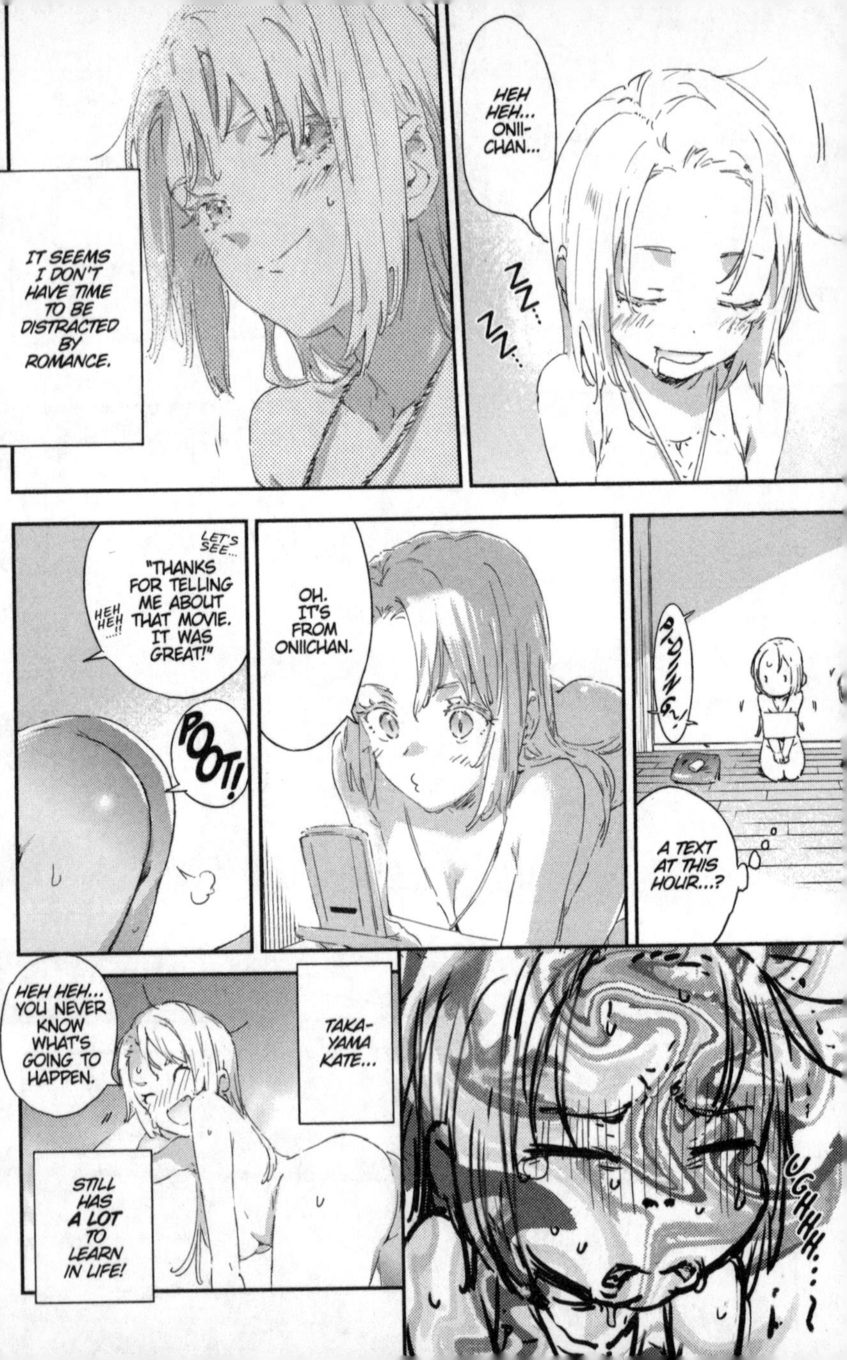
HEH HEH... ONII-CHAN...
ZZ... ZZ...
IT SEEMS I DON'T HAVE TIME TO BE DISTRACTED BY ROMANCE.
P-DING~!
A TEXT AT THIS HOUR...?
OH. IT'S FROM ONIICHAN.
LET'S SEE...
"THANKS FOR TELLING ME ABOUT THAT MOVIE. IT WAS GREAT!"
HEH HEH ...!!
POOT!!
UGHHH...~
TAKA-YAMA KATE...
HEH HEH... YOU NEVER KNOW WHAT'S GOING TO HAPPEN.
STILL HAS A LOT TO LEARN IN LIFE!

I don't have many friends

Haganai I don't have many friends

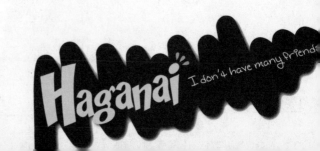

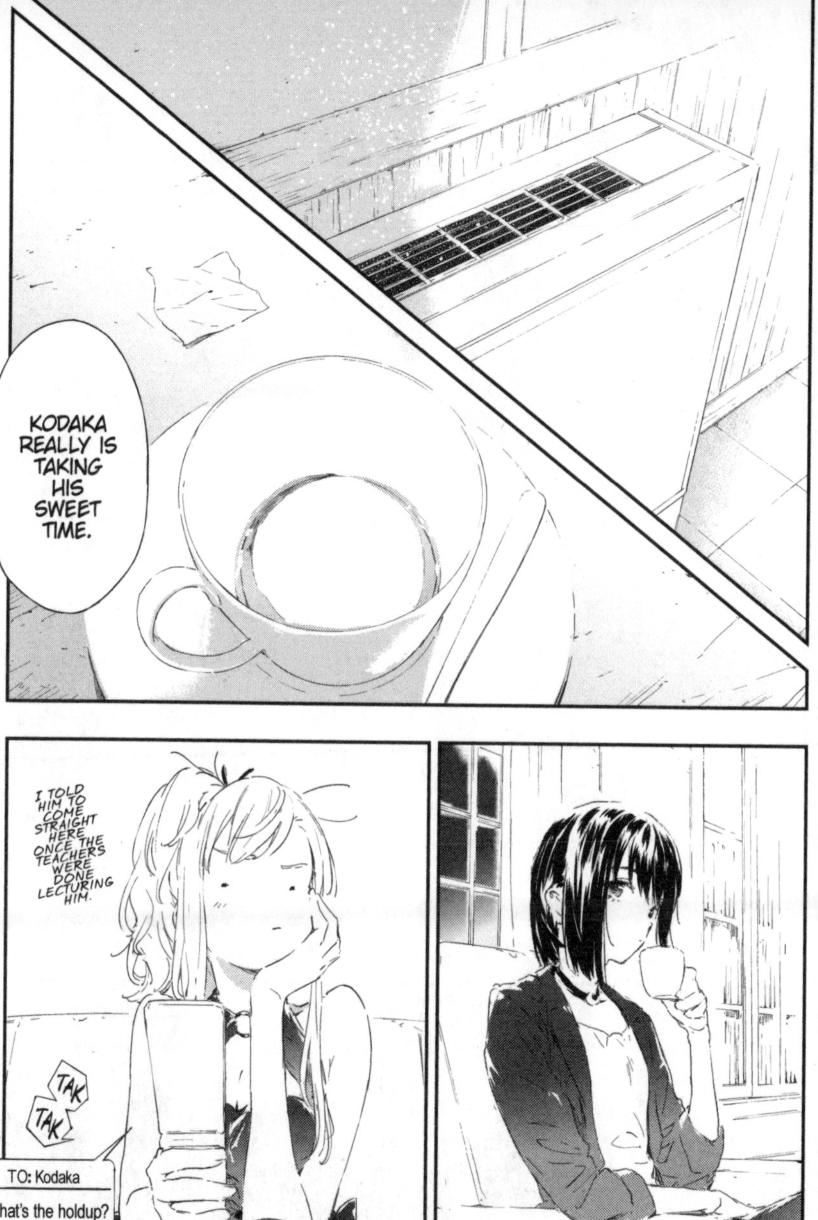
KODAKA REALLY IS TAKING HIS SWEET TIME.
I TOLD HIM TO COME STRAIGHT HERE ONCE THE TEACHERS WERE DONE LECTURING HIM.
TAK TAK
TO: Kodaka
What's the holdup?

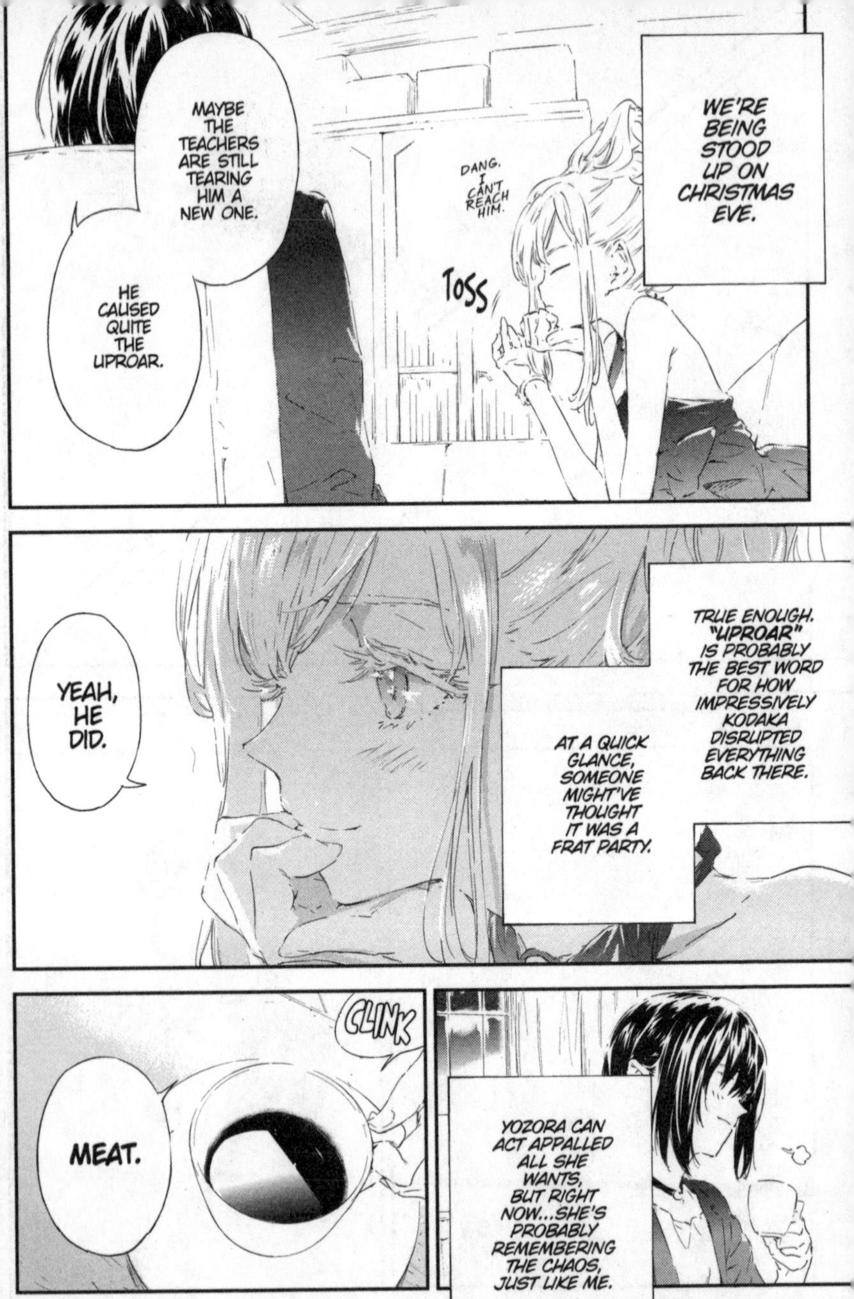
WE'RE BEING STOOD UP ON CHRISTMAS EVE.
DANG. I CAN'T REACH HIM.
TOSS
MAYBE THE TEACHERS ARE STILL TEARING HIM A NEW ONE.
HE CAUSED QUITE THE UPROAR.
TRUE ENOUGH. "UPROAR" IS PROBABLY THE BEST WORD FOR HOW IMPRESSIVELY KODAKA DISRUPTED EVERYTHING BACK THERE.
AT A QUICK GLANCE, SOMEONE MIGHT'VE THOUGHT IT WAS A FRAT PARTY.
YEAH, HE DID.
YOZORA CAN ACT APPALLED ALL SHE WANTS, BUT RIGHT NOW...SHE'S PROBABLY REMEMBERING THE CHAOS, JUST LIKE ME.
CLINK
MEAT.

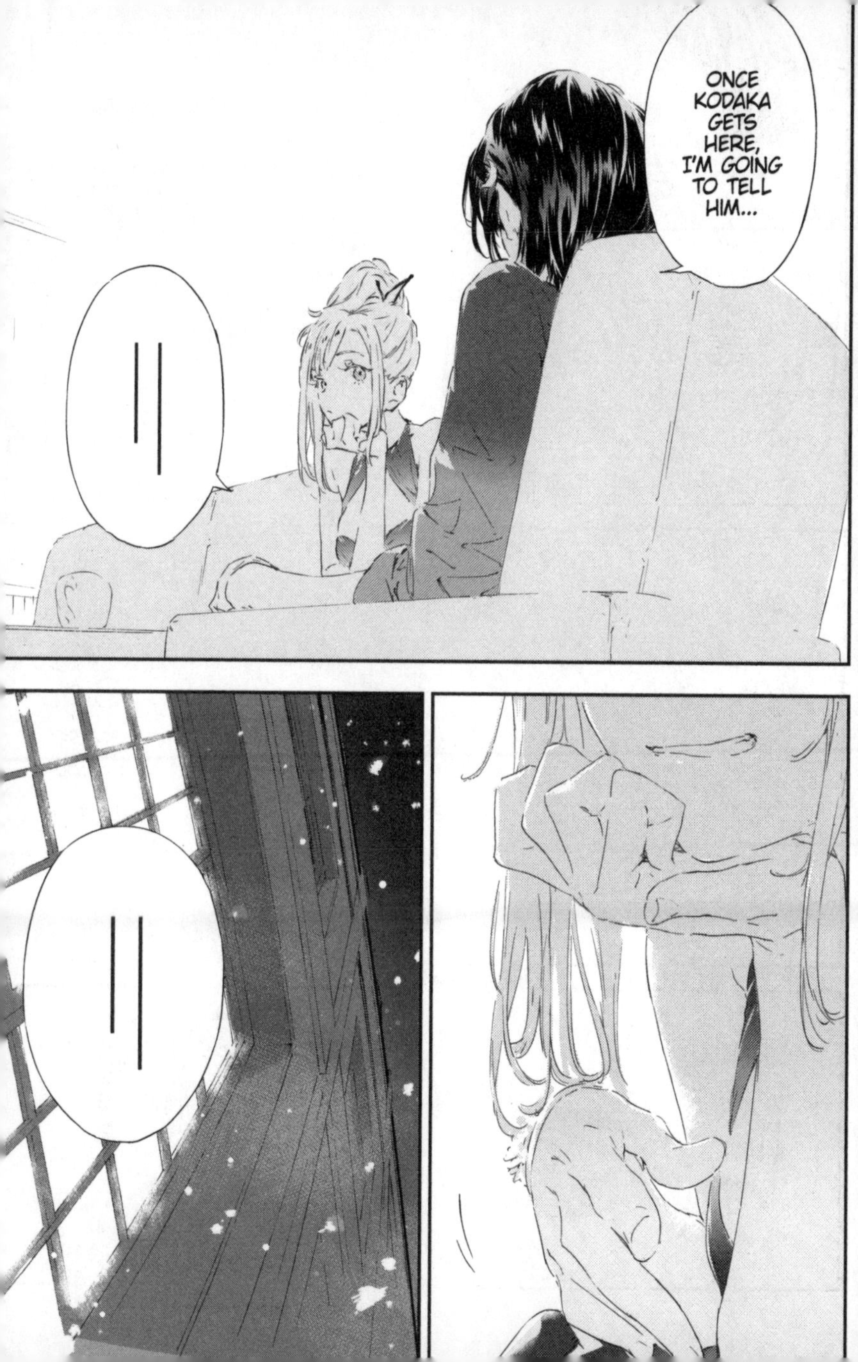
ONCE KODAKA GETS HERE, I'M GOING TO TELL HIM...

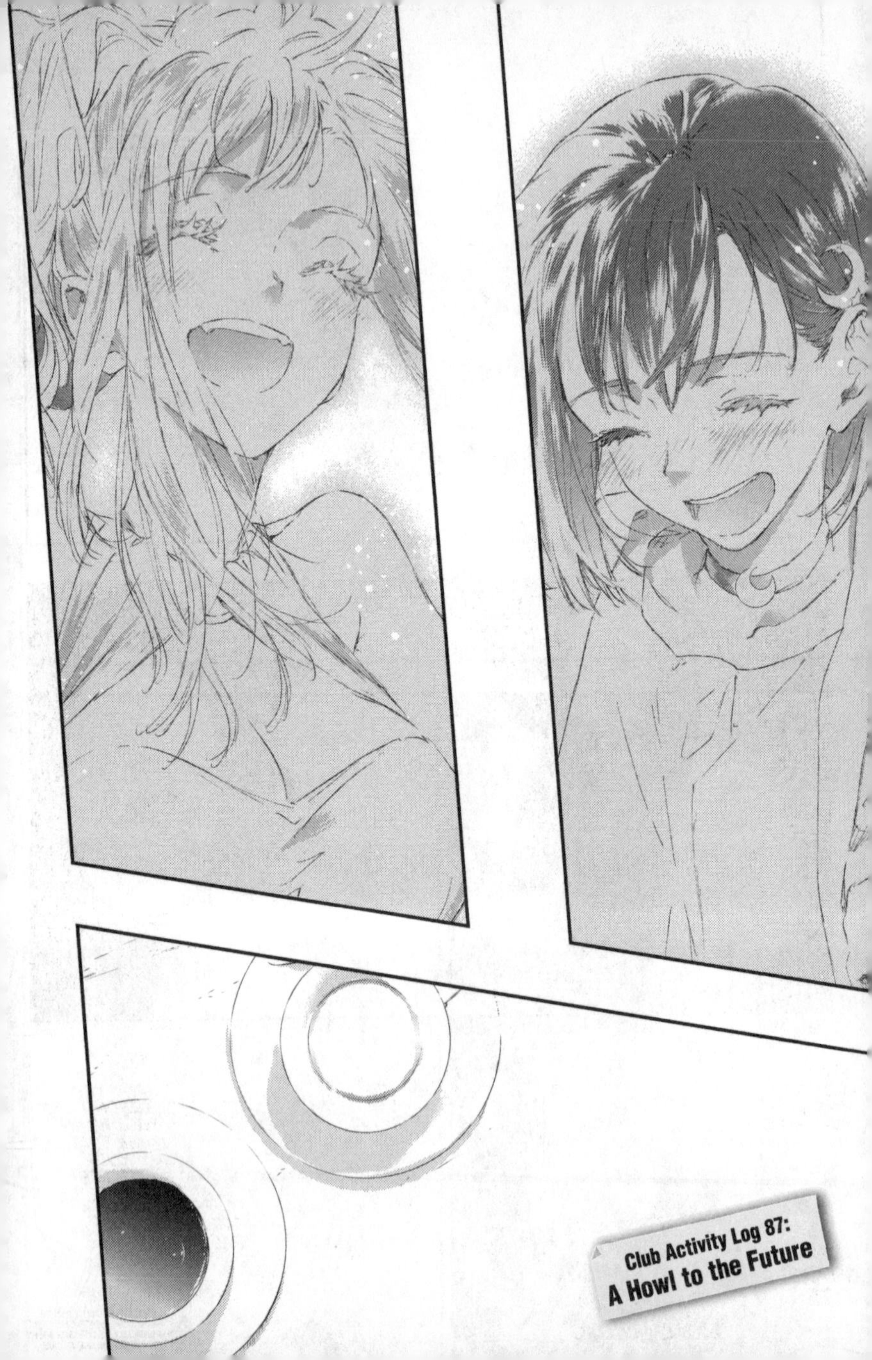
Club Activity Log 87:
A Howl to the Future

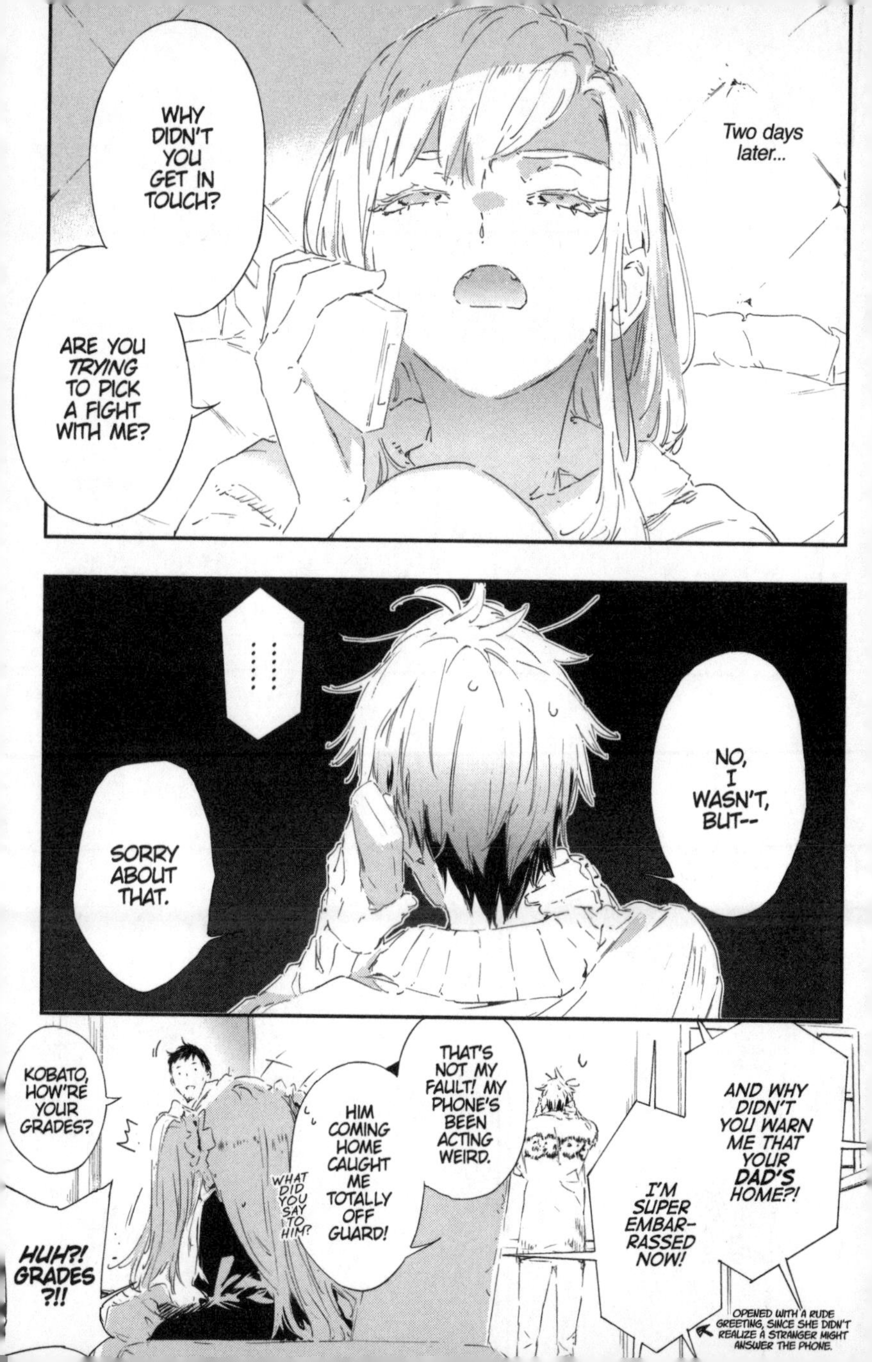
Two days later...
WHY DIDN'T YOU GET IN TOUCH?
ARE YOU *TRYING* TO PICK A FIGHT WITH ME?
......
NO, I WASN'T, BUT--
SORRY ABOUT THAT.
AND WHY DIDN'T YOU WARN ME THAT YOUR **DAD'S** HOME?!
I'M SUPER EMBARRASSED NOW!
OPENED WITH A RUDE GREETING, SINCE SHE DIDN'T REALIZE A STRANGER MIGHT ANSWER THE PHONE.
THAT'S NOT MY FAULT! MY PHONE'S BEEN ACTING WEIRD.
HIM COMING HOME CAUGHT ME TOTALLY OFF GUARD!
WHAT DID YOU SAY TO HIM?
KOBATO, HOW'RE YOUR GRADES?
HUH?! GRADES ?!!

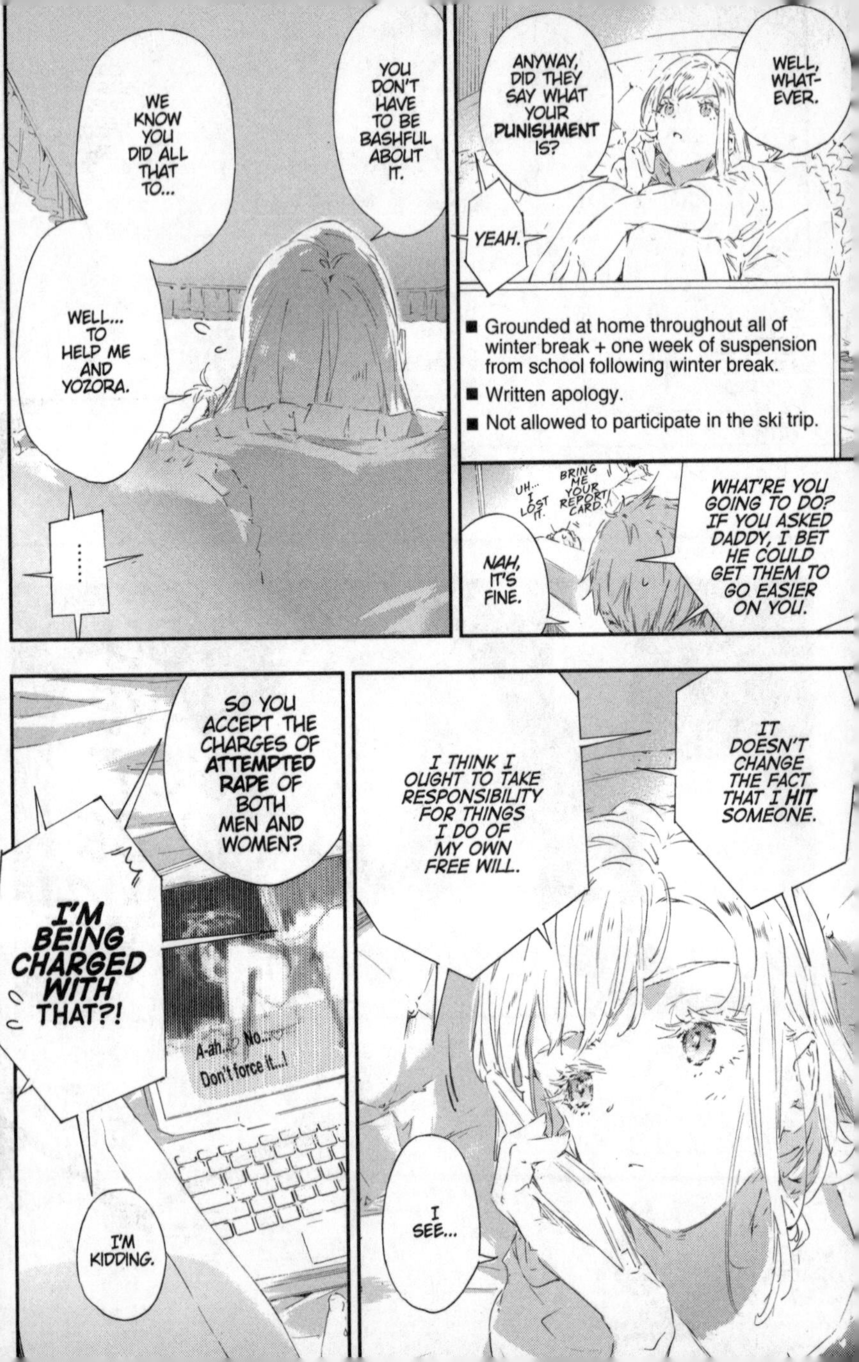
WELL, WHAT-EVER.
ANYWAY, DID THEY SAY WHAT YOUR PUNISHMENT IS?
YEAH.
■ Grounded at home throughout all of winter break + one week of suspension from school following winter break.
■ Written apology.
■ Not allowed to participate in the ski trip.
WHAT'RE YOU GOING TO DO? IF YOU ASKED DADDY, I BET HE COULD GET THEM TO GO EASIER ON YOU.
BRING ME YOUR REPORT CARD.
UH... I LOST IT.
NAH, IT'S FINE.
YOU DON'T HAVE TO BE BASHFUL ABOUT IT.
WE KNOW YOU DID ALL THAT TO...
WELL... TO HELP ME AND YOZORA.
......
IT DOESN'T CHANGE THE FACT THAT I HIT SOMEONE.
I THINK I OUGHT TO TAKE RESPONSIBILITY FOR THINGS I DO OF MY OWN FREE WILL.
I SEE...
SO YOU ACCEPT THE CHARGES OF ATTEMPTED RAPE OF BOTH MEN AND WOMEN?
I'M BEING CHARGED WITH THAT?!
A-ah... No...
Don't force it...!
I'M KIDDING.

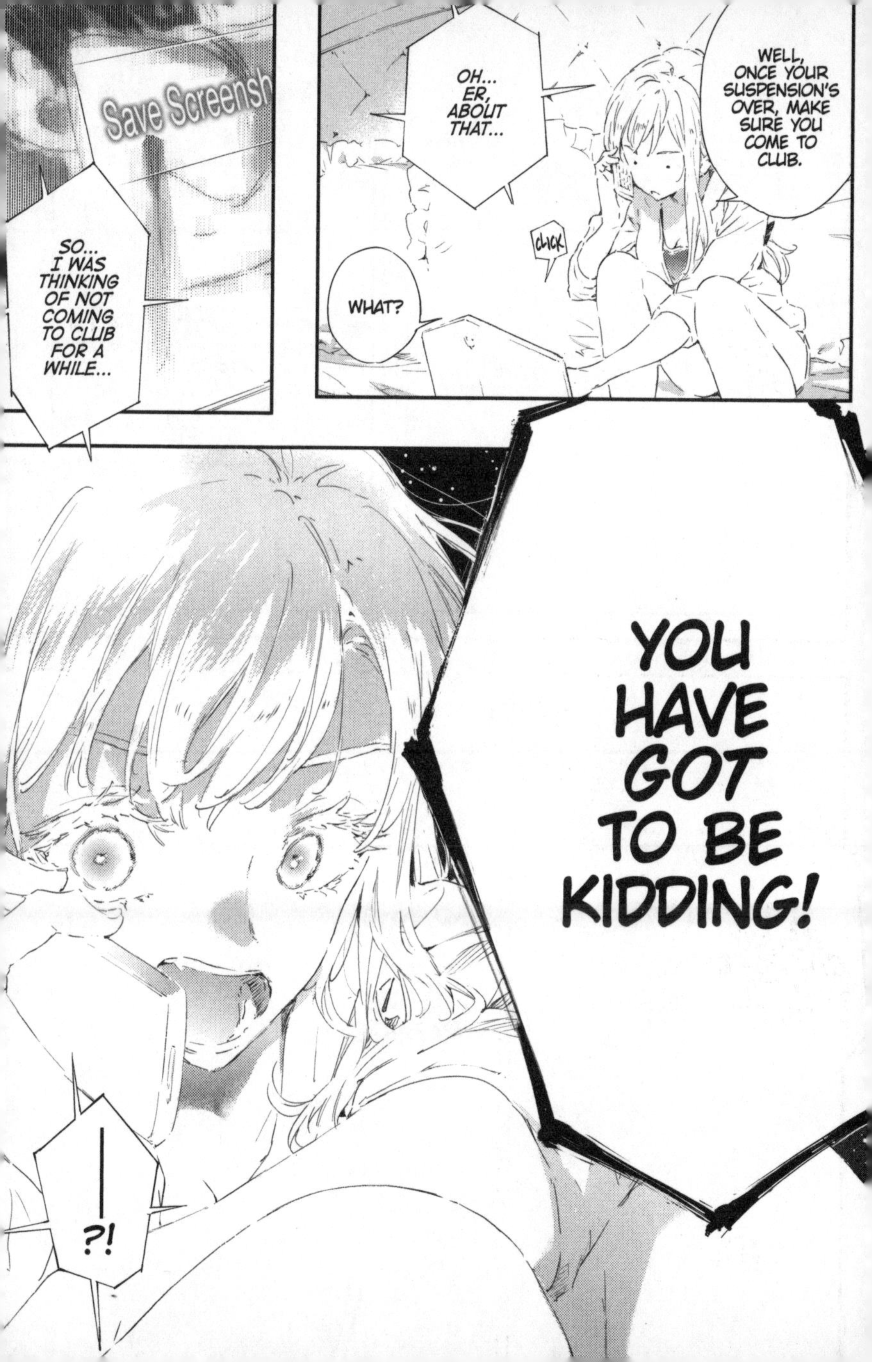
WELL, ONCE YOUR SUSPENSION'S OVER, MAKE SURE YOU COME TO CLUB.
OH... ER, ABOUT THAT...
CLICK
WHAT?
Save Screensh
SO... I WAS THINKING OF NOT COMING TO CLUB FOR A WHILE...
YOU HAVE GOT TO BE KIDDING!
—?!

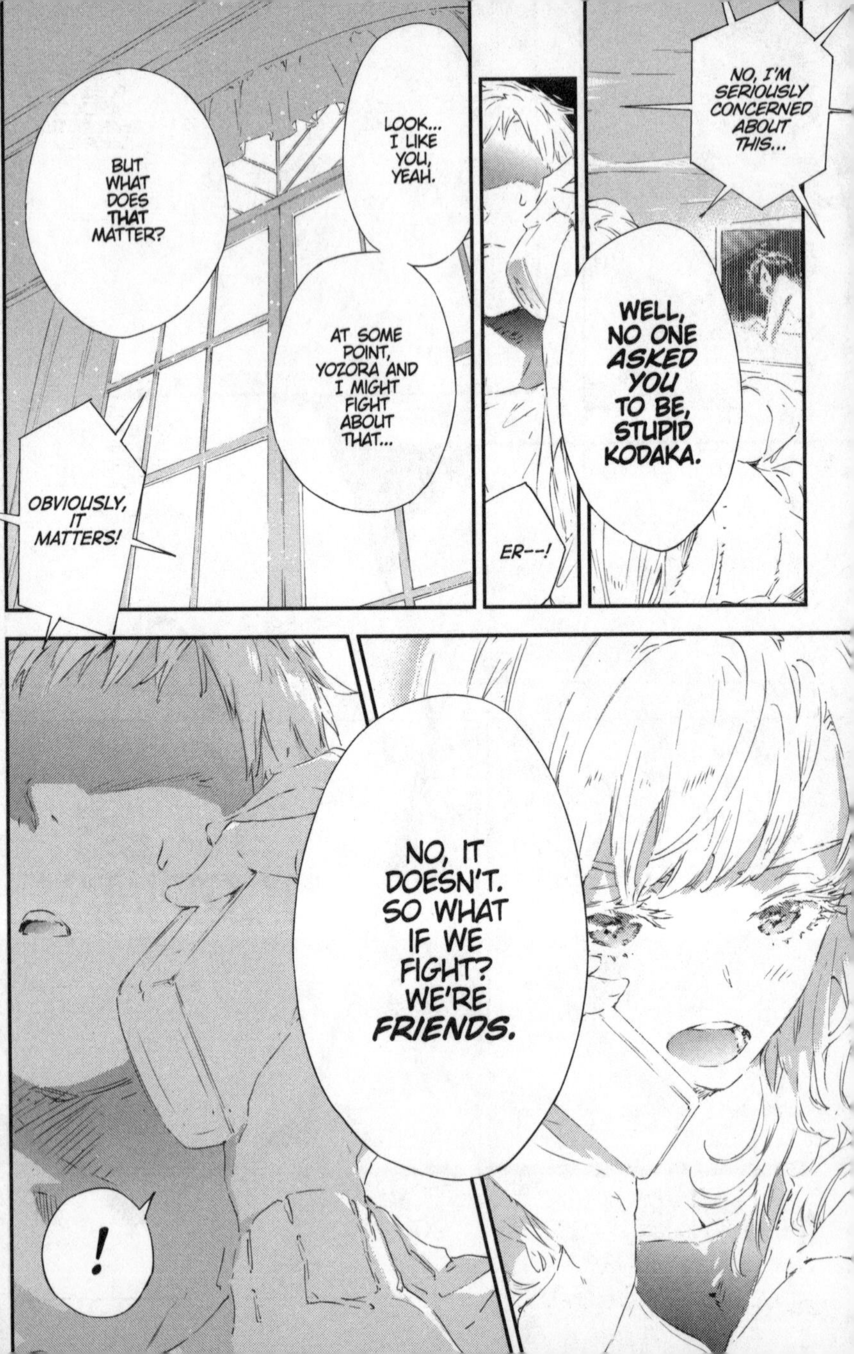
NO, I'M SERIOUSLY CONCERNED ABOUT THIS...
WELL, NO ONE ASKED YOU TO BE, STUPID KODAKA.
ER--!
LOOK... I LIKE YOU, YEAH.
BUT WHAT DOES THAT MATTER?
AT SOME POINT, YOZORA AND I MIGHT FIGHT ABOUT THAT...
OBVIOUSLY, IT MATTERS!
NO, IT DOESN'T. SO WHAT IF WE FIGHT? WE'RE FRIENDS.
!

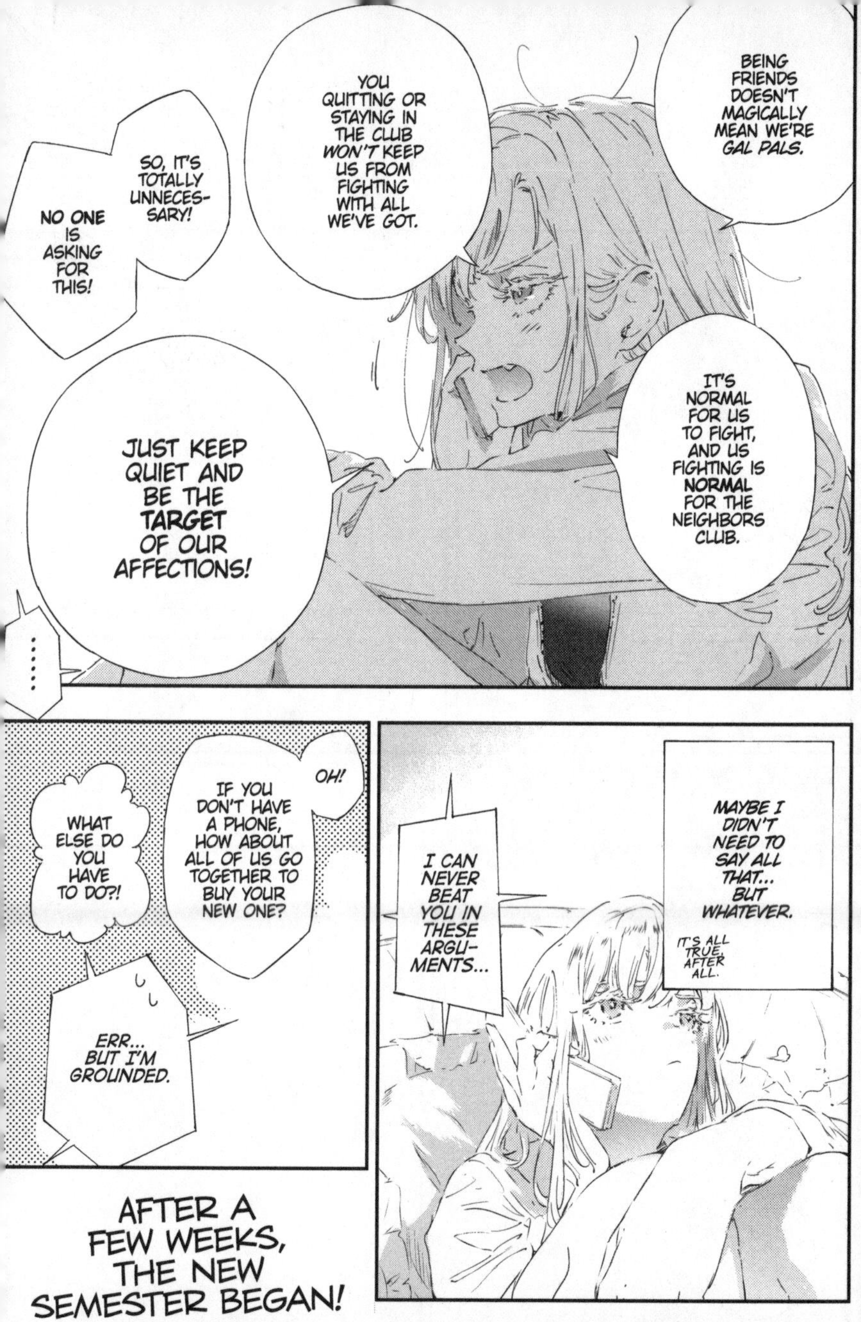
BEING FRIENDS DOESN'T MAGICALLY MEAN WE'RE GAL PALS.
YOU QUITTING OR STAYING IN THE CLUB WON'T KEEP US FROM FIGHTING WITH ALL WE'VE GOT.
SO, IT'S TOTALLY UNNECES-SARY!
NO ONE IS ASKING FOR THIS!
IT'S NORMAL FOR US TO FIGHT, AND US FIGHTING IS NORMAL FOR THE NEIGHBORS CLUB.
JUST KEEP QUIET AND BE THE TARGET OF OUR AFFECTIONS!
......
MAYBE I DIDN'T NEED TO SAY ALL THAT... BUT WHATEVER.
IT'S ALL TRUE, AFTER ALL.
I CAN NEVER BEAT YOU IN THESE ARGU-MENTS...
OH!
IF YOU DON'T HAVE A PHONE, HOW ABOUT ALL OF US GO TOGETHER TO BUY YOUR NEW ONE?
WHAT ELSE DO YOU HAVE TO DO?!
ERR... BUT I'M GROUNDED.
AFTER A FEW WEEKS, THE NEW SEMESTER BEGAN!

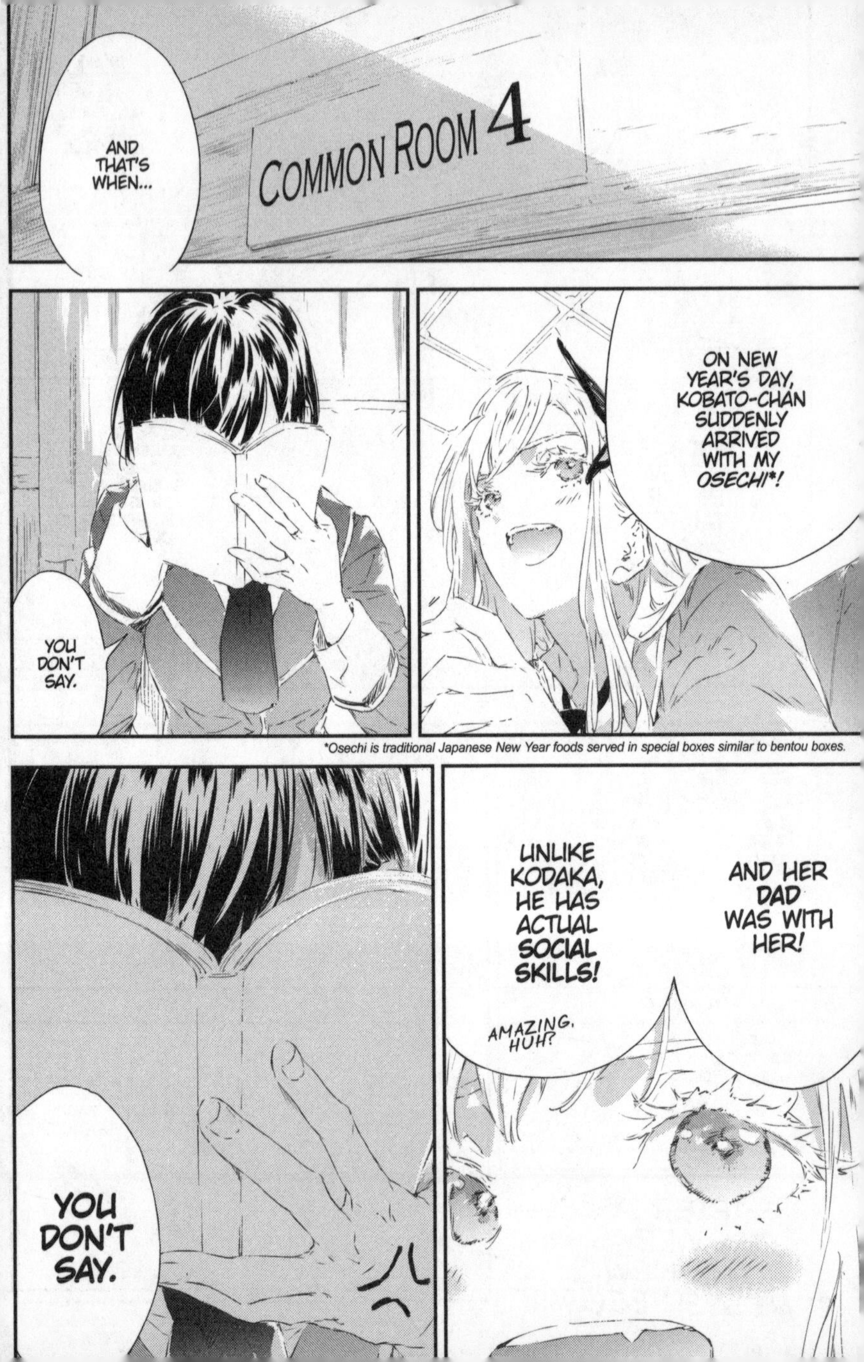
COMMON ROOM 4
AND THAT'S WHEN...
ON NEW YEAR'S DAY, KOBATO-CHAN SUDDENLY ARRIVED WITH MY *OSECHI**!
YOU DON'T SAY.
AND HER DAD WAS WITH HER!
UNLIKE KODAKA, HE HAS ACTUAL SOCIAL SKILLS!
AMAZING, HUH?
YOU DON'T SAY.

**Osechi is traditional Japanese New Year foods served in special boxes similar to bentou boxes.*

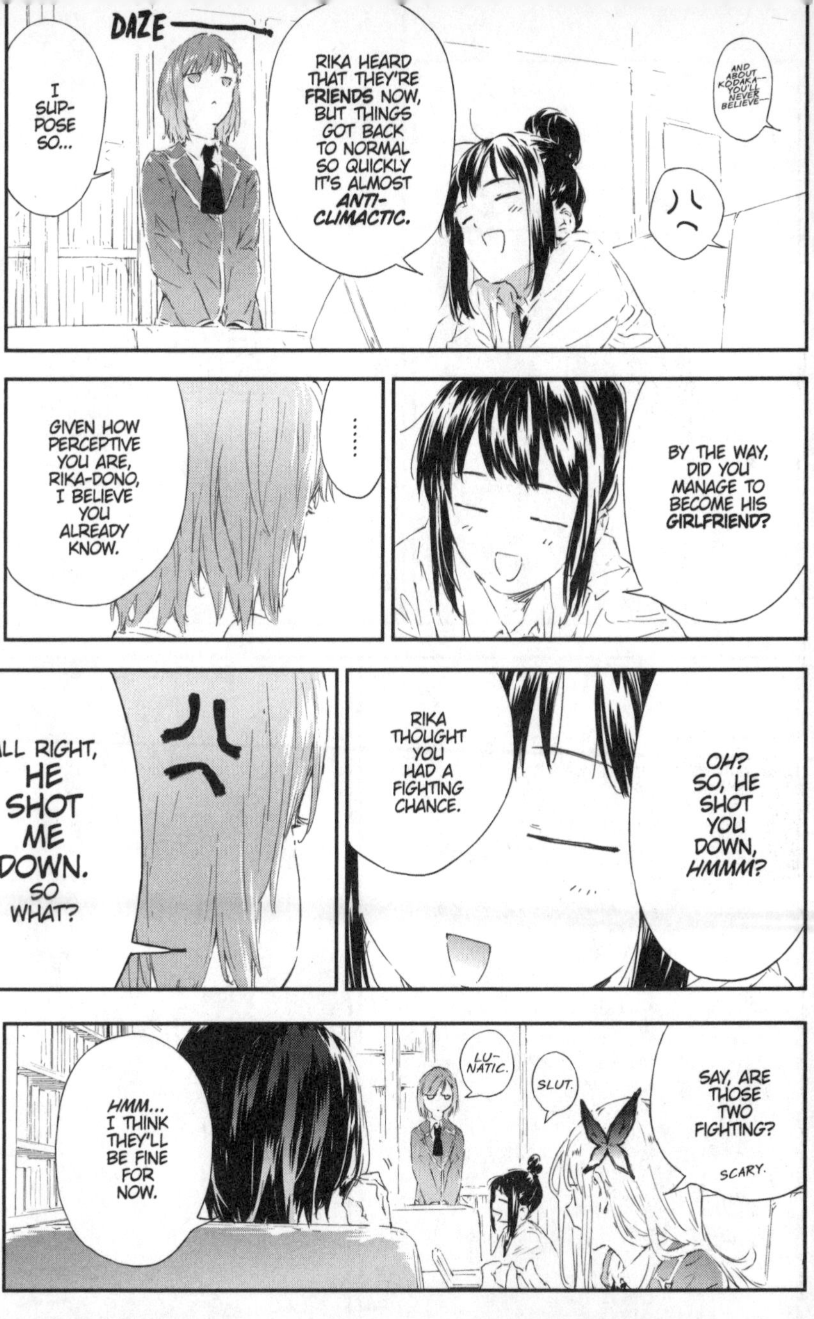
AND ABOUT KODAKA—YOU'LL NEVER BELIEVE—
RIKA HEARD THAT THEY'RE FRIENDS NOW, BUT THINGS GOT BACK TO NORMAL SO QUICKLY IT'S ALMOST ANTI-CLIMACTIC.
DAZE
I SUP-POSE SO...
BY THE WAY, DID YOU MANAGE TO BECOME HIS GIRLFRIEND?
......
GIVEN HOW PERCEPTIVE YOU ARE, RIKA-DONO, I BELIEVE YOU ALREADY KNOW.
OH? SO, HE SHOT YOU DOWN, HMMM?
RIKA THOUGHT YOU HAD A FIGHTING CHANCE.
ALL RIGHT, HE SHOT ME DOWN. SO WHAT?
SAY, ARE THOSE TWO FIGHTING?
SCARY.
SLUT.
LU-NATIC.
HMM... I THINK THEY'LL BE FINE FOR NOW.

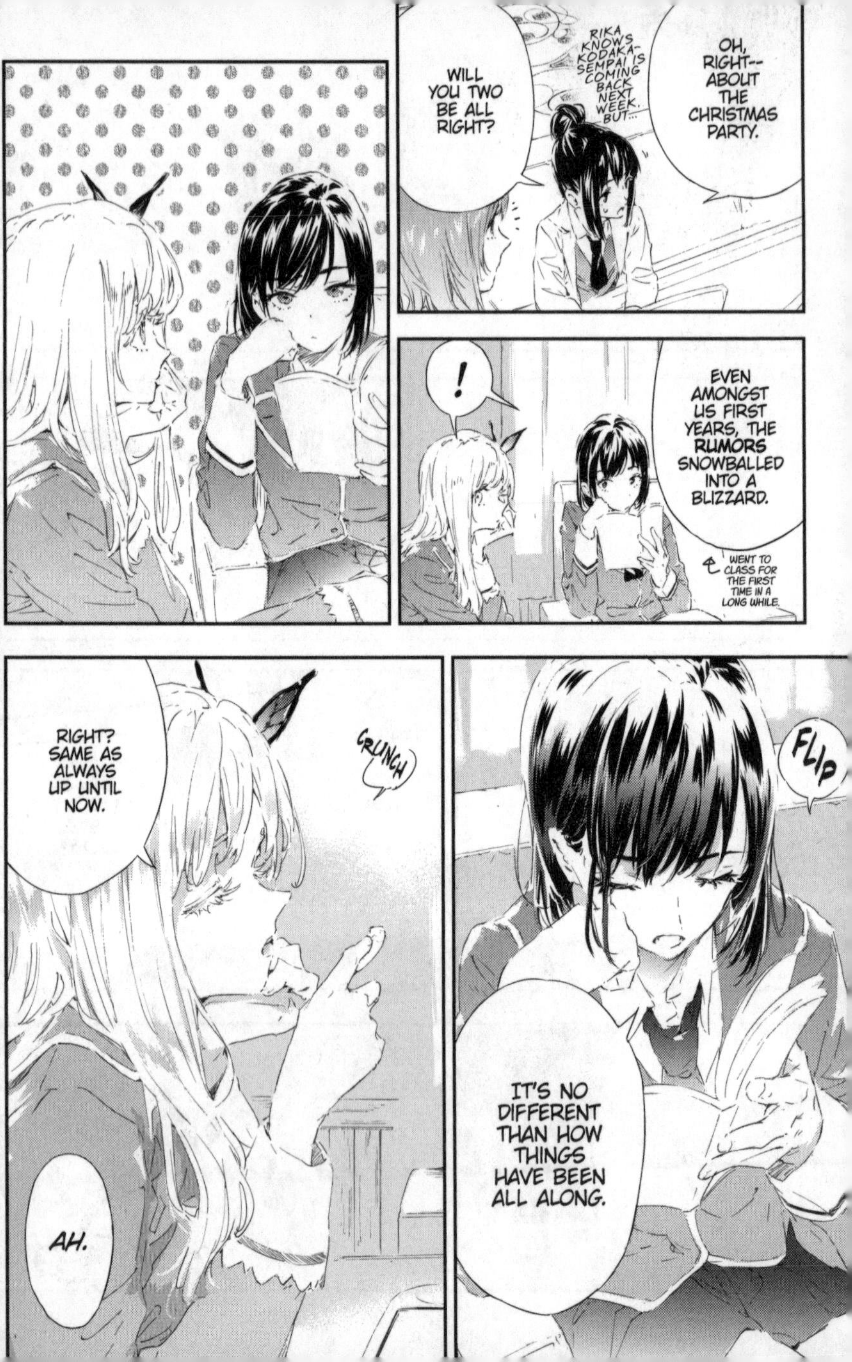
OH, RIGHT-- ABOUT THE CHRISTMAS PARTY.
RIKA KNOWS KODAKA-SEMPAI IS COMING BACK NEXT WEEK, BUT...
WILL YOU TWO BE ALL RIGHT?
EVEN AMONGST US FIRST YEARS, THE RUMORS SNOWBALLED INTO A BLIZZARD.
WENT TO CLASS FOR THE FIRST TIME IN A LONG WHILE.
!
FLIP
IT'S NO DIFFERENT THAN HOW THINGS HAVE BEEN ALL ALONG.
RIGHT? SAME AS ALWAYS UP UNTIL NOW.
CRUNCH
AH.

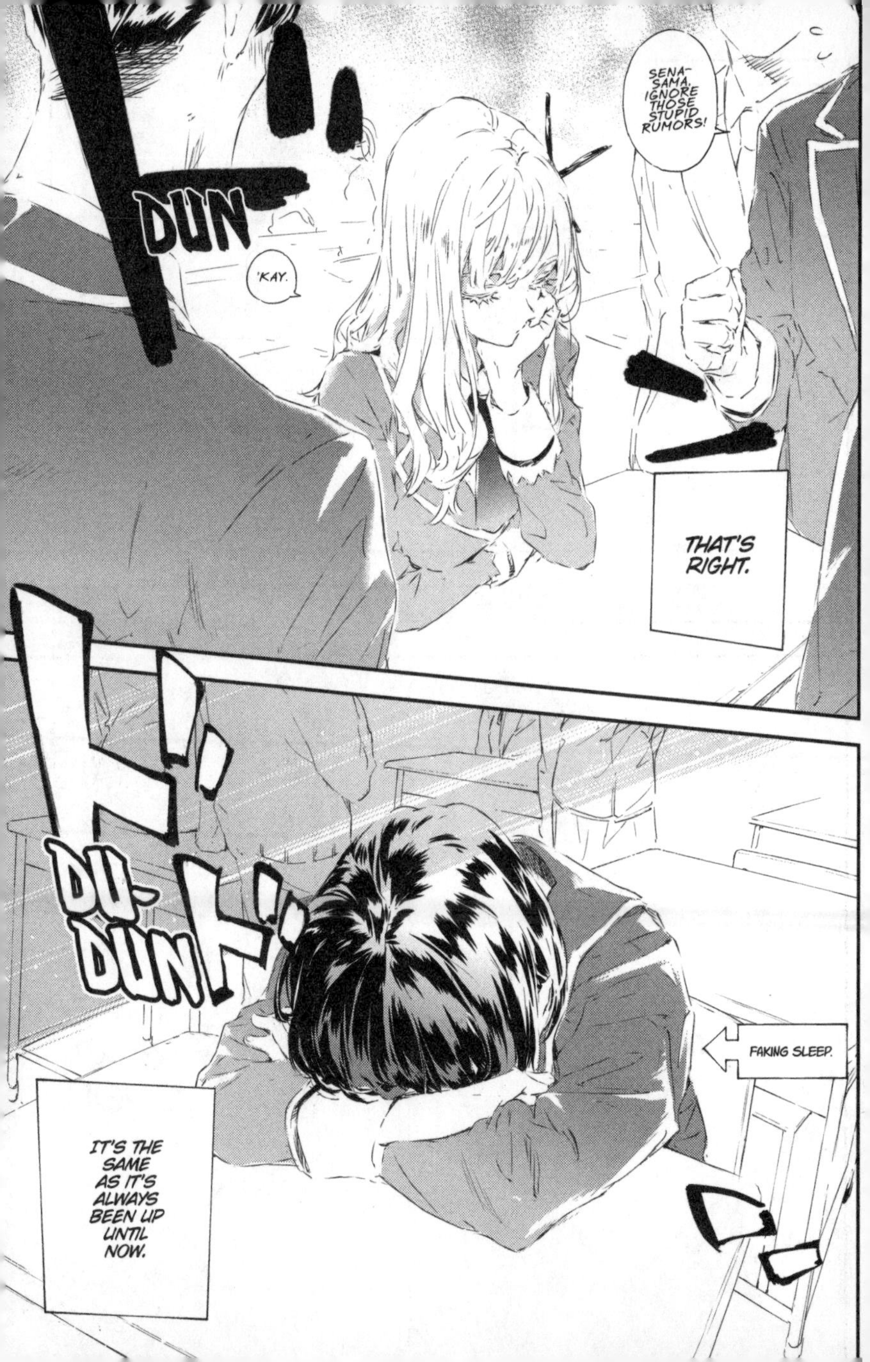
SENA-SAMA, IGNORE THOSE STUPID RUMORS!
DUN
'KAY.
THAT'S RIGHT.
FAKING SLEEP.
DU-DUN
IT'S THE SAME AS IT'S ALWAYS BEEN UP UNTIL NOW.

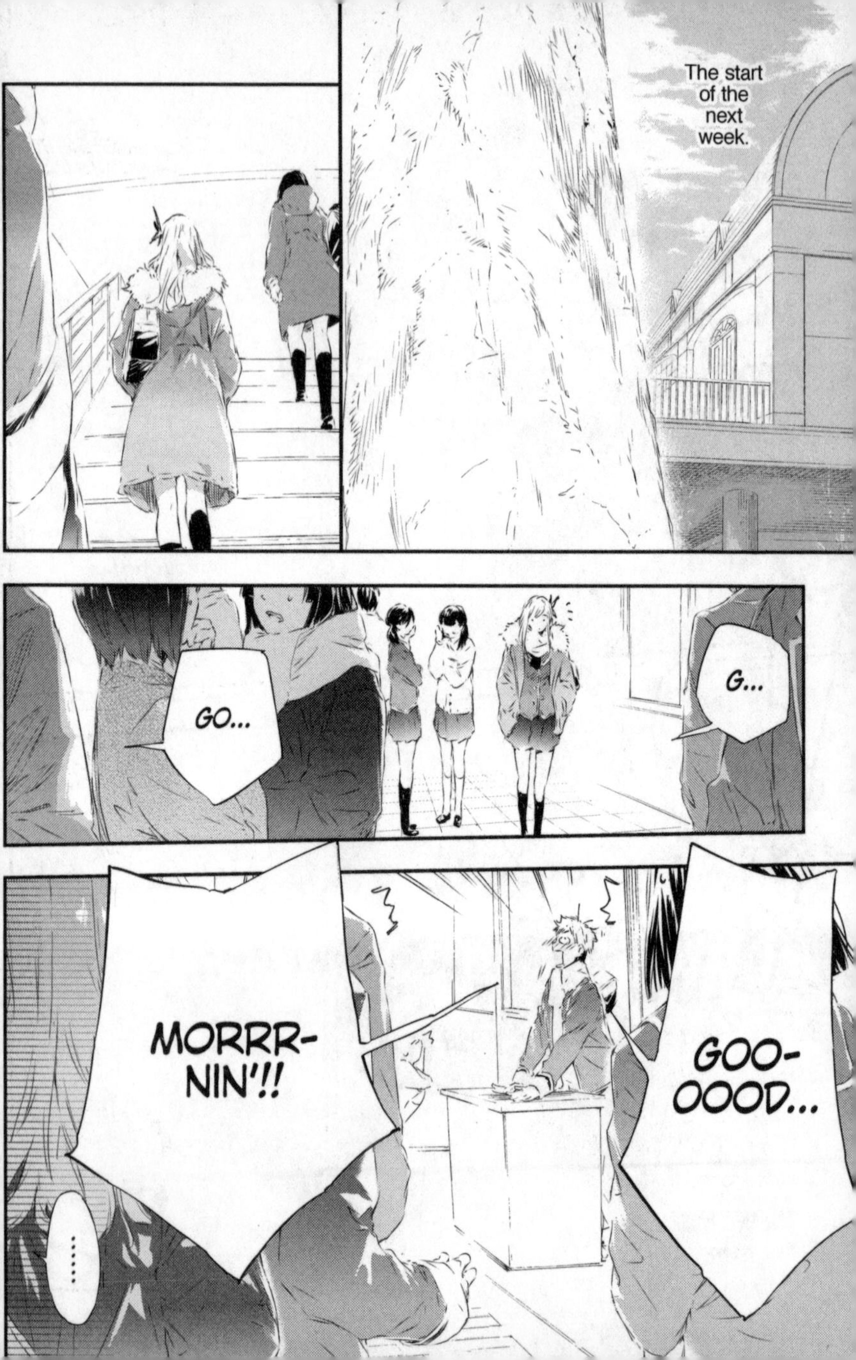
The start of the next week.
G...
GO...
GOO-OOOD...
MORRR-NIN'!!
......

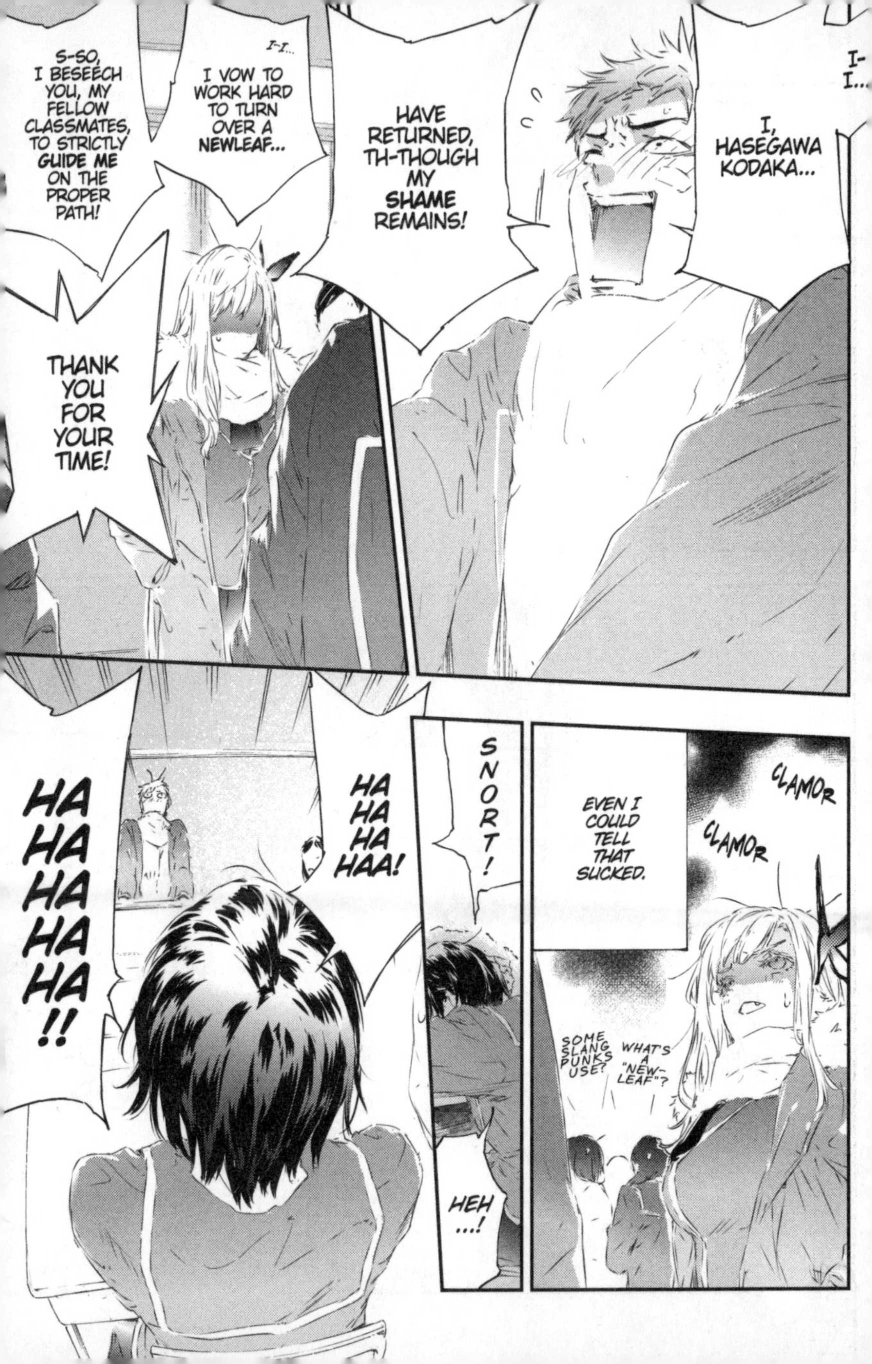
I- I...
I, HASEGAWA KODAKA...
HAVE RETURNED, TH-THOUGH MY SHAME REMAINS!
I-I...
I VOW TO WORK HARD TO TURN OVER A NEWLEAF...
S-SO, I BESEECH YOU, MY FELLOW CLASSMATES, TO STRICTLY GUIDE ME ON THE PROPER PATH!
THANK YOU FOR YOUR TIME!
EVEN I COULD TELL THAT SUCKED.
CLAMOR
CLAMOR
WHAT'S A "NEW-LEAF"?
SOME SLANG PUNKS USE?
SNORT!
HEH ...!
HA HA HA HAA!
HA HA HA HA HA HA!!

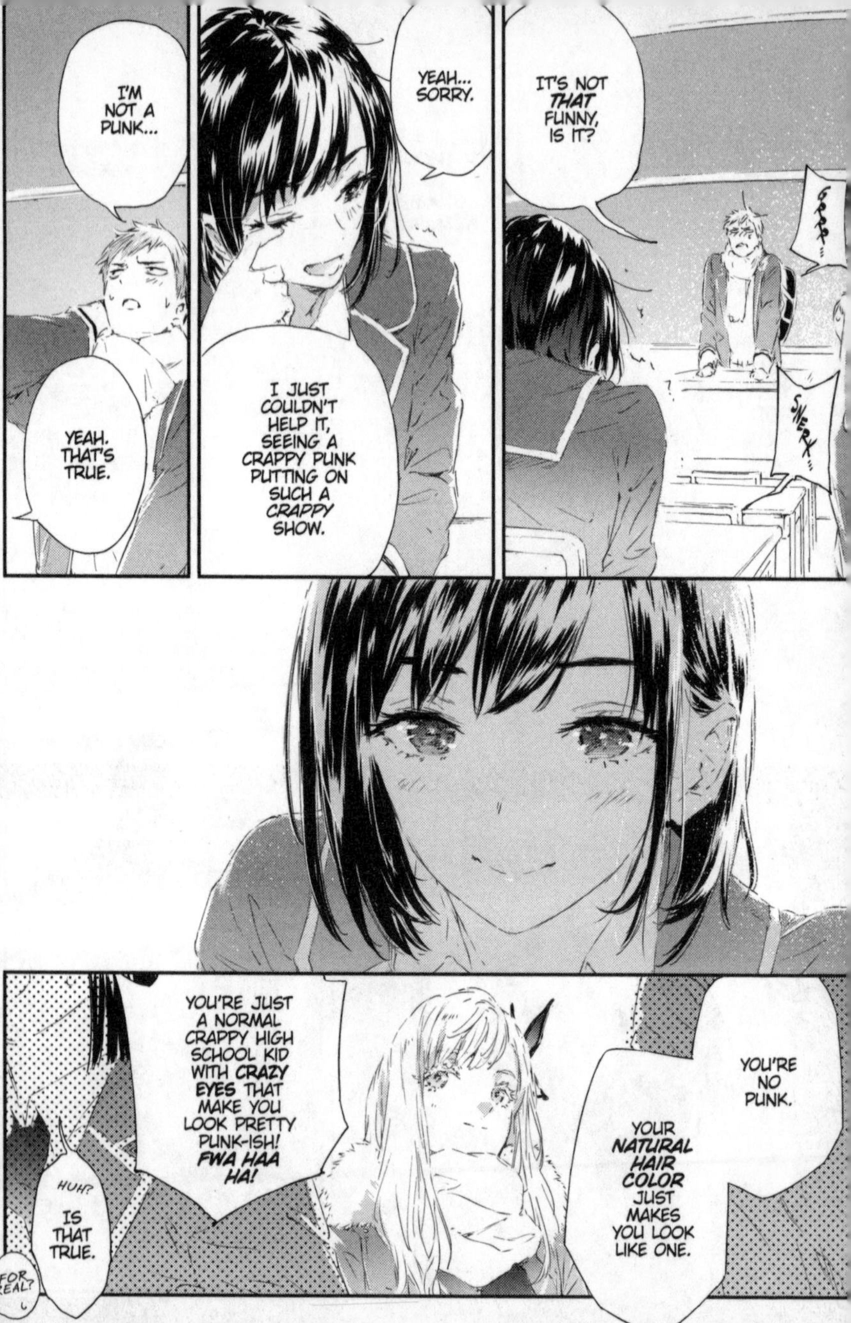
IT'S NOT THAT FUNNY, IS IT?
GRRR...
SNERK...
YEAH... SORRY.
I JUST COULDN'T HELP IT, SEEING A CRAPPY PUNK PUTTING ON SUCH A CRAPPY SHOW.
I'M NOT A PUNK...
YEAH. THAT'S TRUE.
YOU'RE NO PUNK.
YOUR NATURAL HAIR COLOR JUST MAKES YOU LOOK LIKE ONE.
YOU'RE JUST A NORMAL CRAPPY HIGH SCHOOL KID WITH CRAZY EYES THAT MAKE YOU LOOK PRETTY PUNK-ISH! FWA HAA HA!
HUH?
IS THAT TRUE.
FOR REAL?

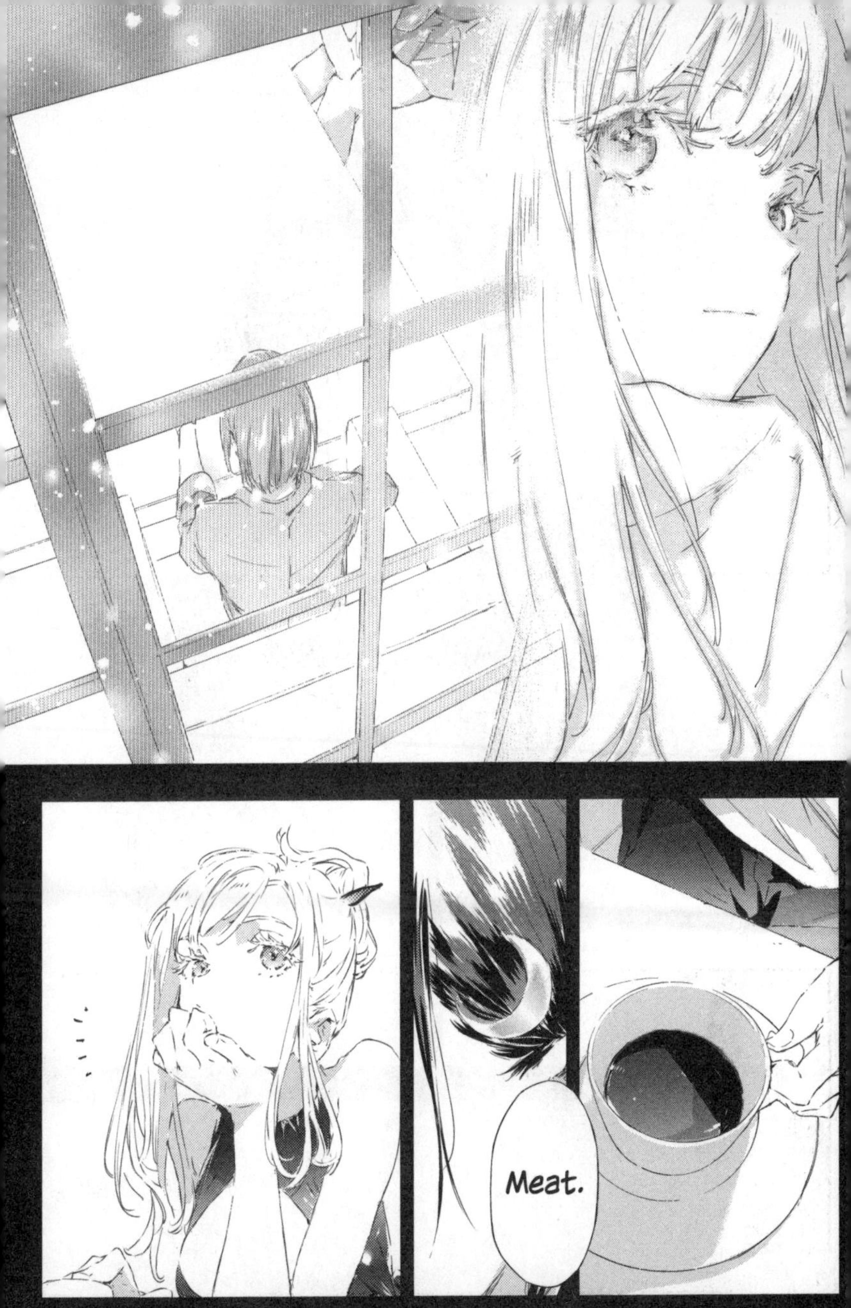
Meat.

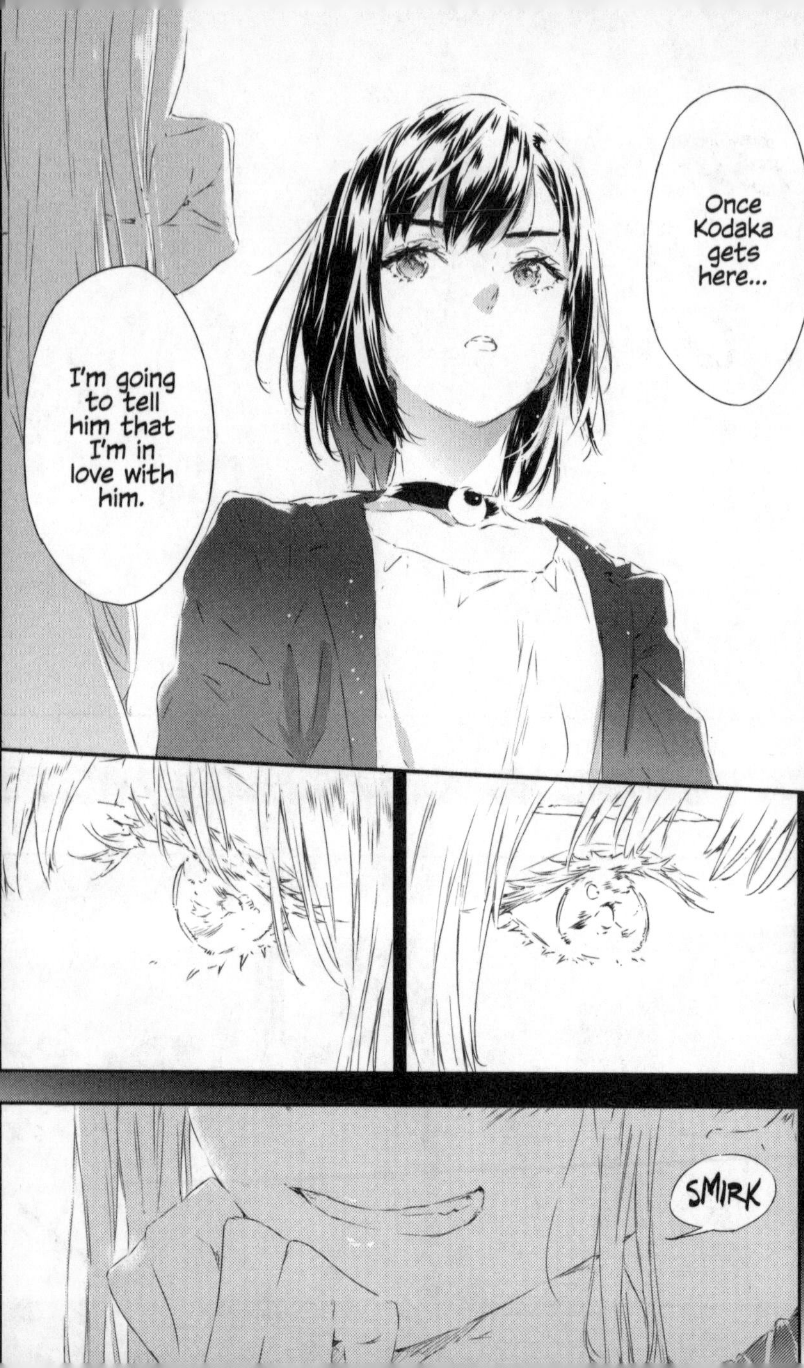
Once Kodaka gets here...
I'm going to tell him that I'm in love with him.
SMIRK

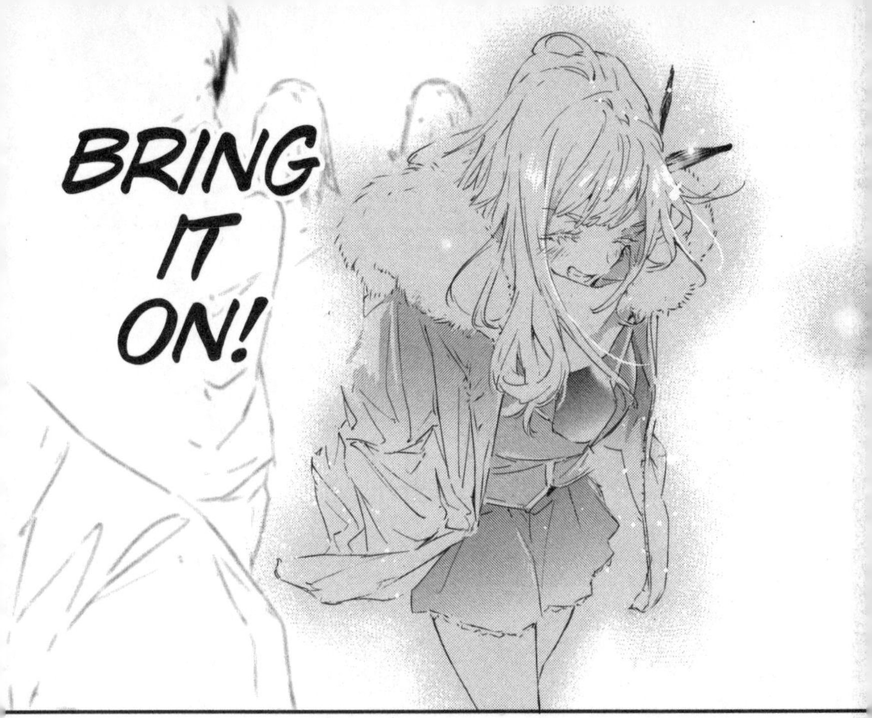
BRING IT ON!

I'M SURE WE'LL KEEP ON ARGUING AS TIME GOES ON.

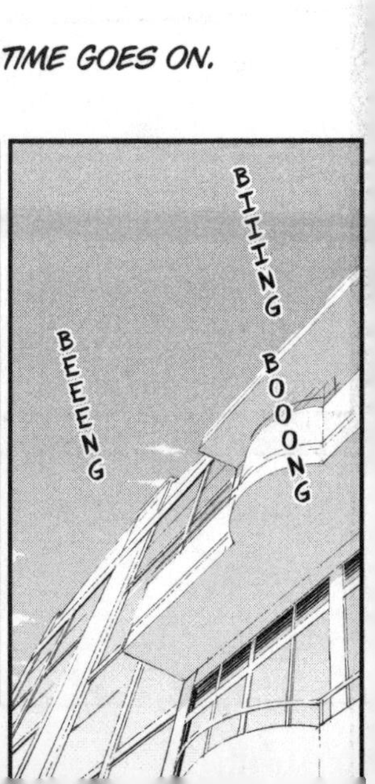
BIIING
BOOONG
BEEENG

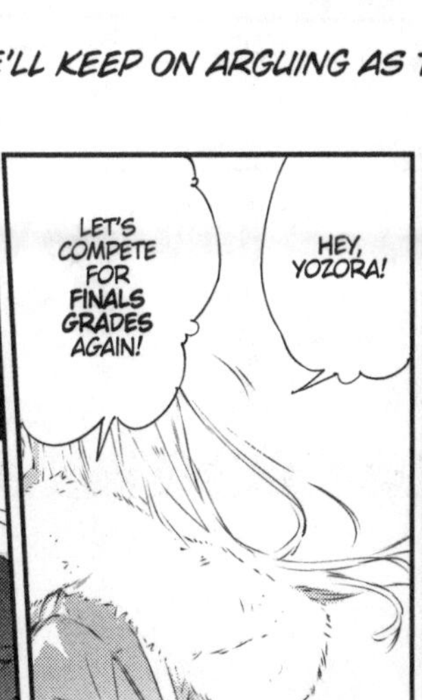
HEY, YOZORA!
LET'S COMPETE FOR FINALS GRADES AGAIN!

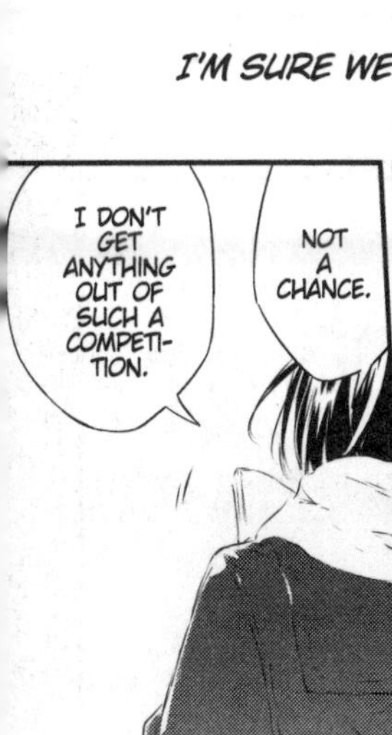
NOT A CHANCE.
I DON'T GET ANYTHING OUT OF SUCH A COMPETITION.

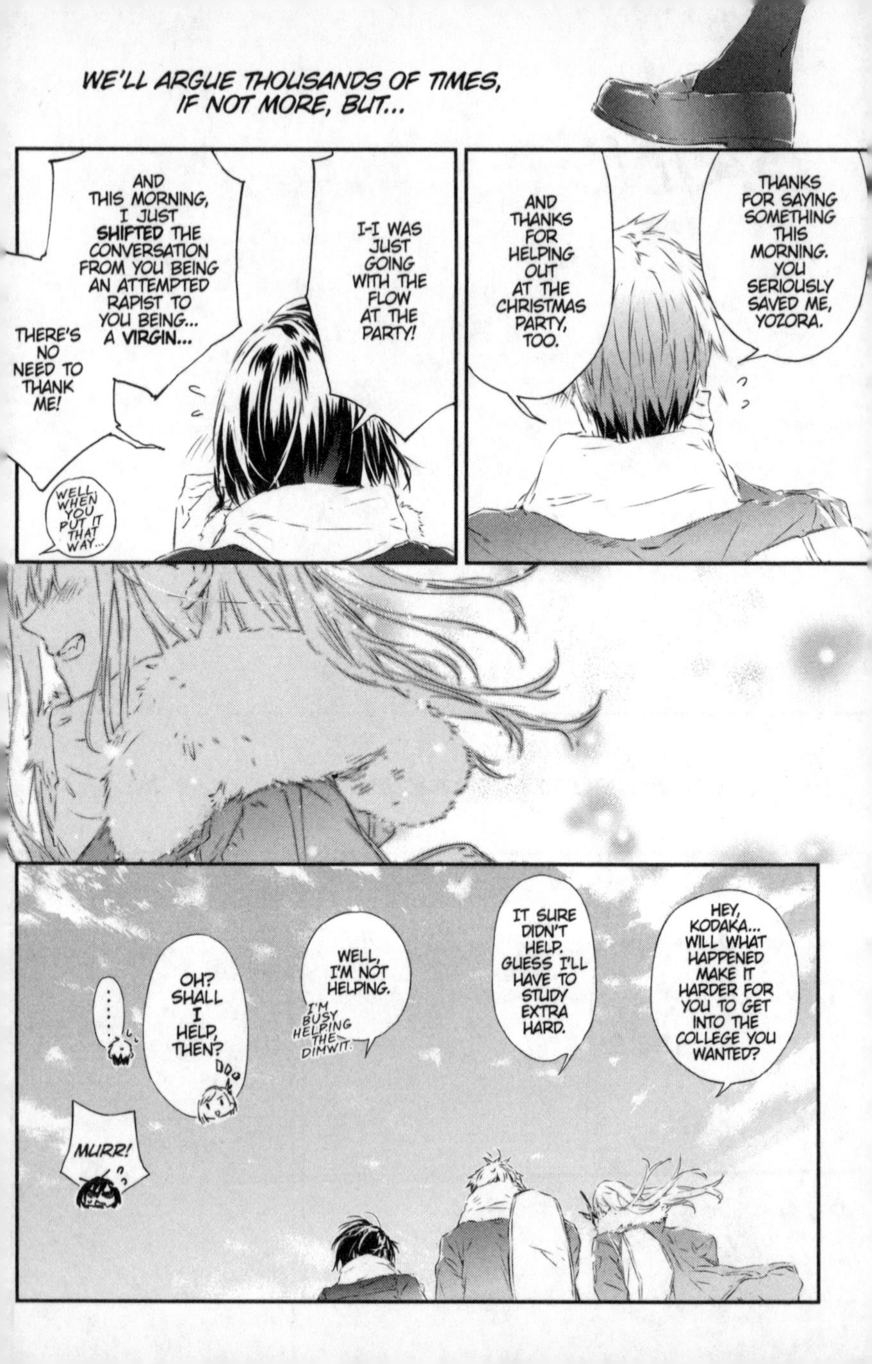
WE'LL ARGUE THOUSANDS OF TIMES, IF NOT MORE, BUT...
THANKS FOR SAYING SOMETHING THIS MORNING. YOU SERIOUSLY SAVED ME, YOZORA.
AND THANKS FOR HELPING OUT AT THE CHRISTMAS PARTY, TOO.
I-I WAS JUST GOING WITH THE FLOW AT THE PARTY!
AND THIS MORNING, I JUST **SHIFTED** THE CONVERSATION FROM YOU BEING AN ATTEMPTED RAPIST TO YOU BEING... A **VIRGIN**...
THERE'S NO NEED TO THANK ME!
WELL, WHEN YOU PUT IT THAT WAY...
HEY, KODAKA... WILL WHAT HAPPENED MAKE IT HARDER FOR YOU TO GET INTO THE COLLEGE YOU WANTED?
IT SURE DIDN'T HELP. GUESS I'LL HAVE TO STUDY EXTRA HARD.
WELL, I'M NOT HELPING.
I'M BUSY HELPING THE DIMWIT.
OH? SHALL **I** HELP, THEN?
......
MURR!

I don't have many friends

Haganai

I don't have many friends

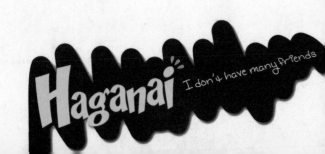

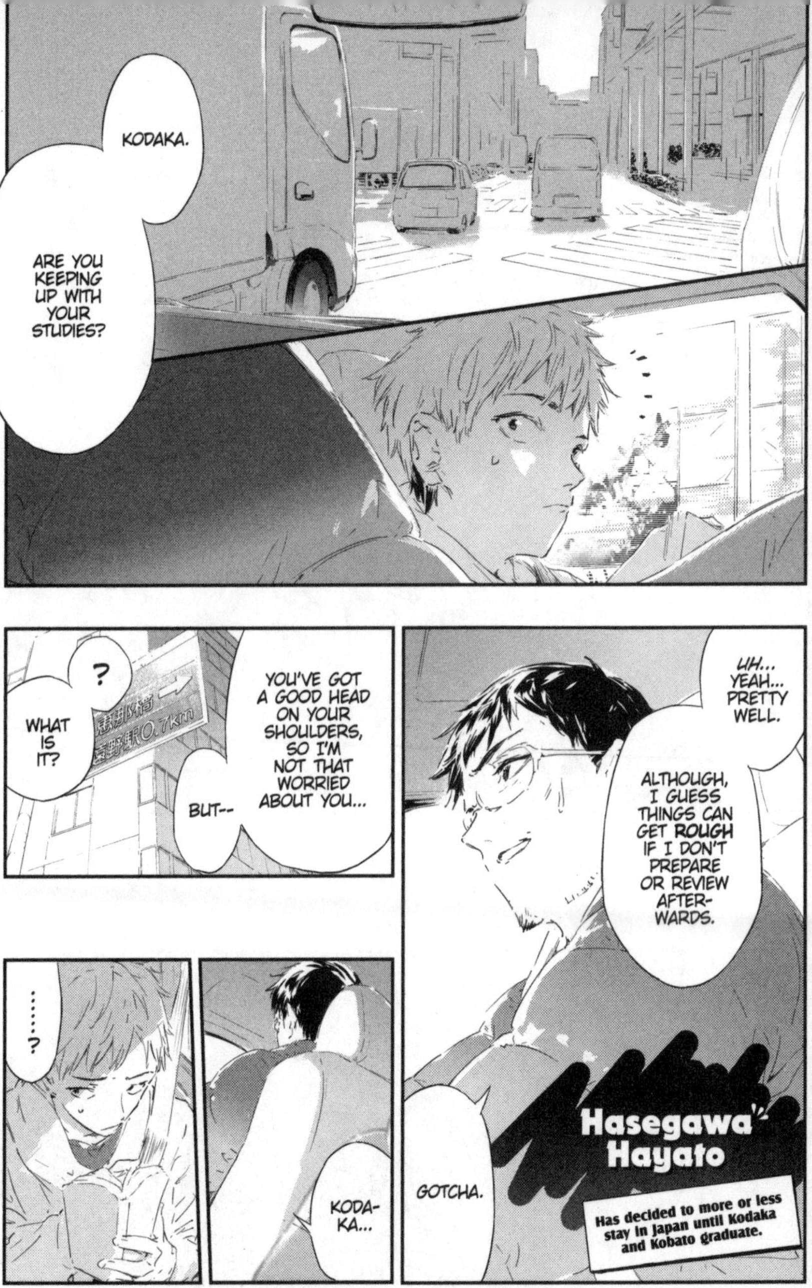
KODAKA.
ARE YOU KEEPING UP WITH YOUR STUDIES?
...
UH... YEAH... PRETTY WELL.
ALTHOUGH, I GUESS THINGS CAN GET **ROUGH** IF I DON'T PREPARE OR REVIEW AFTER-WARDS.
GOTCHA.
Hasegawa Hayato
Has decided to more or less stay in Japan until Kodaka and Kobato graduate.
YOU'VE GOT A GOOD HEAD ON YOUR SHOULDERS, SO I'M NOT THAT WORRIED ABOUT YOU...
BUT--
?
WHAT IS IT?
KODA-KA...
......?

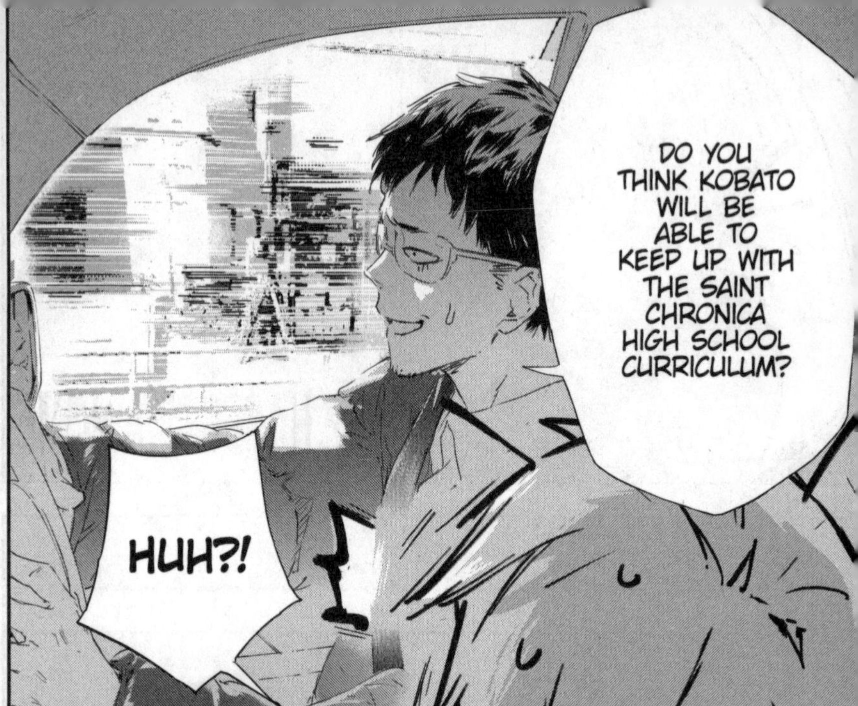
DO YOU THINK KOBATO WILL BE ABLE TO KEEP UP WITH THE SAINT CHRONICA HIGH SCHOOL CURRICULUM?
HUH?!

Club Activity Log 88: The Words We Give

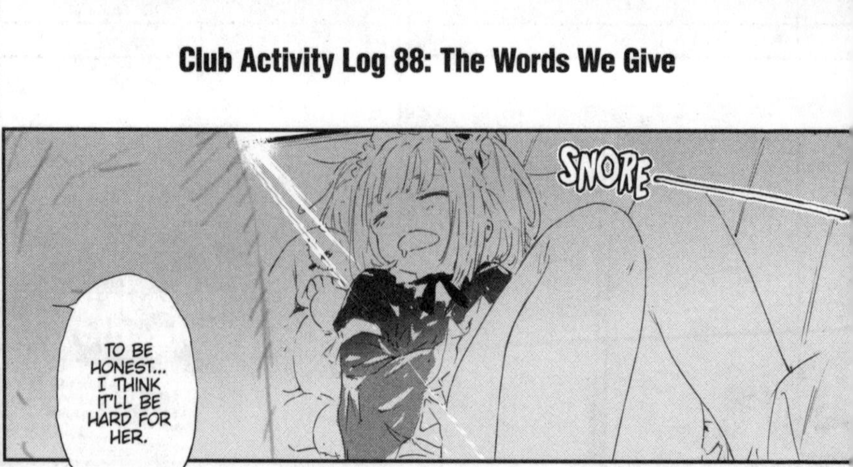
SNORE
TO BE HONEST... I THINK IT'LL BE HARD FOR HER.

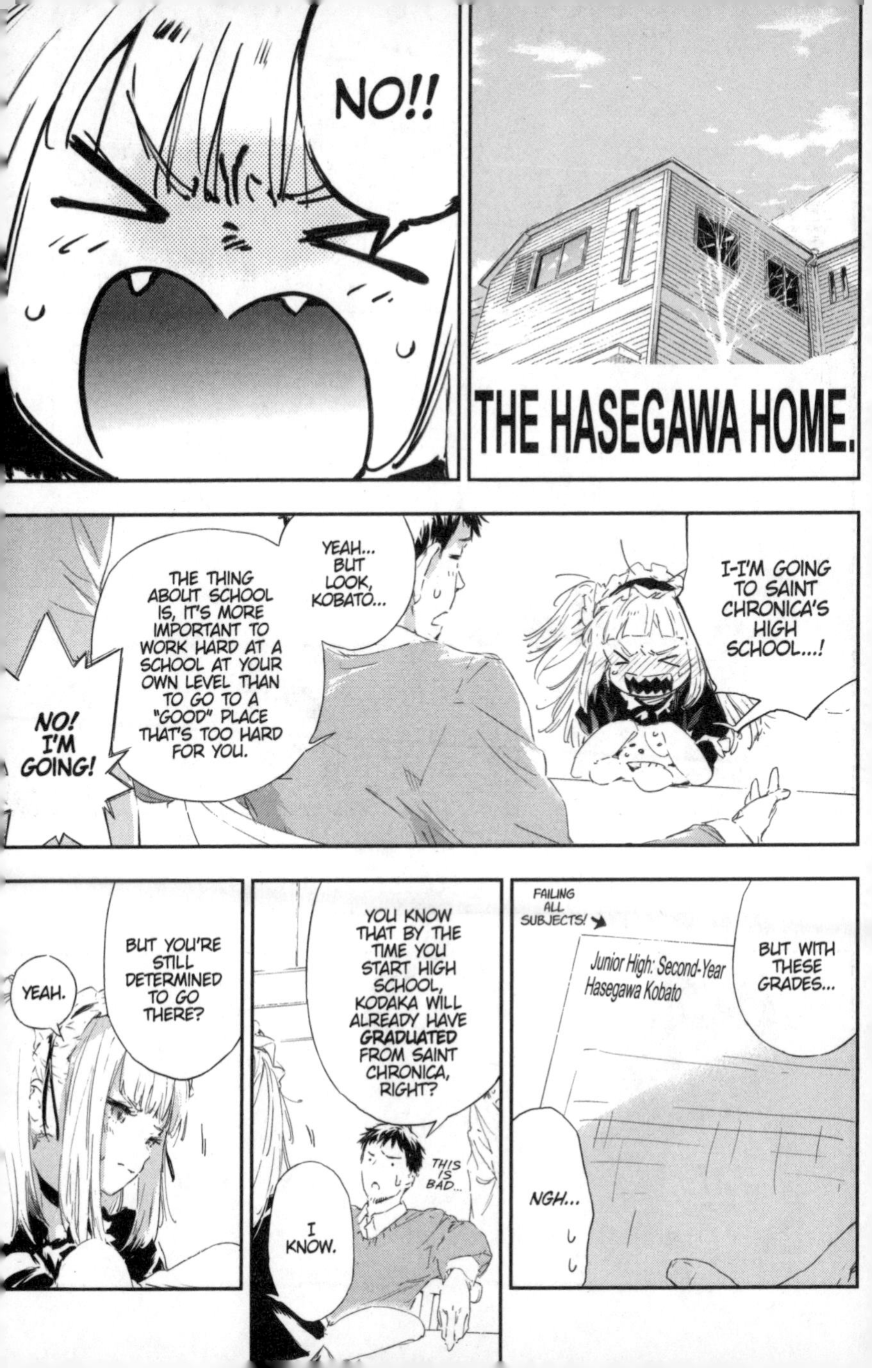
THE HASEGAWA HOME.
NO!!
I-I'M GOING TO SAINT CHRONICA'S HIGH SCHOOL...!
YEAH... BUT LOOK, KOBATO...
THE THING ABOUT SCHOOL IS, IT'S MORE IMPORTANT TO WORK HARD AT A SCHOOL AT YOUR OWN LEVEL THAN TO GO TO A "GOOD" PLACE THAT'S TOO HARD FOR YOU.
NO! I'M GOING!
BUT WITH THESE GRADES...
FAILING ALL SUBJECTS!
Junior High: Second-Year
Hasegawa Kobato
NGH...
YOU KNOW THAT BY THE TIME YOU START HIGH SCHOOL, KODAKA WILL ALREADY HAVE GRADUATED FROM SAINT CHRONICA, RIGHT?
THIS IS BAD...
I KNOW.
BUT YOU'RE STILL DETERMINED TO GO THERE?
YEAH.

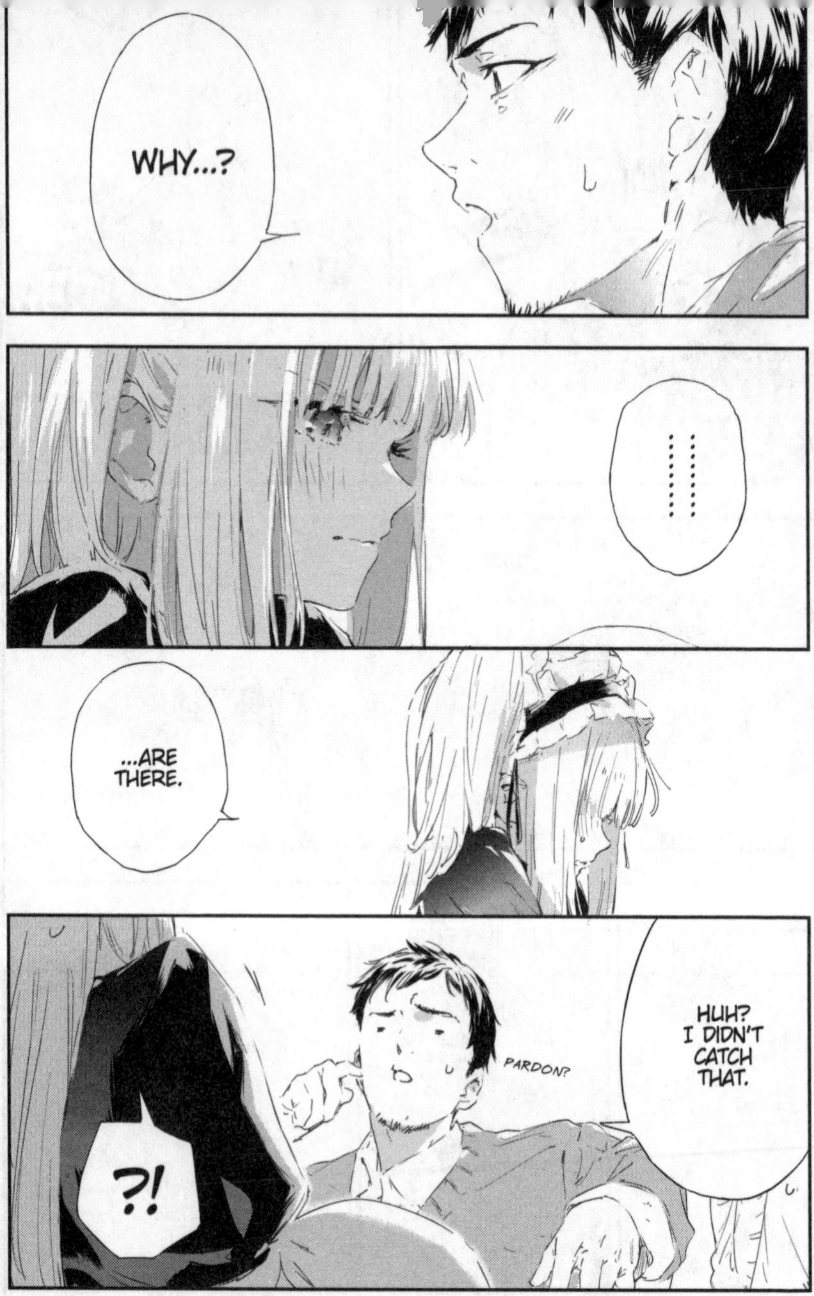
WHY...?
......
...ARE THERE.
HUH? I DIDN'T CATCH THAT.
PARDON?
?!

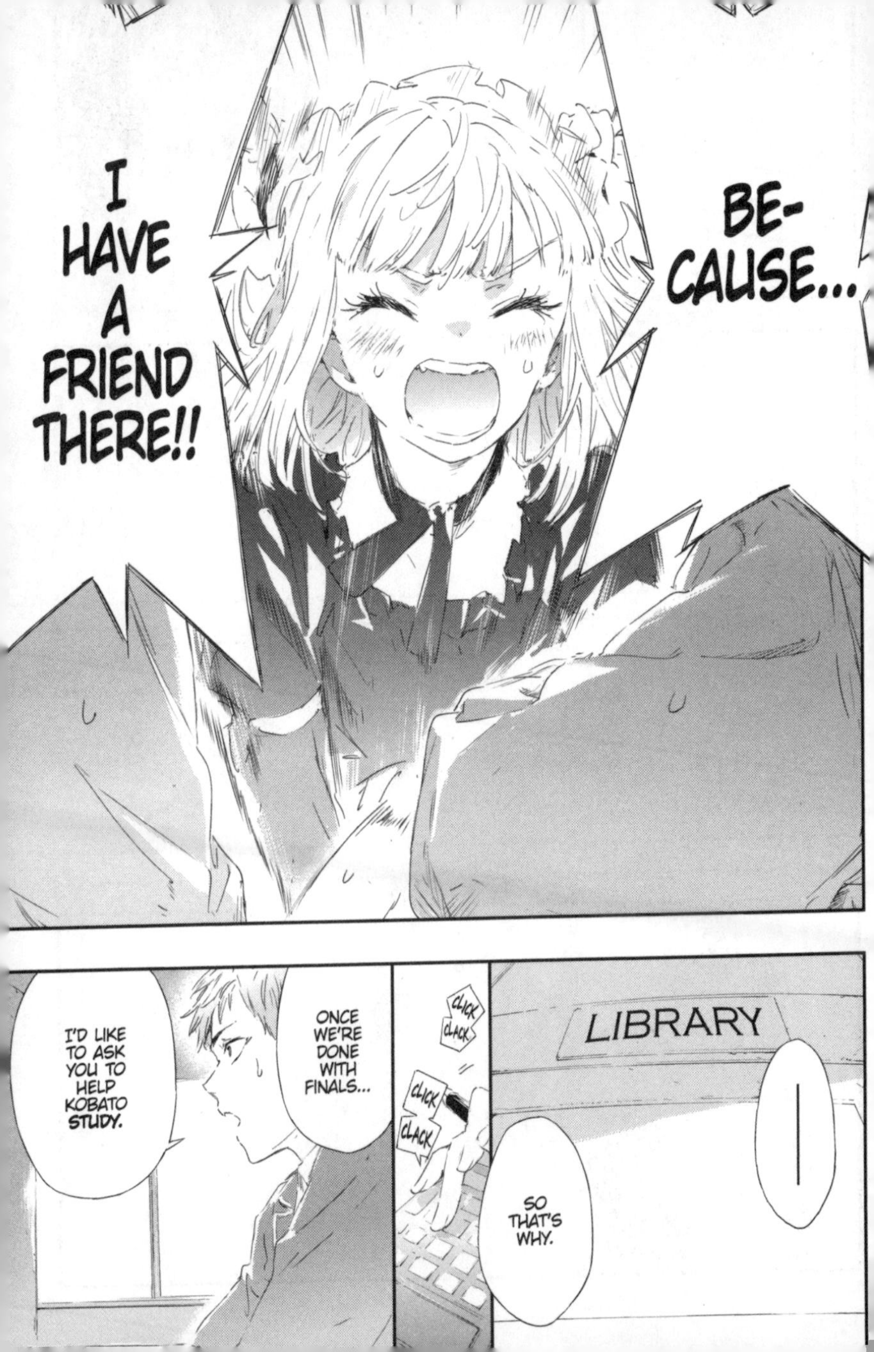
BE-CAUSE...
I HAVE A FRIEND THERE!!
LIBRARY
—
SO THAT'S WHY.
CLICK CLACK
CLICK CLACK
ONCE WE'RE DONE WITH FINALS...
I'D LIKE TO ASK YOU TO HELP KOBATO STUDY.

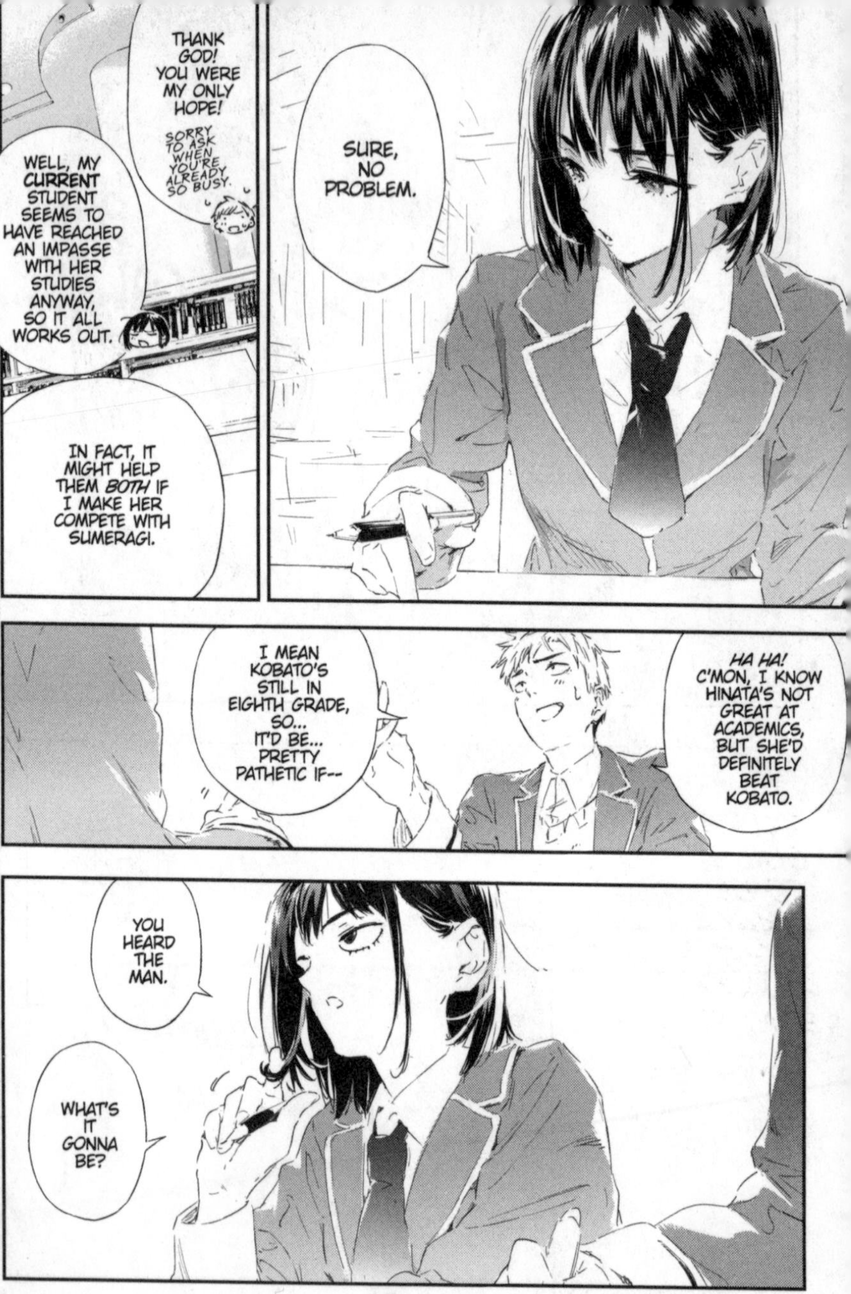
SURE, NO PROBLEM.
THANK GOD! YOU WERE MY ONLY HOPE!
SORRY TO ASK WHEN YOU'RE ALREADY SO BUSY.
WELL, MY **CURRENT** STUDENT SEEMS TO HAVE REACHED AN IMPASSE WITH HER STUDIES ANYWAY, SO IT ALL WORKS OUT.
IN FACT, IT MIGHT HELP THEM *BOTH* IF I MAKE HER COMPETE WITH SUMERAGI.
HA HA! C'MON, I KNOW HINATA'S NOT GREAT AT ACADEMICS, BUT SHE'D DEFINITELY BEAT KOBATO.
I MEAN KOBATO'S STILL IN EIGHTH GRADE, SO... IT'D BE... PRETTY PATHETIC IF--
YOU HEARD THE MAN.
WHAT'S IT GONNA BE?

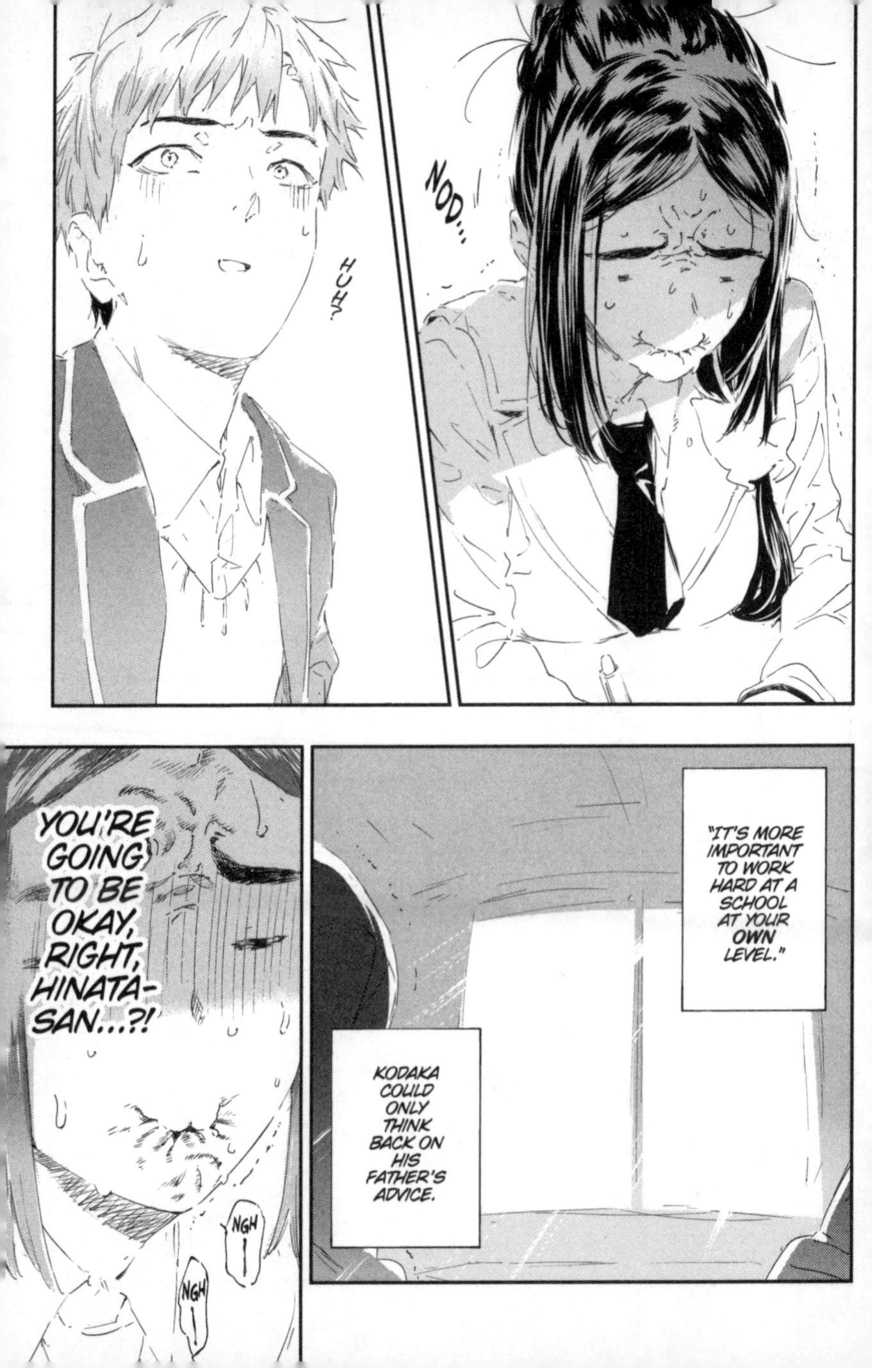
NOD...
HUH?
"IT'S MORE IMPORTANT TO WORK HARD AT A SCHOOL AT YOUR OWN LEVEL."
KODAKA COULD ONLY THINK BACK ON HIS FATHER'S ADVICE.
YOU'RE GOING TO BE OKAY, RIGHT, HINATA-SAN...?!
NGH!
NGH!

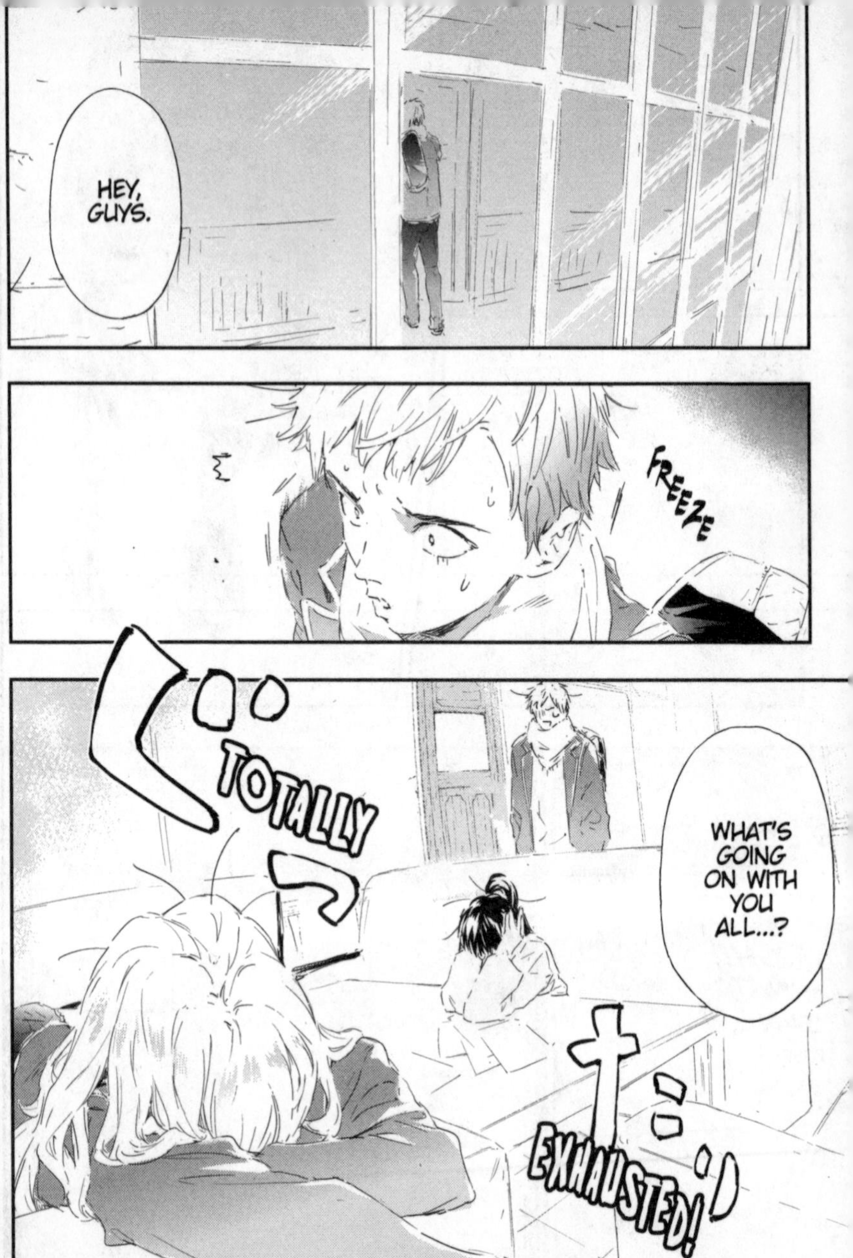
HEY, GUYS.
FREEZE
WHAT'S GOING ON WITH YOU ALL...?
TOTALLY
EXHAUSTED!

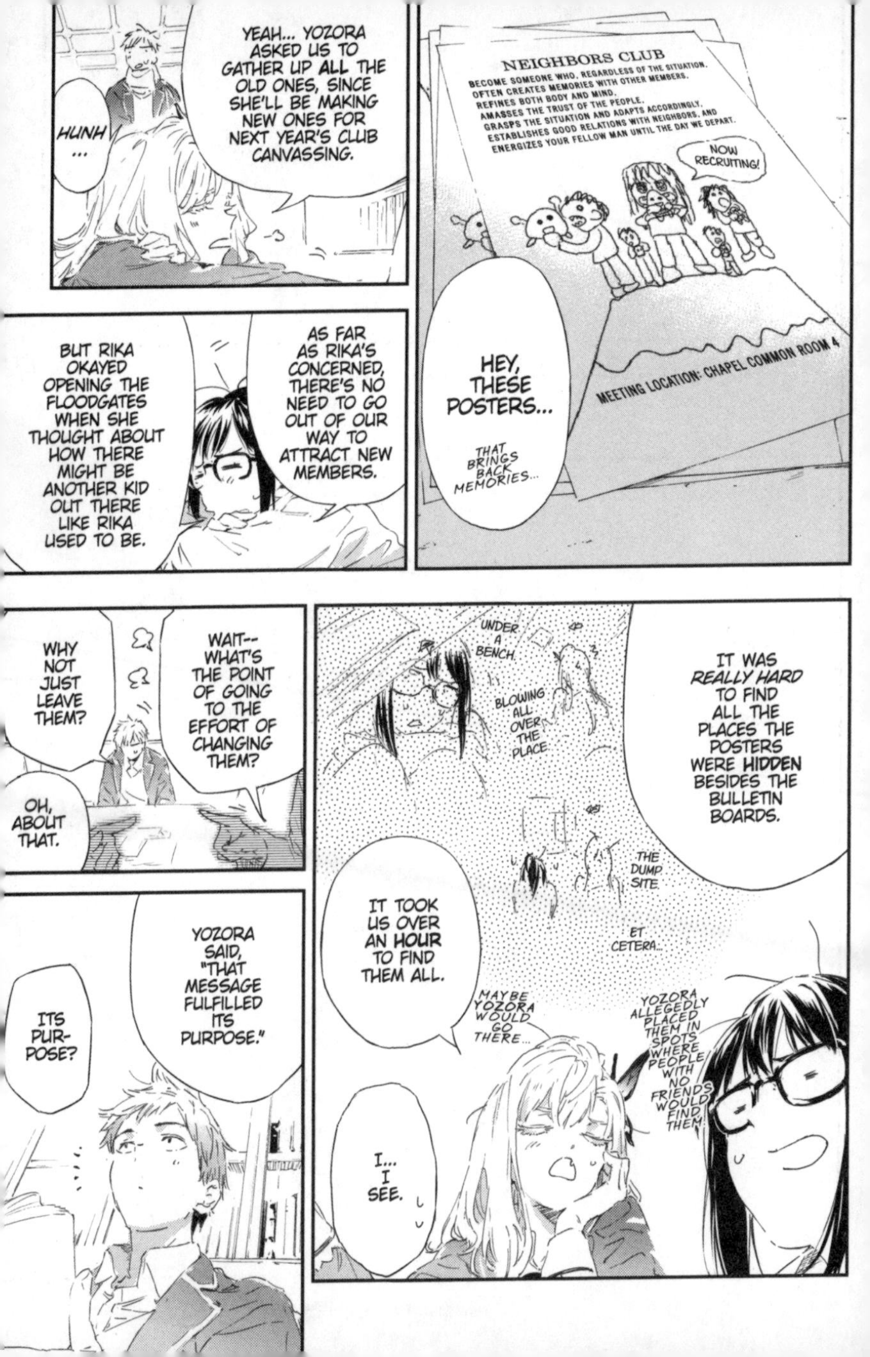
NEIGHBORS CLUB
BECOME SOMEONE WHO, REGARDLESS OF THE SITUATION,
OFTEN CREATES MEMORIES WITH OTHER MEMBERS,
REFINES BOTH BODY AND MIND,
AMASSES THE TRUST OF THE PEOPLE,
GRASPS THE SITUATION AND ADAPTS ACCORDINGLY,
ESTABLISHES GOOD RELATIONS WITH NEIGHBORS, AND
ENERGIZES YOUR FELLOW MAN UNTIL THE DAY WE DEPART.
NOW RECRUITING!
MEETING LOCATION: CHAPEL COMMON ROOM 4
HEY, THESE POSTERS...
THAT BRINGS BACK MEMORIES...
YEAH... YOZORA ASKED US TO GATHER UP ALL THE OLD ONES, SINCE SHE'LL BE MAKING NEW ONES FOR NEXT YEAR'S CLUB CANVASSING.
HUNH...
AS FAR AS RIKA'S CONCERNED, THERE'S NO NEED TO GO OUT OF OUR WAY TO ATTRACT NEW MEMBERS.
BUT RIKA OKAYED OPENING THE FLOODGATES WHEN SHE THOUGHT ABOUT HOW THERE MIGHT BE ANOTHER KID OUT THERE LIKE RIKA USED TO BE.
IT WAS REALLY HARD TO FIND ALL THE PLACES THE POSTERS WERE HIDDEN BESIDES THE BULLETIN BOARDS.
UNDER A BENCH.
BLOWING ALL OVER THE PLACE.
THE DUMP SITE.
ET CETERA...
IT TOOK US OVER AN HOUR TO FIND THEM ALL.
YOZORA ALLEGEDLY PLACED THEM IN SPOTS WHERE PEOPLE WITH NO FRIENDS WOULD FIND THEM!
MAYBE YOZORA WOULD GO THERE...
I... I SEE.
WAIT-- WHAT'S THE POINT OF GOING TO THE EFFORT OF CHANGING THEM?
WHY NOT JUST LEAVE THEM?
OH, ABOUT THAT.
YOZORA SAID, "THAT MESSAGE FULFILLED ITS PURPOSE."
ITS PURPOSE?

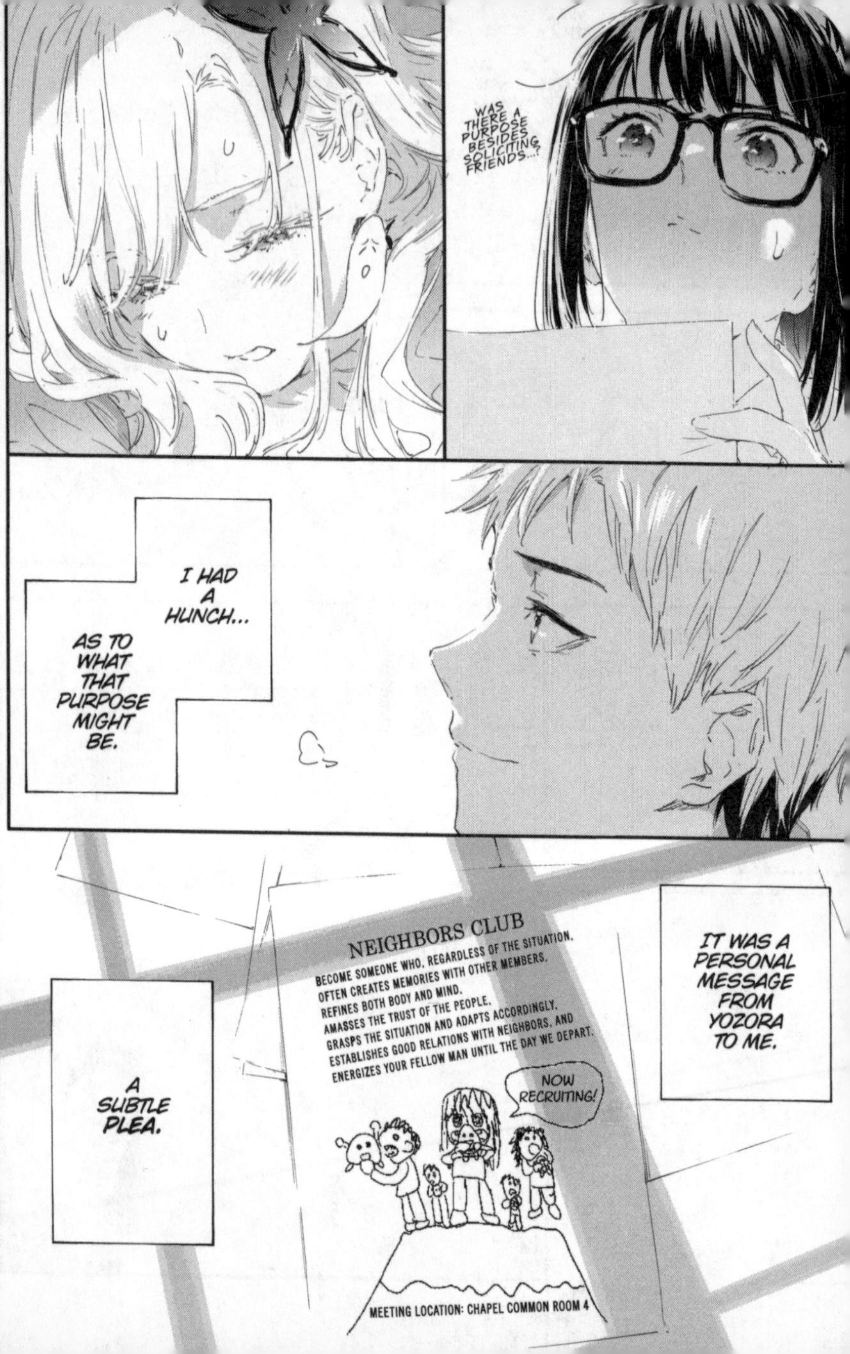
WAS THERE A PURPOSE BESIDES SOLICITING FRIENDS...?
I HAD A HUNCH...
AS TO WHAT THAT PURPOSE MIGHT BE.
IT WAS A PERSONAL MESSAGE FROM YOZORA TO ME.
NEIGHBORS CLUB
BECOME SOMEONE WHO, REGARDLESS OF THE SITUATION,
OFTEN CREATES MEMORIES WITH OTHER MEMBERS,
REFINES BOTH BODY AND MIND,
AMASSES THE TRUST OF THE PEOPLE,
GRASPS THE SITUATION AND ADAPTS ACCORDINGLY,
ESTABLISHES GOOD RELATIONS WITH NEIGHBORS, AND
ENERGIZES YOUR FELLOW MAN UNTIL THE DAY WE DEPART.
NOW RECRUITING!
MEETING LOCATION: CHAPEL COMMON ROOM 4
A SUBTLE PLEA.

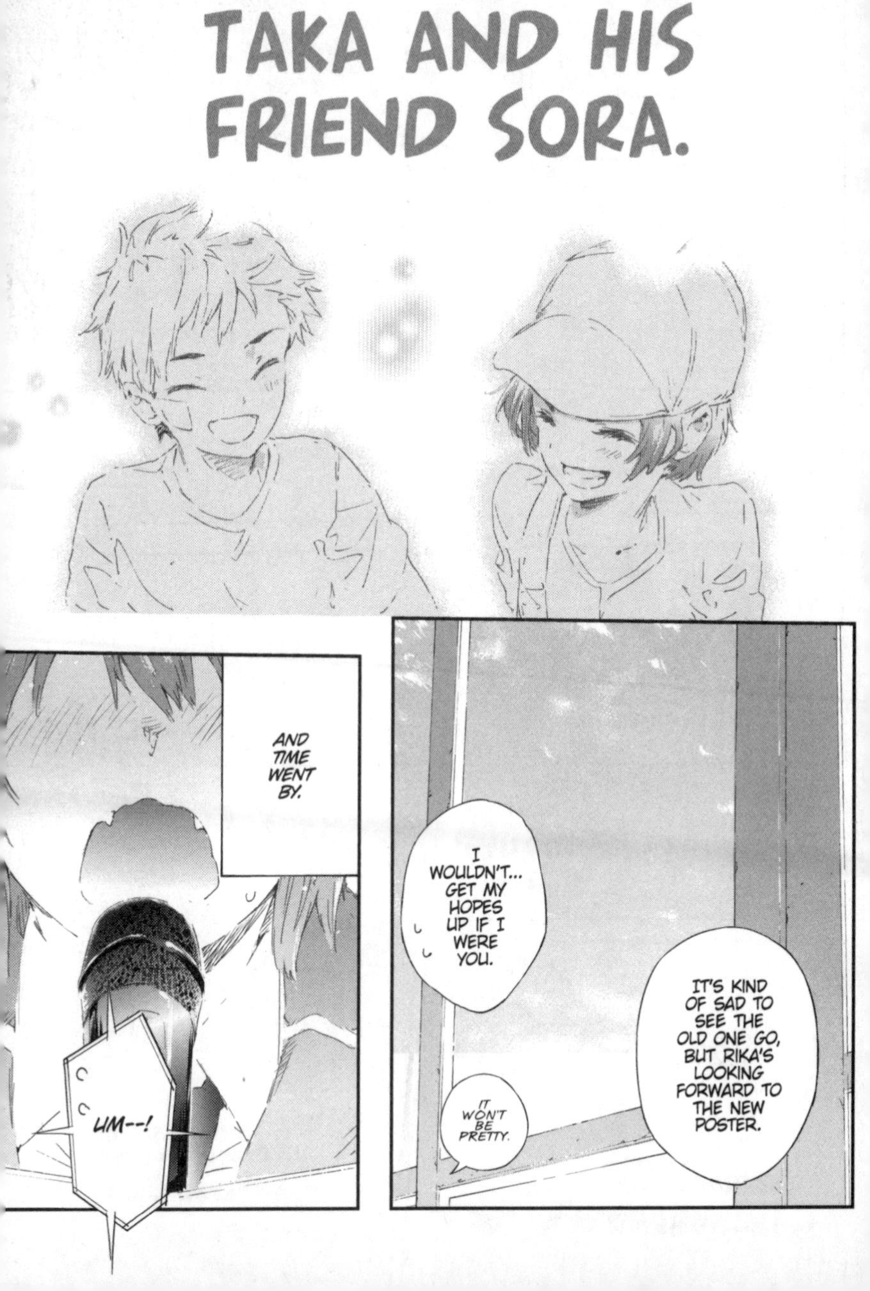
TAKA AND HIS FRIEND SORA.
IT'S KIND OF SAD TO SEE THE OLD ONE GO, BUT RIKA'S LOOKING FORWARD TO THE NEW POSTER.
I WOULDN'T... GET MY HOPES UP IF I WERE YOU.
IT WON'T BE PRETTY.
AND TIME WENT BY.
UM--!

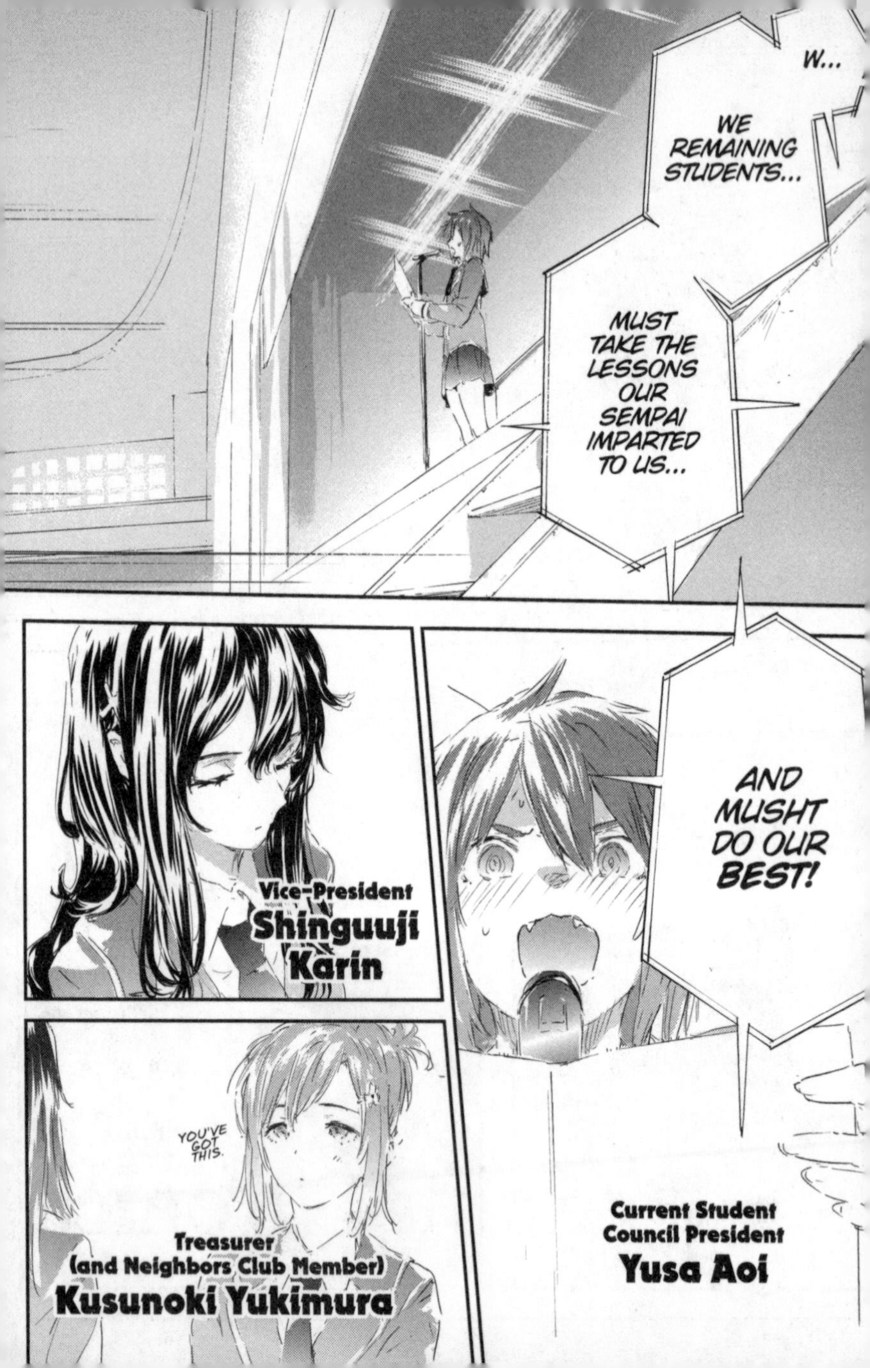
W...
WE REMAINING STUDENTS...
MUST TAKE THE LESSONS OUR SEMPAI IMPARTED TO US...
AND MUSHT DO OUR BEST!
Current Student Council President
Yusa Aoi
Vice-President
Shinguuji Karin
YOU'VE GOT THIS.
Treasurer (and Neighbors Club Member)
Kusunoki Yukimura

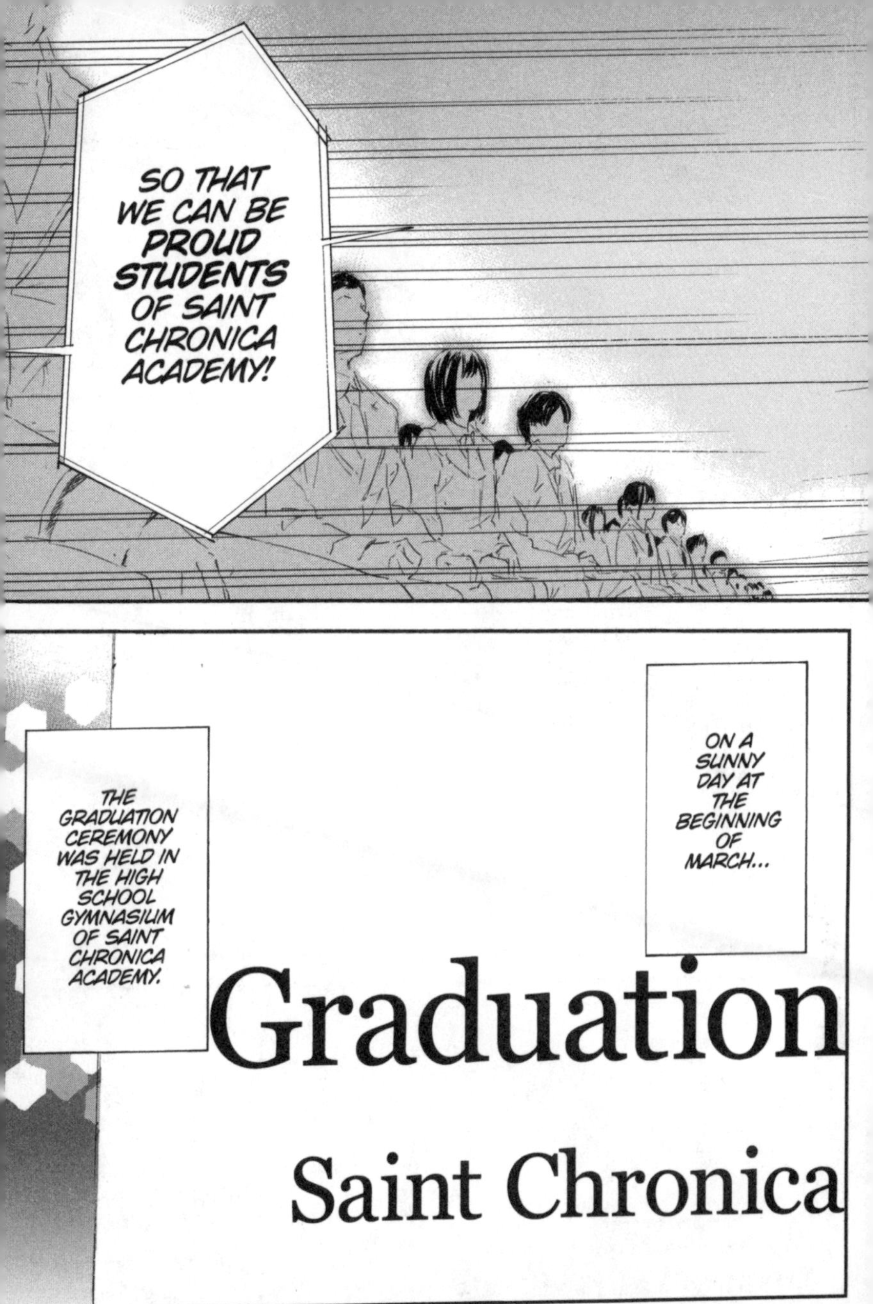
SO THAT WE CAN BE PROUD STUDENTS OF SAINT CHRONICA ACADEMY!
ON A SUNNY DAY AT THE BEGINNING OF MARCH...
THE GRADUATION CEREMONY WAS HELD IN THE HIGH SCHOOL GYMNASIUM OF SAINT CHRONICA ACADEMY.
Graduation
Saint Chronica

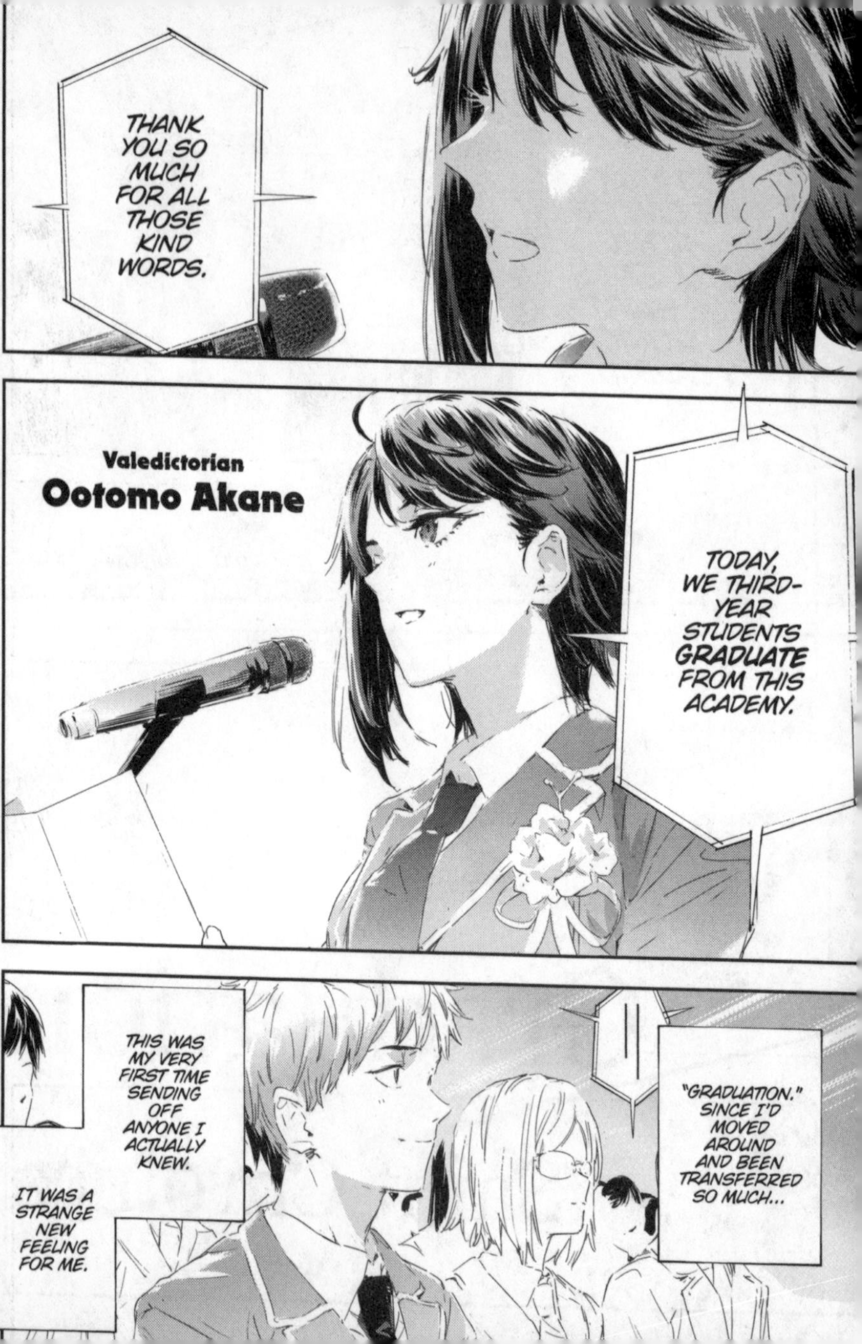
THANK YOU SO MUCH FOR ALL THOSE KIND WORDS.
TODAY, WE THIRD-YEAR STUDENTS GRADUATE FROM THIS ACADEMY.
Valedictorian
Ootomo Akane
"GRADUATION." SINCE I'D MOVED AROUND AND BEEN TRANSFERRED SO MUCH...
THIS WAS MY VERY FIRST TIME SENDING OFF ANYONE I ACTUALLY KNEW.
IT WAS A STRANGE NEW FEELING FOR ME.

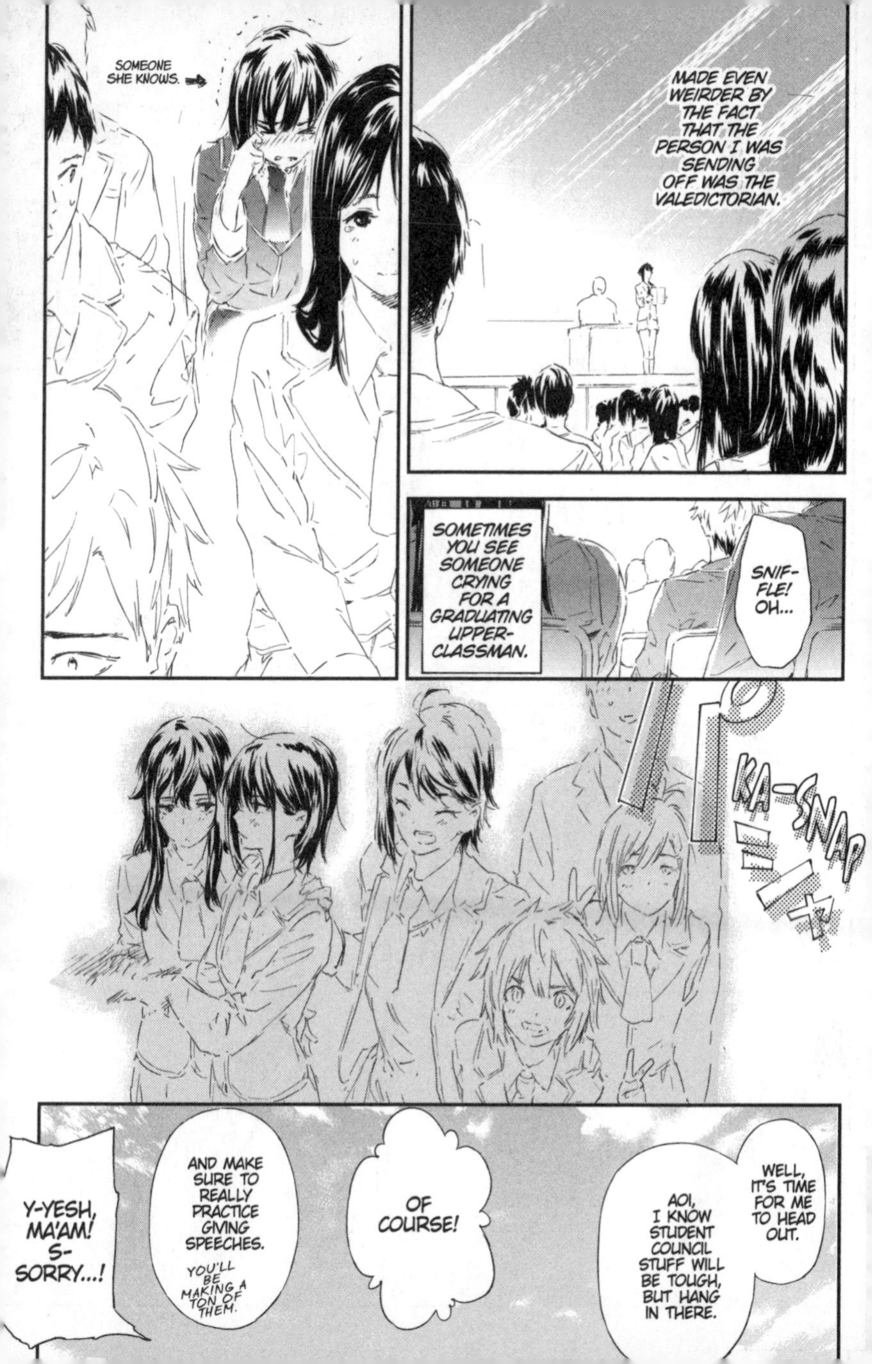
MADE EVEN WEIRDER BY THE FACT THAT THE PERSON I WAS SENDING OFF WAS THE VALEDICTORIAN.
SNIF-FLE! OH...
SOMETIMES YOU SEE SOMEONE CRYING FOR A GRADUATING UPPER-CLASSMAN.
SOMEONE SHE KNOWS.
KA-SNAP
WELL, IT'S TIME FOR ME TO HEAD OUT.
AOI, I KNOW STUDENT COUNCIL STUFF WILL BE TOUGH, BUT HANG IN THERE.
OF COURSE!
AND MAKE SURE TO REALLY PRACTICE GIVING SPEECHES.
YOU'LL BE MAKING A TON OF THEM.
Y-YESH, MA'AM! S-SORRY...!

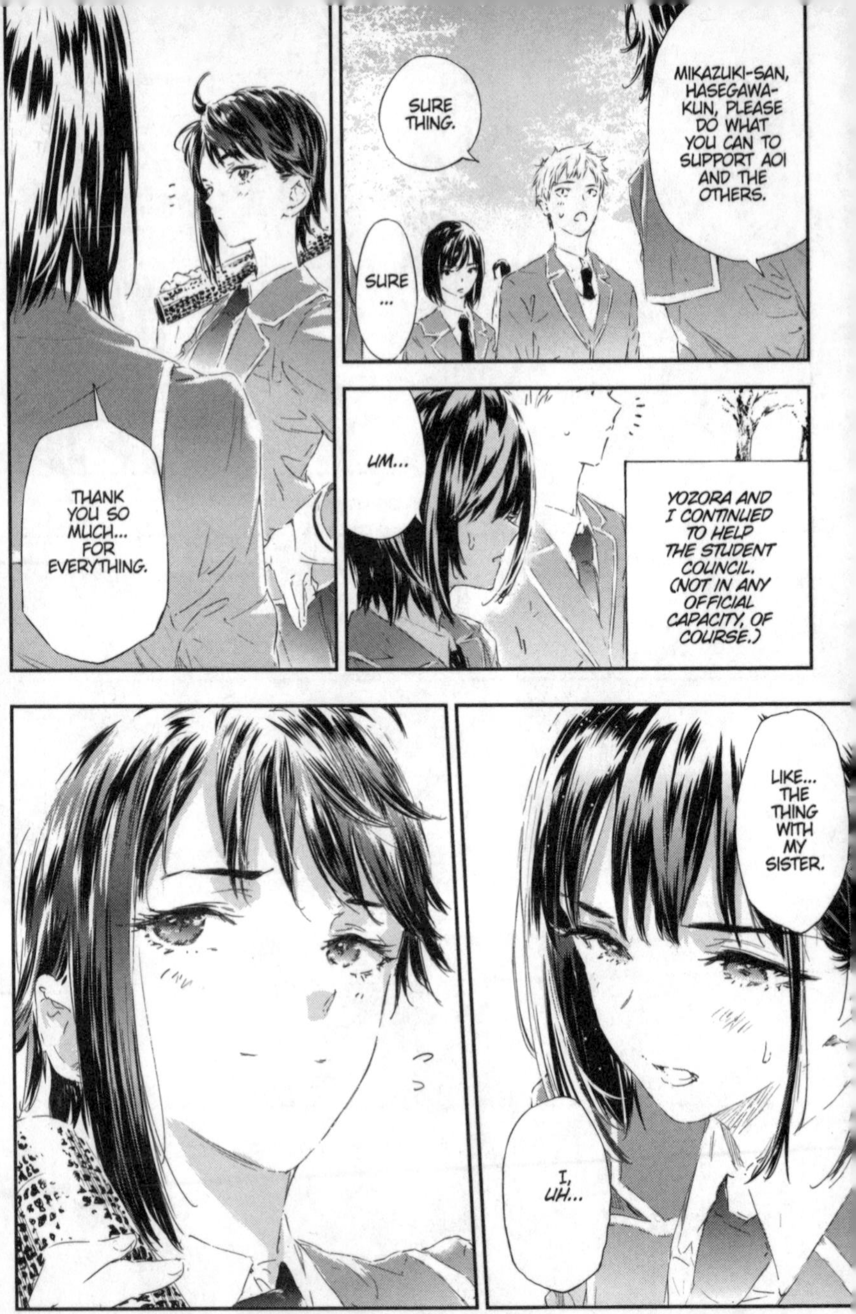
MIKAZUKI-SAN, HASEGAWA-KUN, PLEASE DO WHAT YOU CAN TO SUPPORT AOI AND THE OTHERS.
SURE THING.
SURE ...
YOZORA AND I CONTINUED TO HELP THE STUDENT COUNCIL. (NOT IN ANY OFFICIAL CAPACITY, OF COURSE.)
UM...
THANK YOU SO MUCH... FOR EVERYTHING.
LIKE... THE THING WITH MY SISTER.
I, UH...

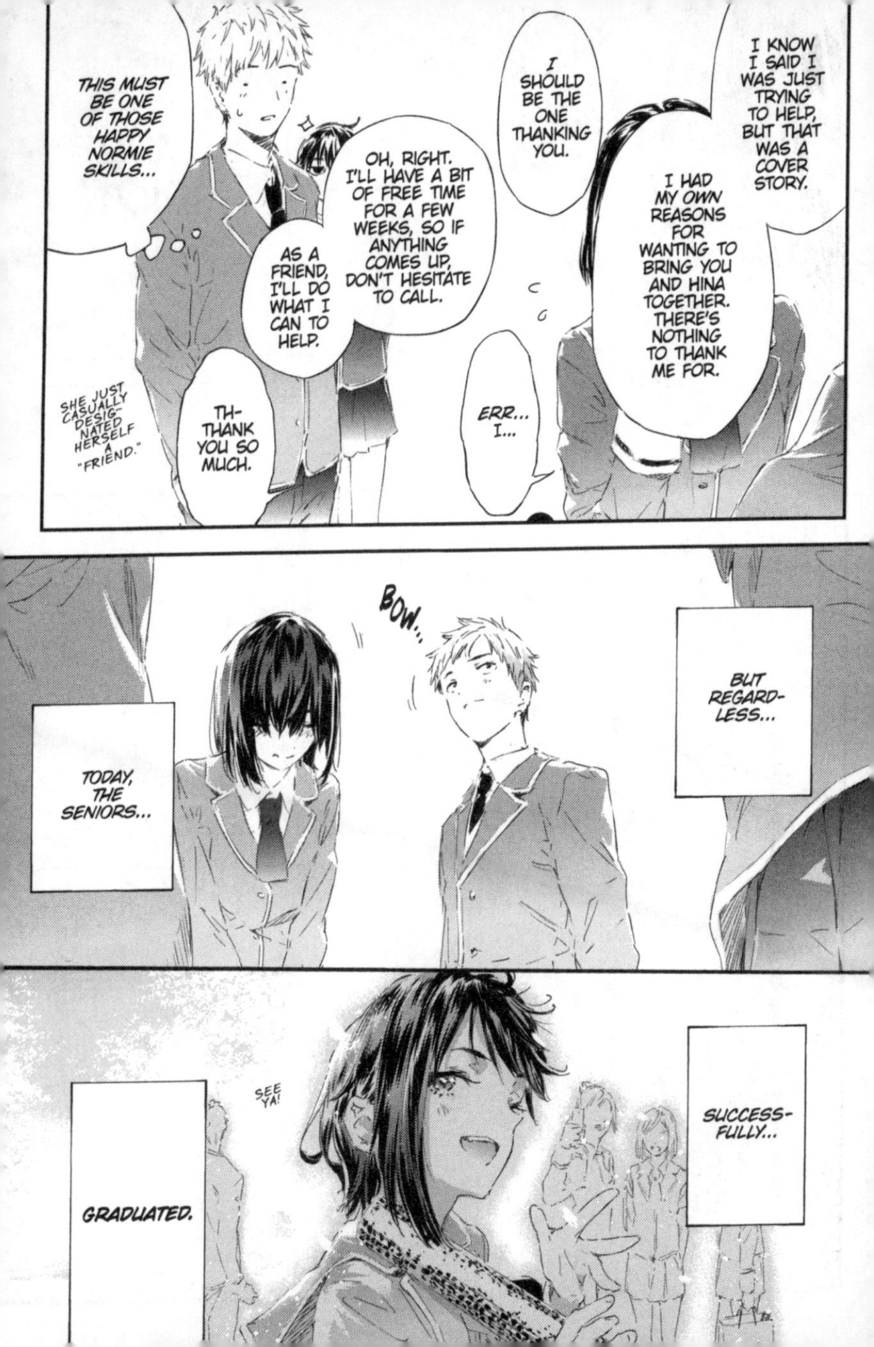
I KNOW I SAID I WAS JUST TRYING TO HELP, BUT THAT WAS A COVER STORY.
I HAD MY OWN REASONS FOR WANTING TO BRING YOU AND HINA TOGETHER. THERE'S NOTHING TO THANK ME FOR.
I SHOULD BE THE ONE THANKING YOU.
ERR... I...
OH, RIGHT. I'LL HAVE A BIT OF FREE TIME FOR A FEW WEEKS, SO IF ANYTHING COMES UP, DON'T HESITATE TO CALL.
AS A FRIEND, I'LL DO WHAT I CAN TO HELP.
TH-THANK YOU SO MUCH.
THIS MUST BE ONE OF THOSE HAPPY NORMIE SKILLS...
SHE JUST CASUALLY DESIGNATED HERSELF A "FRIEND."
BUT REGARDLESS...
BOW...
TODAY, THE SENIORS...
SUCCESSFULLY...
SEE YA!
GRADUATED.

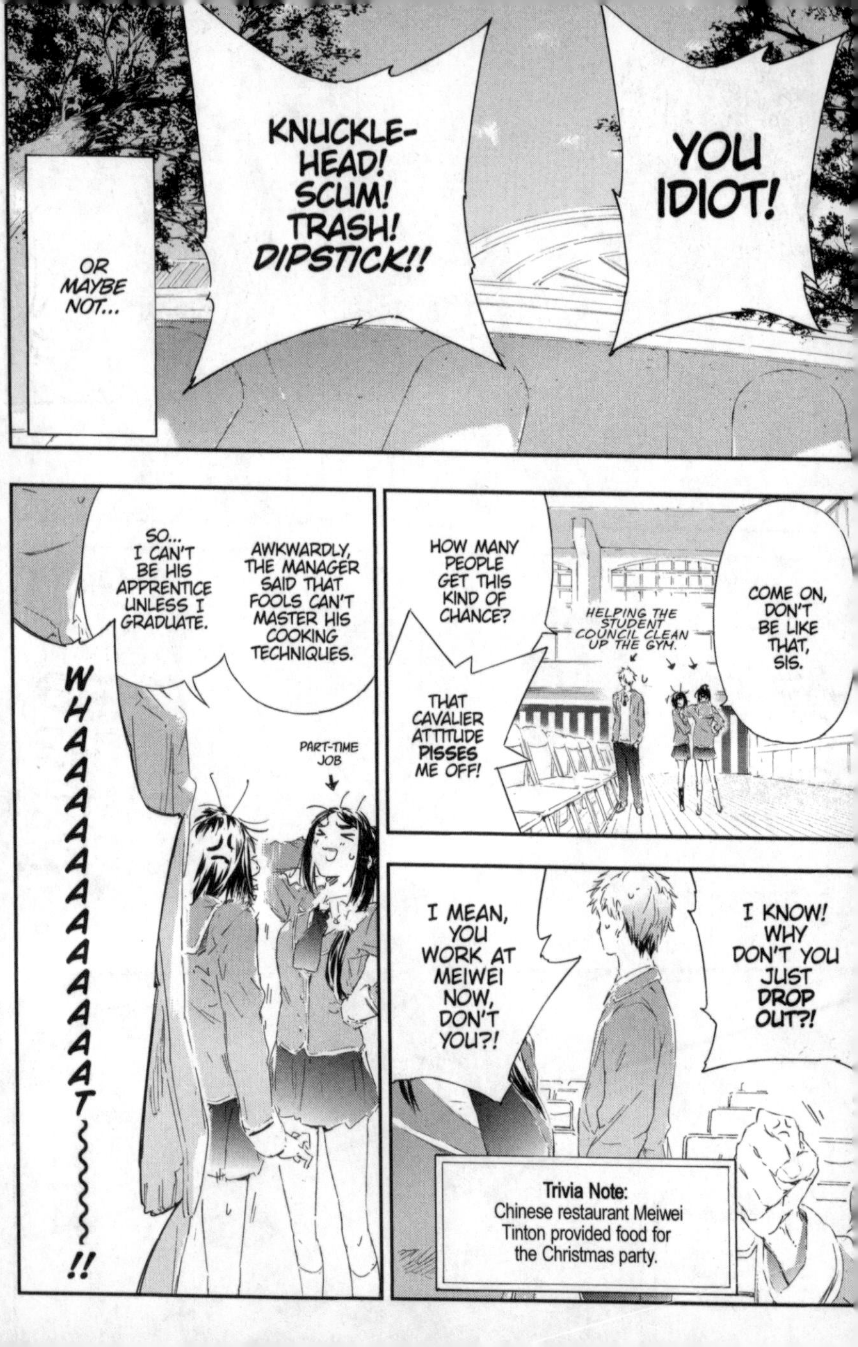
YOU IDIOT!
KNUCKLE-HEAD! SCUM! TRASH! DIPSTICK!!
OR MAYBE NOT...
COME ON, DON'T BE LIKE THAT, SIS.
HELPING THE STUDENT COUNCIL CLEAN UP THE GYM.
HOW MANY PEOPLE GET THIS KIND OF CHANCE?
THAT CAVALIER ATTITUDE PISSES ME OFF!
I KNOW! WHY DON'T YOU JUST DROP OUT?!
I MEAN, YOU WORK AT MEIWEI NOW, DON'T YOU?!
Trivia Note: Chinese restaurant Meiwei Tinton provided food for the Christmas party.
AWKWARDLY, THE MANAGER SAID THAT FOOLS CAN'T MASTER HIS COOKING TECHNIQUES.
SO... I CAN'T BE HIS APPRENTICE UNLESS I GRADUATE.
PART-TIME JOB
WHAAAAAAAAAAAAAT~!!

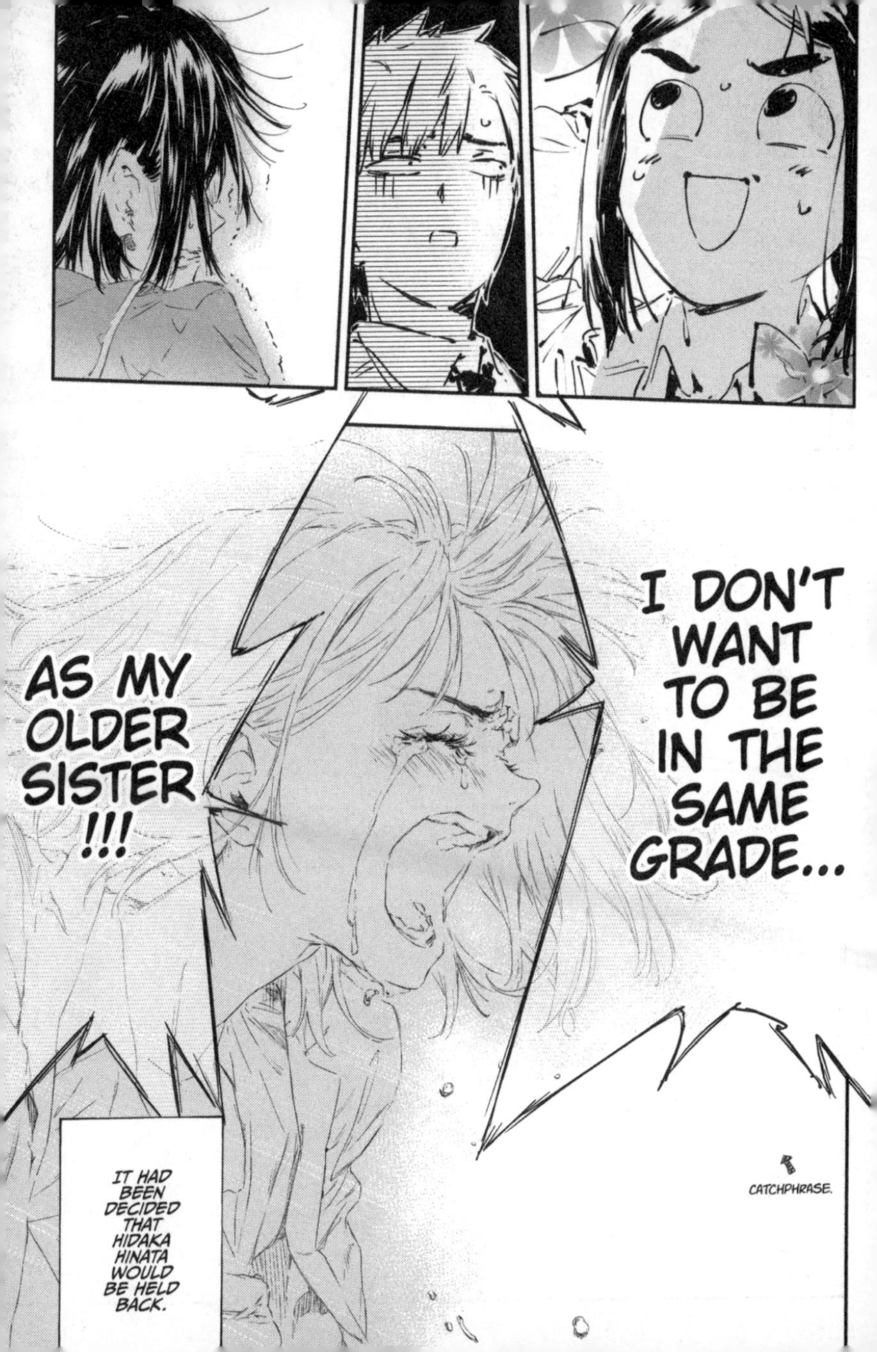
I DON'T WANT TO BE IN THE SAME GRADE...
AS MY OLDER SISTER!!!
CATCHPHRASE.
IT HAD BEEN DECIDED THAT HIDAKA HINATA WOULD BE HELD BACK.

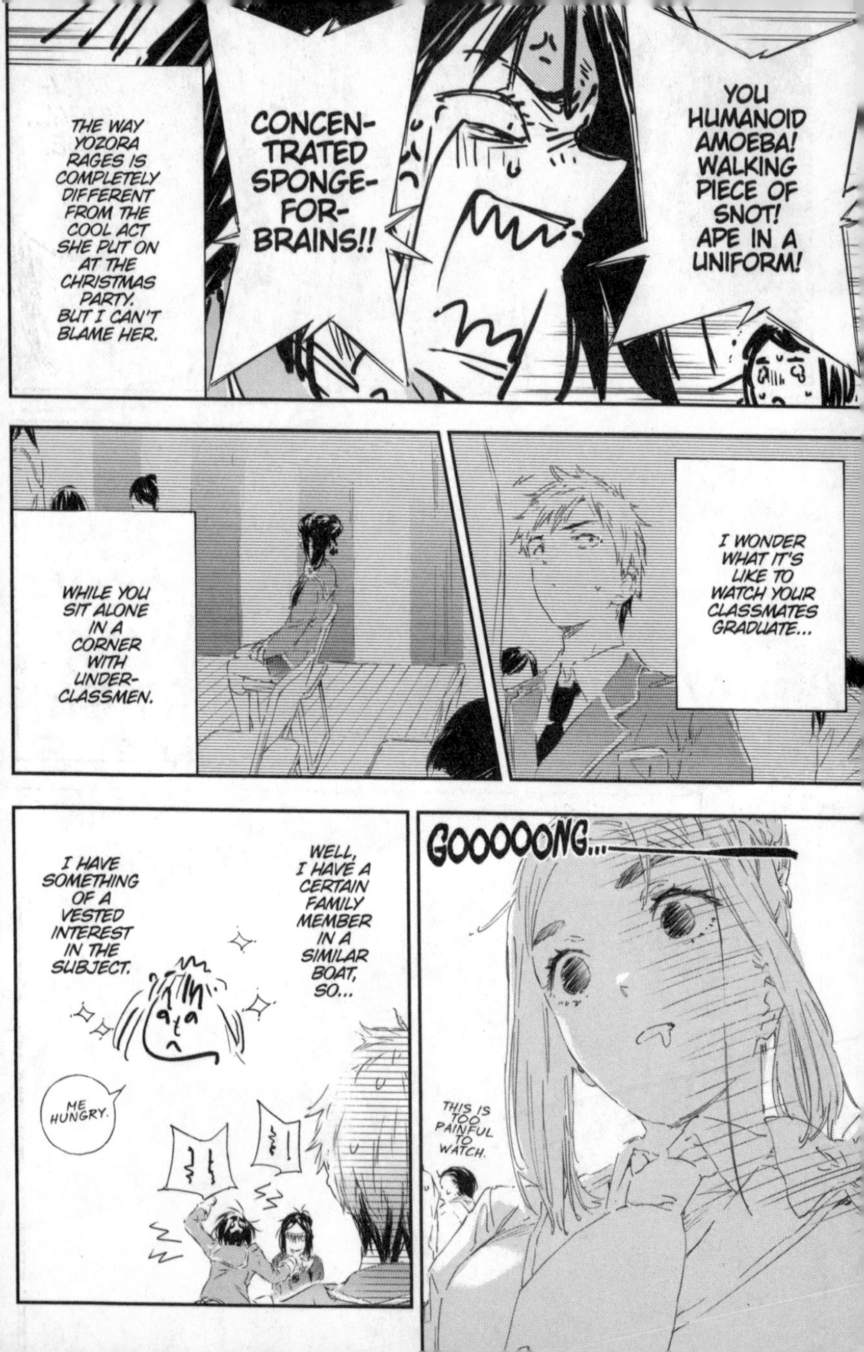
YOU HUMANOID AMOEBA! WALKING PIECE OF SNOT! APE IN A UNIFORM!
CONCEN-TRATED SPONGE-FOR-BRAINS!!
THE WAY YOZORA RAGES IS COMPLETELY DIFFERENT FROM THE COOL ACT SHE PUT ON AT THE CHRISTMAS PARTY. BUT I CAN'T BLAME HER.
I WONDER WHAT IT'S LIKE TO WATCH YOUR CLASSMATES GRADUATE...
WHILE YOU SIT ALONE IN A CORNER WITH UNDER-CLASSMEN.
GOOOOONG...
THIS IS TOO PAINFUL TO WATCH.
WELL, I HAVE A CERTAIN FAMILY MEMBER IN A SIMILAR BOAT, SO...
I HAVE SOMETHING OF A VESTED INTEREST IN THE SUBJECT.
ME HUNGRY.

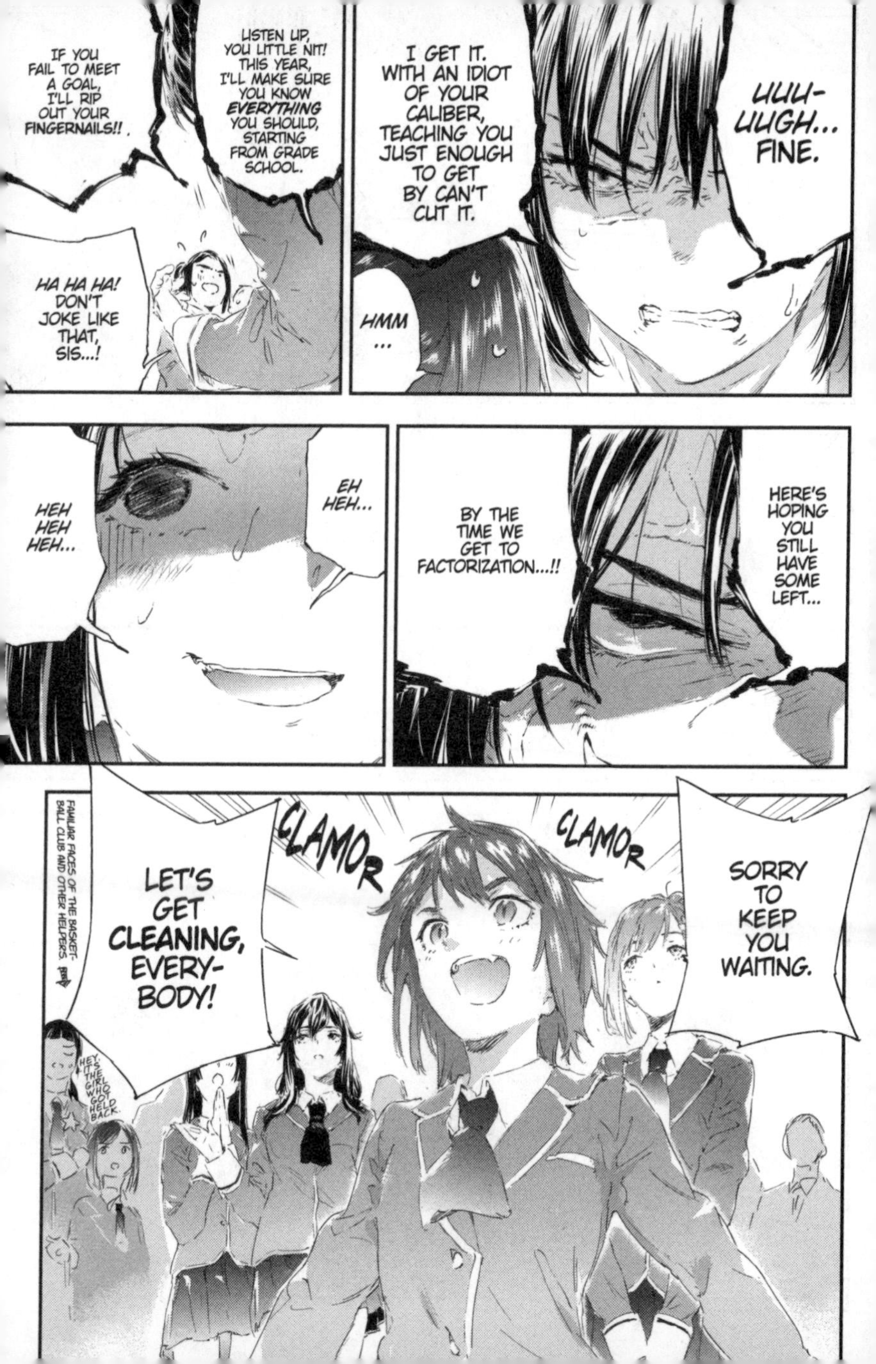
UUU-UUGH... FINE.
I GET IT. WITH AN IDIOT OF YOUR CALIBER, TEACHING YOU JUST ENOUGH TO GET BY CAN'T CUT IT.
HMM...
LISTEN UP, YOU LITTLE NIT! THIS YEAR, I'LL MAKE SURE YOU KNOW *EVERYTHING* YOU SHOULD, STARTING FROM GRADE SCHOOL.
IF YOU FAIL TO MEET A GOAL, I'LL RIP OUT YOUR FINGERNAILS!!
HA HA HA! DON'T JOKE LIKE THAT, SIS...!
HERE'S HOPING YOU STILL HAVE SOME LEFT...
BY THE TIME WE GET TO FACTORIZATION...!!
EH HEH...
HEH HEH HEH...
SORRY TO KEEP YOU WAITING.
CLAMOR
CLAMOR
LET'S GET CLEANING, EVERY-BODY!
HEY, IT'S THE GIRL WHO GOT HELD BACK.
FAMILIAR FACES OF THE BASKET-BALL CLUB AND OTHER HELPERS.

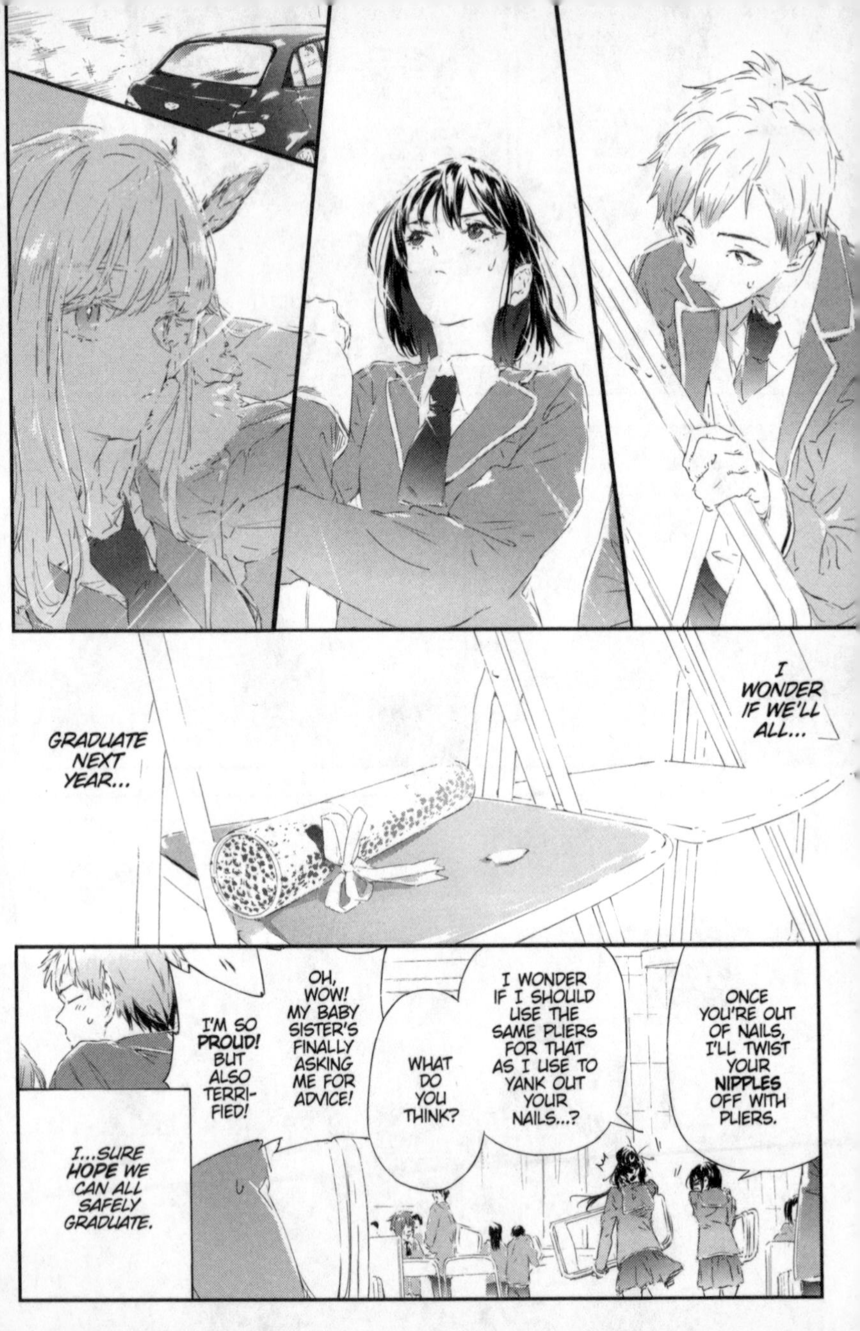
I WONDER IF WE'LL ALL...
GRADUATE NEXT YEAR...
ONCE YOU'RE OUT OF NAILS, I'LL TWIST YOUR NIPPLES OFF WITH PLIERS.
I WONDER IF I SHOULD USE THE SAME PLIERS FOR THAT AS I USE TO YANK OUT YOUR NAILS...?
WHAT DO YOU THINK?
OH, WOW! MY BABY SISTER'S FINALLY ASKING ME FOR ADVICE!
I'M SO PROUD! BUT ALSO TERRIFIED!
I...SURE HOPE WE CAN ALL SAFELY GRADUATE.

I don't have many friends

Haganai I don't have many friends

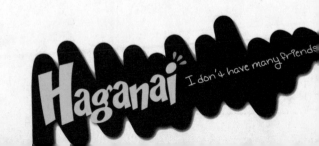

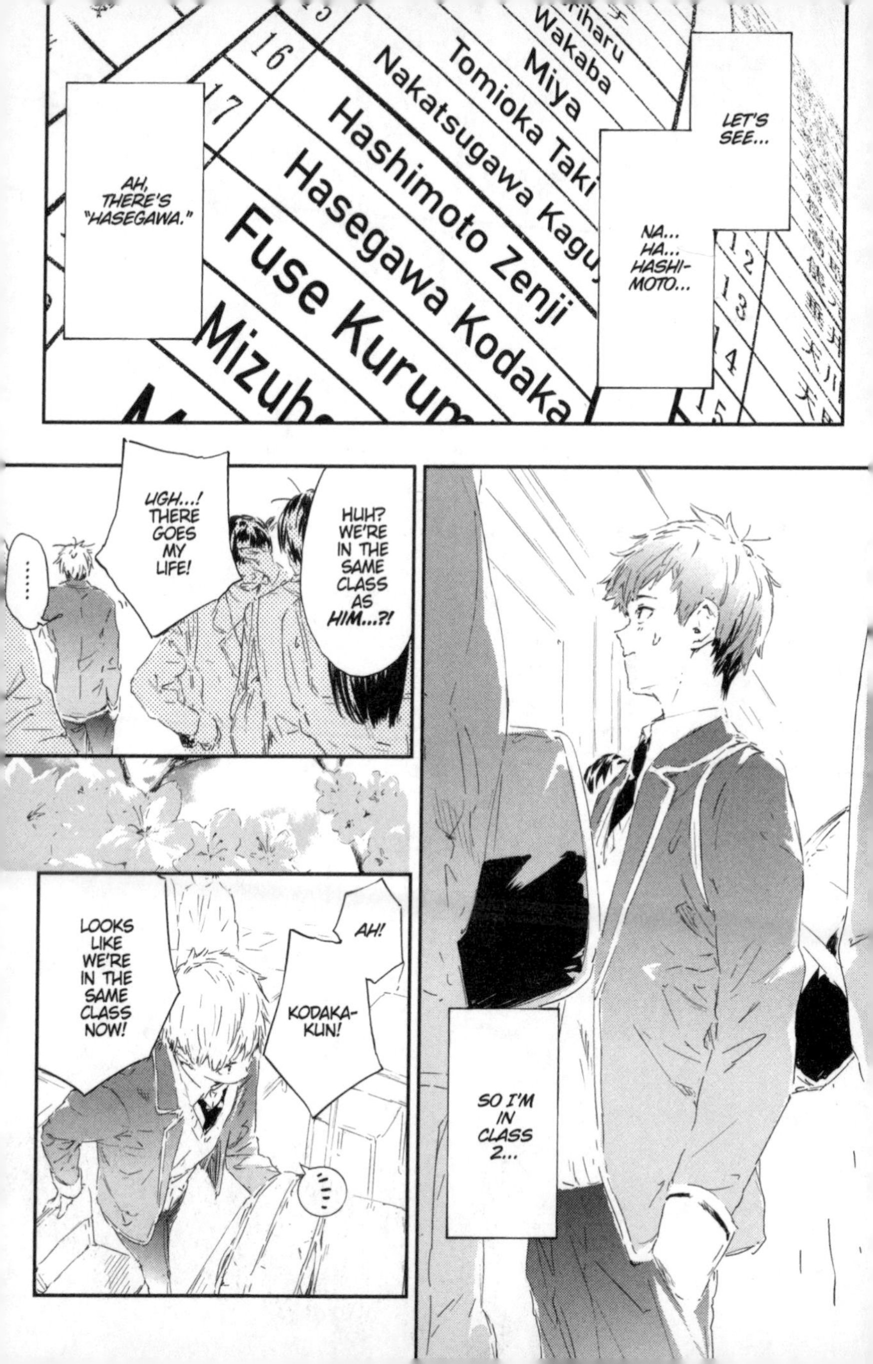
LET'S SEE...
NA... HA... HASHIMOTO...
Wakaba
Miya
Tomioka Taki
Hashimoto Zenji
Hasegawa Kodaka
AH, THERE'S "HASEGAWA."
SO I'M IN CLASS 2...
HUH? WE'RE IN THE SAME CLASS AS HIM...?!
UGH...! THERE GOES MY LIFE!
......
AH!
KODAKA-KUN!
LOOKS LIKE WE'RE IN THE SAME CLASS NOW!
!!

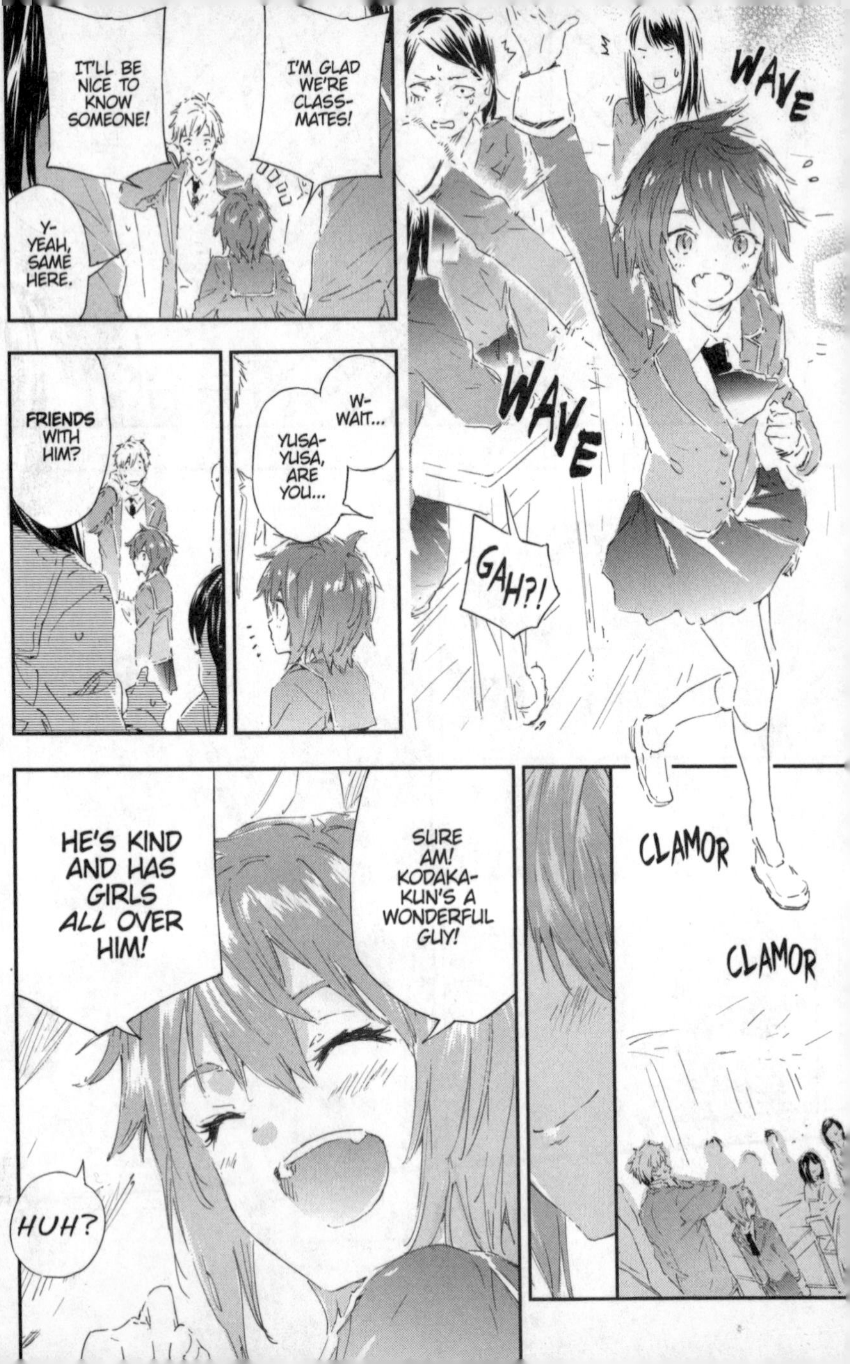
WAVE
WAVE
GAH?!
I'M GLAD WE'RE CLASSMATES!
IT'LL BE NICE TO KNOW SOMEONE!
Y-YEAH, SAME HERE.
W-WAIT... YUSA-YUSA, ARE YOU...
FRIENDS WITH HIM?
CLAMOR
CLAMOR
SURE AM! KODAKA-KUN'S A WONDERFUL GUY!
HE'S KIND AND HAS GIRLS ALL OVER HIM!
HUH?

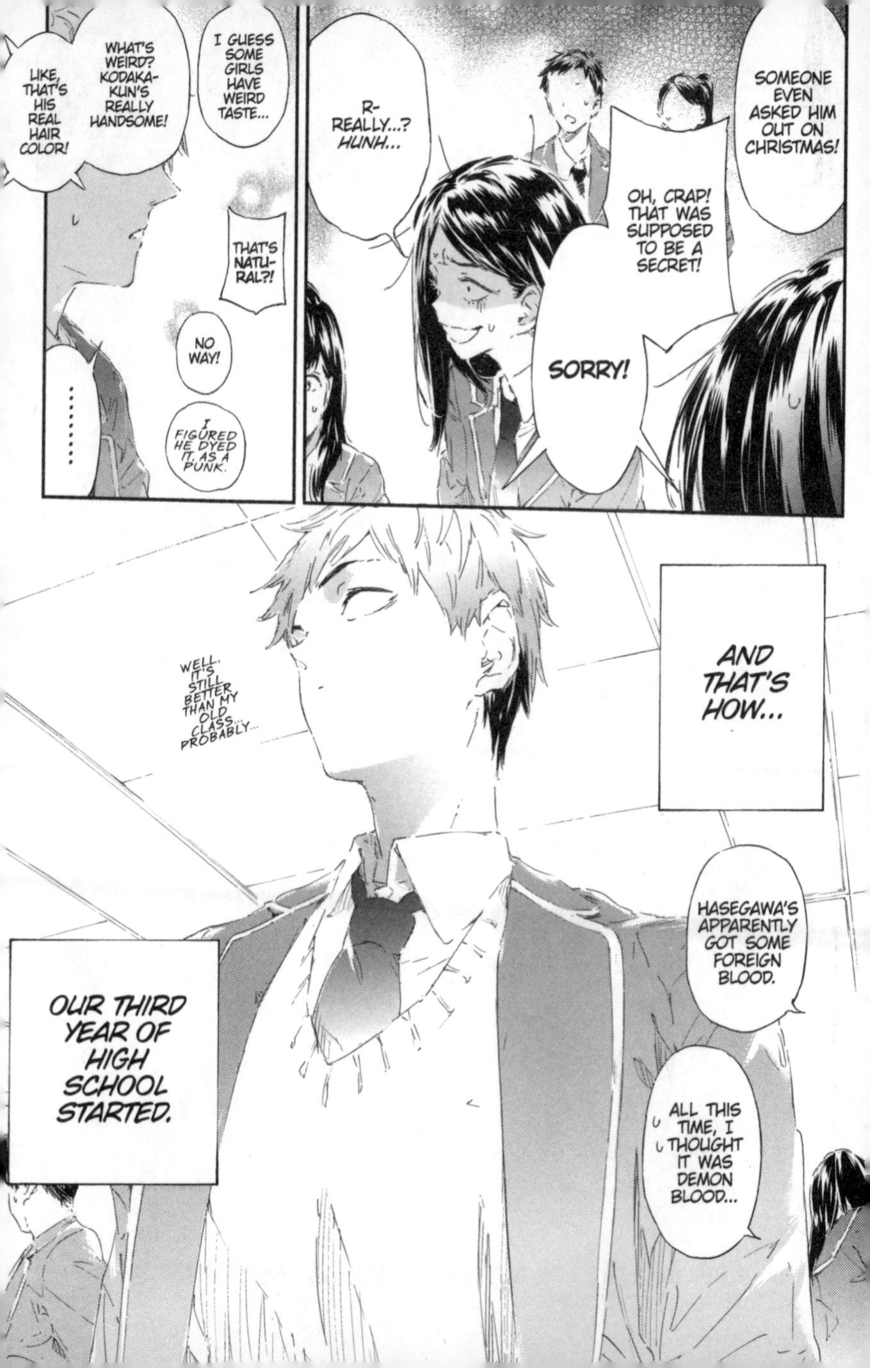
SOMEONE EVEN ASKED HIM OUT ON CHRISTMAS!
R- REALLY...? HUNH...
OH, CRAP! THAT WAS SUPPOSED TO BE A SECRET!
SORRY!
I GUESS SOME GIRLS HAVE WEIRD TASTE...
WHAT'S WEIRD? KODAKA-KUN'S REALLY HANDSOME!
LIKE, THAT'S HIS REAL HAIR COLOR!
THAT'S NATU-RAL?!
NO WAY!
I FIGURED HE DYED IT AS A PUNK.
....
AND THAT'S HOW...
HASEGAWA'S APPARENTLY GOT SOME FOREIGN BLOOD.
ALL THIS TIME, I THOUGHT IT WAS DEMON BLOOD...
WELL, IT'S STILL BETTER THAN MY OLD CLASS... PROBABLY...
OUR THIRD YEAR OF HIGH SCHOOL STARTED.

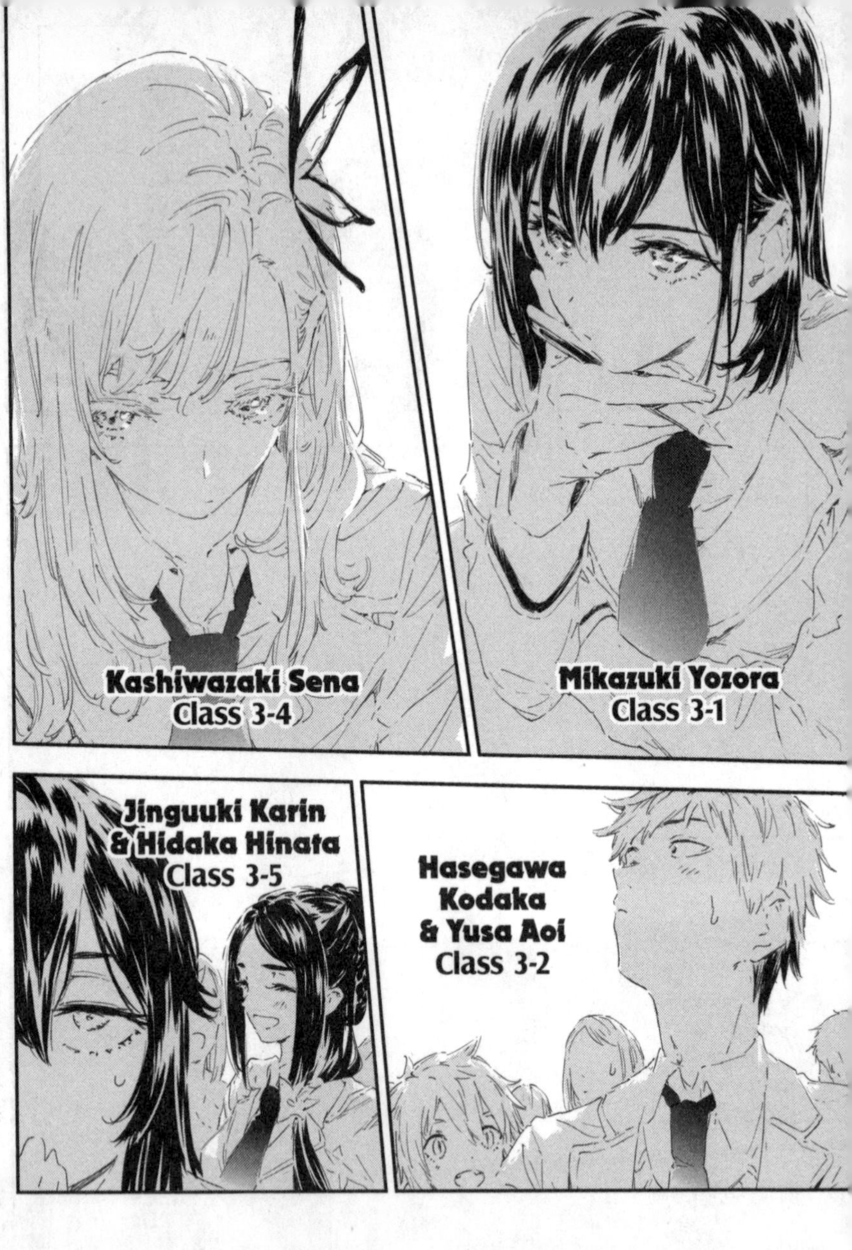
Mikazuki Yozora
Class 3-1
Kashiwazaki Sena
Class 3-4
Hasegawa Kodaka & Yusa Aoi
Class 3-2
Jinguuki Karin & Hidaka Hinata
Class 3-5

Club Activity Log 89: Honest-to-God Seminar (312)

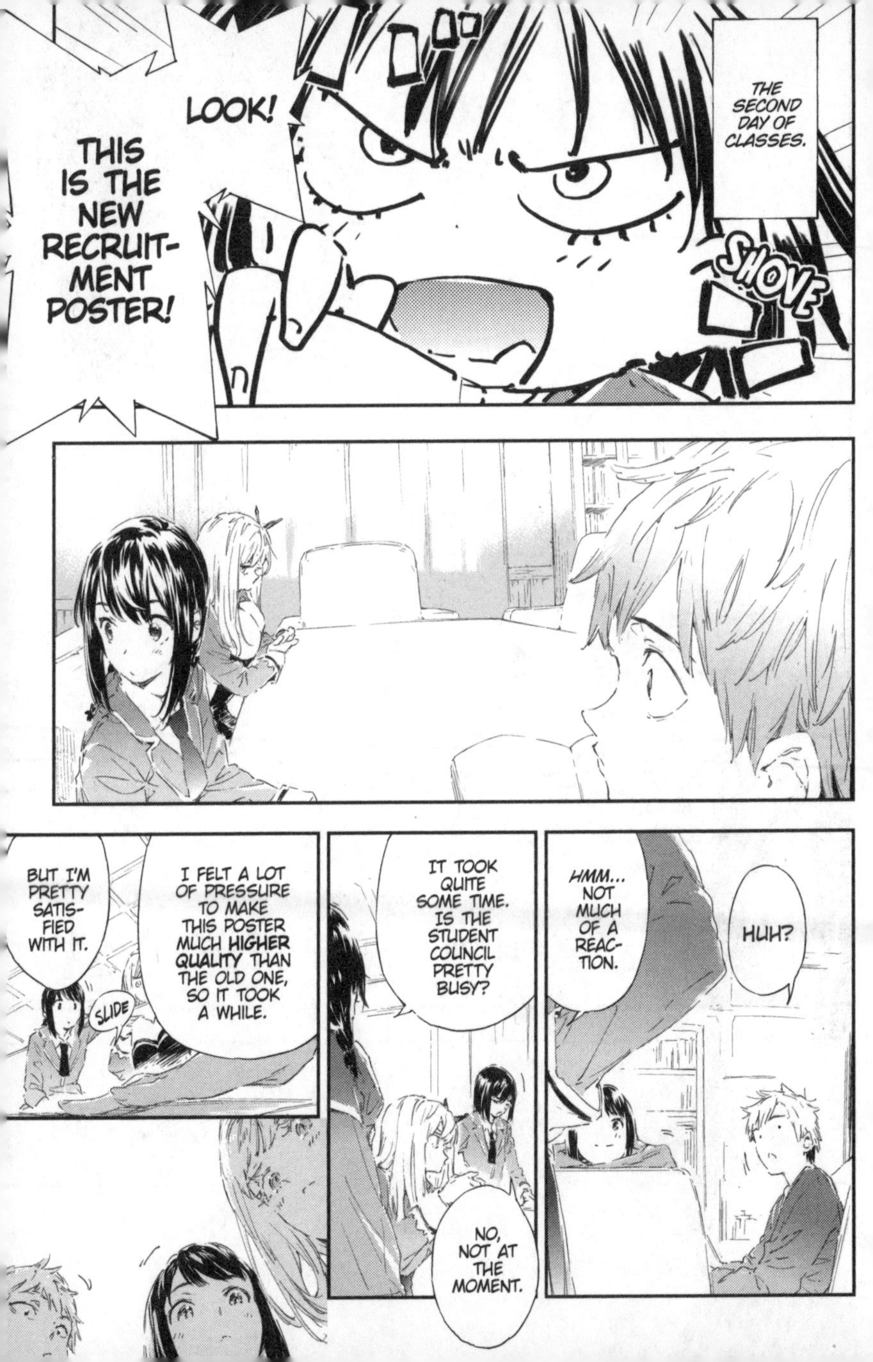
THE SECOND DAY OF CLASSES.
SHOVE
LOOK!
THIS IS THE NEW RECRUIT-MENT POSTER!
HUH?
HMM... NOT MUCH OF A REAC-TION.
IT TOOK QUITE SOME TIME. IS THE STUDENT COUNCIL PRETTY BUSY?
NO, NOT AT THE MOMENT.
I FELT A LOT OF PRESSURE TO MAKE THIS POSTER MUCH HIGHER QUALITY THAN THE OLD ONE, SO IT TOOK A WHILE.
SLIDE
BUT I'M PRETTY SATIS-FIED WITH IT.

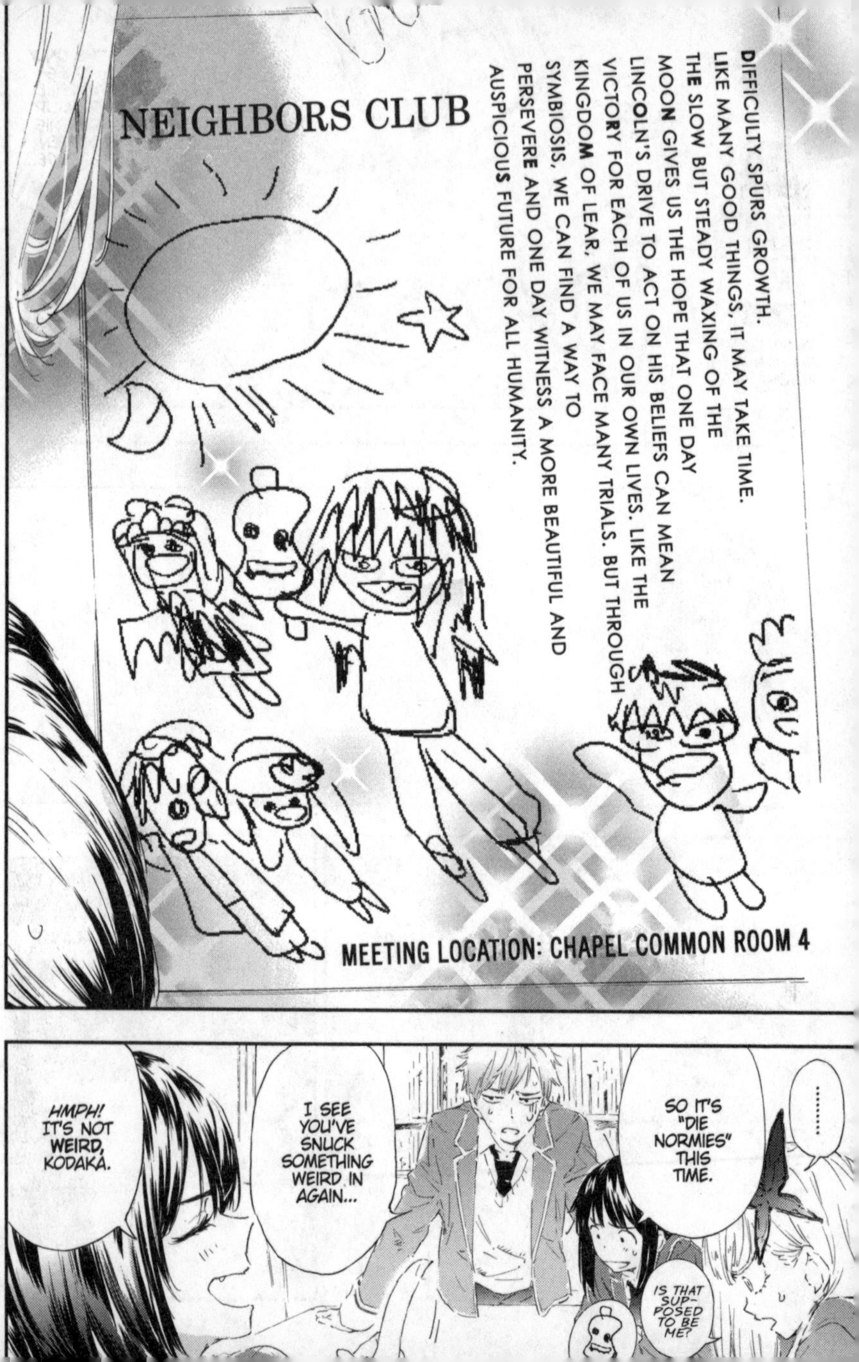
NEIGHBORS CLUB
DIFFICULTY SPURS GROWTH.
LIKE MANY GOOD THINGS, IT MAY TAKE TIME.
THE SLOW BUT STEADY WAXING OF THE
MOON GIVES US THE HOPE THAT ONE DAY
LINCOLN'S DRIVE TO ACT ON HIS BELIEFS CAN MEAN
VICTORY FOR EACH OF US IN OUR OWN LIVES. LIKE THE
KINGDOM OF LEAR, WE MAY FACE MANY TRIALS. BUT THROUGH
SYMBIOSIS, WE CAN FIND A WAY TO
PERSEVERE AND ONE DAY WITNESS A MORE BEAUTIFUL AND
AUSPICIOUS FUTURE FOR ALL HUMANITY.
MEETING LOCATION: CHAPEL COMMON ROOM 4
......
SO IT'S "DIE NORMIES" THIS TIME.
I SEE YOU'VE SNUCK SOMETHING WEIRD IN AGAIN...
HMPH! IT'S NOT WEIRD, KODAKA.
IS THAT SUP-POSED TO BE ME?

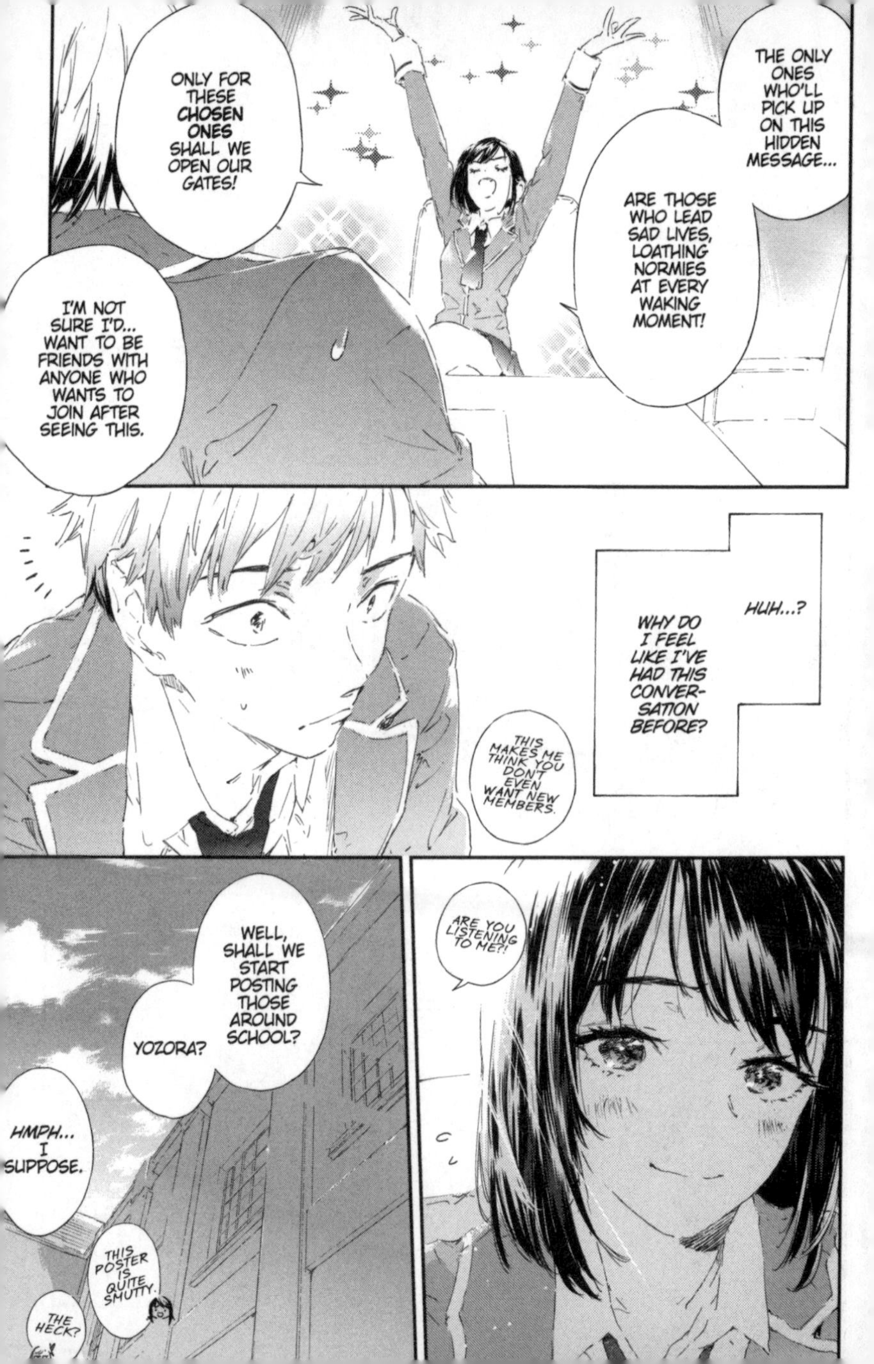
THE ONLY ONES WHO'LL PICK UP ON THIS HIDDEN MESSAGE...
ARE THOSE WHO LEAD SAD LIVES, LOATHING NORMIES AT EVERY WAKING MOMENT!
ONLY FOR THESE **CHOSEN ONES** SHALL WE OPEN OUR GATES!
I'M NOT SURE I'D... WANT TO BE FRIENDS WITH ANYONE WHO WANTS TO JOIN AFTER SEEING THIS.
HUH...?
WHY DO I FEEL LIKE I'VE HAD THIS CONVER-SATION BEFORE?
THIS MAKES ME THINK YOU DON'T EVEN WANT NEW MEMBERS.
ARE YOU LISTENING TO ME?!
WELL, SHALL WE START POSTING THOSE AROUND SCHOOL?
YOZORA?
HMPH... I SUPPOSE.
THIS POSTER IS QUITE SMUTTY.
THE HECK?

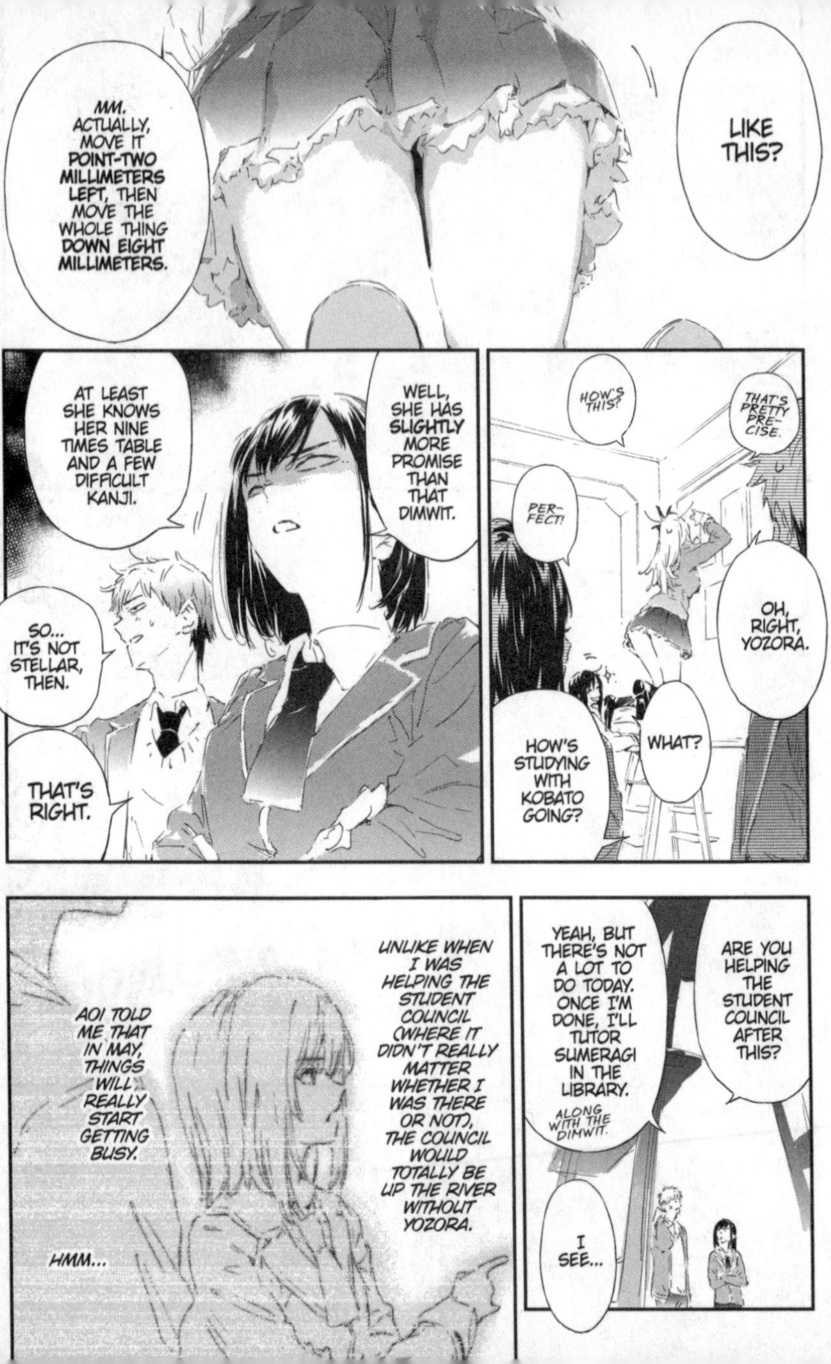
LIKE THIS?
MM. ACTUALLY, MOVE IT POINT-TWO MILLIMETERS LEFT, THEN MOVE THE WHOLE THING DOWN EIGHT MILLIMETERS.
HOW'S THIS?
THAT'S PRETTY PRECISE.
PERFECT!
OH, RIGHT, YOZORA.
WHAT?
HOW'S STUDYING WITH KOBATO GOING?
WELL, SHE HAS SLIGHTLY MORE PROMISE THAN THAT DIMWIT.
AT LEAST SHE KNOWS HER NINE TIMES TABLE AND A FEW DIFFICULT KANJI.
SO... IT'S NOT STELLAR, THEN.
THAT'S RIGHT.
ARE YOU HELPING THE STUDENT COUNCIL AFTER THIS?
YEAH, BUT THERE'S NOT A LOT TO DO TODAY. ONCE I'M DONE, I'LL TUTOR SUMERAGI IN THE LIBRARY.
ALONG WITH THE DIMWIT.
I SEE...
UNLIKE WHEN I WAS HELPING THE STUDENT COUNCIL (WHERE IT DIDN'T REALLY MATTER WHETHER I WAS THERE OR NOT), THE COUNCIL WOULD TOTALLY BE UP THE RIVER WITHOUT YOZORA.
AOI TOLD ME THAT IN MAY, THINGS WILL REALLY START GETTING BUSY.
HMM...

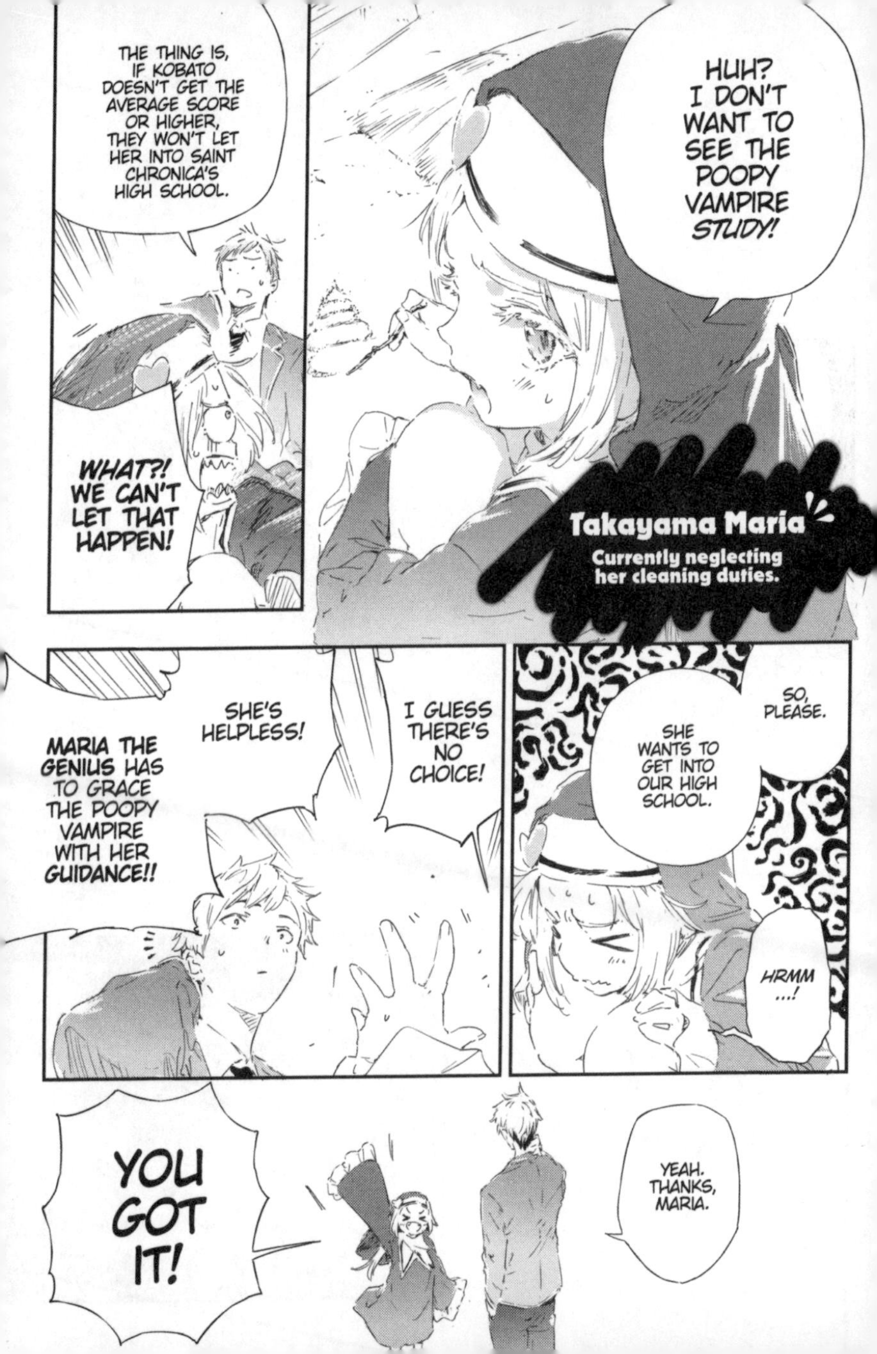
HUH? I DON'T WANT TO SEE THE POOPY VAMPIRE STUDY!
Takayama Maria
Currently neglecting her cleaning duties.
THE THING IS, IF KOBATO DOESN'T GET THE AVERAGE SCORE OR HIGHER, THEY WON'T LET HER INTO SAINT CHRONICA'S HIGH SCHOOL.
WHAT?! WE CAN'T LET THAT HAPPEN!
SO, PLEASE.
SHE WANTS TO GET INTO OUR HIGH SCHOOL.
HRMM ...!
I GUESS THERE'S NO CHOICE!
SHE'S HELPLESS!
MARIA THE GENIUS HAS TO GRACE THE POOPY VAMPIRE WITH HER GUIDANCE!!
YEAH. THANKS, MARIA.
YOU GOT IT!

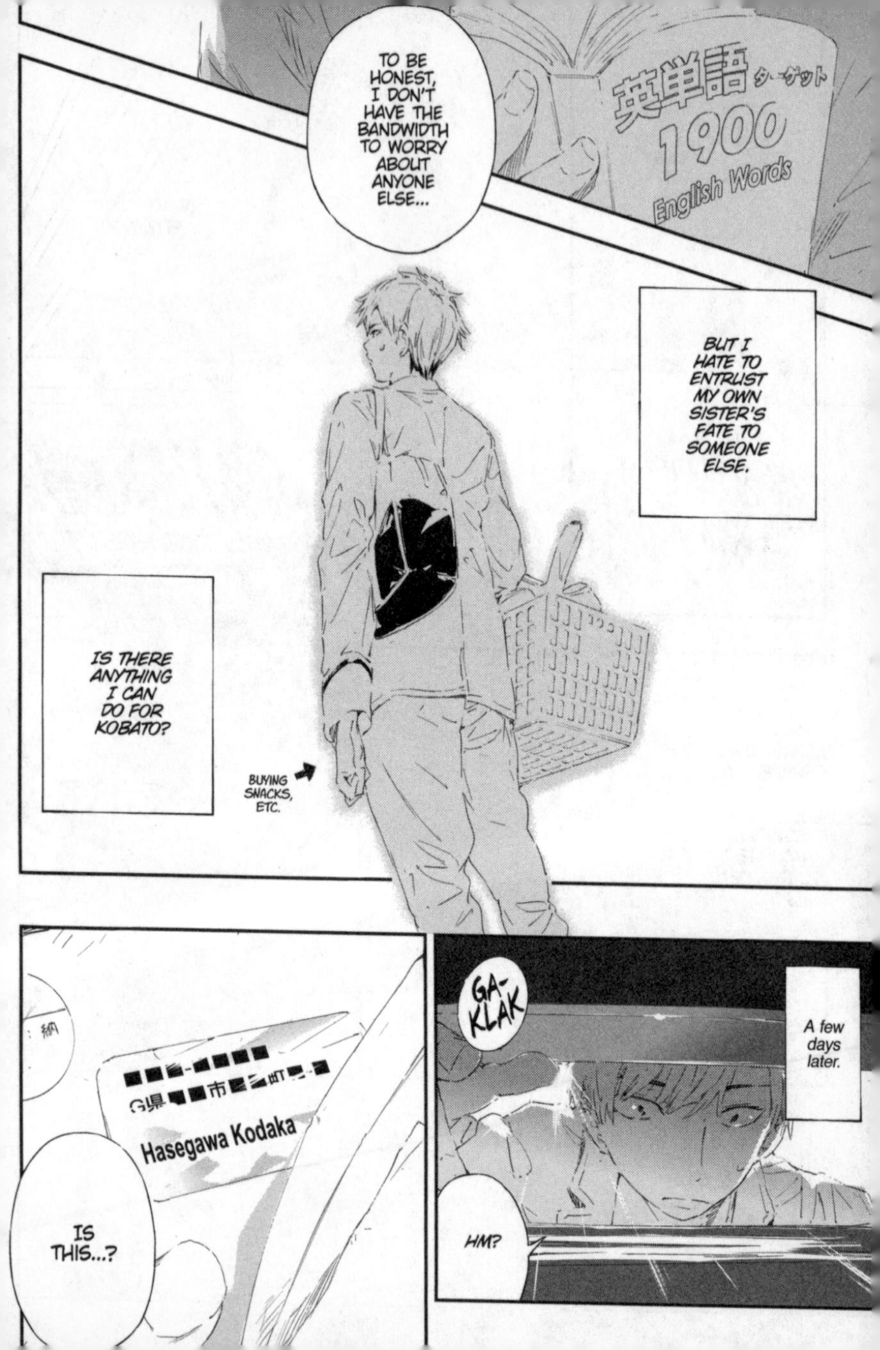
TO BE HONEST, I DON'T HAVE THE BANDWIDTH TO WORRY ABOUT ANYONE ELSE...
英単語 ターゲット
1900
English Words
BUT I HATE TO ENTRUST MY OWN SISTER'S FATE TO SOMEONE ELSE.
IS THERE ANYTHING I CAN DO FOR KOBATO?
BUYING SNACKS, ETC.
A few days later.
GA-KLAK
HM?
納
[redacted]
G県[redacted]市[redacted]町[redacted]
Hasegawa Kodaka
IS THIS...?

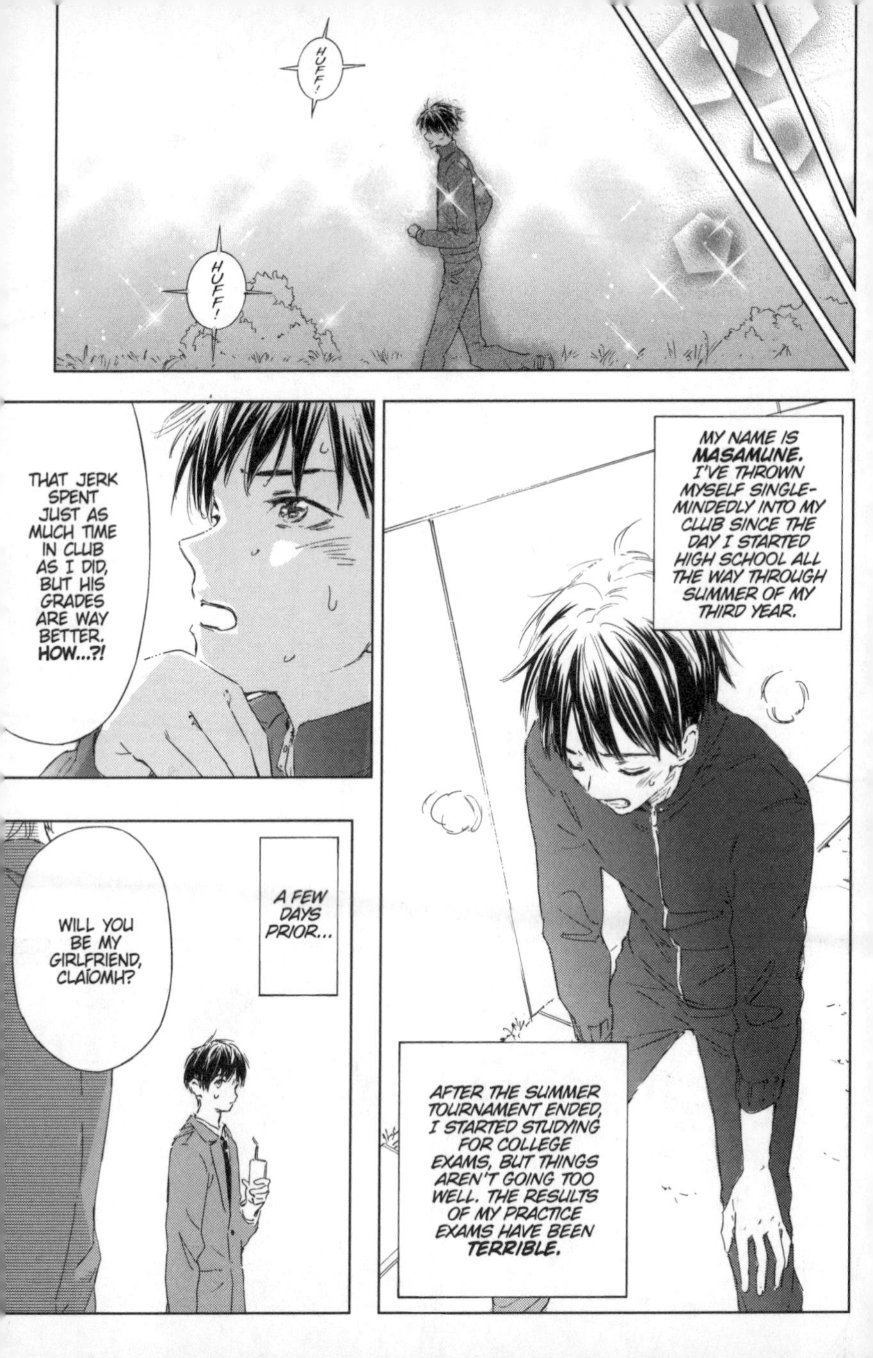
HUFF!
HUFF!
MY NAME IS MASAMUNE. I'VE THROWN MYSELF SINGLE-MINDEDLY INTO MY CLUB SINCE THE DAY I STARTED HIGH SCHOOL ALL THE WAY THROUGH SUMMER OF MY THIRD YEAR.
AFTER THE SUMMER TOURNAMENT ENDED, I STARTED STUDYING FOR COLLEGE EXAMS, BUT THINGS AREN'T GOING TOO WELL. THE RESULTS OF MY PRACTICE EXAMS HAVE BEEN TERRIBLE.
THAT JERK SPENT JUST AS MUCH TIME IN CLUB AS I DID, BUT HIS GRADES ARE WAY BETTER. HOW...?!
A FEW DAYS PRIOR...
WILL YOU BE MY GIRLFRIEND, CLAÍOMH?

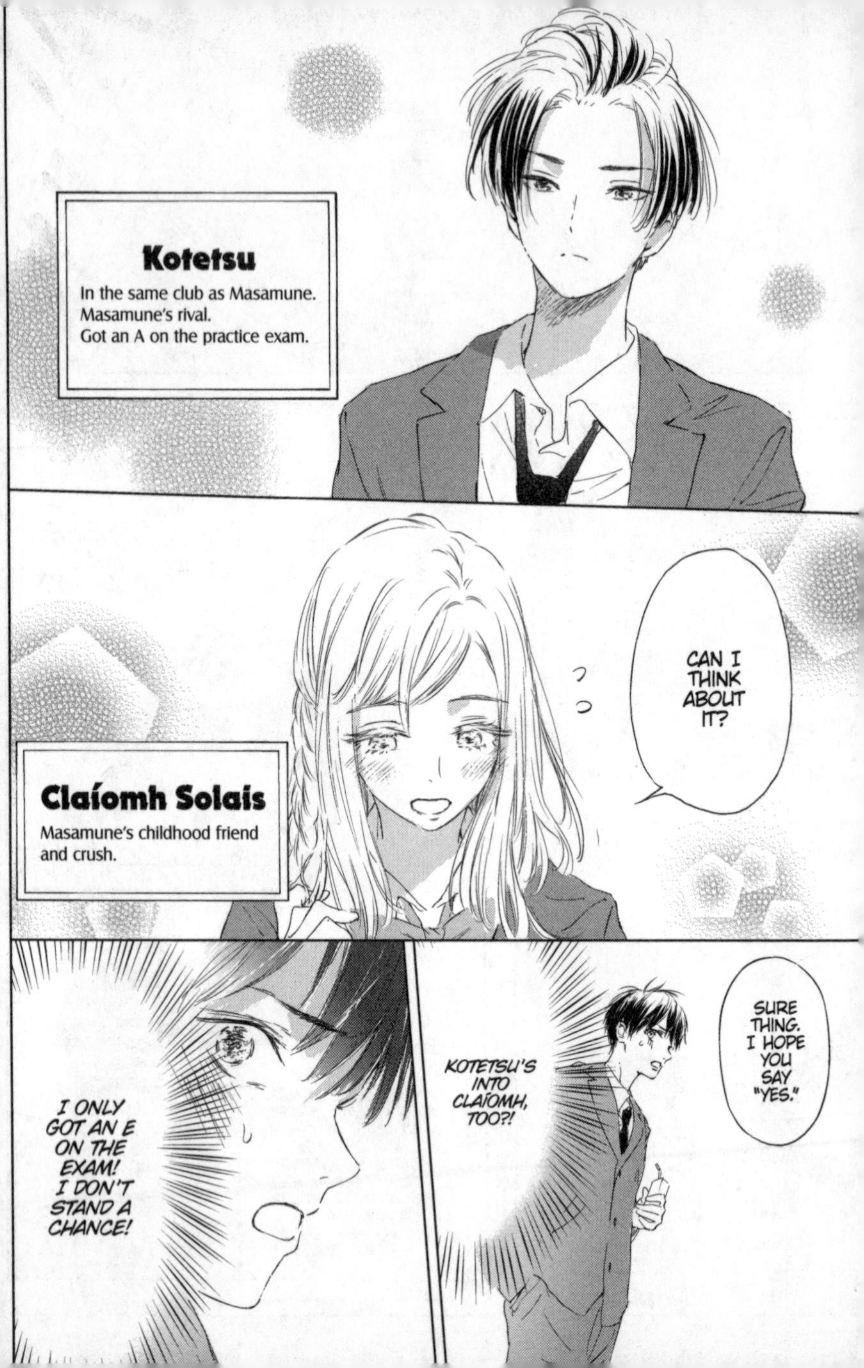

Kotetsu
In the same club as Masamune.
Masamune's rival.
Got an A on the practice exam.
CAN I THINK ABOUT IT?
Claíomh Solais
Masamune's childhood friend and crush.
SURE THING. I HOPE YOU SAY "YES."
KOTETSU'S INTO CLAÍOMH, TOO?!
I ONLY GOT AN E ON THE EXAM! I DON'T STAND A CHANCE!

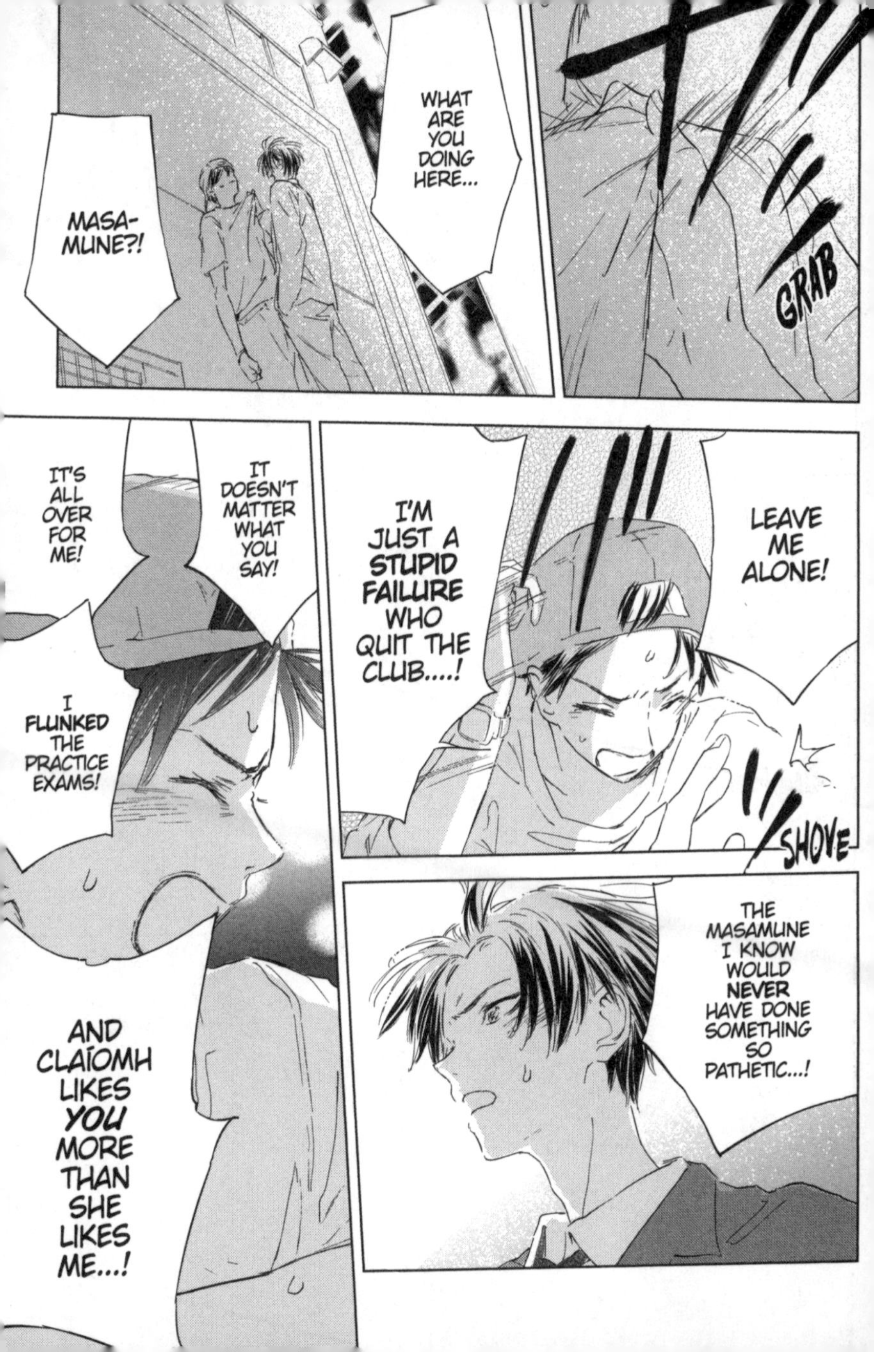
GRAB
WHAT ARE YOU DOING HERE...
MASA-MUNE?!
LEAVE ME ALONE!
I'M JUST A **STUPID FAILURE** WHO QUIT THE CLUB....!
SHOVE
THE MASAMUNE I KNOW WOULD **NEVER** HAVE DONE SOMETHING SO PATHETIC...!
IT DOESN'T MATTER WHAT YOU SAY!
IT'S ALL OVER FOR ME!
I FLUNKED THE PRACTICE EXAMS!
AND CLAÍOMH LIKES ***YOU*** MORE THAN SHE LIKES ME...!

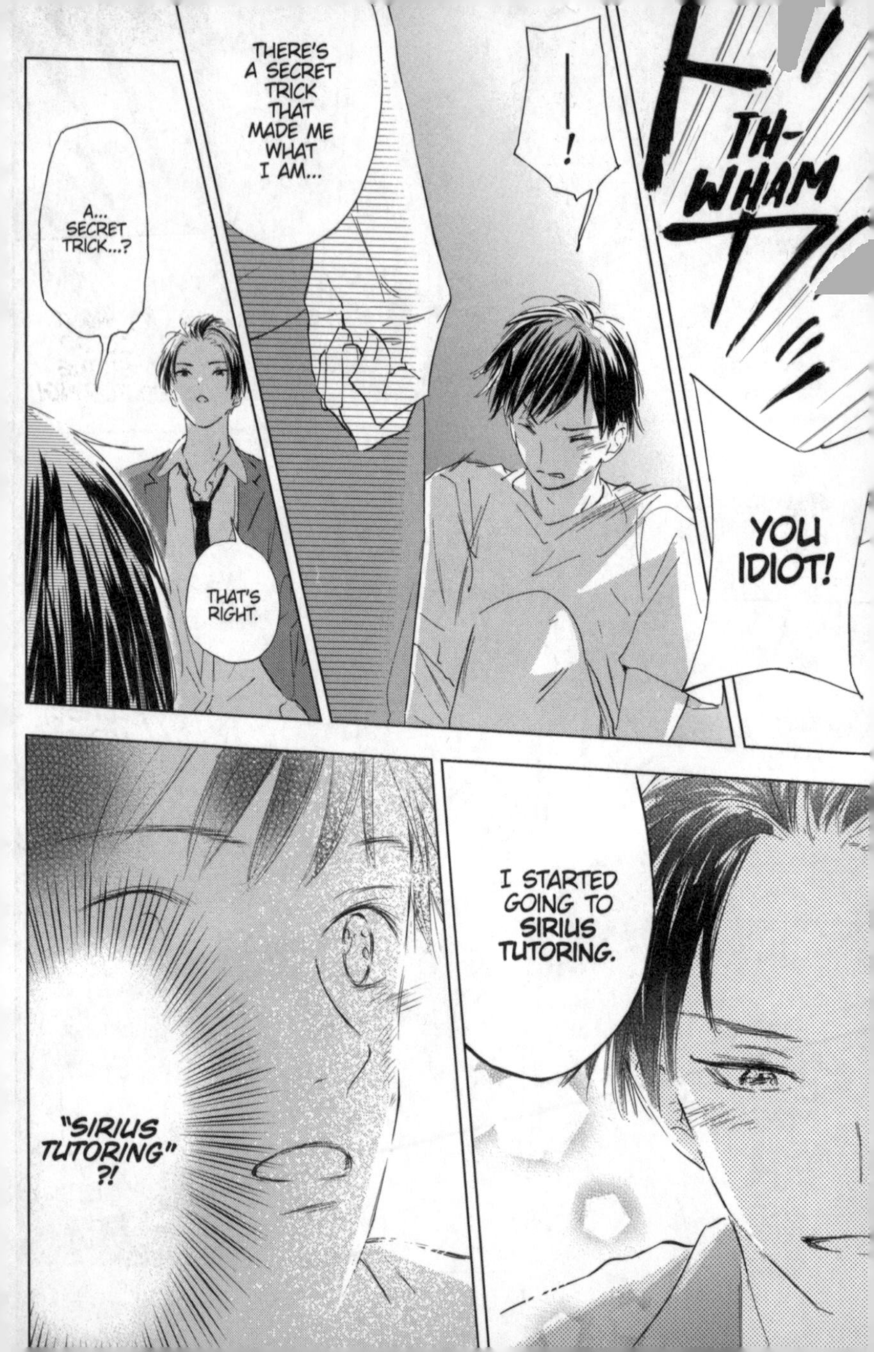
TH-WHAM
YOU IDIOT!
—!
THERE'S A SECRET TRICK THAT MADE ME WHAT I AM...
A... SECRET TRICK...?
THAT'S RIGHT.
I STARTED GOING TO SIRIUS TUTORING.
"SIRIUS TUTORING" ?!

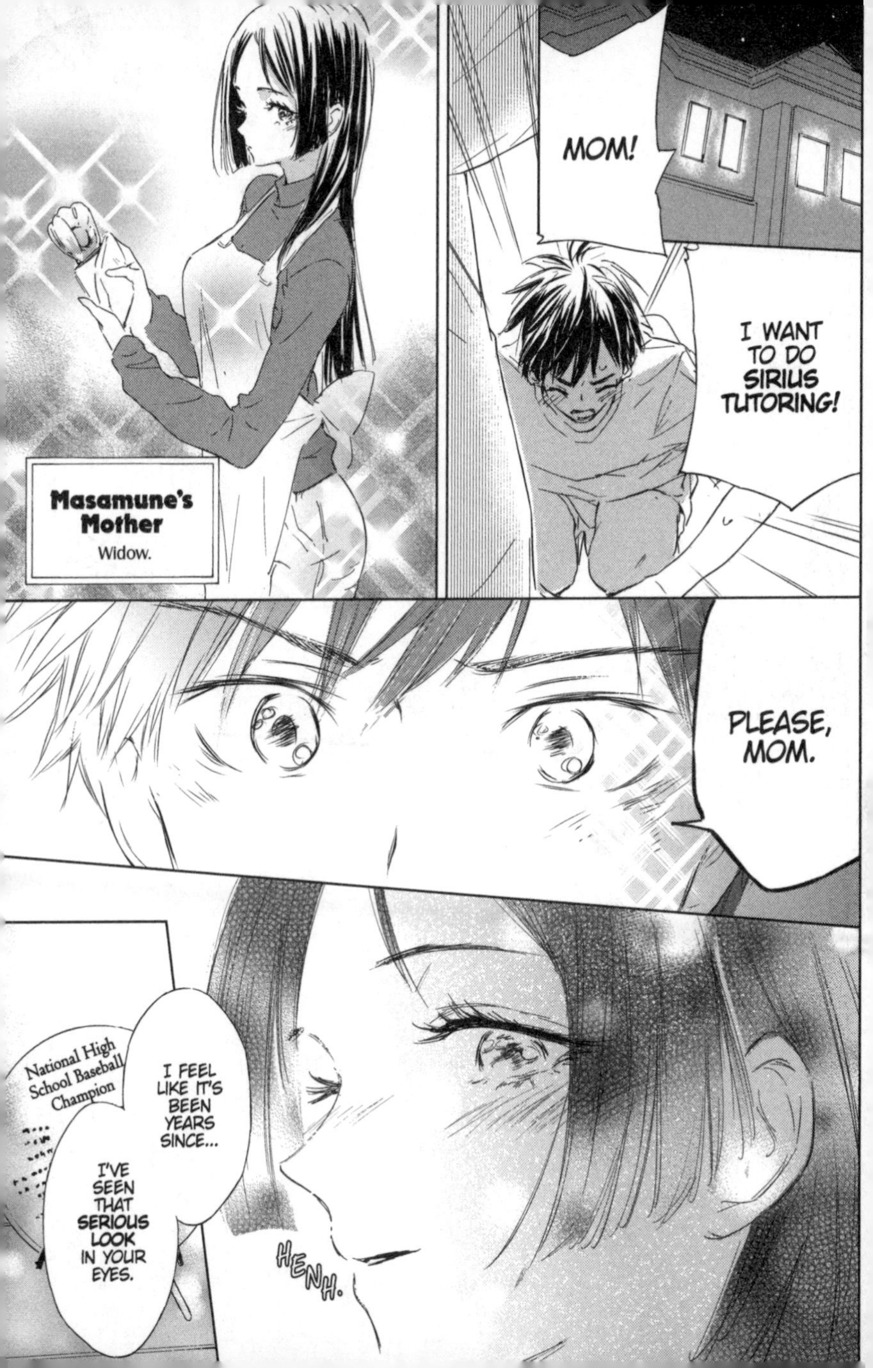
MOM!
I WANT TO DO SIRIUS TUTORING!
Masamune's Mother
Widow.
PLEASE, MOM.
I FEEL LIKE IT'S BEEN YEARS SINCE...
National High School Baseball Champion
I'VE SEEN THAT SERIOUS LOOK IN YOUR EYES.
HENH.

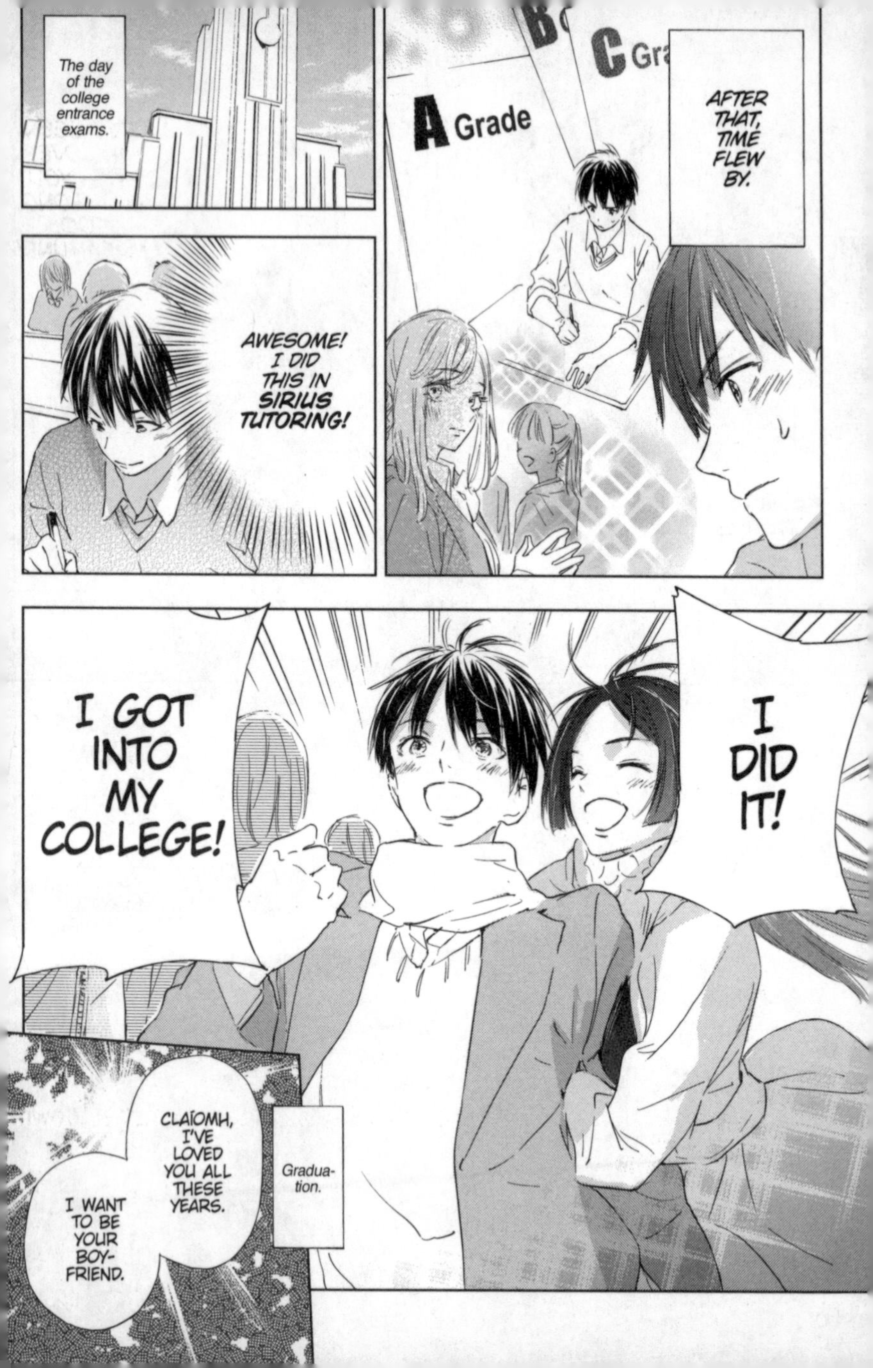
AFTER THAT, TIME FLEW BY.
A Grade
The day of the college entrance exams.
AWESOME! I DID THIS IN SIRIUS TUTORING!
I DID IT!
I GOT INTO MY COLLEGE!
Gradua-tion.
CLAÍOMH, I'VE LOVED YOU ALL THESE YEARS.
I WANT TO BE YOUR BOY-FRIEND.

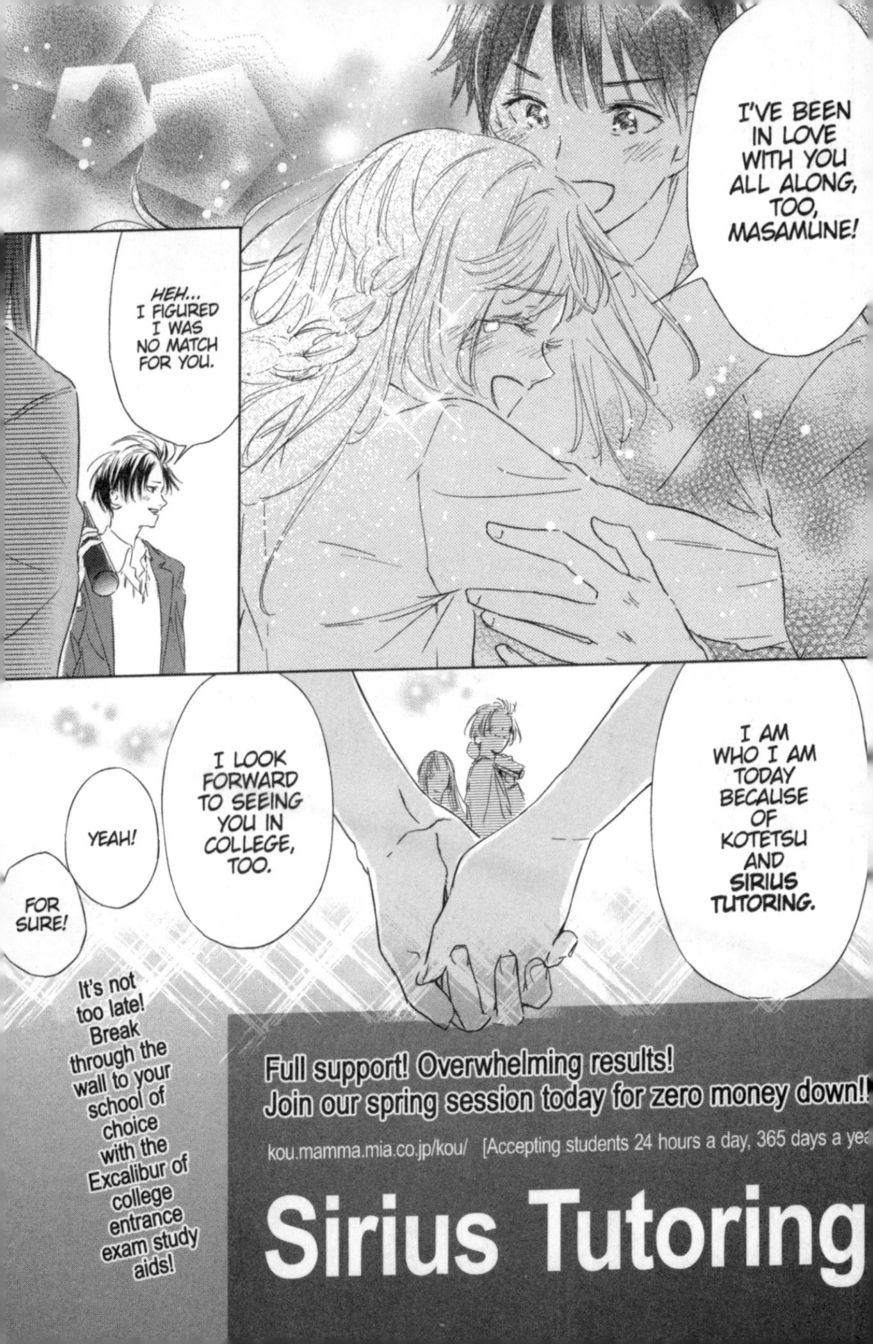
I'VE BEEN IN LOVE WITH YOU ALL ALONG, TOO, MASAMUNE!
HEH... I FIGURED I WAS NO MATCH FOR YOU.
I AM WHO I AM TODAY BECAUSE OF KOTETSU AND SIRIUS TUTORING.
I LOOK FORWARD TO SEEING YOU IN COLLEGE, TOO.
YEAH!
FOR SURE!
It's not too late! Break through the wall to your school of choice with the Excalibur of college entrance exam study aids!
Full support! Overwhelming results!
Join our spring session today for zero money down!!
kou.mamma.mia.co.jp/kou/ [Accepting students 24 hours a day, 365 days a yea
Sirius Tutoring

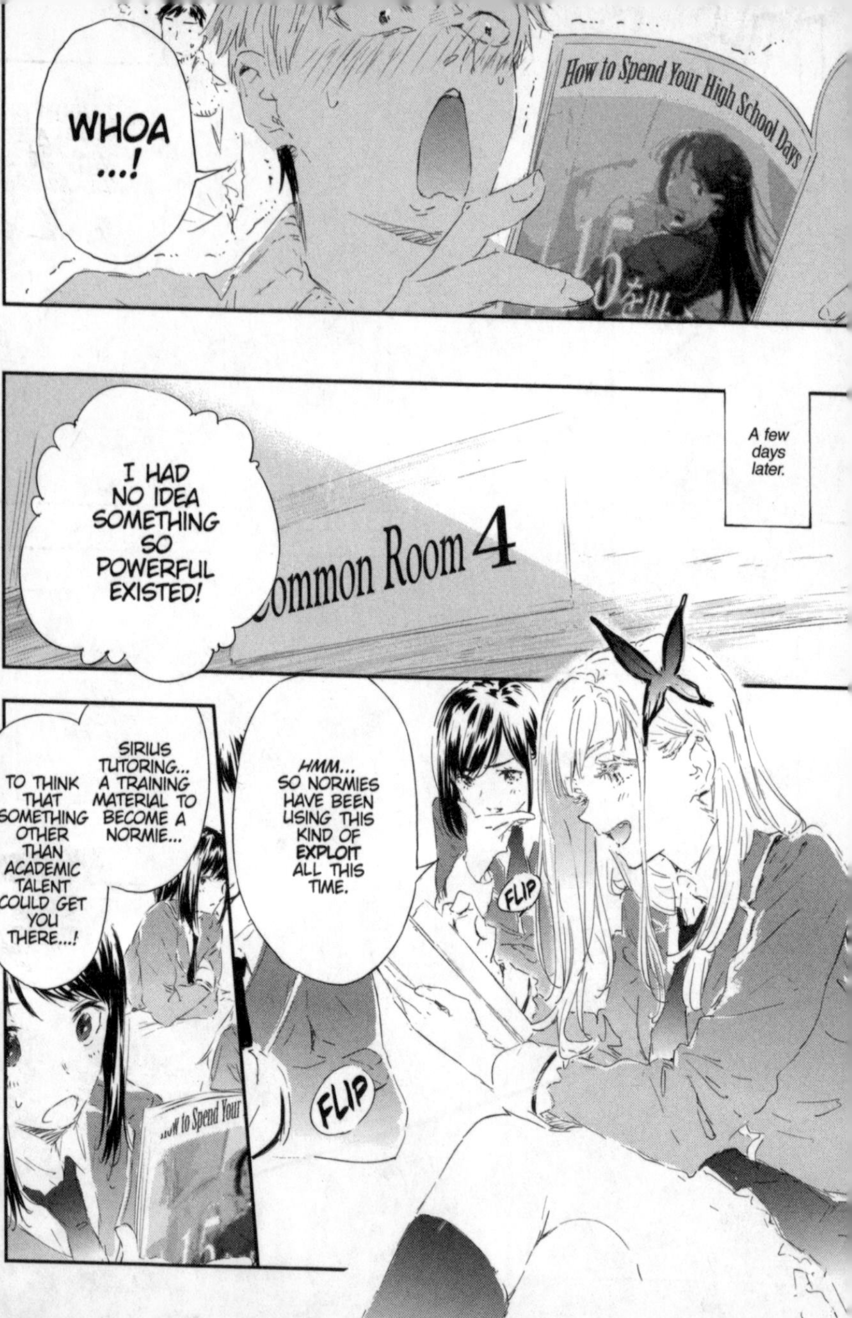
How to Spend Your High School Days
WHOA ...!
A few days later.
Common Room 4
I HAD NO IDEA SOMETHING SO POWERFUL EXISTED!
HMM... SO NORMIES HAVE BEEN USING THIS KIND OF EXPLOIT ALL THIS TIME.
FLIP
FLIP
SIRIUS TUTORING... A TRAINING MATERIAL TO BECOME A NORMIE...
TO THINK THAT SOMETHING OTHER THAN ACADEMIC TALENT COULD GET YOU THERE...!
How to Spend Your

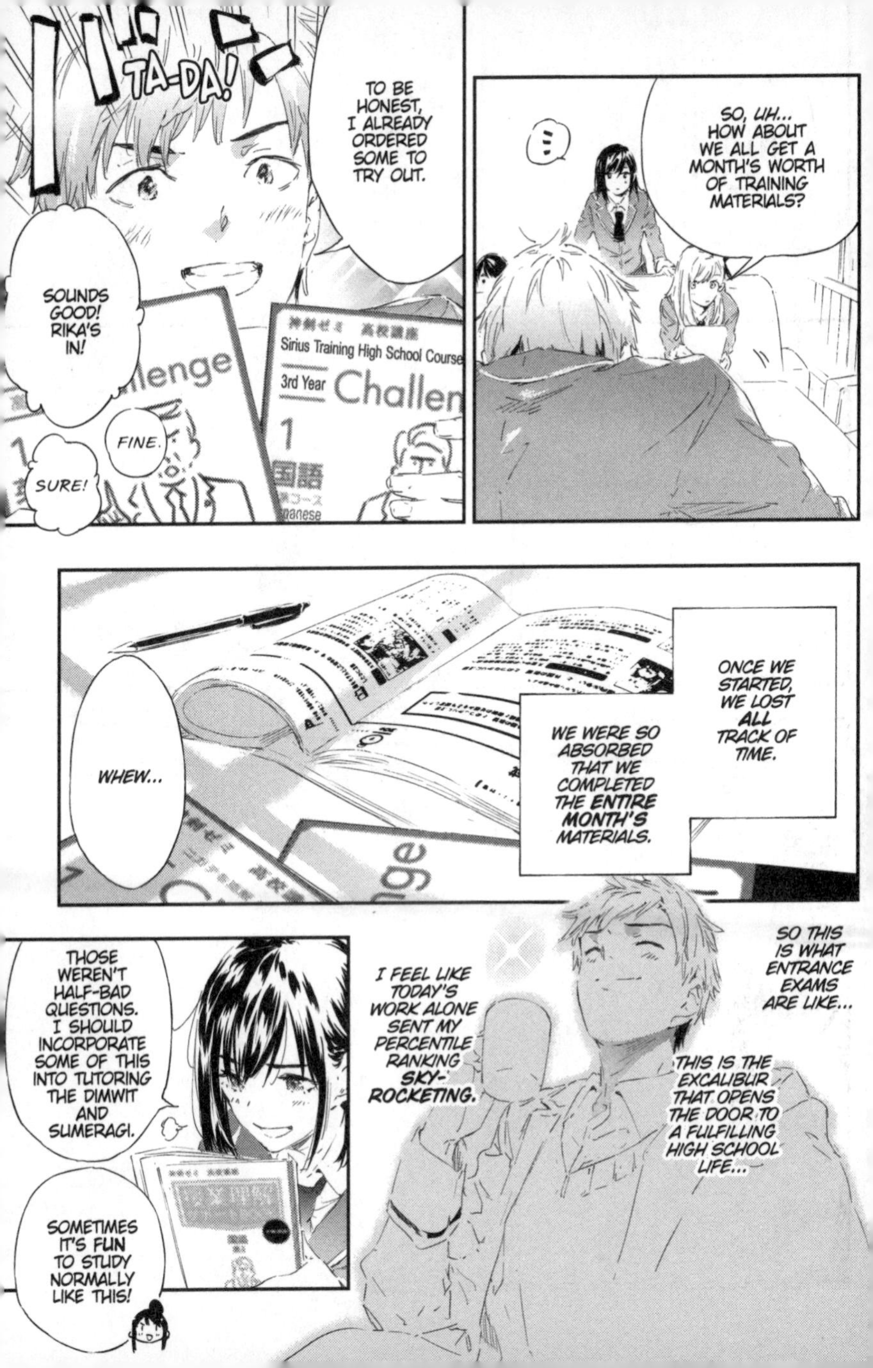

...
SO, UH... HOW ABOUT WE ALL GET A MONTH'S WORTH OF TRAINING MATERIALS?
TA-DA!
TO BE HONEST, I ALREADY ORDERED SOME TO TRY OUT.
Sirius Training High School Course
3rd Year
Challen
国語
SOUNDS GOOD! RIKA'S IN!
FINE.
SURE!
ONCE WE STARTED, WE LOST ALL TRACK OF TIME.
WE WERE SO ABSORBED THAT WE COMPLETED THE ENTIRE MONTH'S MATERIALS.
WHEW...
SO THIS IS WHAT ENTRANCE EXAMS ARE LIKE...
THIS IS THE EXCALIBUR THAT OPENS THE DOOR TO A FULFILLING HIGH SCHOOL LIFE...
I FEEL LIKE TODAY'S WORK ALONE SENT MY PERCENTILE RANKING SKY-ROCKETING.
THOSE WEREN'T HALF-BAD QUESTIONS. I SHOULD INCORPORATE SOME OF THIS INTO TUTORING THE DIMWIT AND SUMERAGI.
SOMETIMES IT'S FUN TO STUDY NORMALLY LIKE THIS!

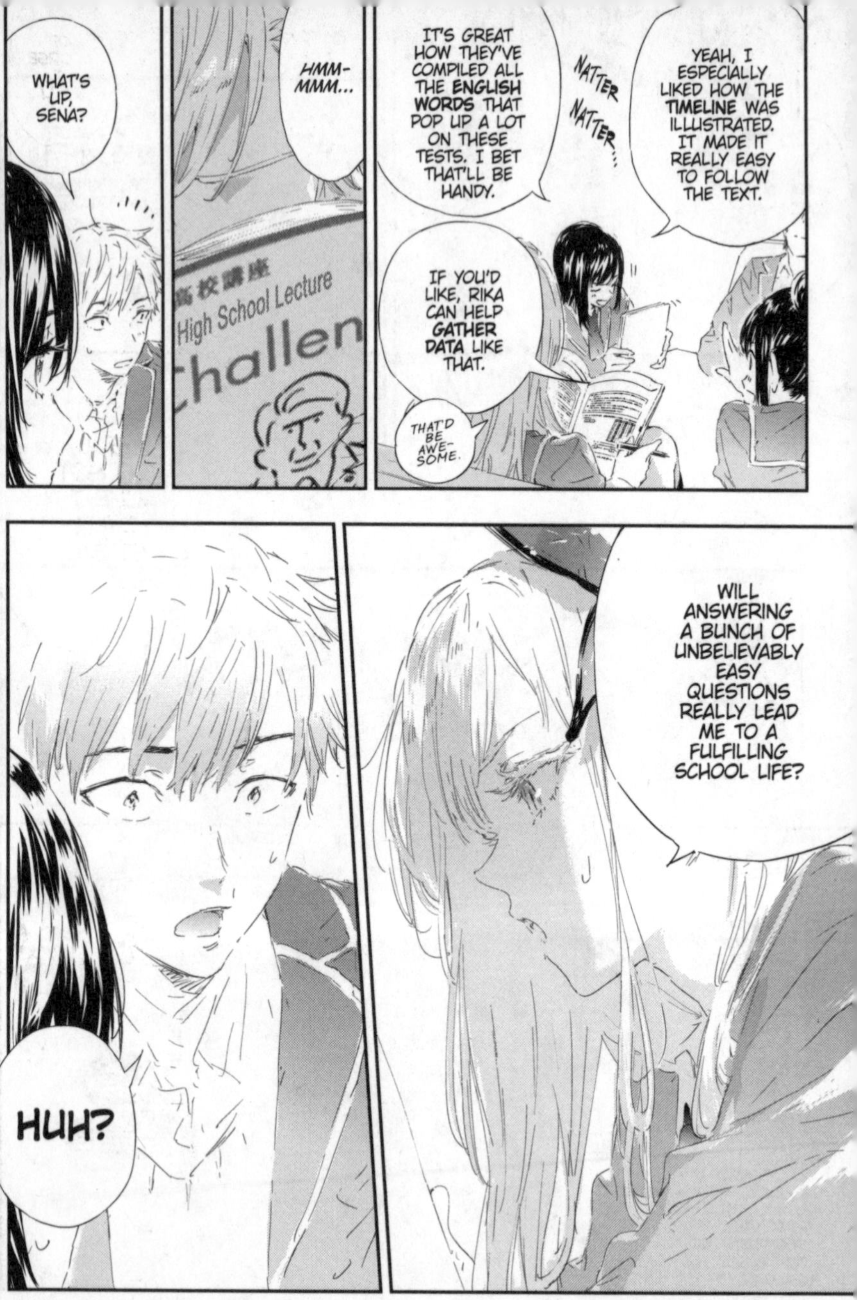
YEAH, I ESPECIALLY LIKED HOW THE TIMELINE WAS ILLUSTRATED. IT MADE IT REALLY EASY TO FOLLOW THE TEXT.
NATTER NATTER...
IT'S GREAT HOW THEY'VE COMPILED ALL THE ENGLISH WORDS THAT POP UP A LOT ON THESE TESTS. I BET THAT'LL BE HANDY.
IF YOU'D LIKE, RIKA CAN HELP GATHER DATA LIKE THAT.
THAT'D BE AWE-SOME.
HMM-MMM...
High School Lecture
Challen
WHAT'S UP, SENA?
WILL ANSWERING A BUNCH OF UNBELIEVABLY EASY QUESTIONS REALLY LEAD ME TO A FULFILLING SCHOOL LIFE?
HUH?

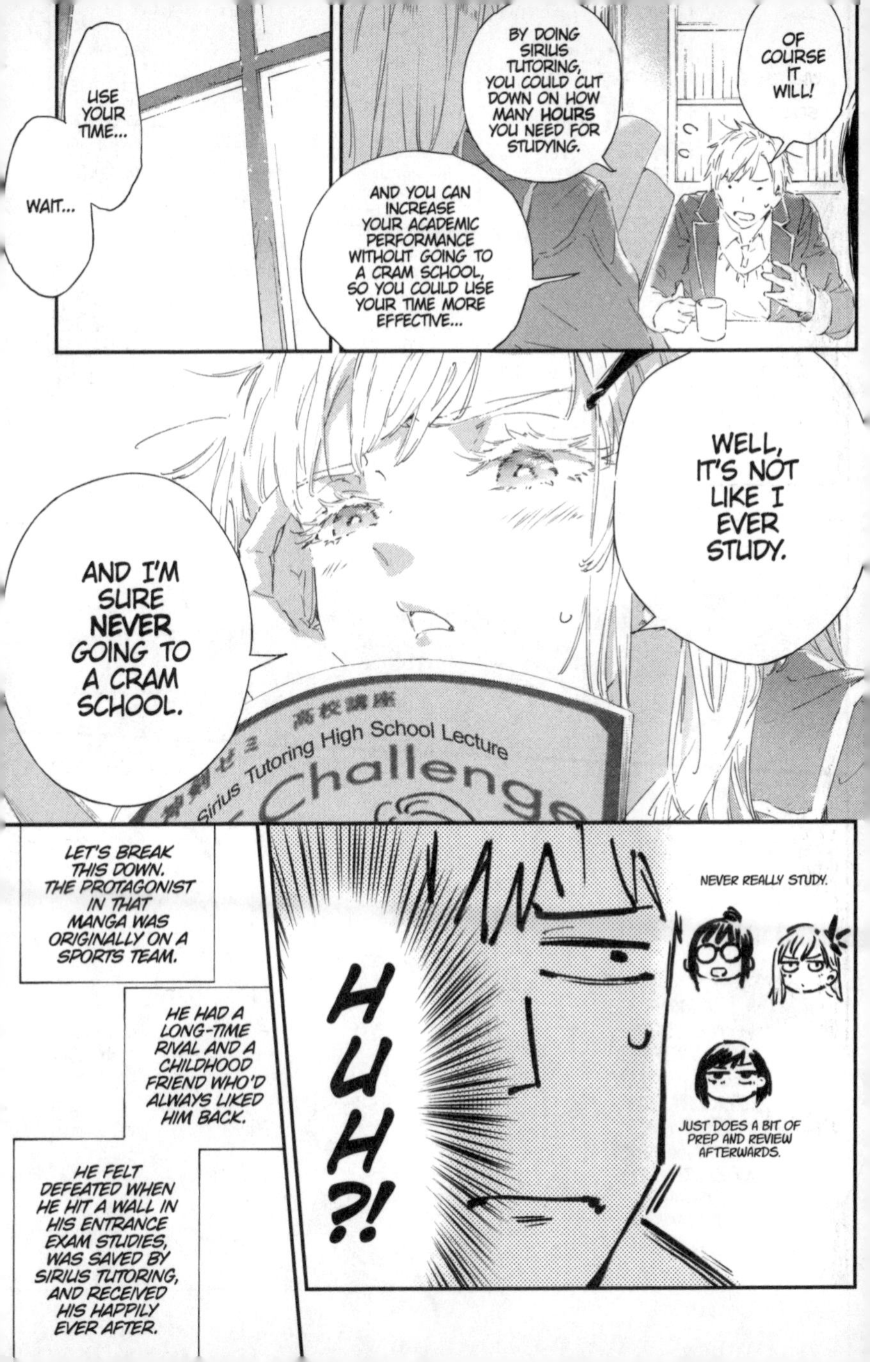
OF COURSE IT WILL!
BY DOING SIRIUS TUTORING, YOU COULD CUT DOWN ON HOW MANY HOURS YOU NEED FOR STUDYING.
AND YOU CAN INCREASE YOUR ACADEMIC PERFORMANCE WITHOUT GOING TO A CRAM SCHOOL, SO YOU COULD USE YOUR TIME MORE EFFECTIVE...
USE YOUR TIME...
WAIT...
WELL, IT'S NOT LIKE I EVER STUDY.
AND I'M SURE NEVER GOING TO A CRAM SCHOOL.
高校講座
Sirius Tutoring High School Lecture
NEVER REALLY STUDY.
JUST DOES A BIT OF PREP AND REVIEW AFTERWARDS.
HUH?!
LET'S BREAK THIS DOWN. THE PROTAGONIST IN THAT MANGA WAS ORIGINALLY ON A SPORTS TEAM.
HE HAD A LONG-TIME RIVAL AND A CHILDHOOD FRIEND WHO'D ALWAYS LIKED HIM BACK.
HE FELT DEFEATED WHEN HE HIT A WALL IN HIS ENTRANCE EXAM STUDIES, WAS SAVED BY SIRIUS TUTORING, AND RECEIVED HIS HAPPILY EVER AFTER.

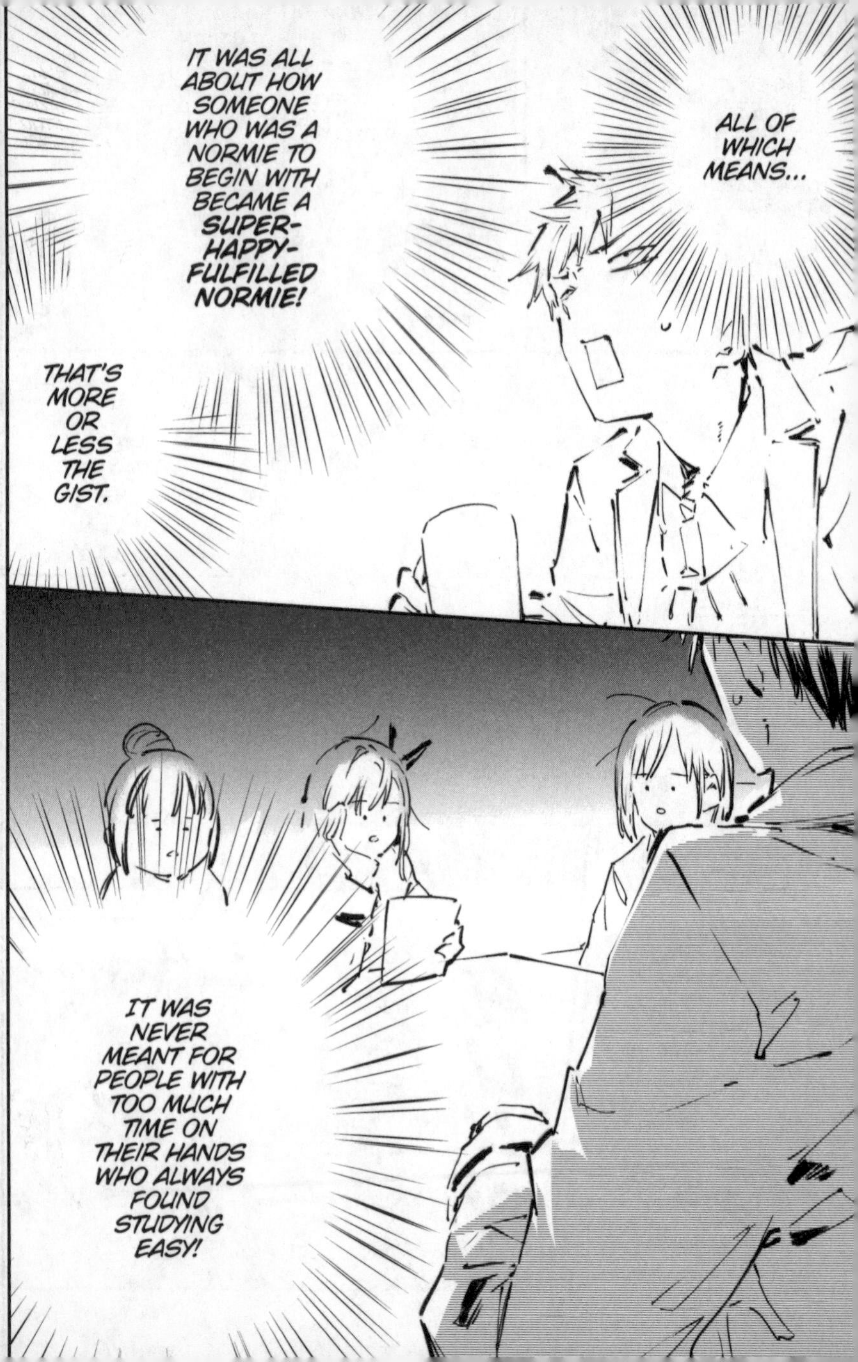
IT WAS ALL ABOUT HOW SOMEONE WHO WAS A NORMIE TO BEGIN WITH BECAME A SUPER-HAPPY-FULFILLED NORMIE!
THAT'S MORE OR LESS THE GIST.
ALL OF WHICH MEANS...
IT WAS NEVER MEANT FOR PEOPLE WITH TOO MUCH TIME ON THEIR HANDS WHO ALWAYS FOUND STUDYING EASY!

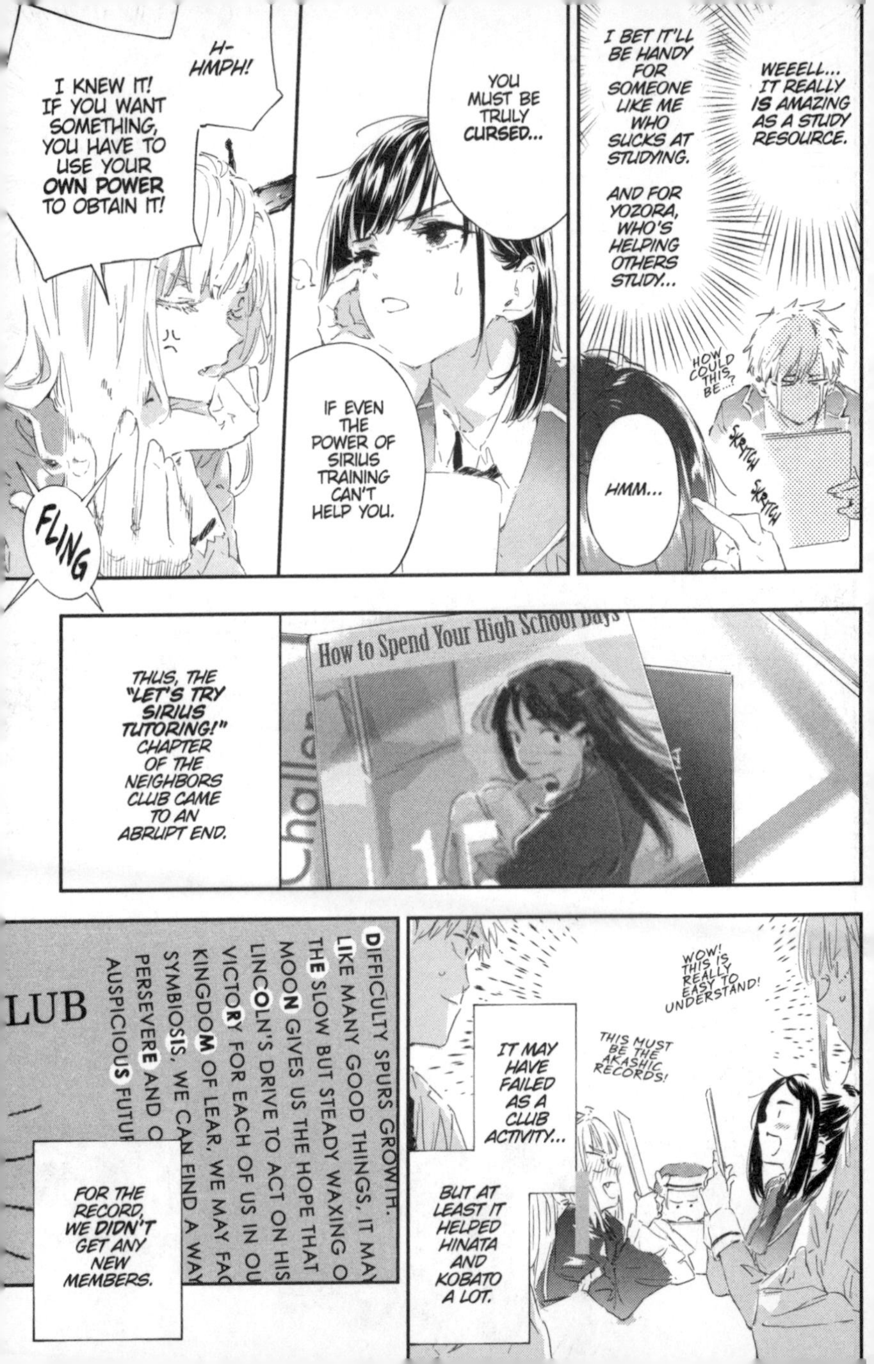
WEEELL... IT REALLY IS AMAZING AS A STUDY RESOURCE.
I BET IT'LL BE HANDY FOR SOMEONE LIKE ME WHO SUCKS AT STUDYING.
AND FOR YOZORA, WHO'S HELPING OTHERS STUDY...
HOW COULD THIS BE...?
SKRITCH
SKRITCH
HMM...
YOU MUST BE TRULY CURSED...
IF EVEN THE POWER OF SIRIUS TRAINING CAN'T HELP YOU.
H-HMPH!
I KNEW IT! IF YOU WANT SOMETHING, YOU HAVE TO USE YOUR OWN POWER TO OBTAIN IT!
FLING
How to Spend Your High School Days
THUS, THE "LET'S TRY SIRIUS TUTORING!" CHAPTER OF THE NEIGHBORS CLUB CAME TO AN ABRUPT END.
WOW! THIS IS REALLY EASY TO UNDERSTAND!
THIS MUST BE THE AKASHIC RECORDS!
IT MAY HAVE FAILED AS A CLUB ACTIVITY...
BUT AT LEAST IT HELPED HINATA AND KOBATO A LOT.
LUB
DIFFICULTY SPURS GROWTH.
LIKE MANY GOOD THINGS. IT MA
THE SLOW BUT STEADY WAXING O
MOON GIVES US THE HOPE THAT
LINCOLN'S DRIVE TO ACT ON HIS
VICTORY FOR EACH OF US IN OU
KINGDOM OF LEAR. WE MAY FAC
SYMBIOSIS, WE CAN FIND A WAY
PERSEVERE AND O
AUSPICIOUS FUTUR
FOR THE RECORD, WE DIDN'T GET ANY NEW MEMBERS.

Haganai

I don't have many friends

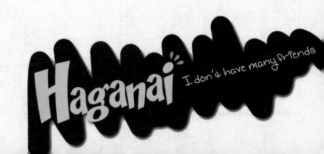

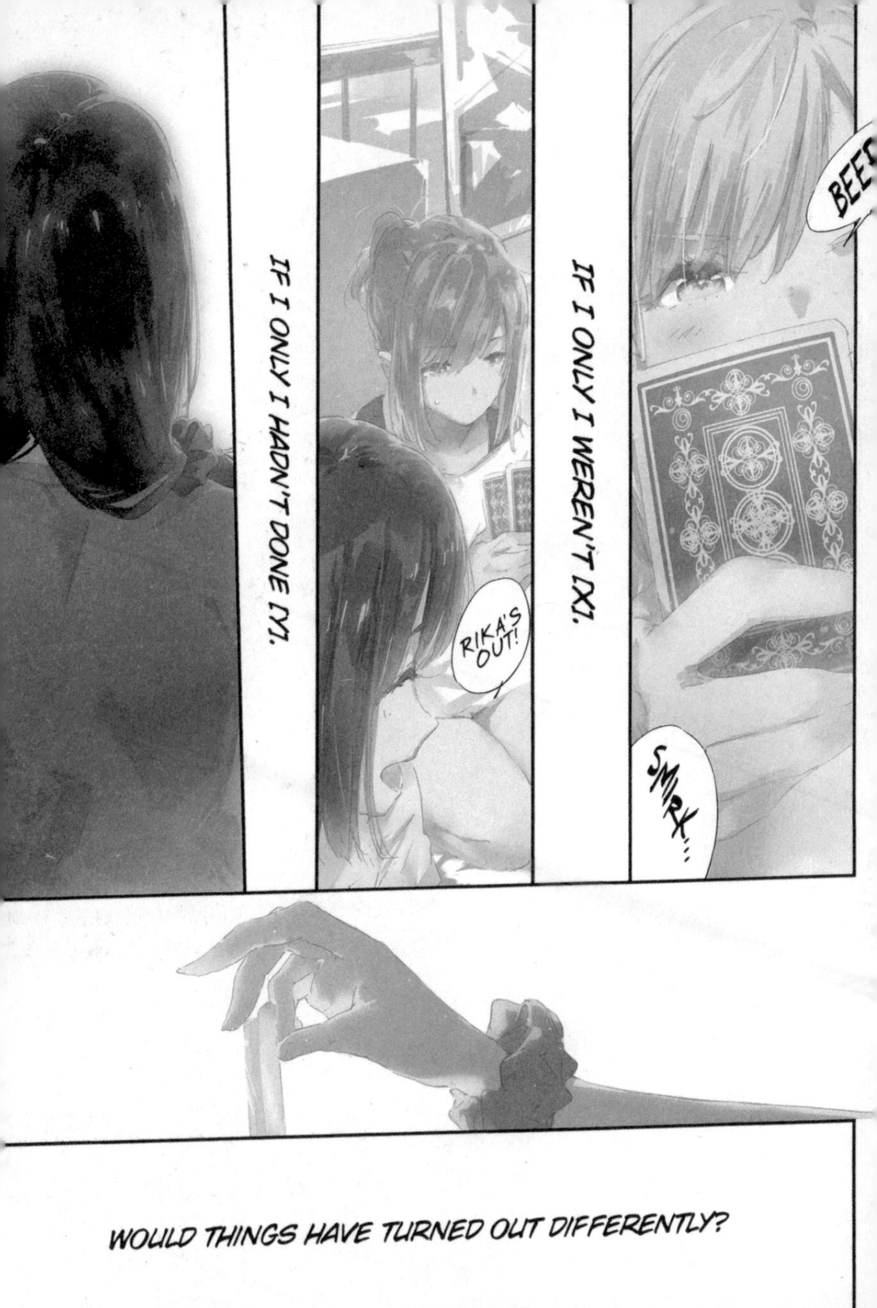
BEE
SMIRK...
IF I ONLY I WEREN'T [X].
RIKA'S OUT!
IF I ONLY I HADN'T DONE [Y].
WOULD THINGS HAVE TURNED OUT DIFFERENTLY?

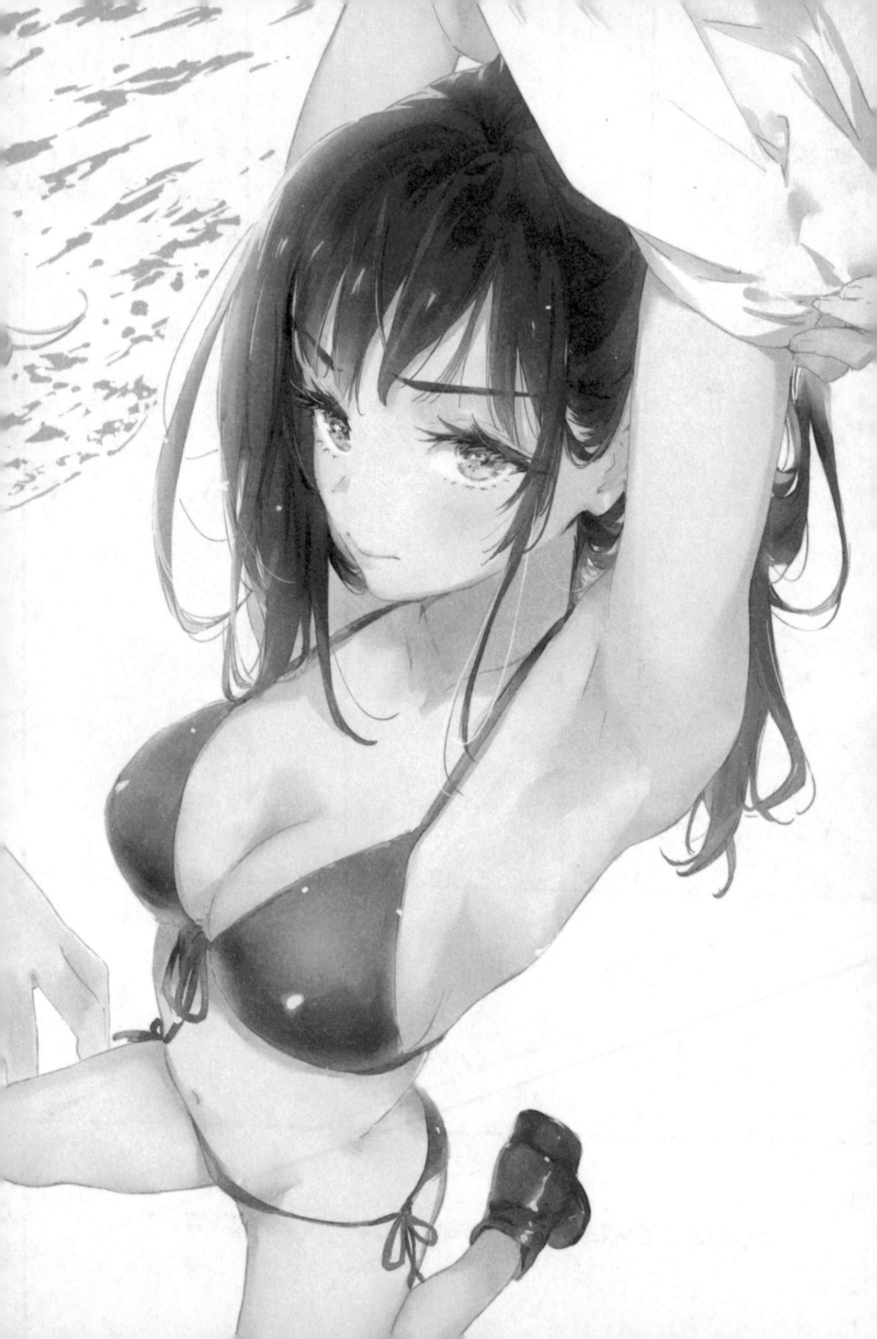

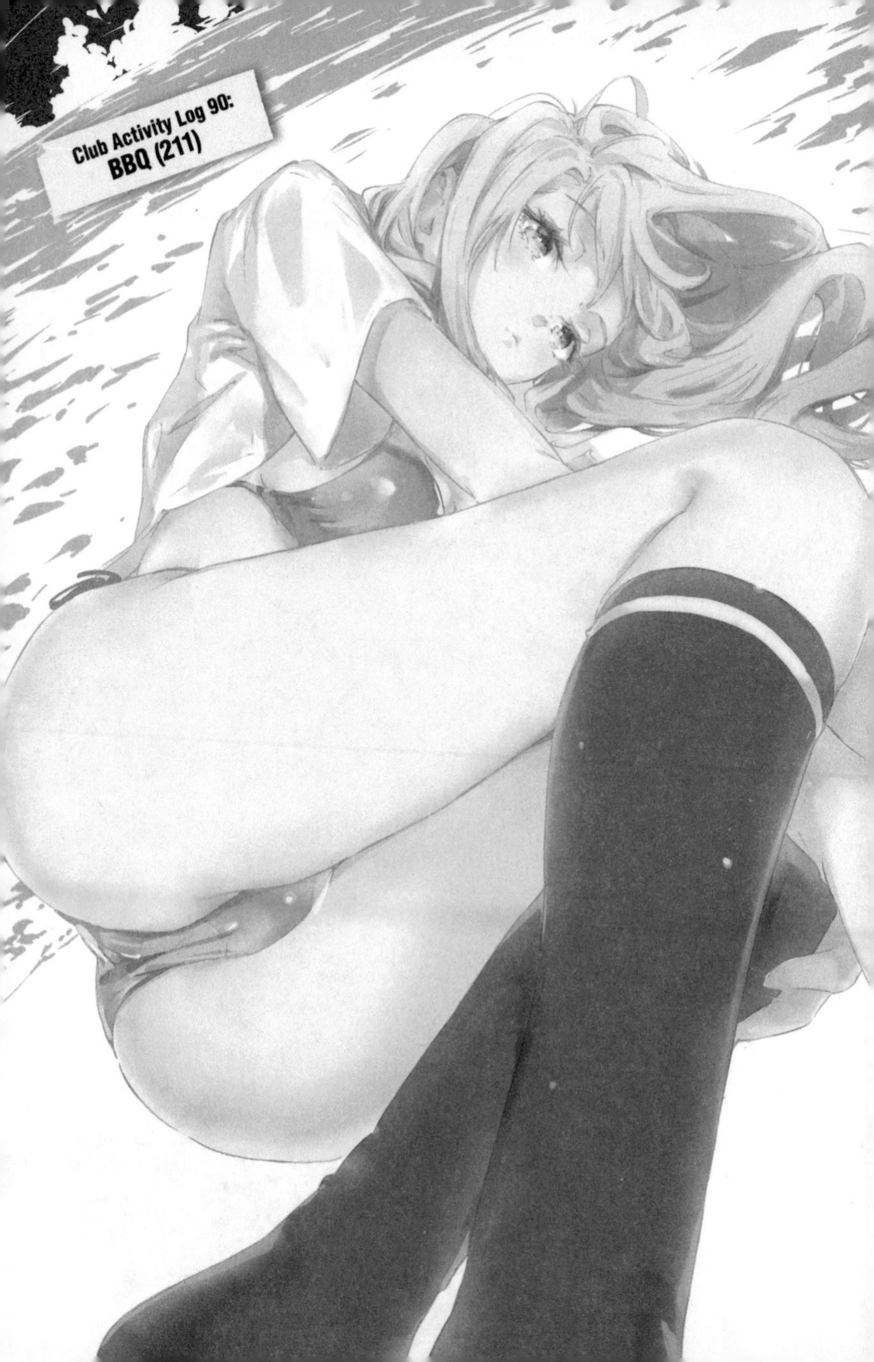
Club Activity Log 90:
BBQ (211)

Haganai

I don't have many friends

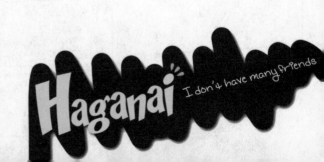

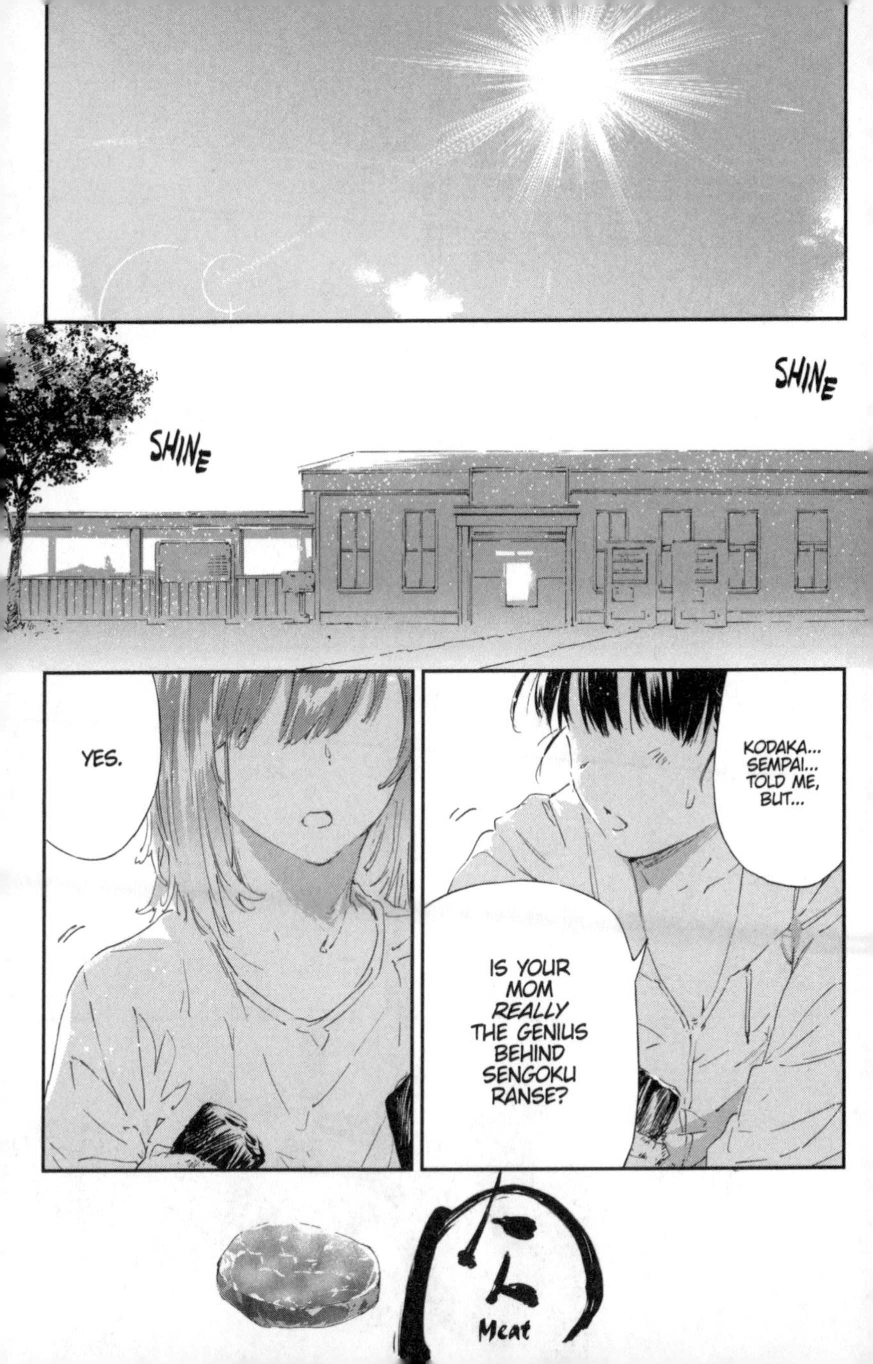
SHINE
SHINE
KODAKA... SEMPAI... TOLD ME, BUT...
IS YOUR MOM *REALLY* THE GENIUS BEHIND SENGOKU RANSE?
YES.
Meat

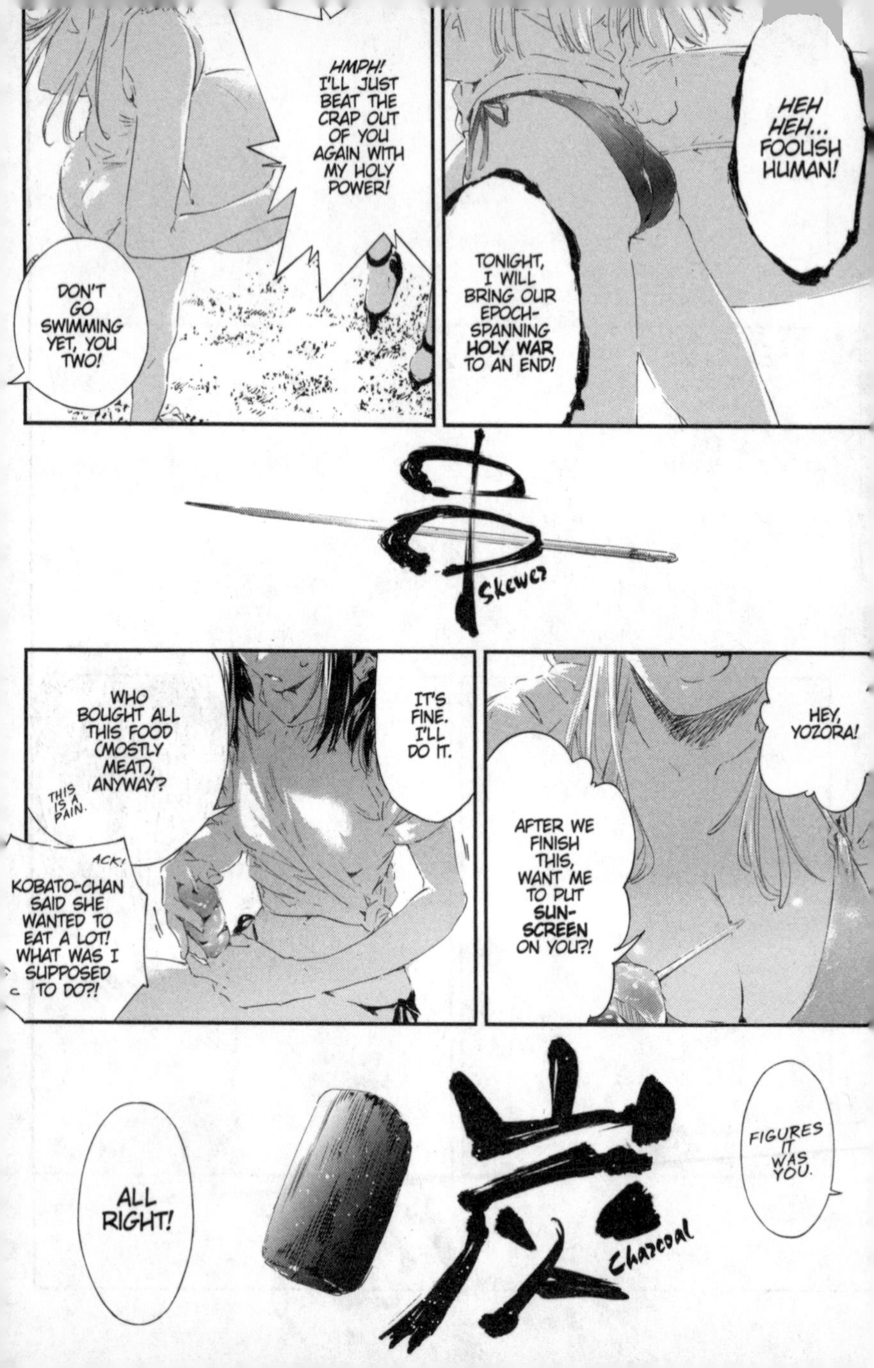
HEH HEH... FOOLISH HUMAN!
TONIGHT, I WILL BRING OUR EPOCH-SPANNING HOLY WAR TO AN END!
HMPH! I'LL JUST BEAT THE CRAP OUT OF YOU AGAIN WITH MY HOLY POWER!
DON'T GO SWIMMING YET, YOU TWO!
Skewer
HEY, YOZORA!
AFTER WE FINISH THIS, WANT ME TO PUT SUN-SCREEN ON YOU?!
IT'S FINE. I'LL DO IT.
WHO BOUGHT ALL THIS FOOD (MOSTLY MEAT), ANYWAY?
THIS IS A PAIN.
ACK!
KOBATO-CHAN SAID SHE WANTED TO EAT A LOT! WHAT WAS I SUPPOSED TO DO?!
FIGURES IT WAS YOU.
Charcoal
ALL RIGHT!

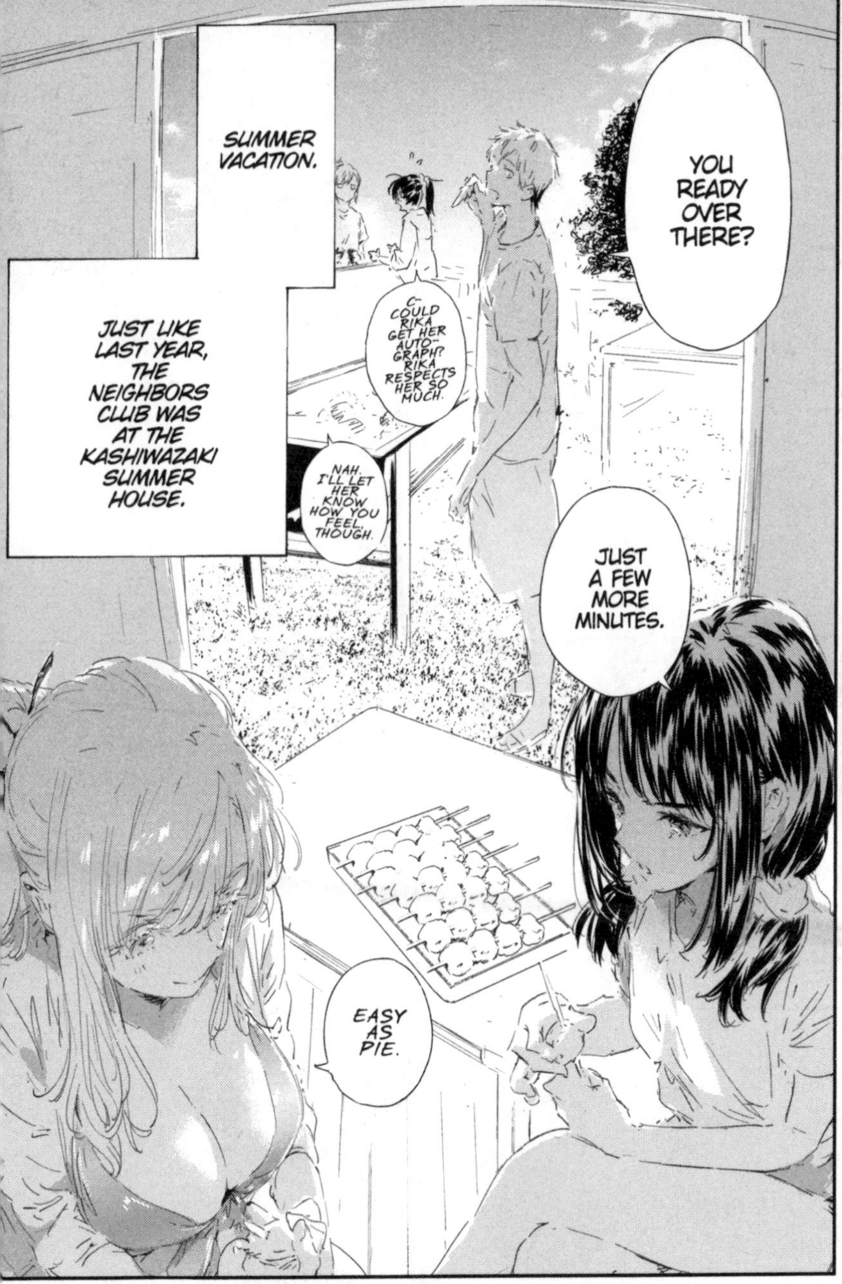
YOU READY OVER THERE?
SUMMER VACATION.
JUST LIKE LAST YEAR, THE NEIGHBORS CLUB WAS AT THE KASHIWAZAKI SUMMER HOUSE.
C-COULD RIKA GET HER AUTO-GRAPH? RIKA RESPECTS HER SO MUCH.
NAH. I'LL LET HER KNOW HOW YOU FEEL, THOUGH.
JUST A FEW MORE MINUTES.
EASY AS PIE.

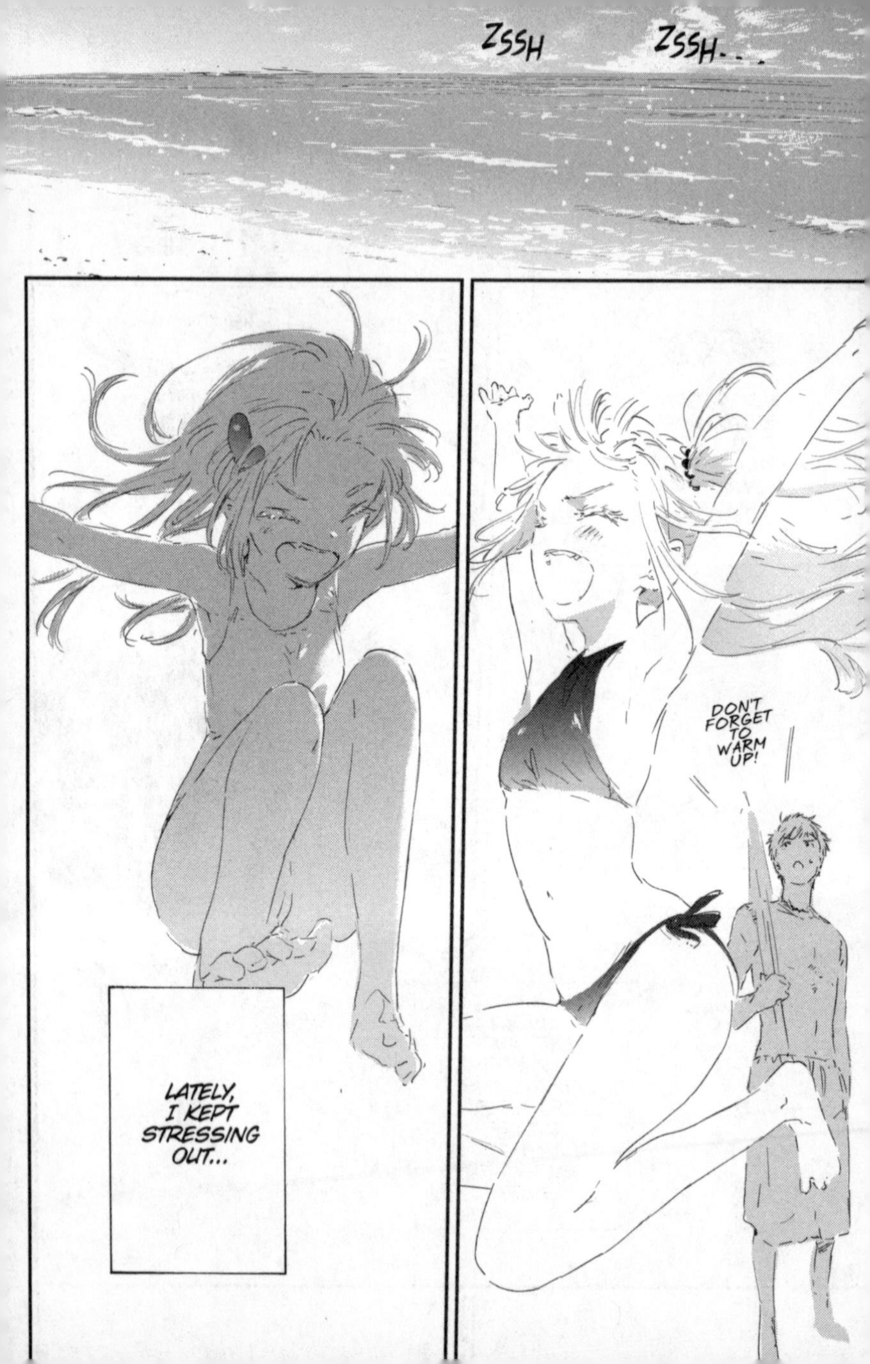
ZSSH ZSSH...
DON'T FORGET TO WARM UP!
LATELY, I KEPT STRESSING OUT...

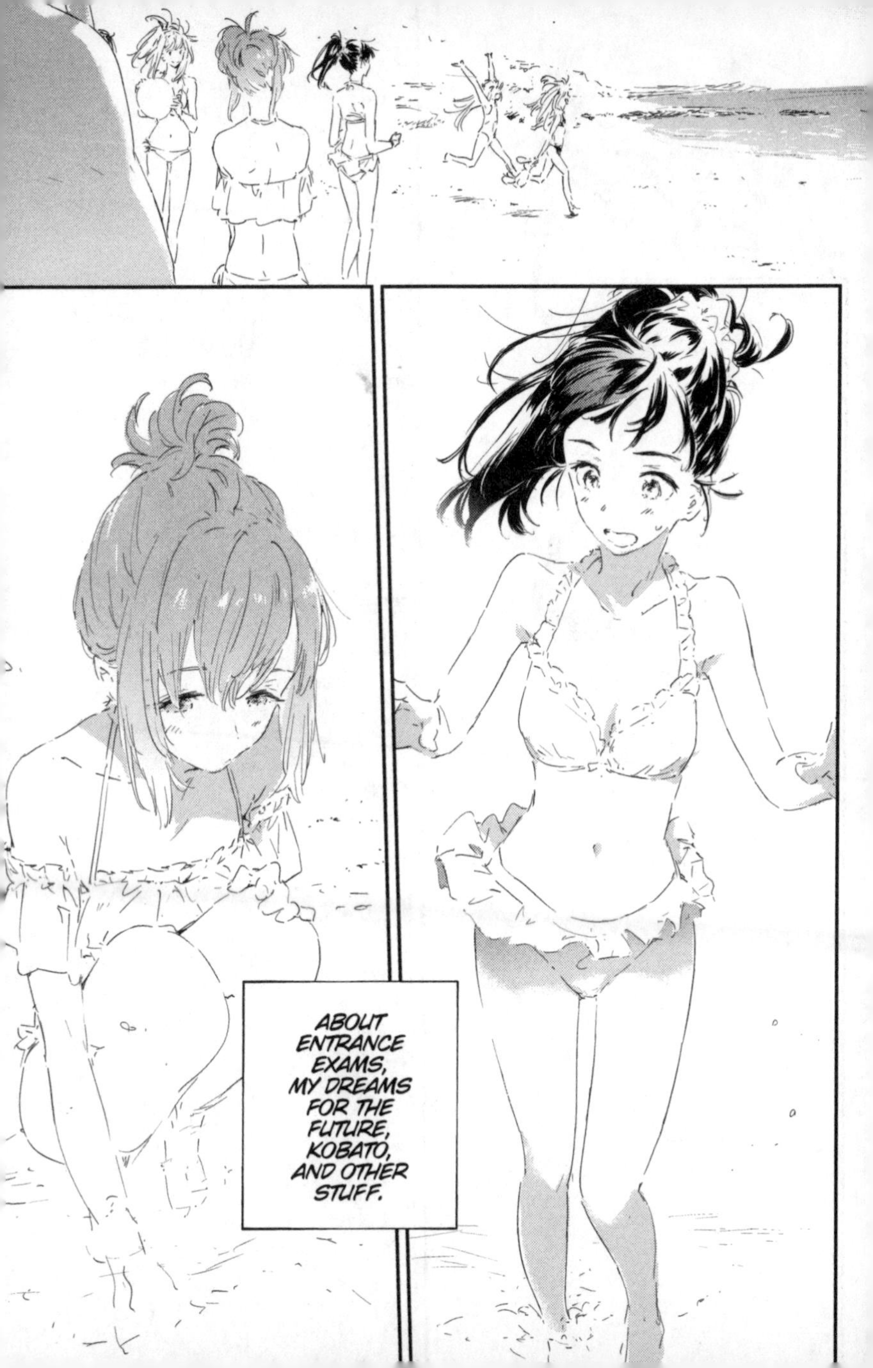
ABOUT ENTRANCE EXAMS, MY DREAMS FOR THE FUTURE, KOBATO, AND OTHER STUFF.

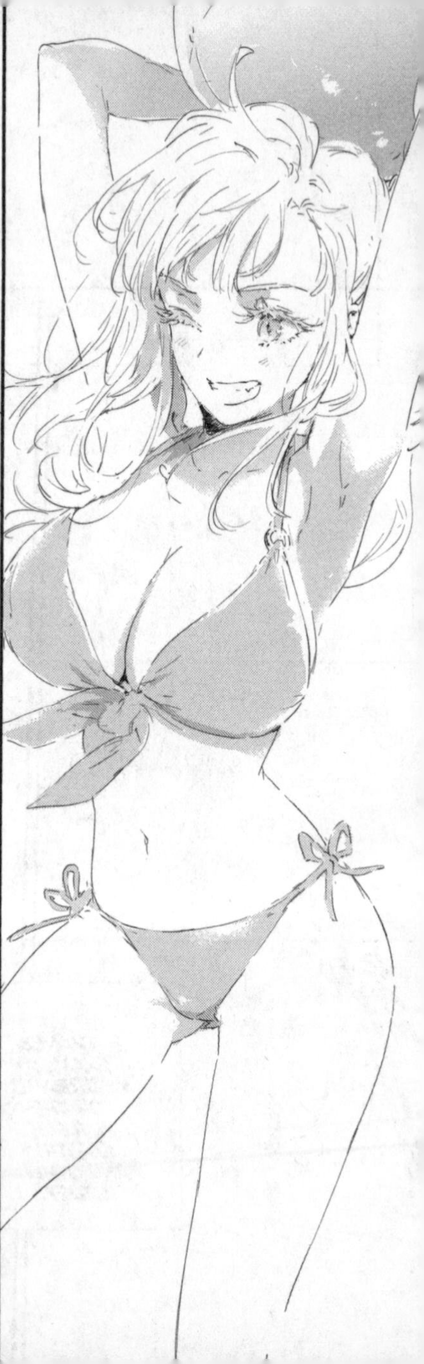
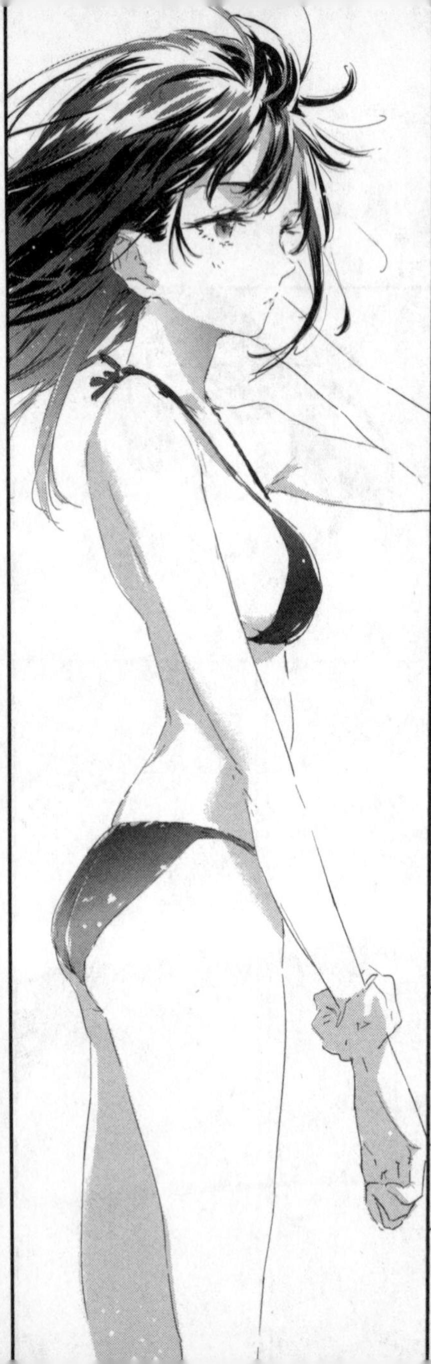

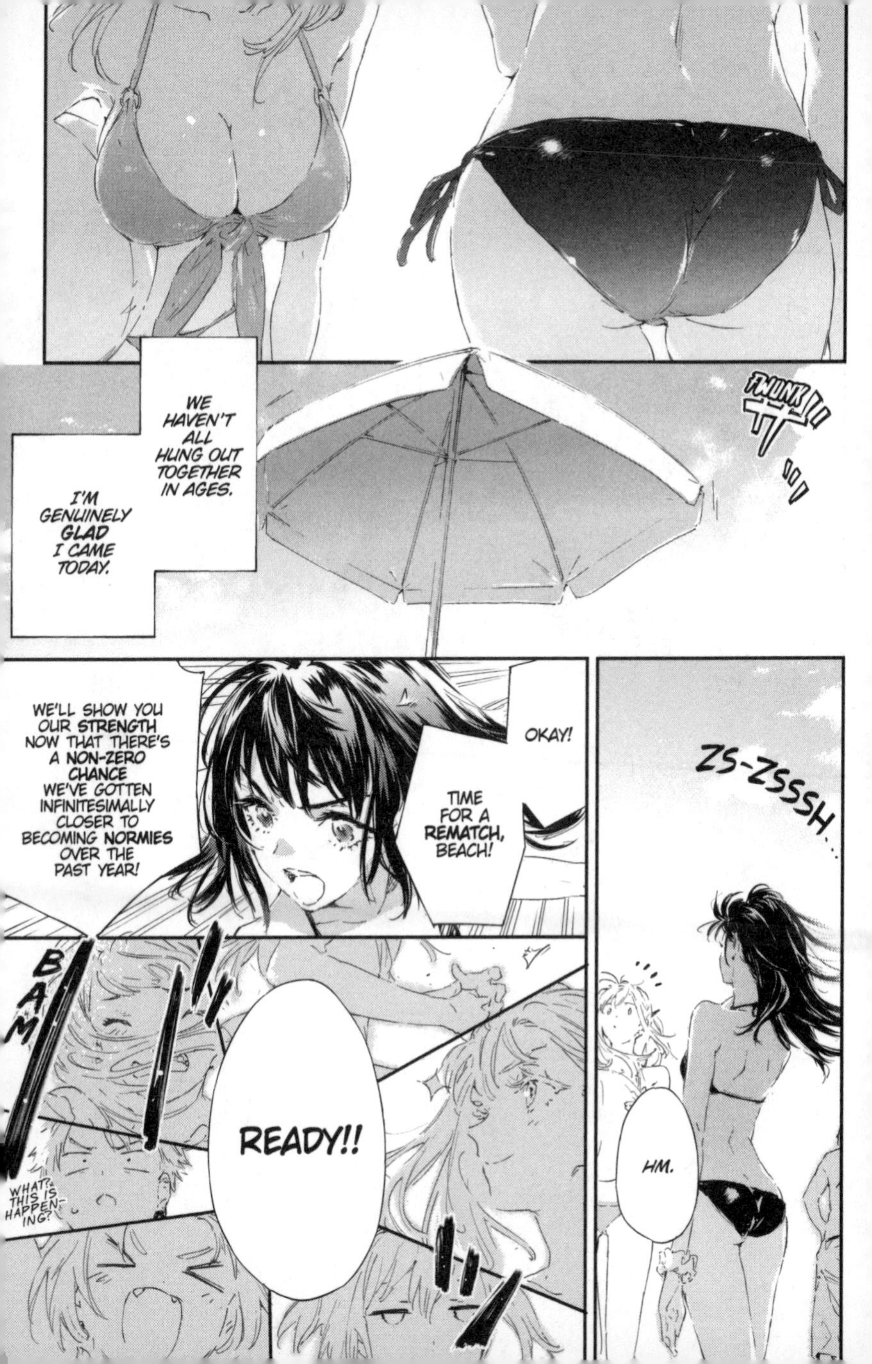
FWUNK
WE HAVEN'T ALL HUNG OUT TOGETHER IN AGES.
I'M GENUINELY GLAD I CAME TODAY.
ZS-ZSSSH...
HM.
OKAY!
TIME FOR A REMATCH, BEACH!
WE'LL SHOW YOU OUR STRENGTH NOW THAT THERE'S A NON-ZERO CHANCE WE'VE GOTTEN INFINITESIMALLY CLOSER TO BECOMING NORMIES OVER THE PAST YEAR!
READY!!
BAM
WHAT? THIS IS HAPPENING?

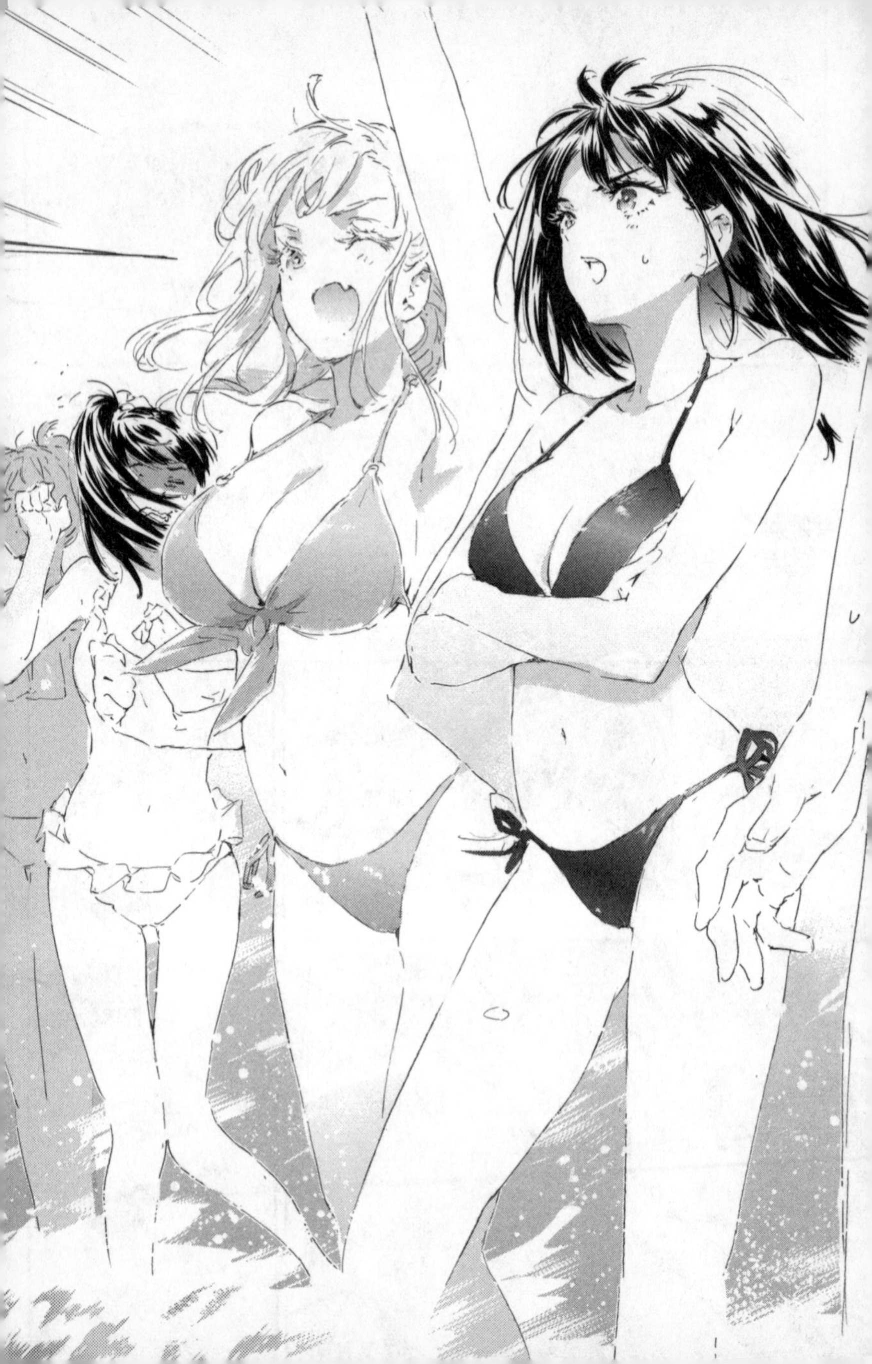

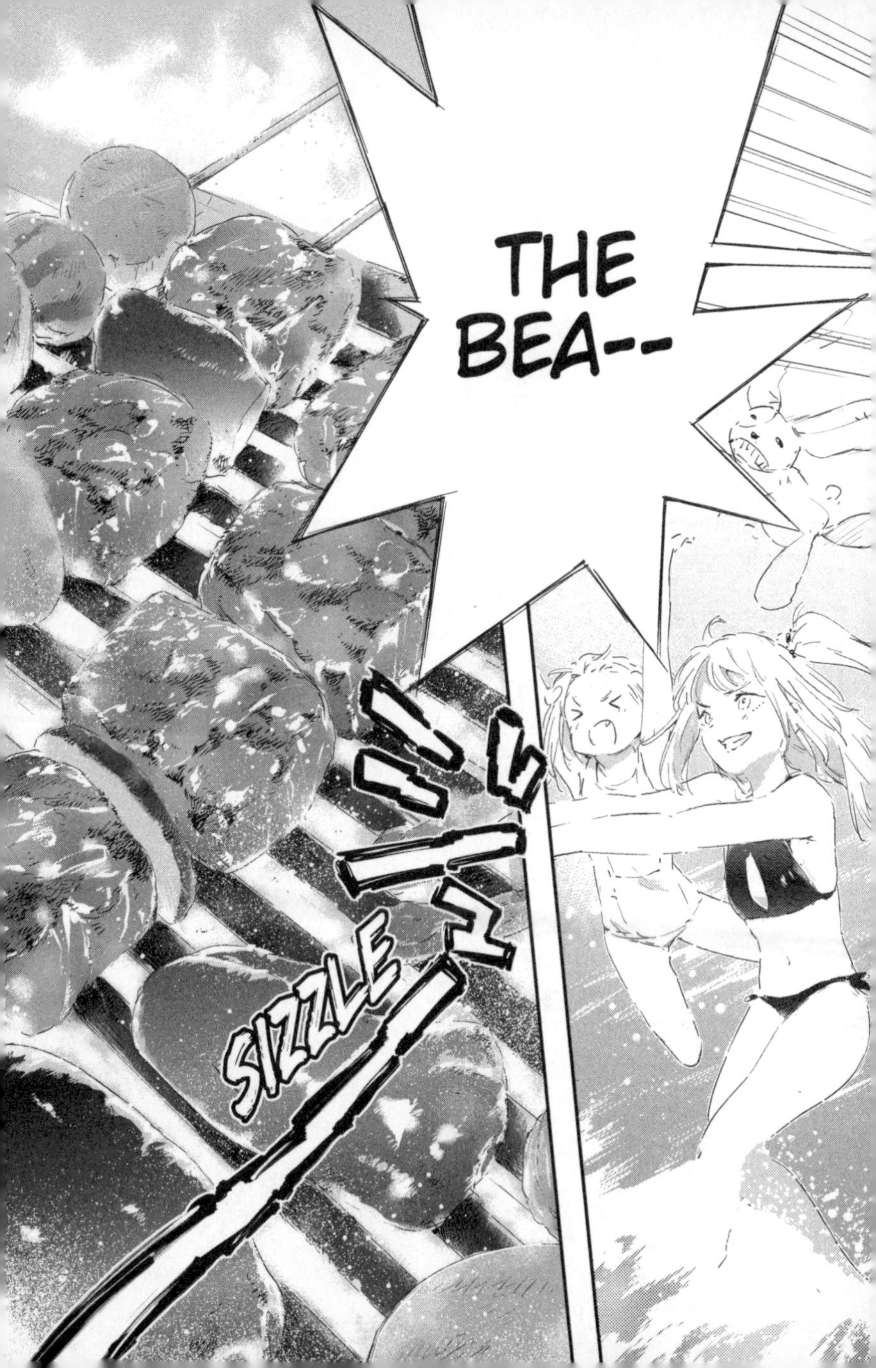
THE BEA--
SIZZLE

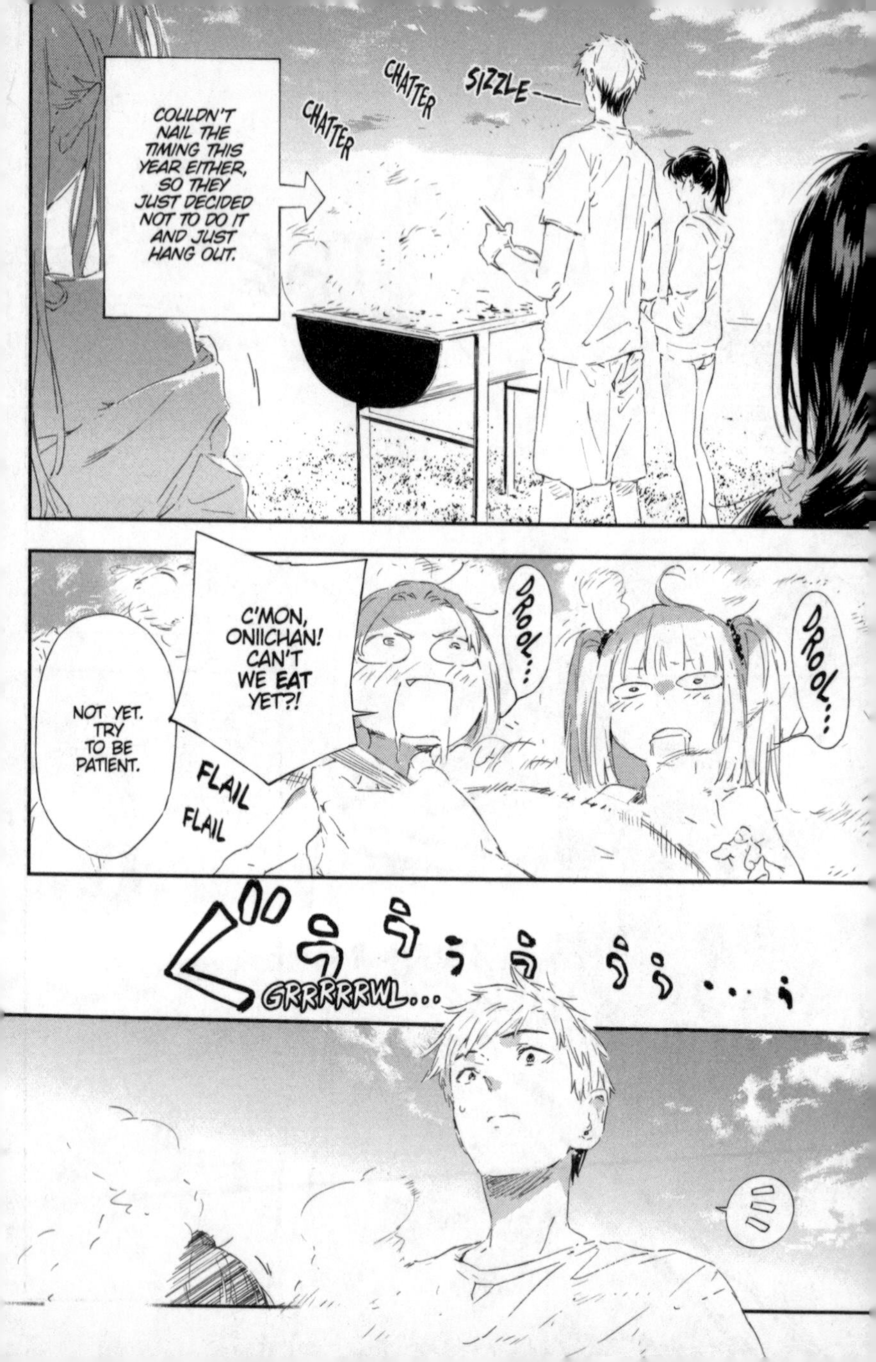
SIZZLE
CHATTER
CHATTER
COULDN'T NAIL THE TIMING THIS YEAR EITHER, SO THEY JUST DECIDED NOT TO DO IT AND JUST HANG OUT.
DROOL...
DROOL...
C'MON, ONIICHAN! CAN'T WE EAT YET?!
NOT YET. TRY TO BE PATIENT.
FLAIL
FLAIL
GRRRRRWL...

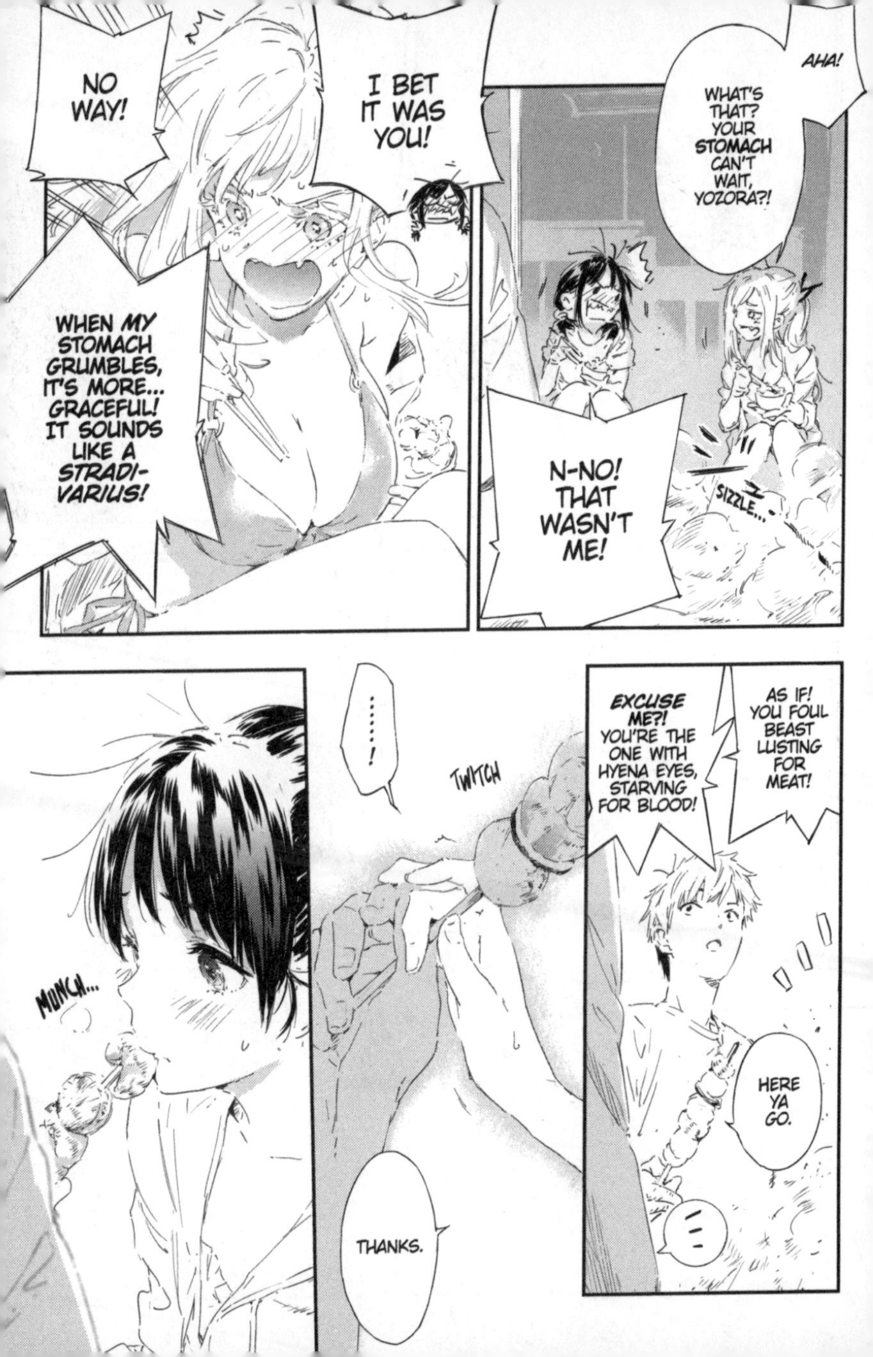
AHA!
WHAT'S THAT? YOUR STOMACH CAN'T WAIT, YOZORA?!
N-NO! THAT WASN'T ME!
SIZZLE...
I BET IT WAS YOU!
NO WAY!
WHEN *MY* STOMACH GRUMBLES, IT'S MORE... GRACEFUL! IT SOUNDS LIKE A *STRADI-VARIUS!*
AS IF! YOU FOUL BEAST LUSTING FOR MEAT!
EXCUSE ME?! YOU'RE THE ONE WITH HYENA EYES, STARVING FOR BLOOD!
HERE YA GO.
...
......!
TWITCH
THANKS.
MUNCH...

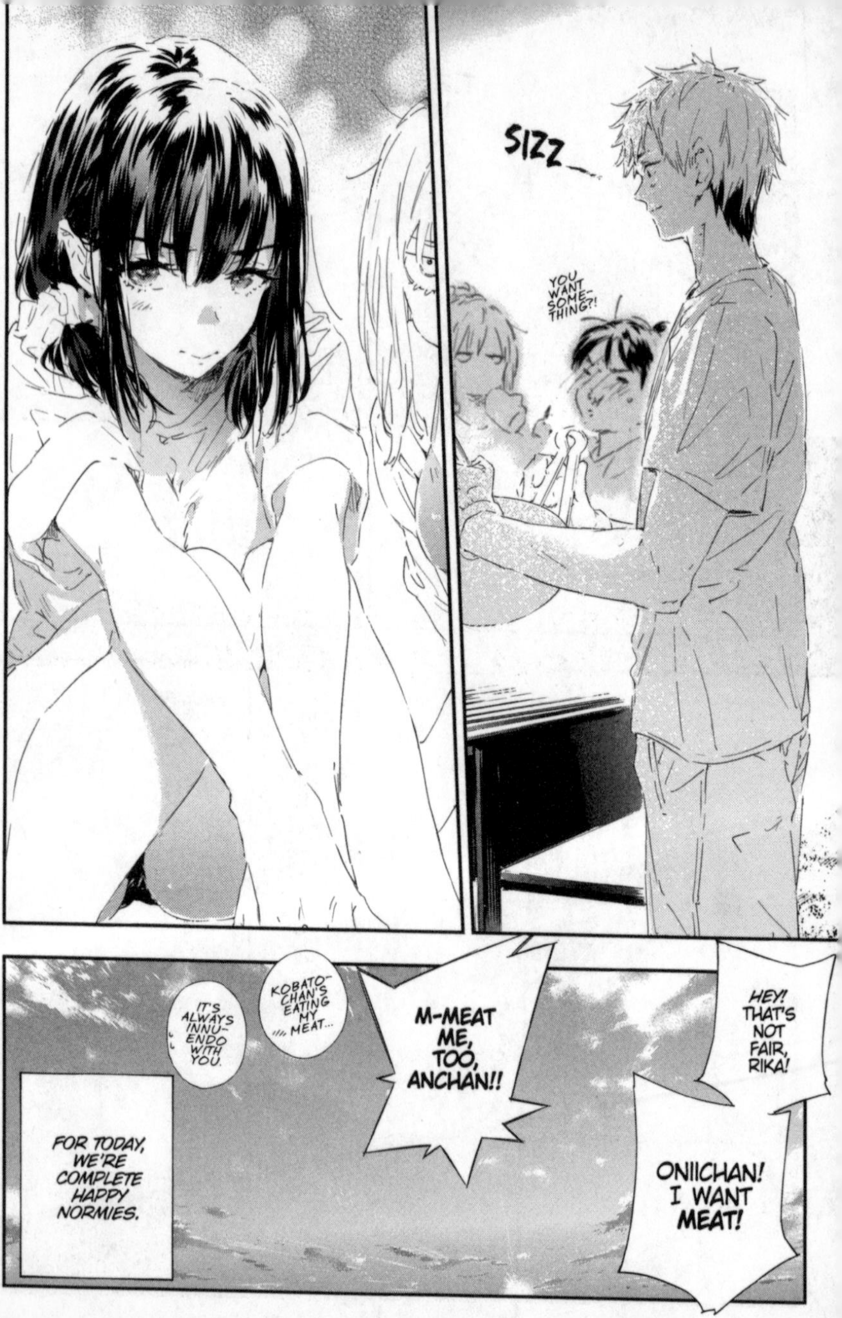
SIZZ
YOU WANT SOMETHING?!
HEY! THAT'S NOT FAIR, RIKA!
ONIICHAN! I WANT MEAT!
M-MEAT ME, TOO, ANCHAN!!
KOBATO-CHAN'S EATING MY MEAT...
IT'S ALWAYS INNUENDO WITH YOU.
FOR TODAY, WE'RE COMPLETE HAPPY NORMIES.

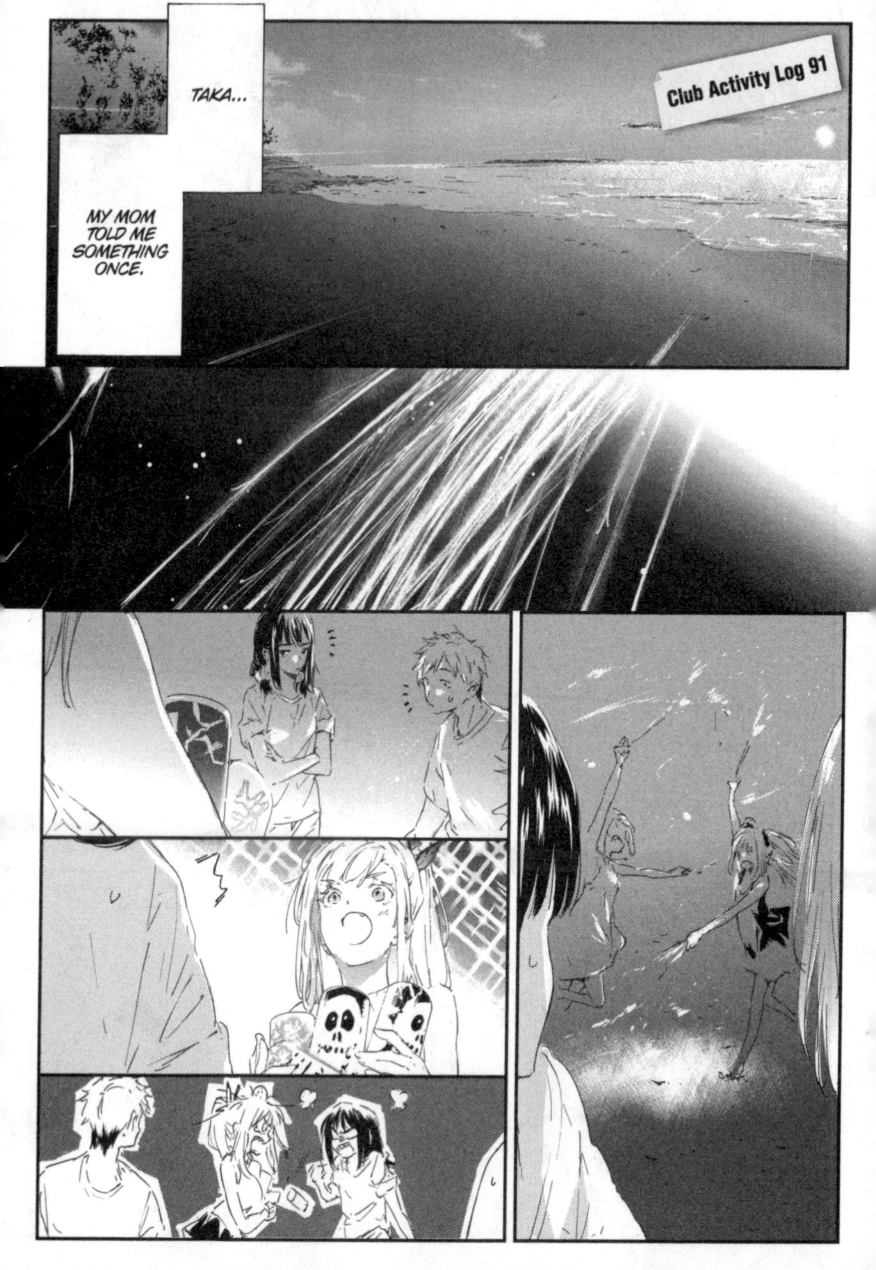
Club Activity Log 91
TAKA...
MY MOM TOLD ME SOMETHING ONCE.

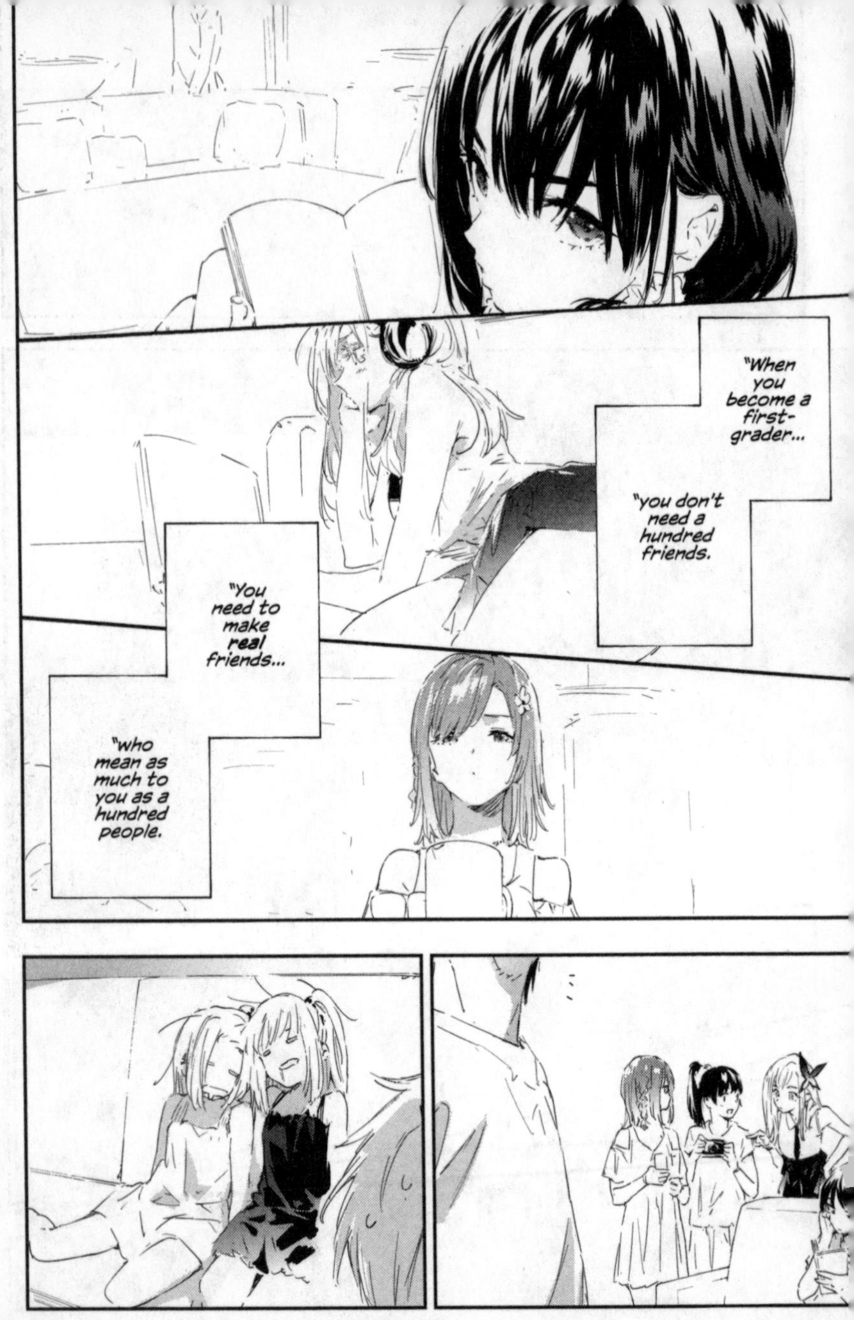
"When you become a first-grader...
"you don't need a hundred friends.
"You need to make real friends...
"who mean as much to you as a hundred people.

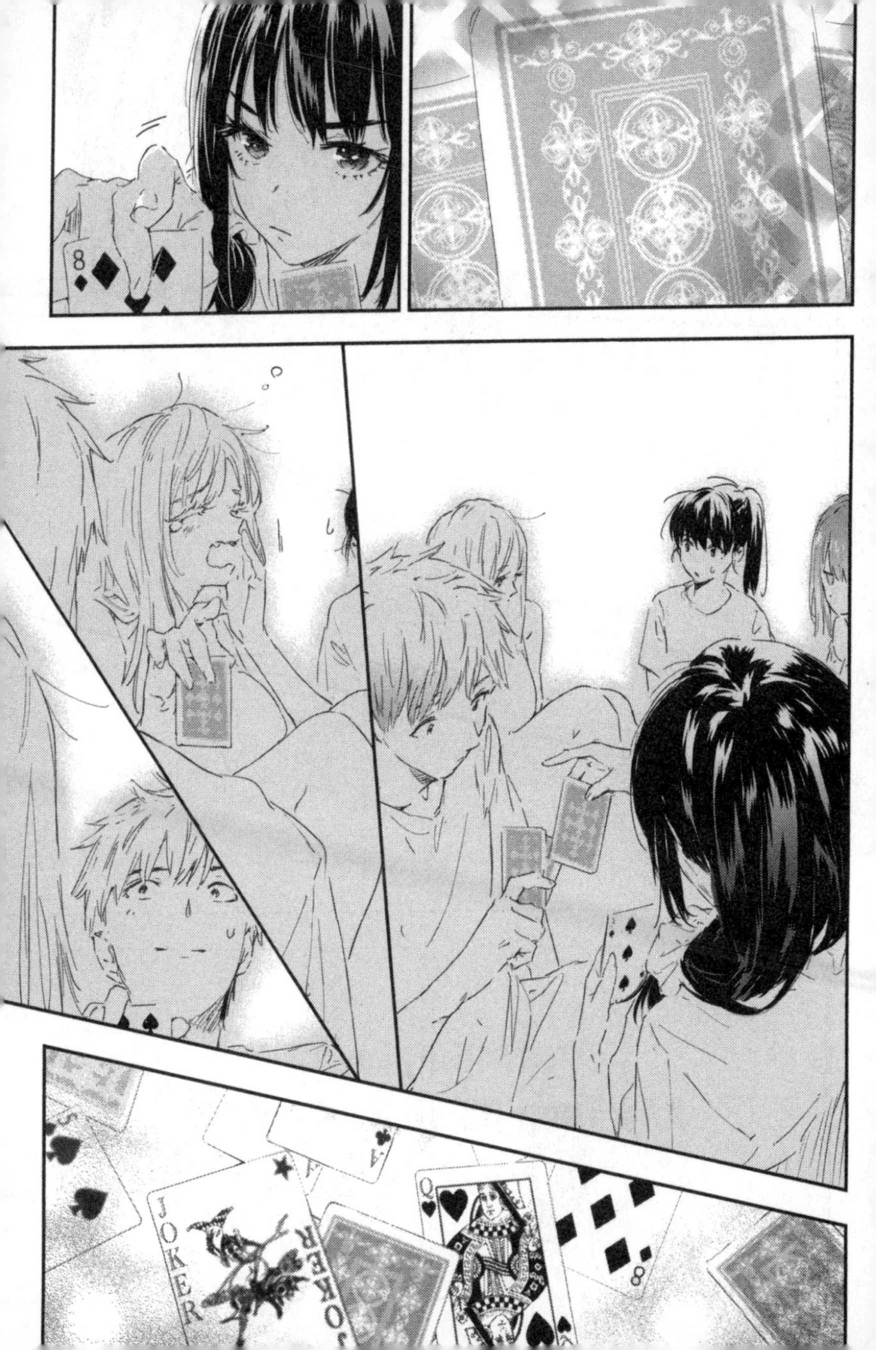
JOKER

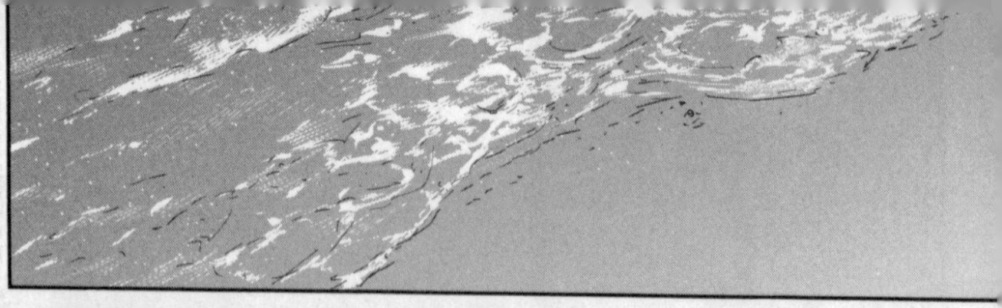

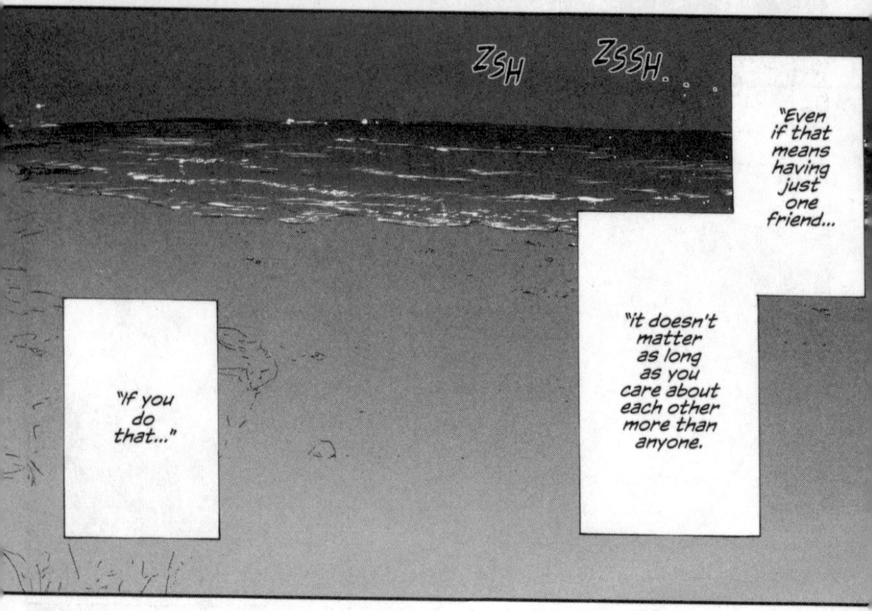
"Even if that means having just one friend...
ZSSH.
ZSH
"it doesn't matter as long as you care about each other more than anyone.
"If you do that..."

Club Activity Log 91:

And Then Dawn Broke (210)

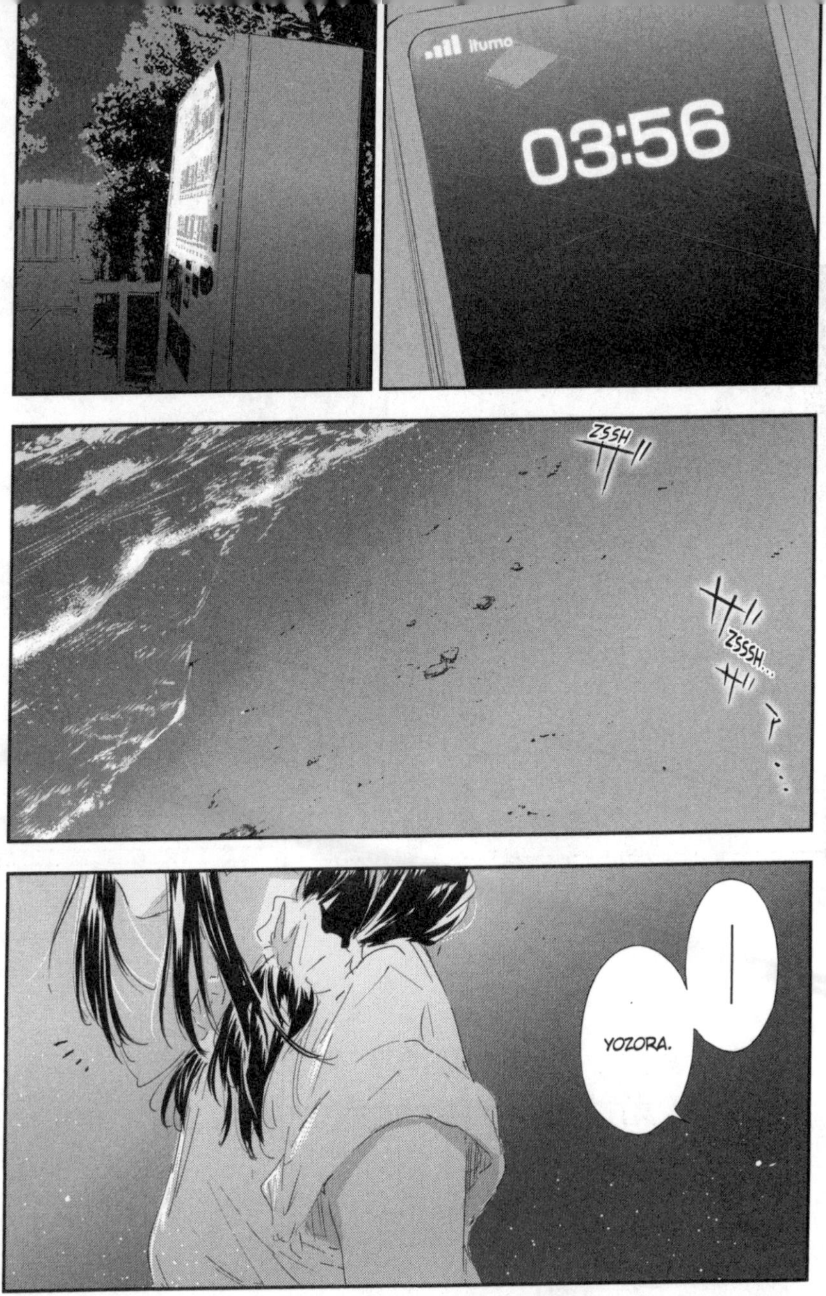

itumo
03:56
ZSSH
ZSSSH...
—
YOZORA.

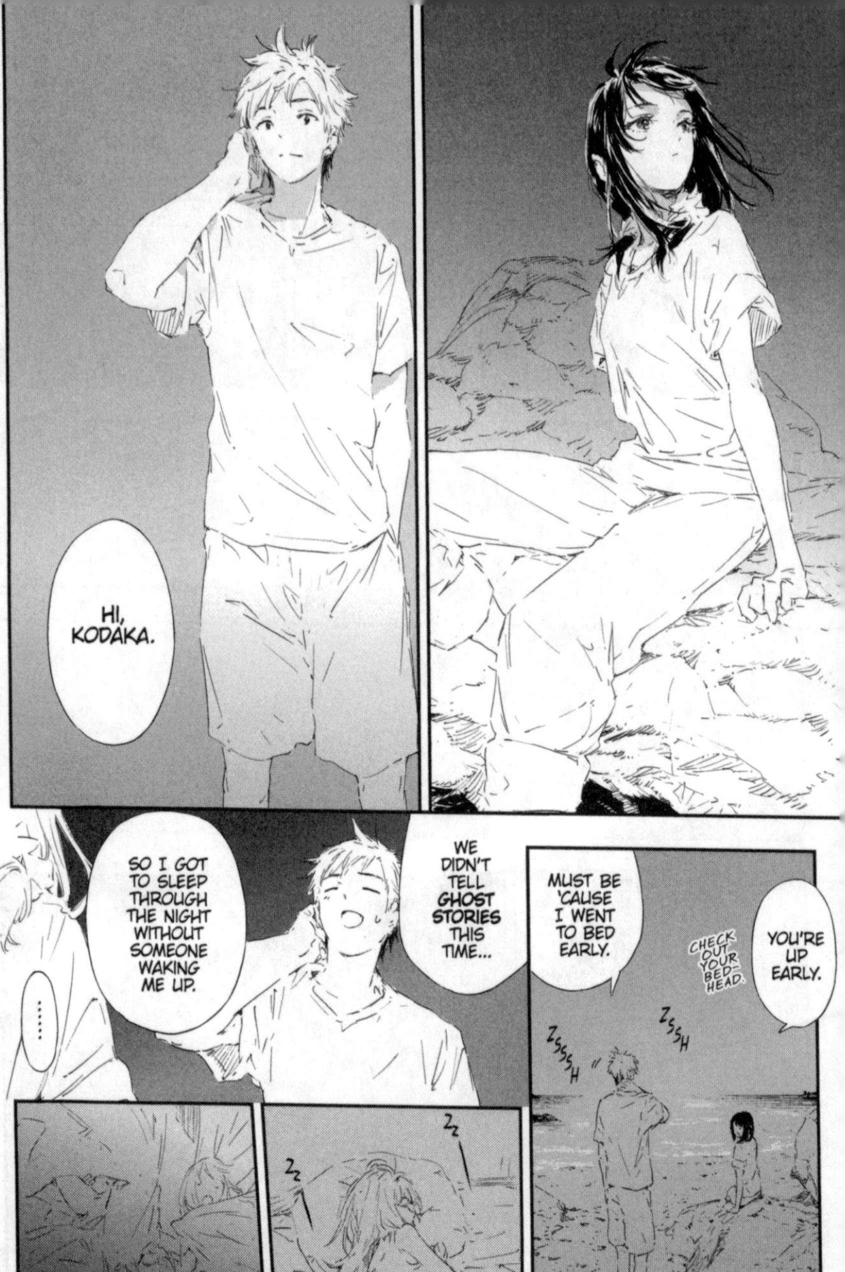
HI, KODAKA.
YOU'RE UP EARLY.
CHECK OUT YOUR BED-HEAD.
MUST BE 'CAUSE I WENT TO BED EARLY.
ZSSSH
ZSSSH
WE DIDN'T TELL GHOST STORIES THIS TIME...
SO I GOT TO SLEEP THROUGH THE NIGHT WITHOUT SOMEONE WAKING ME UP.
......
ZZ
ZZ

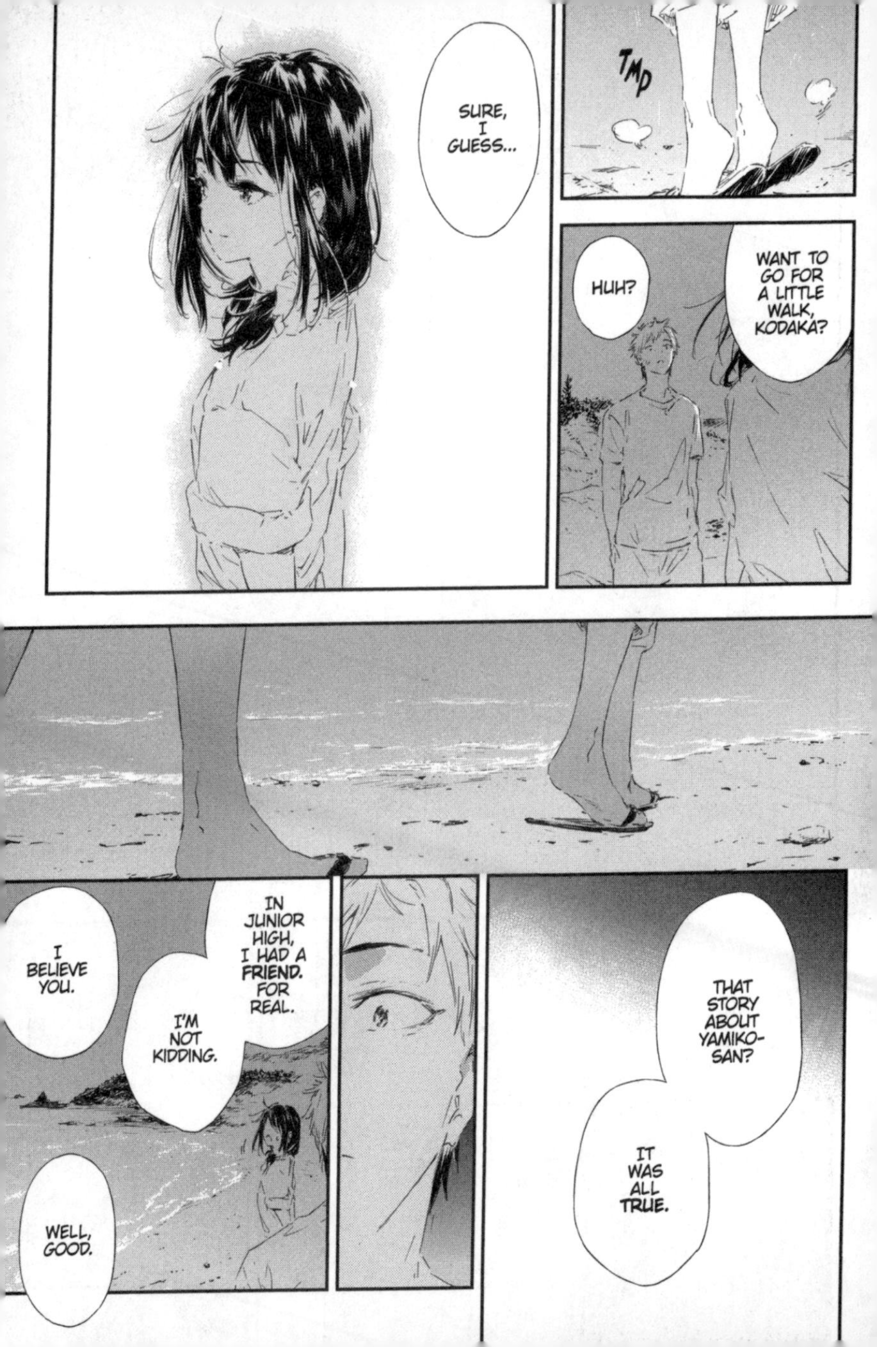
TMP
WANT TO GO FOR A LITTLE WALK, KODAKA?
HUH?
SURE, I GUESS...
THAT STORY ABOUT YAMIKO-SAN?
IT WAS ALL TRUE.
IN JUNIOR HIGH, I HAD A FRIEND. FOR REAL.
I'M NOT KIDDING.
I BELIEVE YOU.
WELL, GOOD.

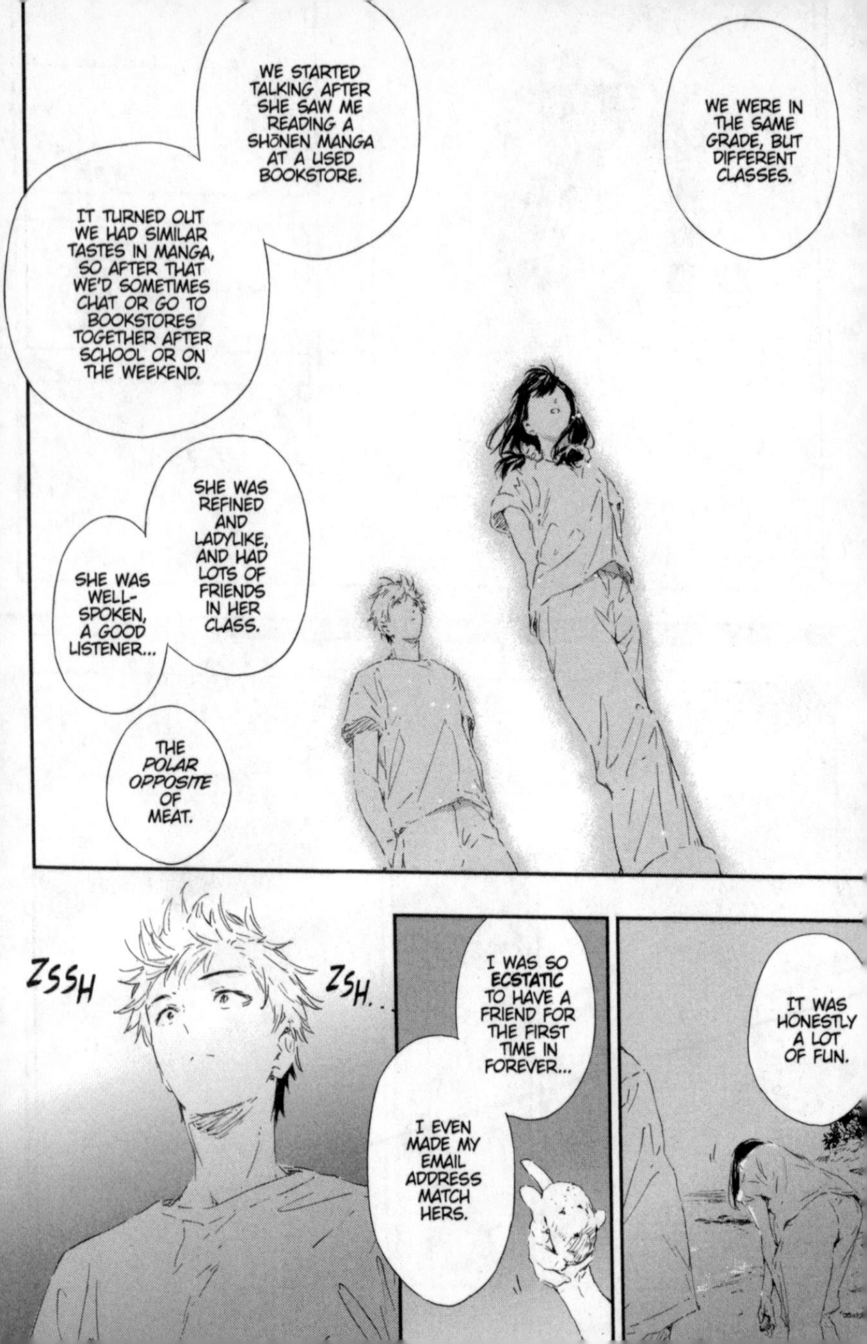
WE WERE IN THE SAME GRADE, BUT DIFFERENT CLASSES.
WE STARTED TALKING AFTER SHE SAW ME READING A SHŌNEN MANGA AT A USED BOOKSTORE.
IT TURNED OUT WE HAD SIMILAR TASTES IN MANGA, SO AFTER THAT WE'D SOMETIMES CHAT OR GO TO BOOKSTORES TOGETHER AFTER SCHOOL OR ON THE WEEKEND.
SHE WAS REFINED AND LADYLIKE, AND HAD LOTS OF FRIENDS IN HER CLASS.
SHE WAS WELL-SPOKEN, A GOOD LISTENER...
THE *POLAR OPPOSITE* OF MEAT.
IT WAS HONESTLY A LOT OF FUN.
I WAS SO *ECSTATIC* TO HAVE A FRIEND FOR THE FIRST TIME IN FOREVER...
I EVEN MADE MY EMAIL ADDRESS MATCH HERS.
ZSH...
ZSSH

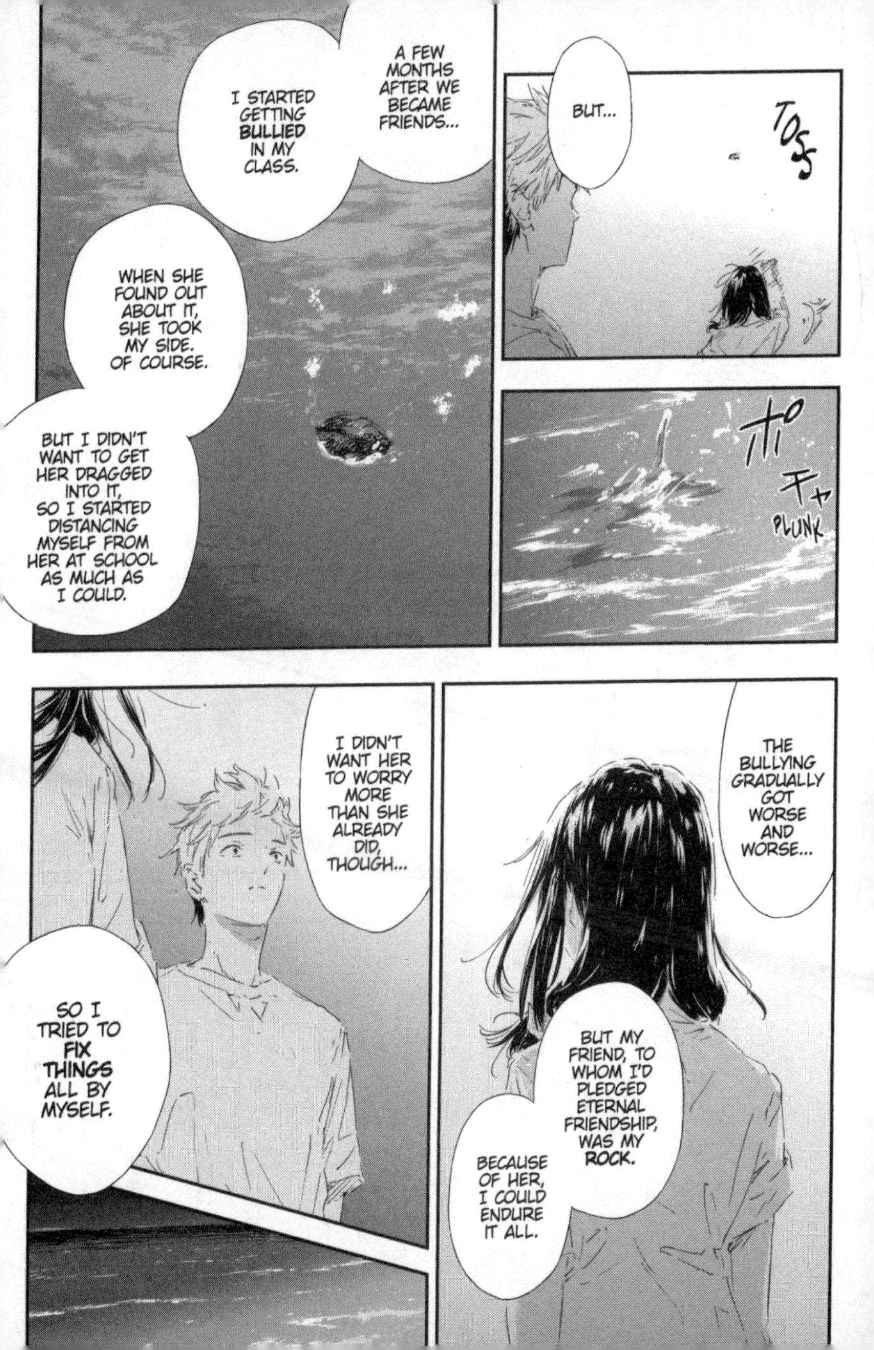
BUT...
TOSS
ポチャ
PLUNK
A FEW MONTHS AFTER WE BECAME FRIENDS...
I STARTED GETTING BULLIED IN MY CLASS.
WHEN SHE FOUND OUT ABOUT IT, SHE TOOK MY SIDE. OF COURSE.
BUT I DIDN'T WANT TO GET HER DRAGGED INTO IT, SO I STARTED DISTANCING MYSELF FROM HER AT SCHOOL AS MUCH AS I COULD.
THE BULLYING GRADUALLY GOT WORSE AND WORSE...
BUT MY FRIEND, TO WHOM I'D PLEDGED ETERNAL FRIENDSHIP, WAS MY ROCK.
BECAUSE OF HER, I COULD ENDURE IT ALL.
I DIDN'T WANT HER TO WORRY MORE THAN SHE ALREADY DID, THOUGH...
SO I TRIED TO FIX THINGS ALL BY MYSELF.

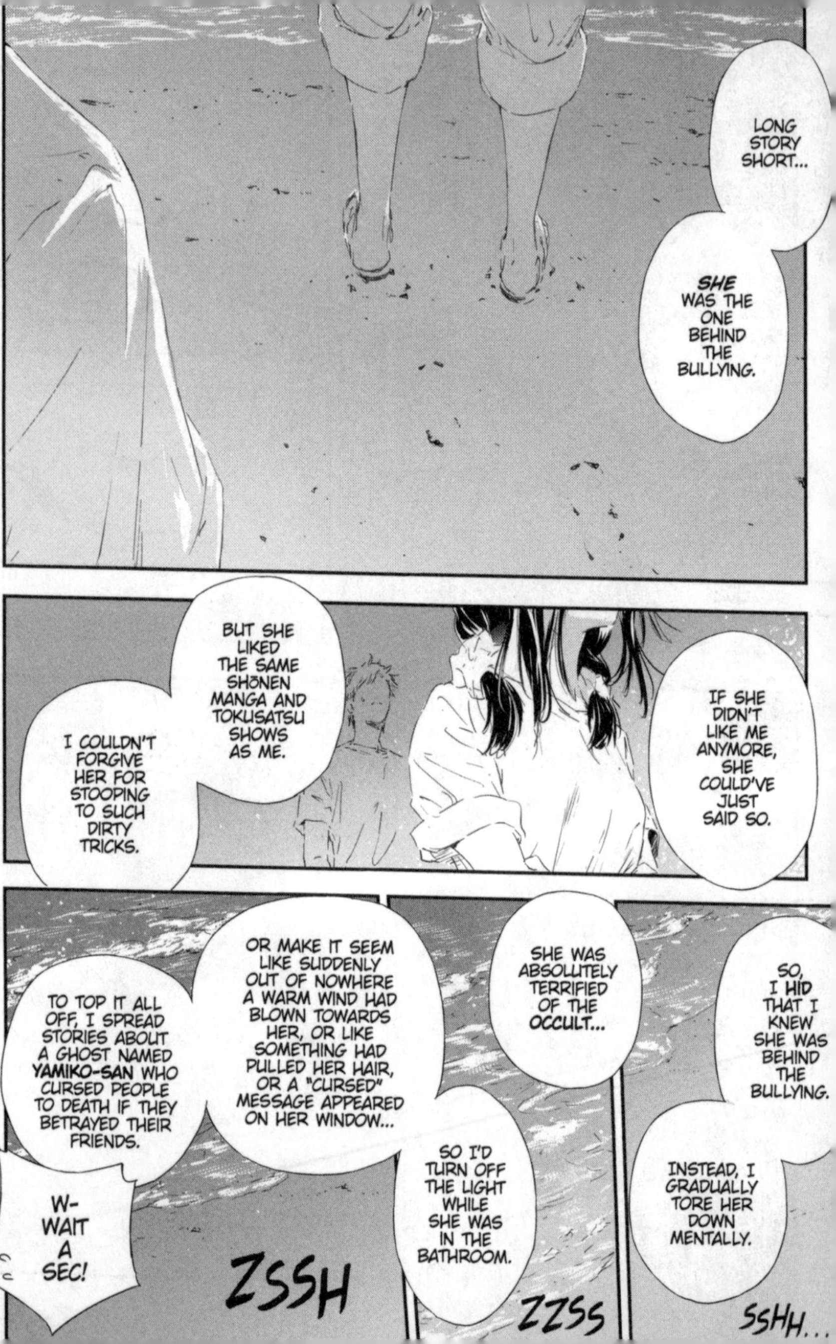
LONG STORY SHORT...
SHE WAS THE ONE BEHIND THE BULLYING.
IF SHE DIDN'T LIKE ME ANYMORE, SHE COULD'VE JUST SAID SO.
BUT SHE LIKED THE SAME SHŌNEN MANGA AND TOKUSATSU SHOWS AS ME.
I COULDN'T FORGIVE HER FOR STOOPING TO SUCH DIRTY TRICKS.
SO, I HID THAT I KNEW SHE WAS BEHIND THE BULLYING.
INSTEAD, I GRADUALLY TORE HER DOWN MENTALLY.
SSHH...
SHE WAS ABSOLUTELY TERRIFIED OF THE OCCULT...
SO I'D TURN OFF THE LIGHT WHILE SHE WAS IN THE BATHROOM.
ZZSS
OR MAKE IT SEEM LIKE SUDDENLY OUT OF NOWHERE A WARM WIND HAD BLOWN TOWARDS HER, OR LIKE SOMETHING HAD PULLED HER HAIR, OR A "CURSED" MESSAGE APPEARED ON HER WINDOW...
TO TOP IT ALL OFF, I SPREAD STORIES ABOUT A GHOST NAMED YAMIKO-SAN WHO CURSED PEOPLE TO DEATH IF THEY BETRAYED THEIR FRIENDS.
W-WAIT A SEC!
ZSSH

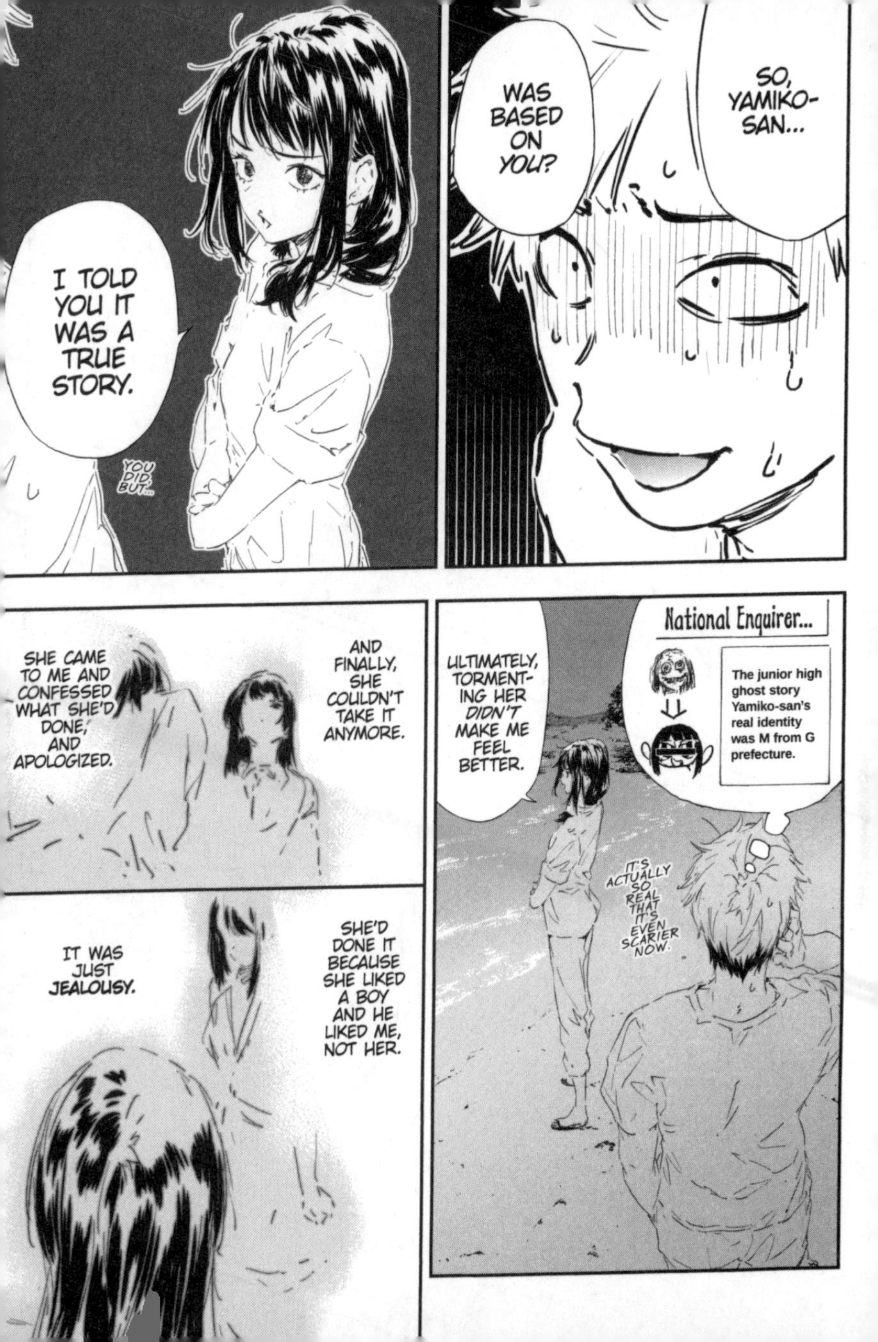
SO, YAMIKO-SAN...
WAS BASED ON YOU?
I TOLD YOU IT WAS A TRUE STORY.
YOU DID, BUT...
ULTIMATELY, TORMENTING HER DIDN'T MAKE ME FEEL BETTER.
National Enquirer...
The junior high ghost story Yamiko-san's real identity was M from G prefecture.
IT'S ACTUALLY SO REAL THAT IT'S EVEN SCARIER NOW.
AND FINALLY, SHE COULDN'T TAKE IT ANYMORE.
SHE CAME TO ME AND CONFESSED WHAT SHE'D DONE, AND APOLOGIZED.
SHE'D DONE IT BECAUSE SHE LIKED A BOY AND HE LIKED ME, NOT HER.
IT WAS JUST JEALOUSY.

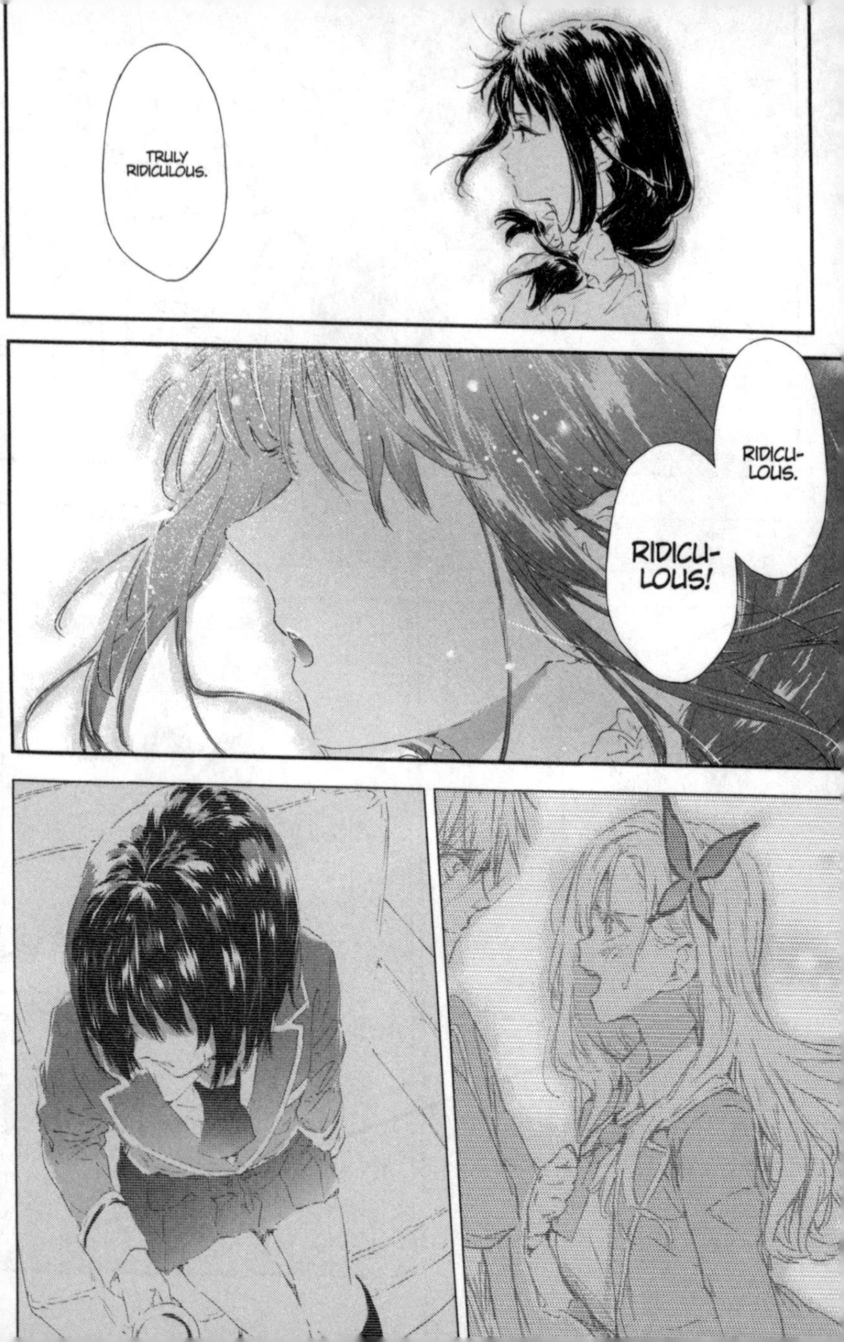
TRULY RIDICULOUS.
RIDICU-LOUS.
RIDICU-LOUS!

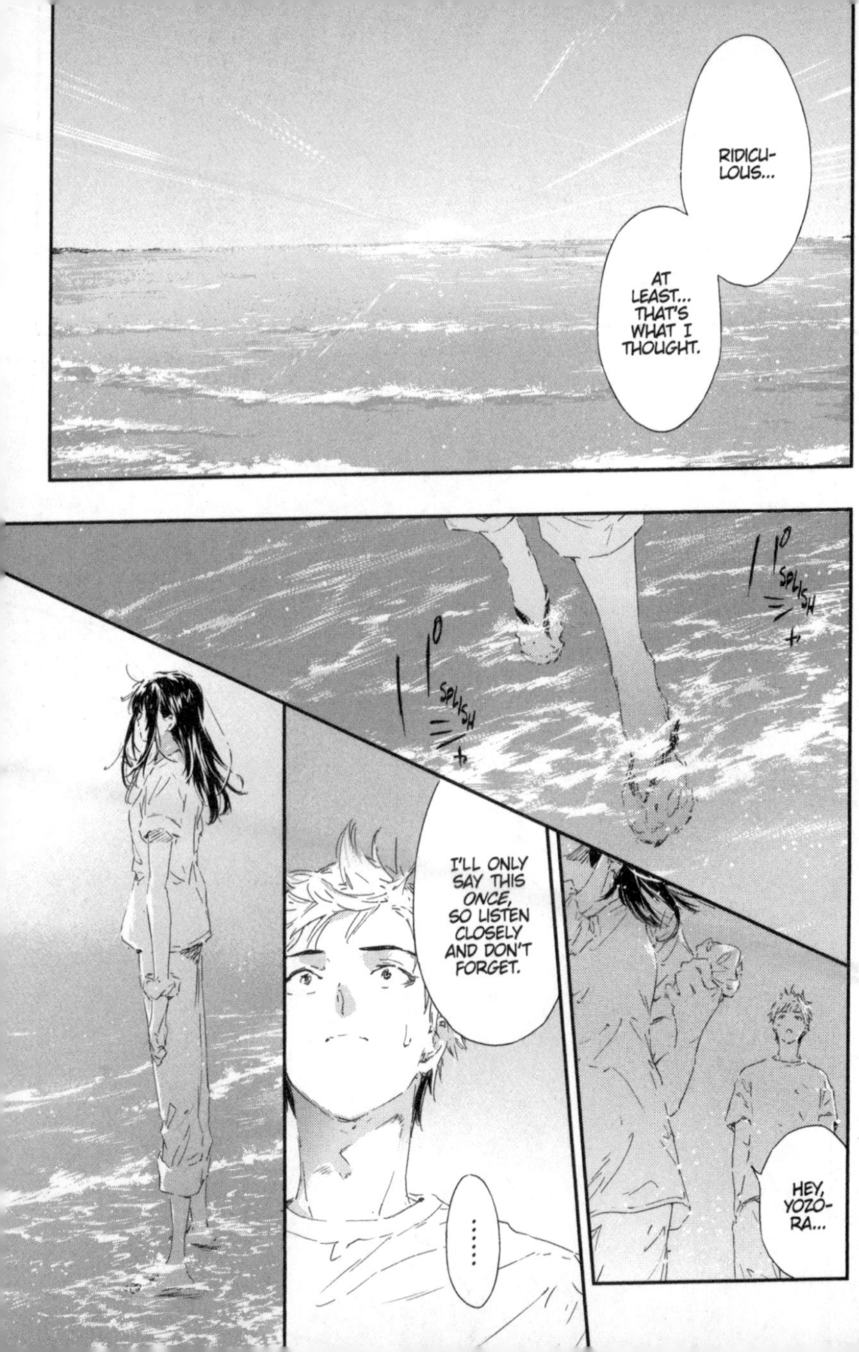
RIDICULOUS...
AT LEAST... THAT'S WHAT I THOUGHT.
SPLISH
SPLISH
HEY, YOZORA...
I'LL ONLY SAY THIS ONCE, SO LISTEN CLOSELY AND DON'T FORGET.
......

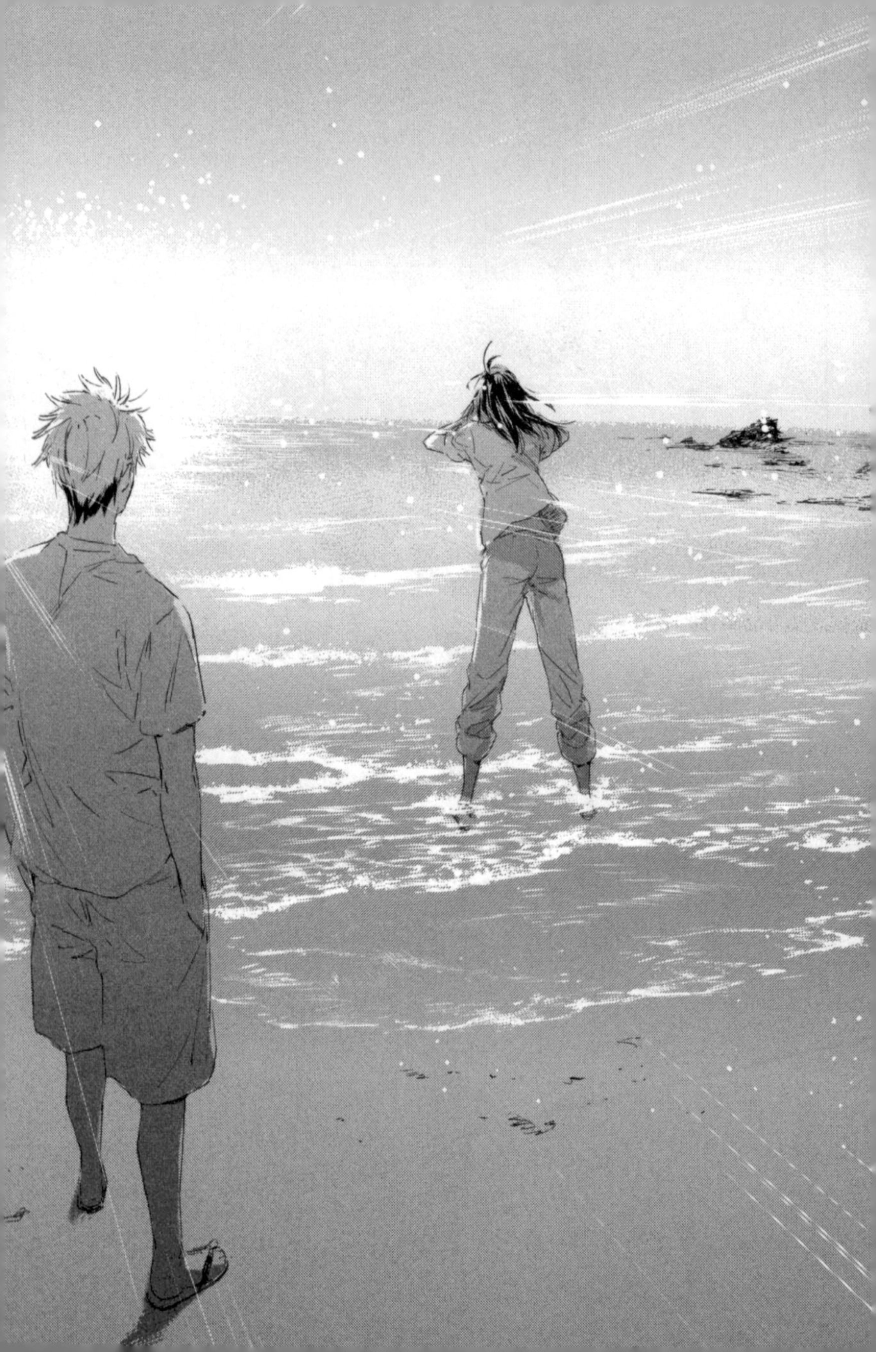

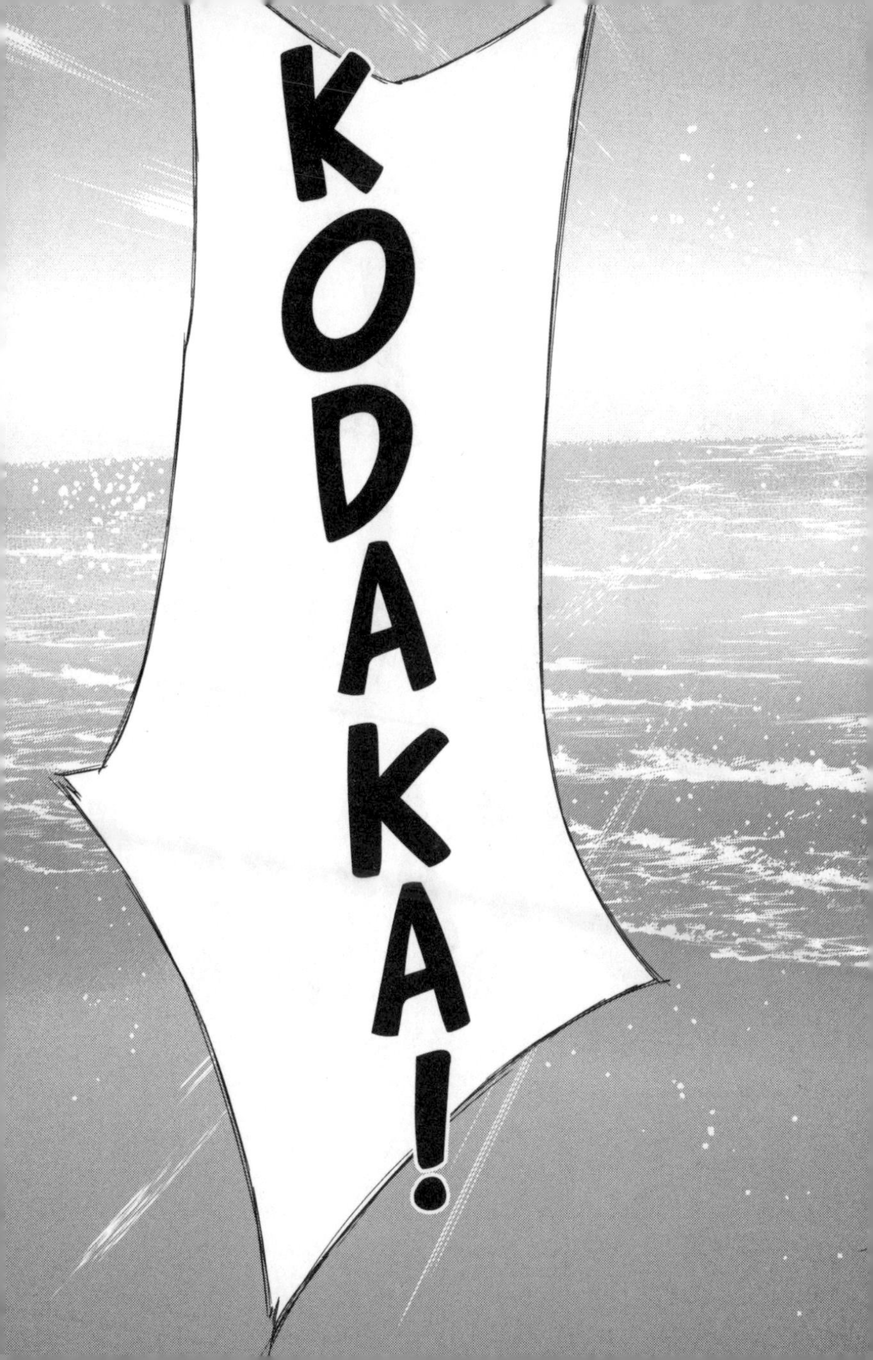
KODAKA!

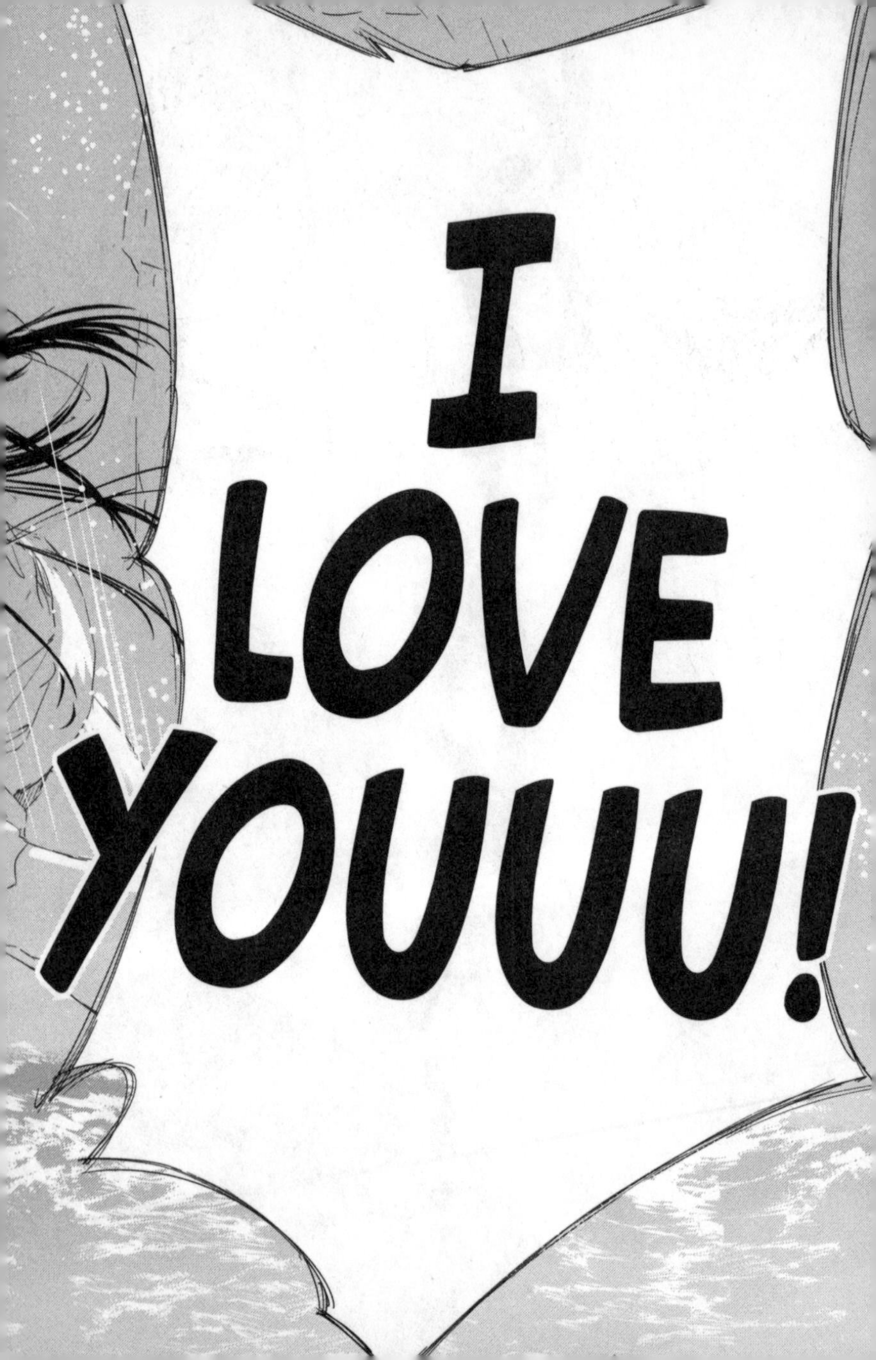
I LOVE YOUUU!

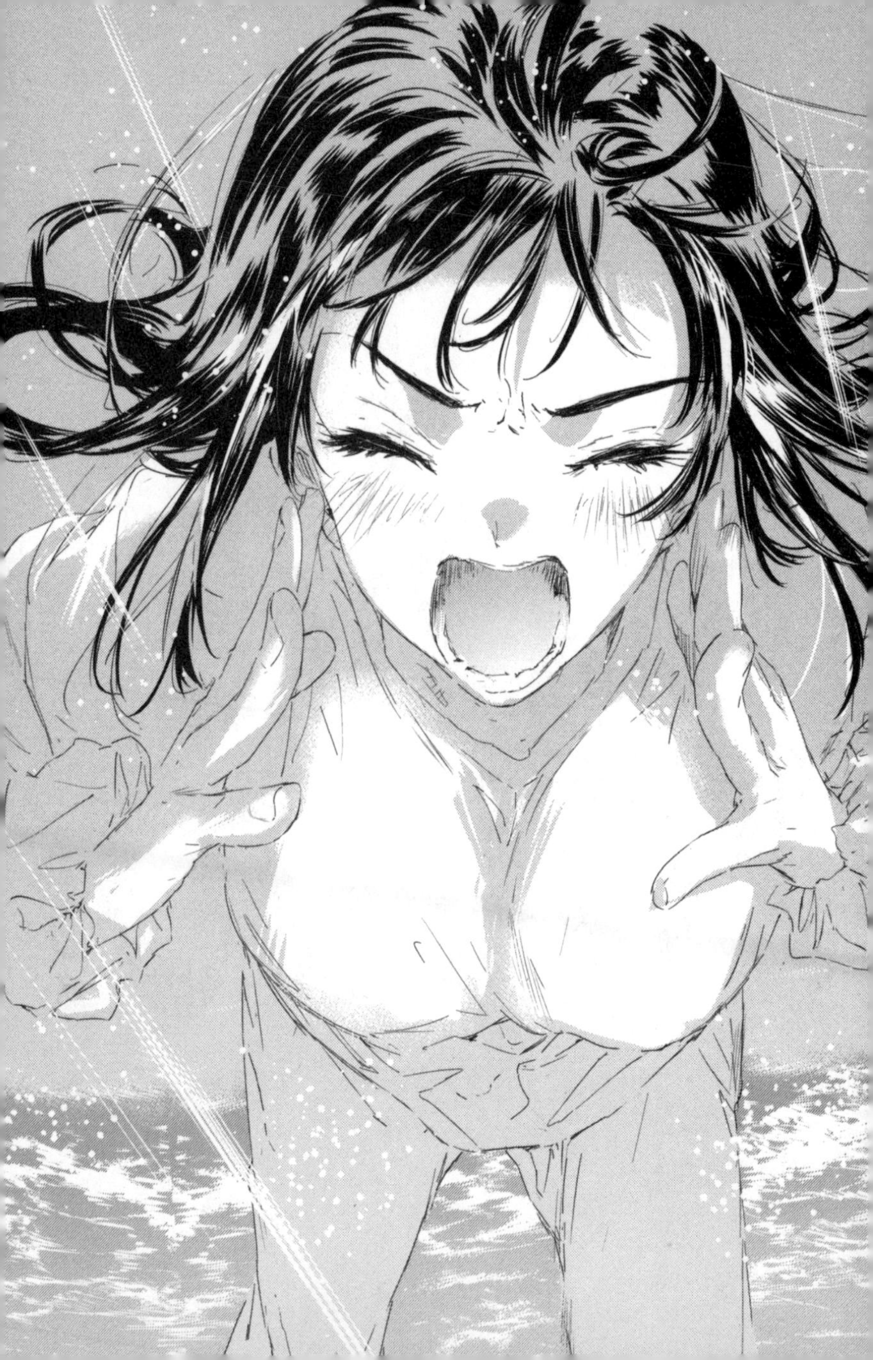

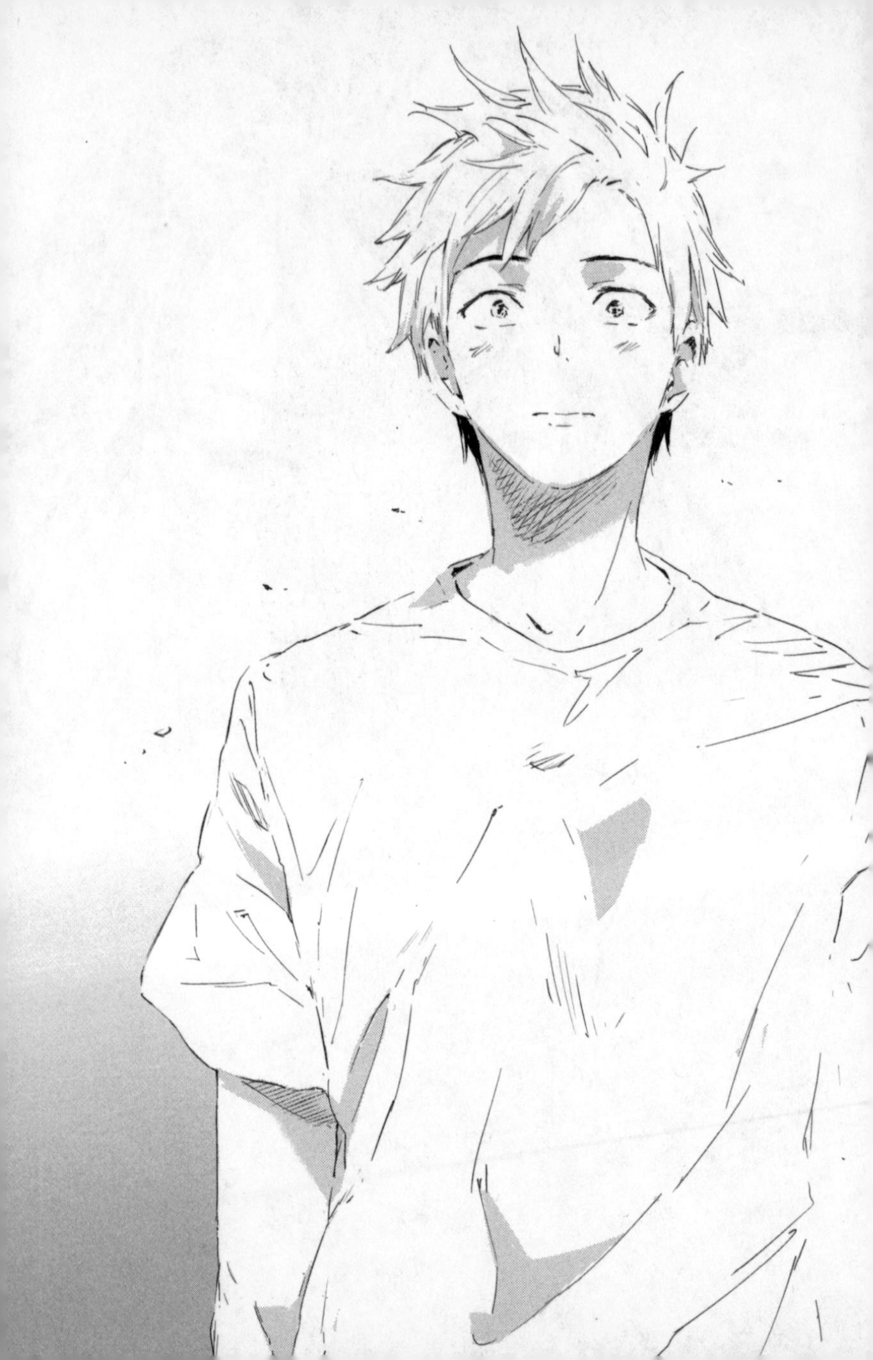

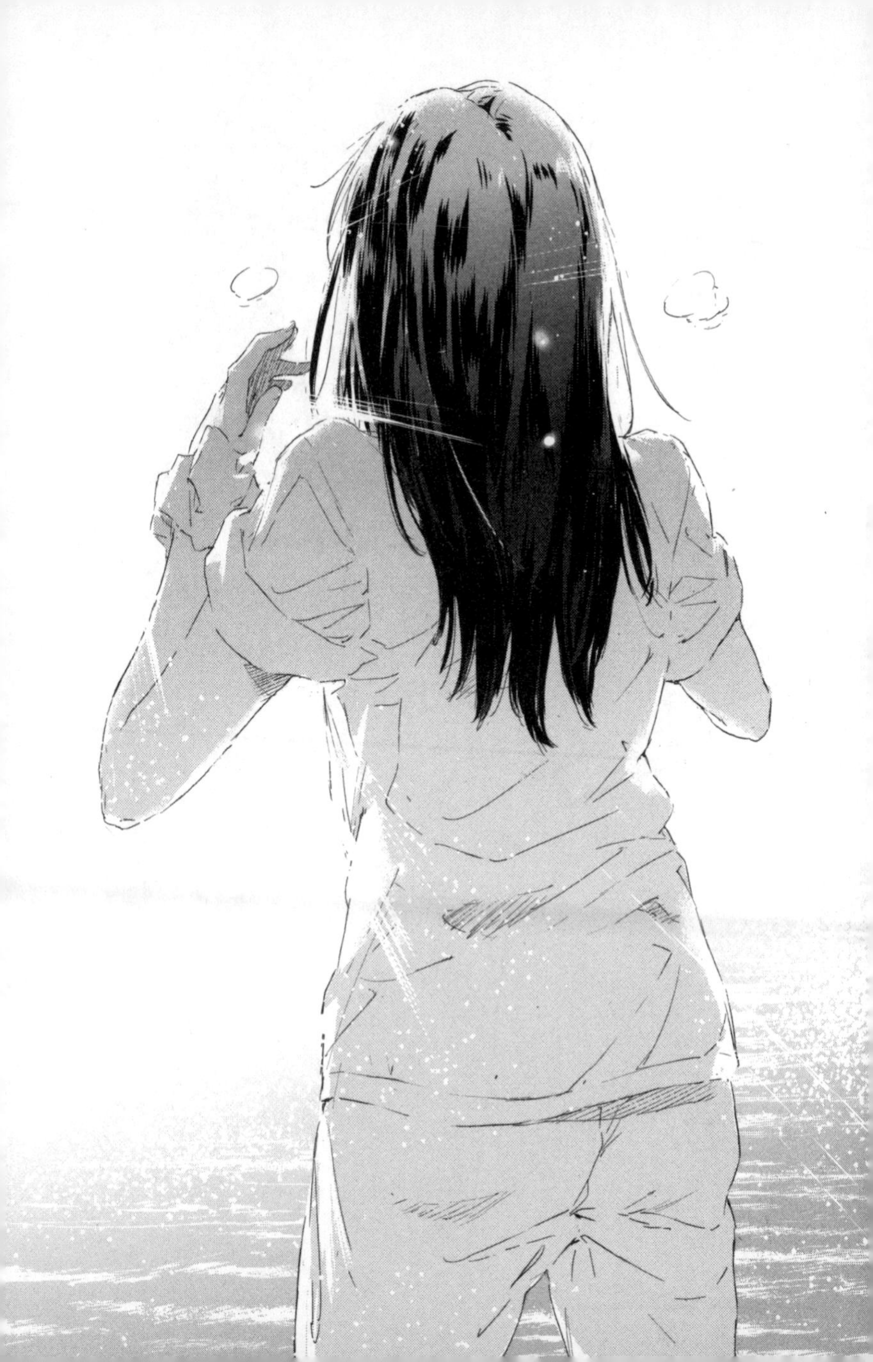

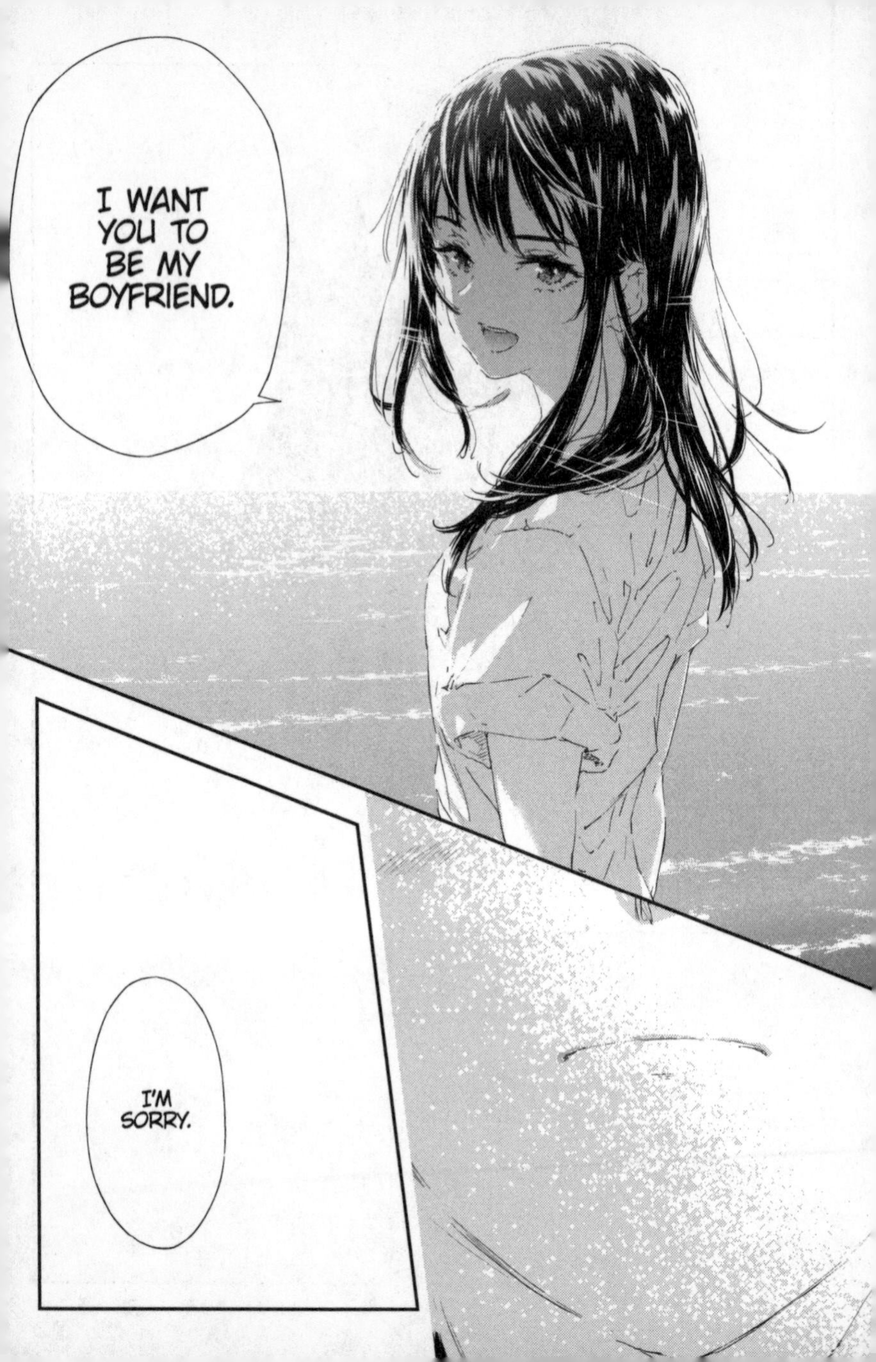
I WANT YOU TO BE MY BOYFRIEND.
I'M SORRY.

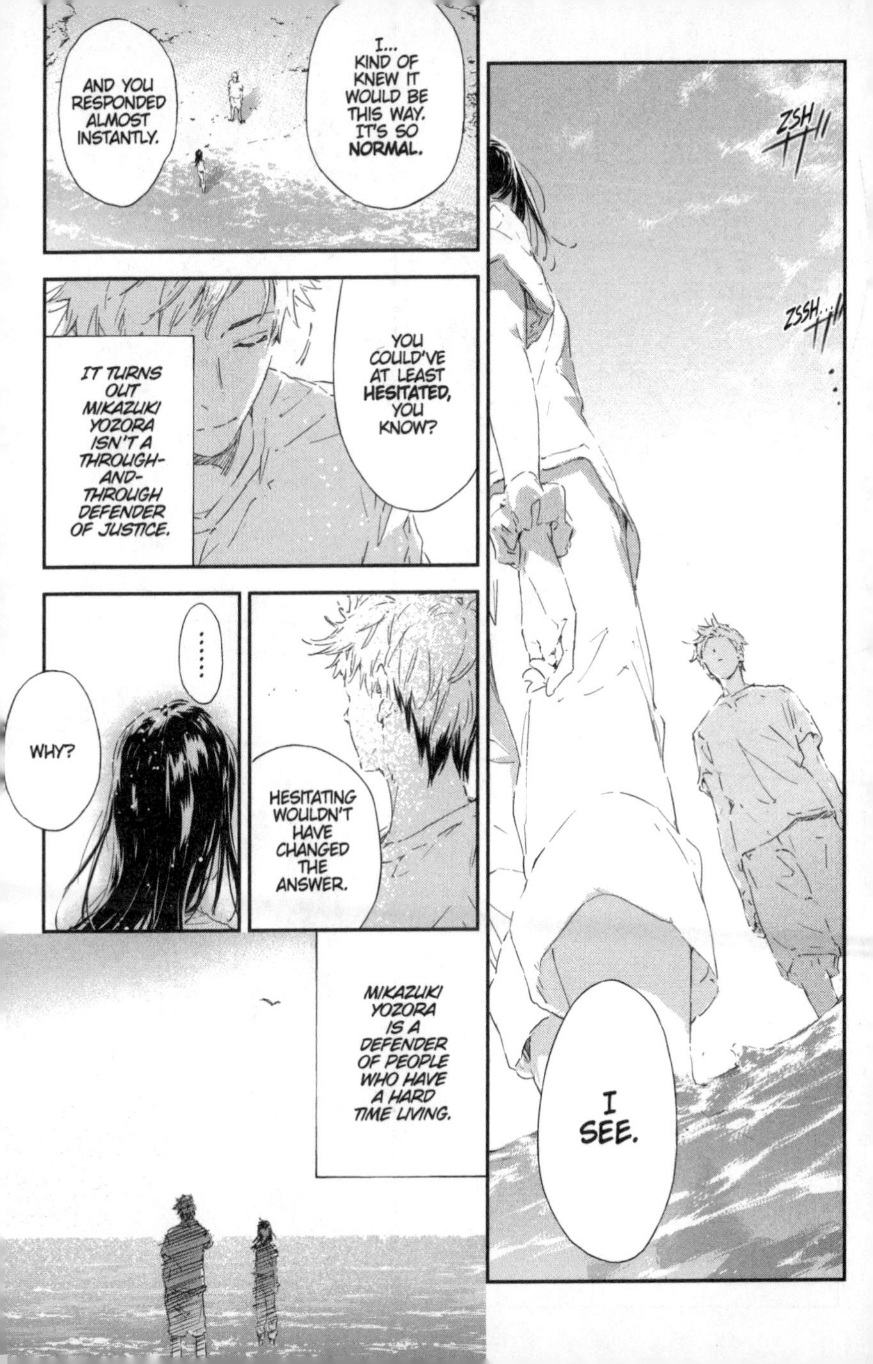
ZSH
ZSSH...
I SEE.
I... KIND OF KNEW IT WOULD BE THIS WAY. IT'S SO **NORMAL**.
AND YOU RESPONDED ALMOST INSTANTLY.
YOU COULD'VE AT LEAST **HESITATED**, YOU KNOW?
IT TURNS OUT MIKAZUKI YOZORA ISN'T A THROUGH-AND-THROUGH DEFENDER OF JUSTICE.
HESITATING WOULDN'T HAVE CHANGED THE ANSWER.
......
WHY?
MIKAZUKI YOZORA IS A DEFENDER OF PEOPLE WHO HAVE A HARD TIME LIVING.

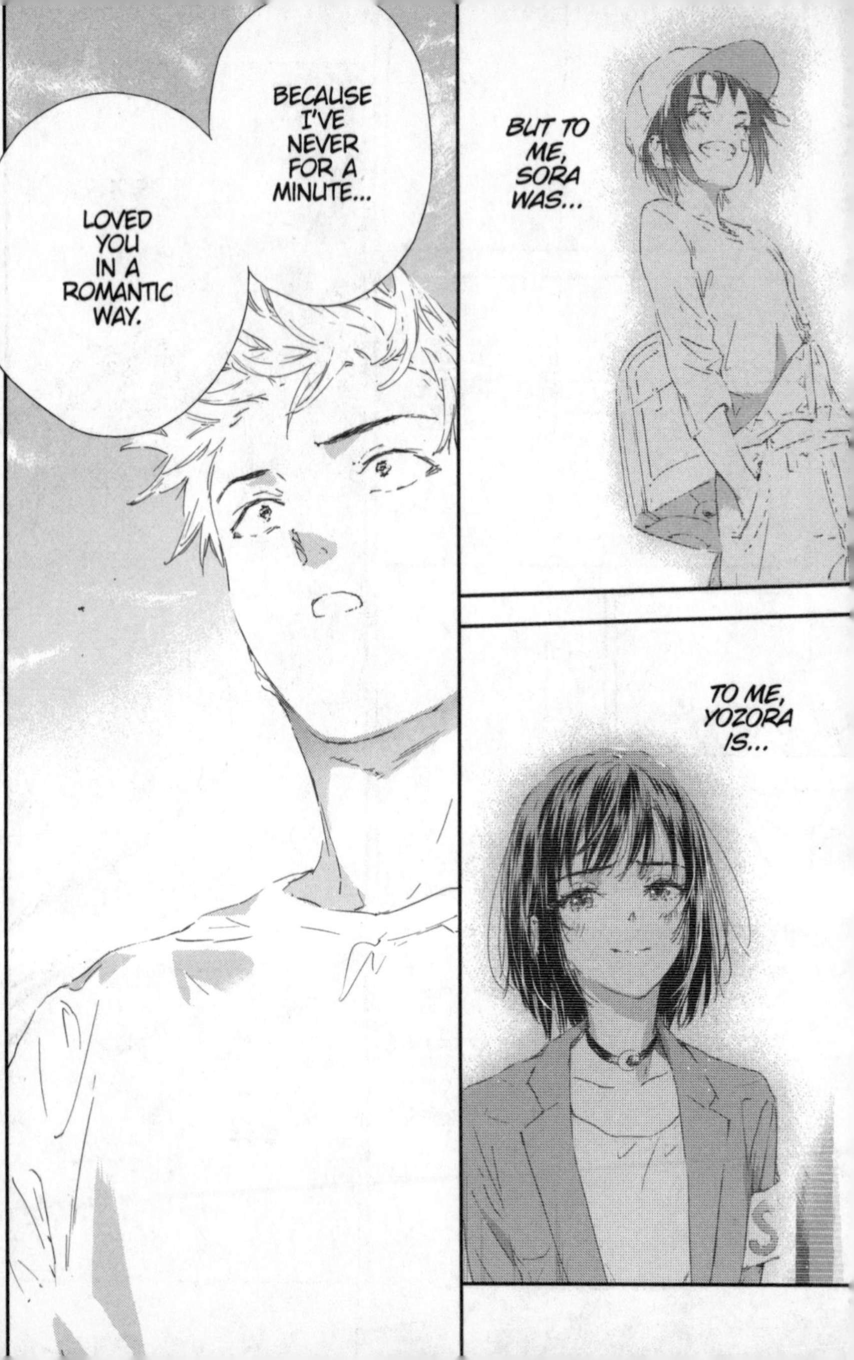
BUT TO ME, SORA WAS...
TO ME, YOZORA IS...
BECAUSE I'VE NEVER FOR A MINUTE...
LOVED YOU IN A ROMANTIC WAY.

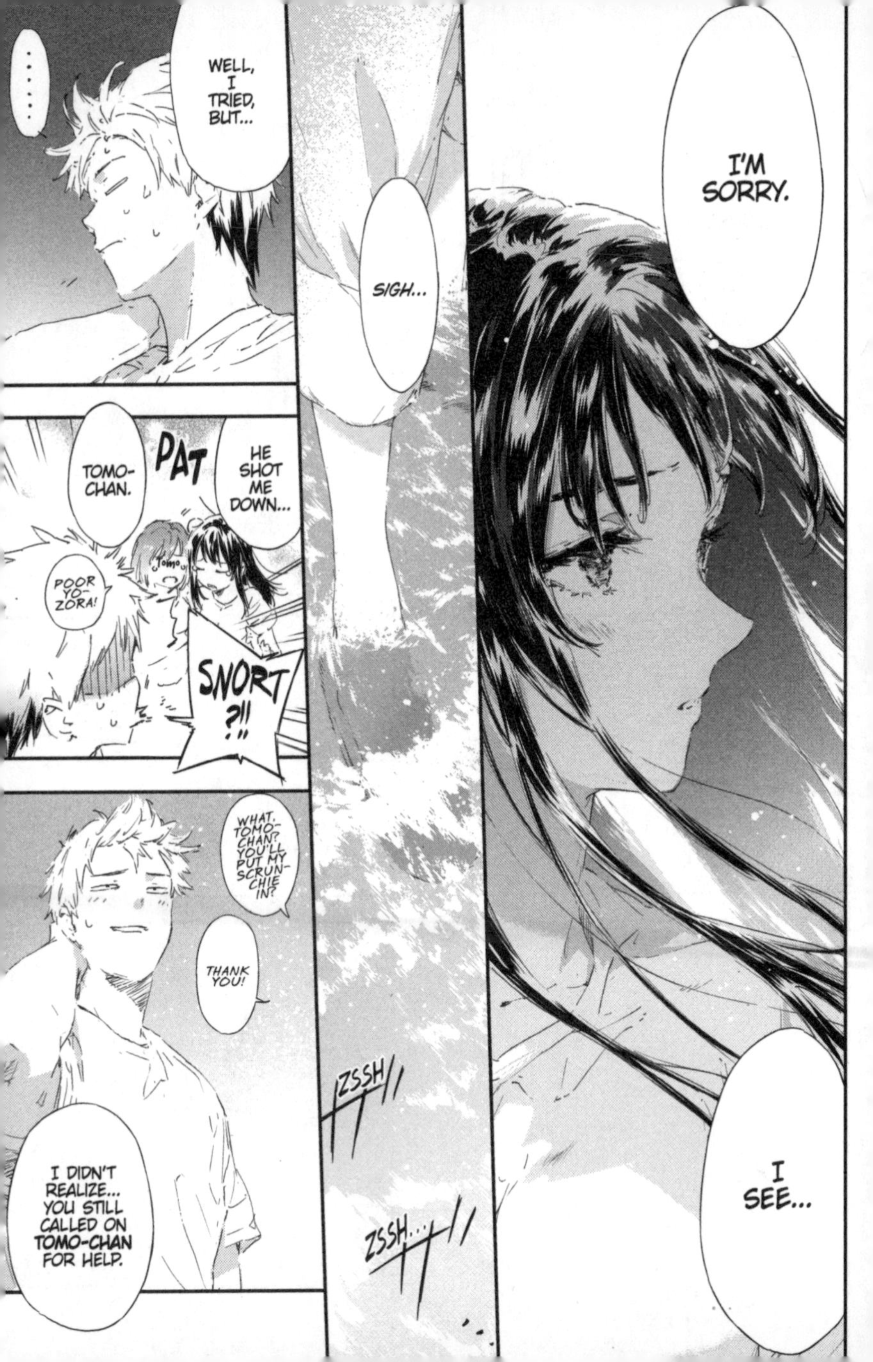
I'M SORRY.
I SEE...
SIGH...
ZSSH
ZSSH...
WELL, I TRIED, BUT...
......
HE SHOT ME DOWN...
PAT
TOMO-CHAN.
Tomo
POOR YO-ZORA!
SNORT ?!!
WHAT, TOMO-CHAN? YOU'LL PUT MY SCRUN-CHIE IN?
THANK YOU!
I DIDN'T REALIZE... YOU STILL CALLED ON TOMO-CHAN FOR HELP.

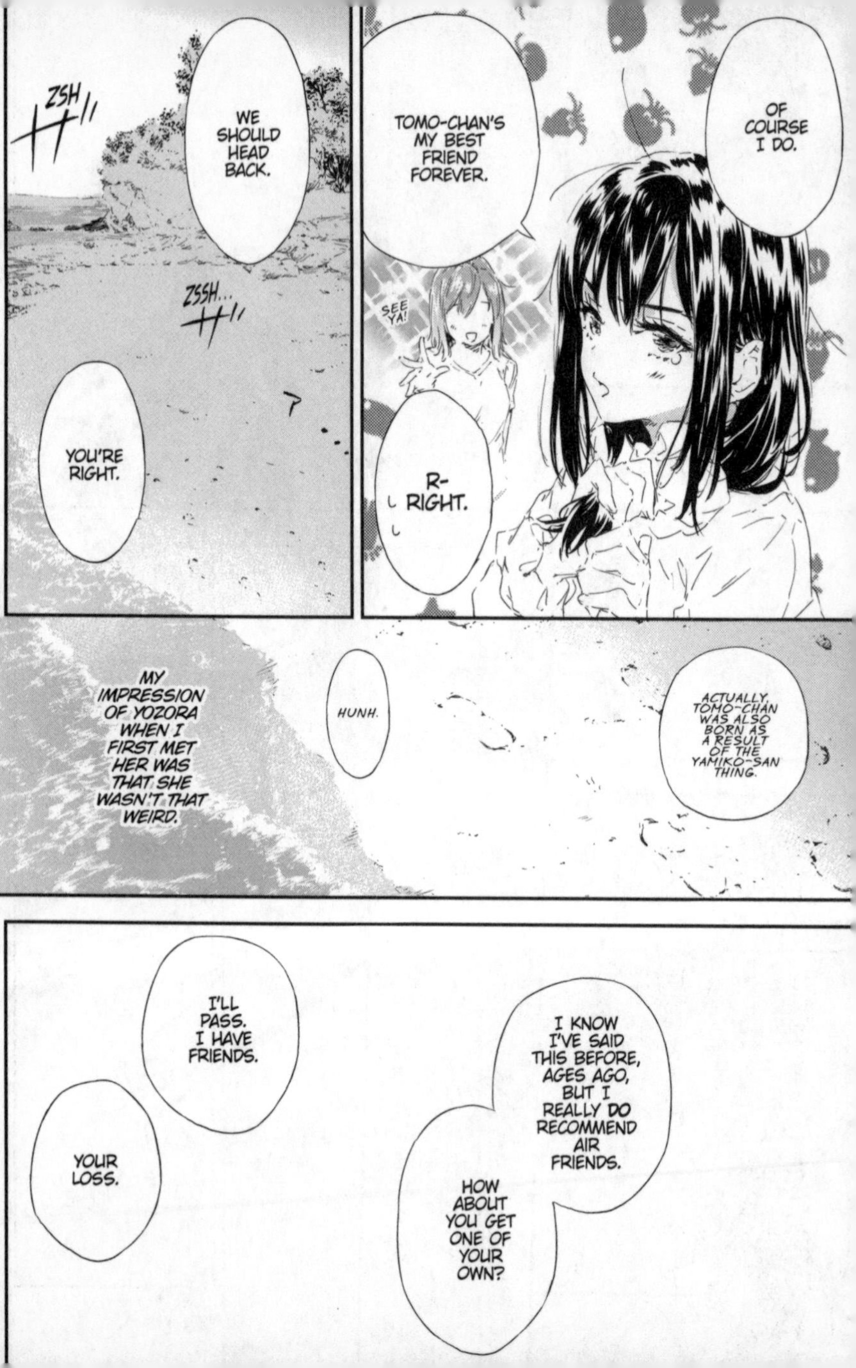
OF COURSE I DO.
TOMO-CHAN'S MY BEST FRIEND FOREVER.
SEE YA!
R-RIGHT.
WE SHOULD HEAD BACK.
ZSH
ZSSH...
YOU'RE RIGHT.
ACTUALLY, TOMO-CHAN WAS ALSO BORN AS A RESULT OF THE YAMIKO-SAN THING.
HUNH.
MY IMPRESSION OF YOZORA WHEN I FIRST MET HER WAS THAT SHE WASN'T THAT WEIRD.
I KNOW I'VE SAID THIS BEFORE, AGES AGO, BUT I REALLY DO RECOMMEND AIR FRIENDS.
HOW ABOUT YOU GET ONE OF YOUR OWN?
I'LL PASS. I HAVE FRIENDS.
YOUR LOSS.

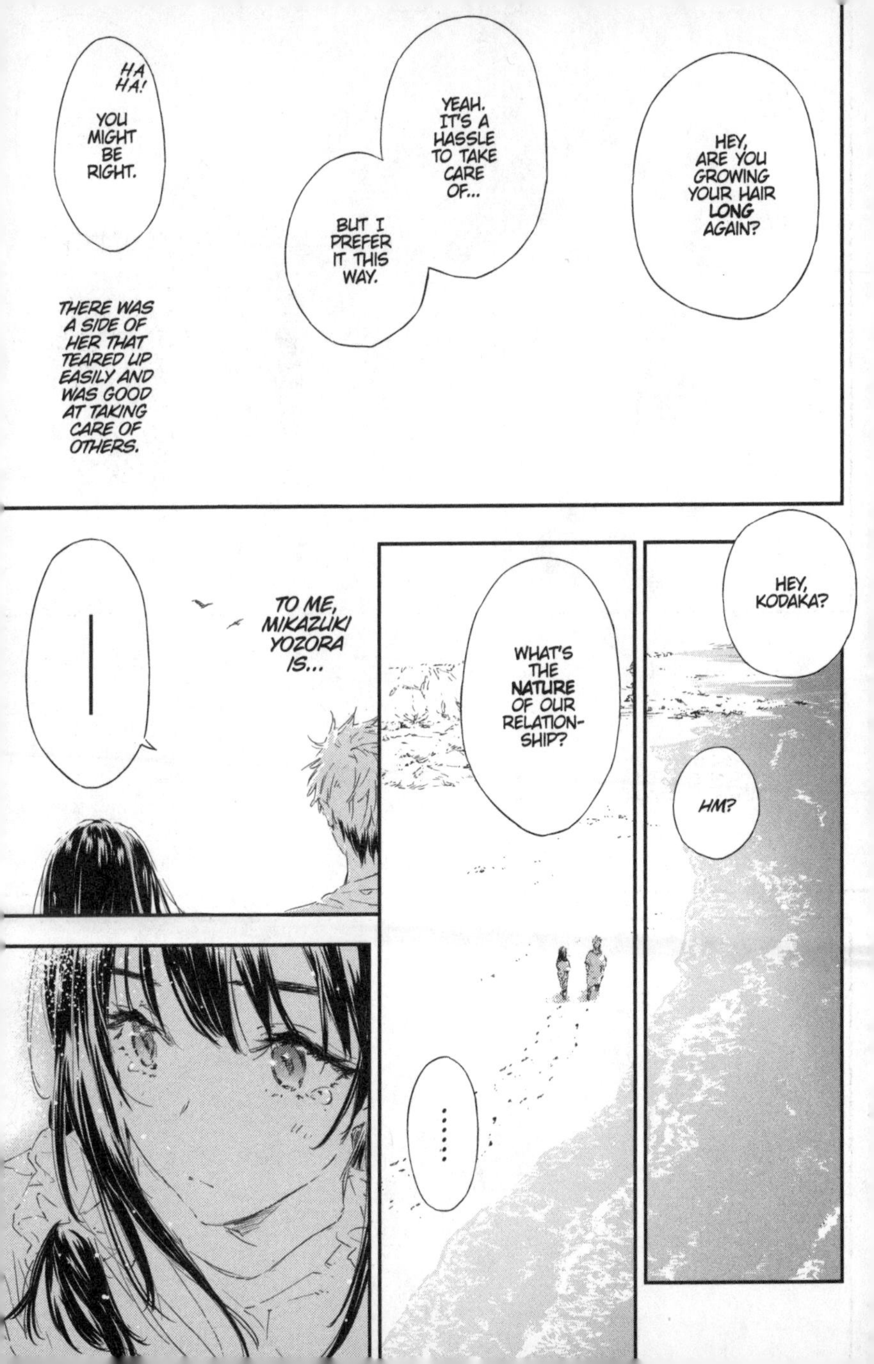
HEY, ARE YOU GROWING YOUR HAIR LONG AGAIN?
YEAH. IT'S A HASSLE TO TAKE CARE OF...
BUT I PREFER IT THIS WAY.
HA HA! YOU MIGHT BE RIGHT.
THERE WAS A SIDE OF HER THAT TEARED UP EASILY AND WAS GOOD AT TAKING CARE OF OTHERS.
HEY, KODAKA?
HM?
WHAT'S THE NATURE OF OUR RELATIONSHIP?
......
TO ME, MIKAZUKI YOZORA IS...
—

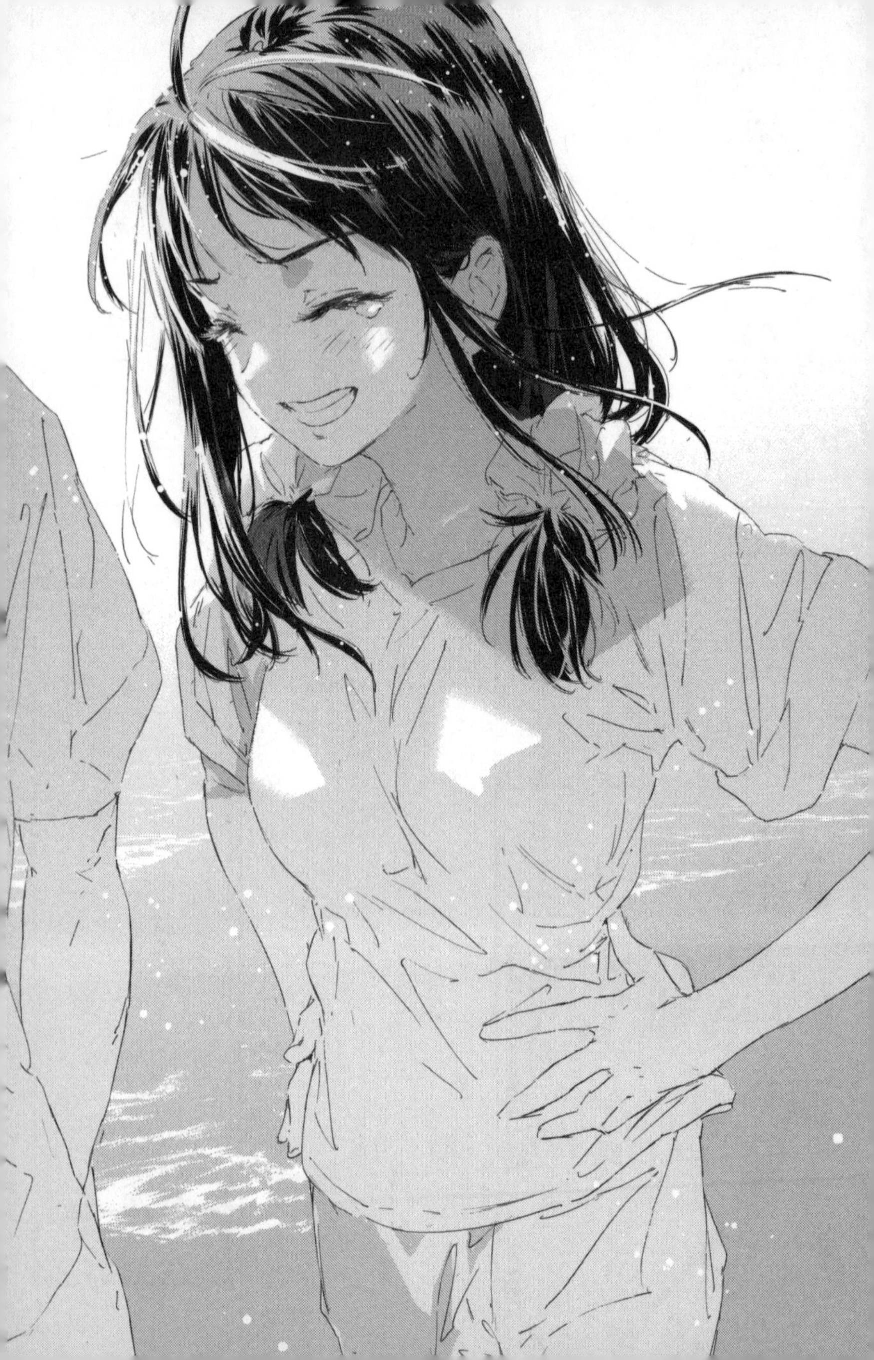

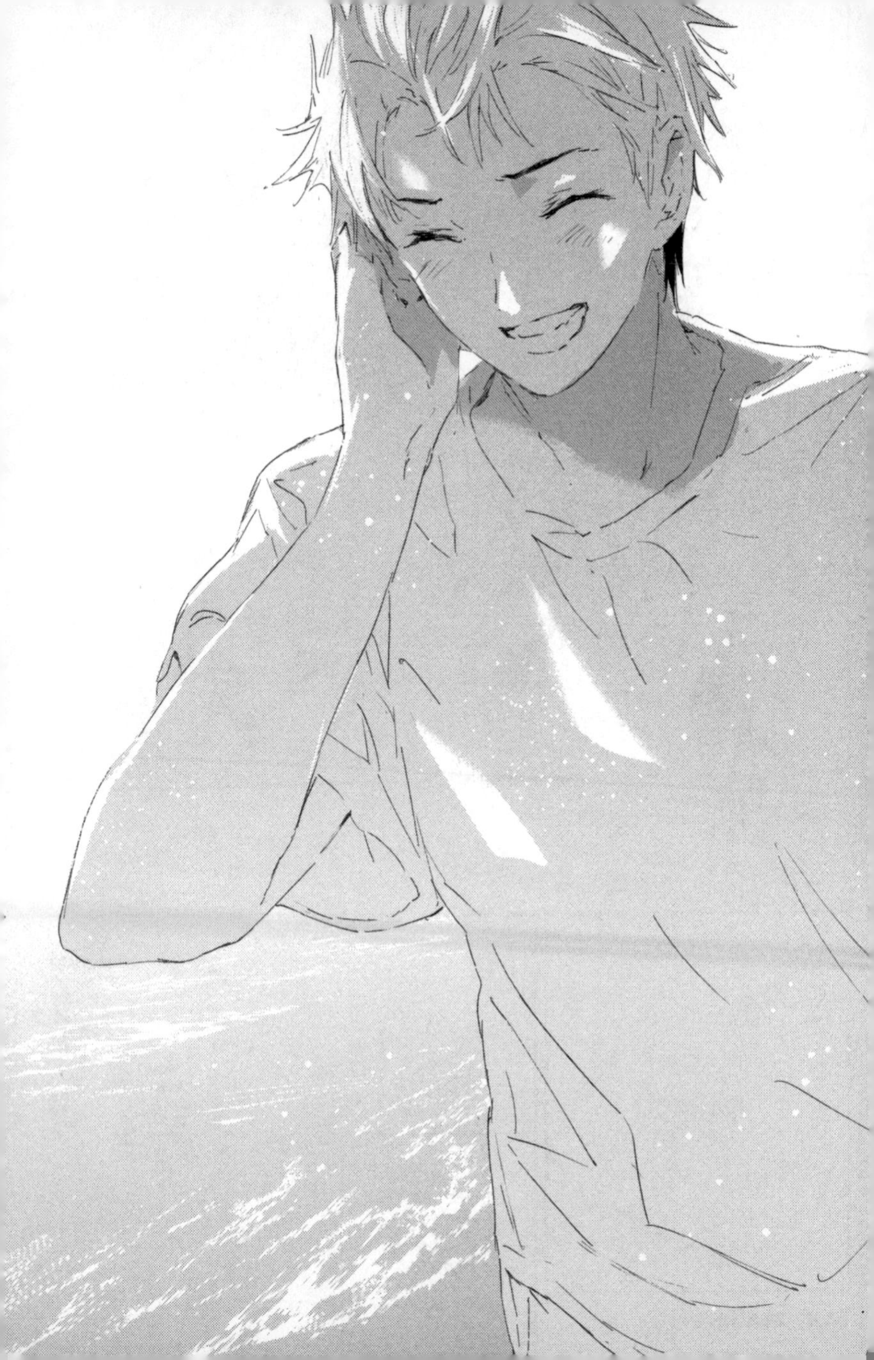

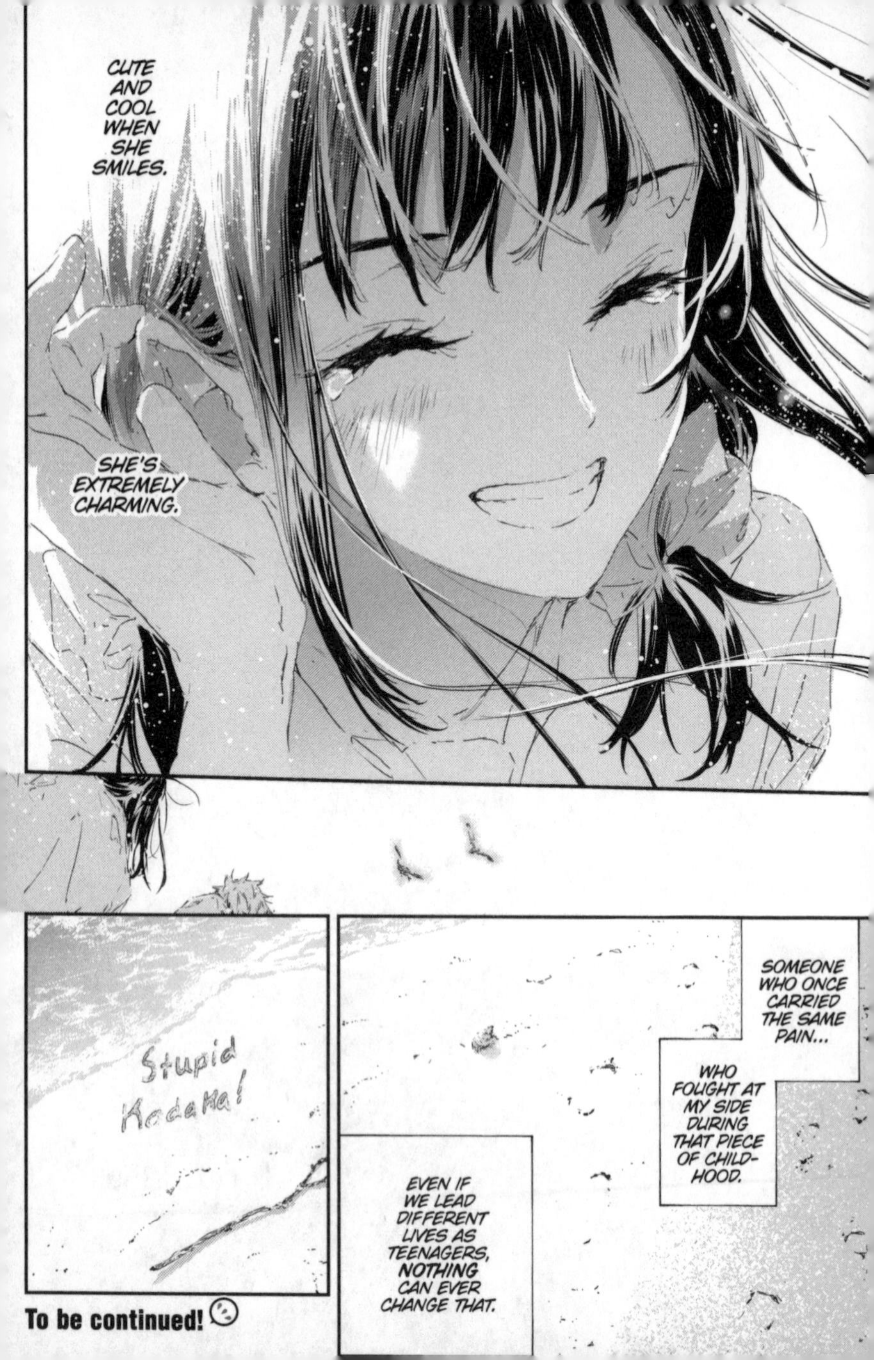
CUTE AND COOL WHEN SHE SMILES.
SHE'S EXTREMELY CHARMING.
SOMEONE WHO ONCE CARRIED THE SAME PAIN...
WHO FOUGHT AT MY SIDE DURING THAT PIECE OF CHILD-HOOD.
EVEN IF WE LEAD DIFFERENT LIVES AS TEENAGERS, NOTHING CAN EVER CHANGE THAT.
Stupid Kodama!
To be continued!

I don't have many friends

Afterword

Thank you for picking up Volume 19!

When I first received the offer to work on the manga version of *Haganai,* I never dreamed the series would be serialized for this long! But now, at long last, I've managed to approach the finish line. The next volume will be the last one. Just one year left with our beloved characters before they graduate... I'd appreciate it if you watch over them together with me.

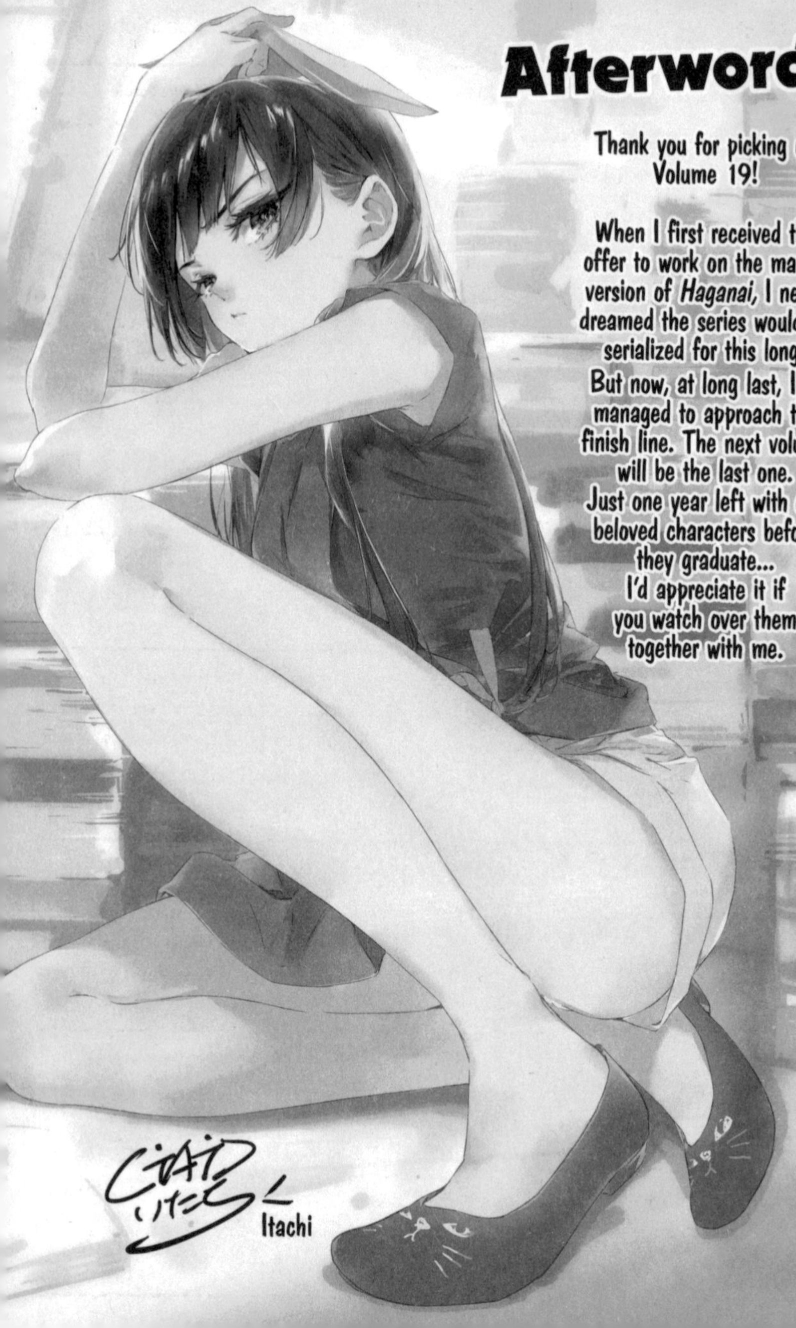

Itachi